Group Benefits:
Basic Concepts and
Alternatives

$1.08

Huebner School Series

Group Benefits: Basic Concepts and Alternatives

14th Edition

Juliana H. York

HS325-14

This publication is designed to provide accurate and authoritative information about the subject covered. While every precaution has been taken in the preparation of this material, the authors, and The American College assume no liability for damages resulting from the use of the information contained in this publication. The American College is not engaged in rendering legal, accounting, or other professional advice. If legal or other expert advice is required, the services of an appropriate professional should be sought.

© 2016 The American College Press
270 S. Bryn Mawr Avenue
Bryn Mawr, PA 19010
(888) AMERCOL (263-7265)
theamericancollege.edu
ISSN: 1945-242X
ISBN-10: 1-58293-236-0
ISBN-13: 978-1-58293-236-1
Printed in the United States of America

Dedication

To my husband, James.

J.H.Y.

Table of Contents

Topic 2

Topic 8.

Pg 2 – Pg 4

Topic 1

Topic 1

Topic 5.
P.6.1 - P.6.5
Topic 6
P.6.5 - P.6.2?

Topic 7.

Topic 3.

Topic 3. **Employee Benefit Marketing, Plan Design, and Administration. 12.1**

~~P12.14.   P15-17 P12.1T P20 P20-P4.~~

About the Author

Juliana York, CLU,® ChFC,® CEBS, RHU,® REBC,® ChHC,® CCP, CSCP

Juliana is an Adjunct Assistant Professor of Health Insurance at The American College. She received her BS in Management from the University of North Carolina-Asheville and a Masters of Risk Management and Insurance from Georgia State University in Atlanta, GA. Julie has worked in the insurance and managed care industry for more than 35 years, holding positions related to Worker's Compensation, TPA Administration, Group Health Sales and Account Management, Member Services, Marketing and Sales Operations, and Sales Incentive Compensation with major insurance companies and managed care organizations. Julie was a part-time instructor in the Risk Management and Insurance Department of Georgia State University in Atlanta for seventeen years where she taught junior and senior level undergraduate courses. She began teaching the HS 325, HS 340, and HS 344 classes for the Atlanta Association of Health Underwriters in 2001 and continues the program through the National Association of Health Underwriters since 2008.

The American College

The American College®is an independent, nonprofit, accredited institution founded in 1927 that offers professional certification and graduate-degree distance education to men and women seeking career growth in financial services.

The Center for Financial Advisor Education at The American College offers both the LUTCF and the Financial Services Specialist (FSS) professional designations to introduce students in a classroom environment to the technical side of financial services, while at the same time providing them with the requisite sales-training skills.

The Solomon S. Huebner School®of The American College administers the Chartered Life Underwriter (CLU®); the Chartered Financial Consultant (ChFC®); the Chartered Advisor for Senior Living (CASL®); the Registered Health Underwriter (RHU®); the Registered Employee Benefits Consultant (REBC®); the Chartered Healthcare Consultant™and the Chartered Leadership Fellow®(CLF®) professional designation programs. In addition, the Huebner School also administers The College's CFP Board—registered education program for those individuals interested in pursuing CFP®certification, the CFP®Certification Curriculum.

The Richard D. Irwin Graduate School®of The American College offers the master of science in financial services (MSFS) degree, the Graduate Financial Planning Track (another CFP[†] Board-registered education program), and several graduate-level certificates that concentrate on specific subject areas. It also offers the Chartered Advisor in Philanthropy (CAP®) and the master of science in management (MSM), a one-year program with an emphasis in leadership. The National Association of Estate Planners & Councils has named The College as the provider of the education required to earn its prestigious AEP designation.

The American College is accredited by The Middle States Commission on Higher Education, 3624 Market Street, Philadelphia, PA 19104 at telephone number 267.284.5000.

The Middle States Commission on Higher Education is a regional accrediting agency recognized by the U.S. Secretary of Education and the Commission on Recognition of Postsecondary Accreditation. Middle States accreditation is an expression of confidence in an institution's mission and goals, performance, and resources. It attests that in the judgment of the Commission on Higher Education, based on the results of an internal institutional self-study and an evaluation by a team of outside peer observers assigned by the Commission, an institution is guided by well-defined and appropriate goals; that it has established

---

†   Certified Financial Planner Board of Standards, Inc., owns the certification marks CFP®, CERTIFIED FINANCIAL PLANNER™, and CFP (with flame logo)®, which it awards to individuals who successfully complete initial and ongoing certification requirements.

conditions and procedures under which its goals can be realized; that it is accomplishing them substantially; that it is so organized, staffed, and supported that it can be expected to continue to do so; and that it meets the standards of the Middle States Association. The American College has been accredited since 1978.

The American College does not discriminate on the basis of race, religion, sex, handicap, or national and ethnic origin in its admissions policies, educational programs and activities, or employment policies.

The American College is located at 270 S. Bryn Mawr Avenue, Bryn Mawr, PA 19010. The toll-free number of the Office of Professional Education is (888) AMERCOL (263-7265); the fax number is (610) 526-1465; and the home page address is theamericancollege.edu.

Chapter 1

Introduction to Group Benefits

Learning Objectives

An understanding of the material in this chapter should enable the student to

1. **Identify the categories of benefits that can be included in a broad definition of employee benefits, and explain their significance.**

2. **Understand the factors that have influenced the growth of group benefits, and discuss the significance of each factor.**

3. **Briefly describe the benefit planning process.**

employee benefits

Although few would dispute that employee benefits are a major part of the overall compensation for working, even employee benefit specialists disagree over the precise meaning of the term **employee benefits**. However, regardless of the definition used, those in the field agree that the significance of the term has increased in recent years.

The narrowest definition of employee benefits includes only employer-provided benefits for situations involving death, accident, sickness, retirement, or unemployment. Even this narrow interpretation produces disagreement over whether the definition should include benefits that are financed by employer contributions but are provided under social insurance programs, such as workers' compensation insurance, unemployment insurance, Social Security, and Medicare.[1]

On the other hand, the broadest definition of employee benefits includes all benefits and services, other than wages for time worked, that employees receive in whole or in part from their employers. This book uses a broad definition and defines employee benefits as including the following five categories:[2]

- legally required payments for government programs. These include employer contributions to such programs as

  - Social Security

  - Medicare

  - unemployment compensation insurance

---

1. The Social Security Administration uses a narrow definition in its studies of employee benefit plans. Its definition includes only benefits not underwritten or paid directly by federal, state, or local governments.

2. This definition is similar to those used by the U.S. Chamber of Commerce and the Bureau of Labor Statistics.

SMUW

- workers' compensation insurance
- temporary disability insurance

- payments for private insurance and retirement plans. These include the cost of establishing such plans, as well as contributions in the form of insurance premiums or payments through alternative funding arrangements. Benefits are provided under these plans for personal loss exposures, such as

  - old age
  - death
  - disability
  - long-term care expenses
  - medical expenses
  - dental expenses
  - legal expenses
  - property and liability losses

- payments or other benefits for time not worked. These include

  - vacations
  - holidays
  - jury duty
  - maternity/paternity leave
  - reserve/National Guard duty
  - military leave

- extra cash payments, other than wages and bonuses based on performance, to employees. Benefits in this category include

  - educational assistance
  - moving expenses
  - suggestion awards
  - Christmas bonuses

- cost of services to employees, such as

  - subsidized cafeterias
  - employee discounts

- wellness programs
- employee-assistance programs
- day care programs
- adoption assistance
- financial planning programs
- retirement counseling
- free parking

group benefits

welfare benefits

The first category is usually referred to as social insurance, and it is covered only briefly in this book. The last four categories are commonly called **group benefits**. This book covers all types of group benefits except for retirement plans, which are beyond the scope of this text. The legal term that is often applied to the benefits covered is **welfare benefits**. The major emphasis is on group benefits that provide life insurance, disability income insurance, and medical expense insurance. The briefer treatment of numerous other types of benefits, however, should not diminish their importance.

SIGNIFICANCE OF GROUP BENEFITS

Looking at data of LIMRA can best show the significance of employee benefits. These data come from surveys conducted by LIMRA and are periodically updated. It often takes a year or more to collect and tabulate these statistics, and the data shown are for the latest survey years available at the time this book was revised.

LIMRA

LIMRA is a membership organization of life insurance and financial services organizations that provides marketing and distribution information and advice to its over 800 members. The data it gathers and the reports it issues are on its website: limra.com. However, much of its data is proprietary and is accessible only to members.

A recent LIMRA report[3] examined current employee benefit practices. One portion of that report contains statistics about the percentage of employers that provide certain group insurance benefits to at least some of their employees. This information, broken down by employer size, is based on a survey of 1,467 employers. The table below shows a portion of these statistics.

Table 1-1 Percentage of Employers Offering Selected Group Insurance Benefits, by Size of Employer as of January 1, 2014						
	Size (by Number of Employees)					
Group Insurance Benefit	10–19	20–99	100–499	500–999	1,000–4,999	5,000 or more
Life Insurance	42	60	77	78	85	90
Medical expense	74	85	92	88	94	93
Accidental death and dismemberment	27	49	70	81	81	75
Dental	51	68	83	77	88	94
Vision	39	58	72	78	78	90
Short-term disability income	32	55	73	73	74	85
Long-term disability income	32	51	64	77	84	81

FACTORS IN THE GROWTH OF GROUP BENEFITS

There is no single reason for the substantial growth in group benefits over time. Rather, this growth has resulted from a combination of factors, many of which are applicable to employee benefits in general. Frequently mentioned factors include (1) industrialization, (2) the influence of organized labor, (3) wage controls, (4) cost advantages, (5) inflation, and (6) state and federal legislation.

Industrialization

During the nineteenth century, the United States made the transition from an agrarian economy to one characterized by increasing industrialization and urbanization. The economic consequences of death, sickness, accidents, and old age became more significant as individuals began to depend more on monetary wages than on self-reliance and family ties

---

3. LIMRA. Employee Benefits At A Crossroads. *Employer Perspectives,* Technical Report, Volume 1, 2014, pg. 49.

to meet their basic needs. As a result, some employers began to provide retirement, death, and medical benefits to their employees. Not only did such benefits improve morale and productivity, they also reduced employee turnover and the expenses associated with it.

Although some of the earlier benefits were paid directly by employers, the development of group insurance enabled them to fund these benefits with systematic payments to an insurance company. As group insurance became more common, employers were faced with adopting new or better plans to remain competitive in attracting and keeping employees. This competition in employee benefits continues to exist.

Industrialization also led to more government benefits, such as Social Security, Medicare, unemployment insurance, and workers' compensation insurance.

Organized Labor

Since a Supreme Court ruling in 1949, there has been no question about the right of labor unions to legally negotiate for employee benefits. Although union pressures prior to that time often resulted in the establishment or broadening of employee benefit plans, this ruling strengthened the influence of labor unions.

Labor unions have also affected benefits for nonunion employees. Employers with both union and nonunion employees often provide the same benefits for the nonunion employees as those stipulated in the union contracts.

Wage Controls

Employee benefit plans grew substantially during World War II and the Korean War. Although the federal government froze wages, they imposed no restrictions on employee benefits, thus making them an important factor in attracting and retaining employees in labor markets with little unemployment. When these conflicts ended, the new and enhanced benefits remained.

Cost and Tax Advantages

nondiscrimination rules

Because of the economies associated with group underwriting and administration, employees can usually obtain benefits at a lower cost through group insurance rather than through separately purchased individual insurance policies. Employers can realize similar savings by directly providing employees with certain services, such as financial planning, day-care centers, and subsidized meals. The Internal Revenue Code also provides favorable tax treatment to employer contributions for certain types of group benefits. The employer may deduct most contributions as usual business expenses, and employees often have no taxable income because of employer contributions on their behalf. In addition, employees may receive tax-free benefits from certain types of group benefit plans and payments or services from many other types of group benefit programs, even if provided by employer contributions. However, there are often **nondiscrimination rules** that deny favorable tax treatment to some employees if the benefit plan does not provide equitable benefits to a large cross section of employees.

It is important to note here that the types of group benefits with the most favorable tax treatment also tend to be the most prevalent.

Inflation

Inflation also affects group benefits. When benefit levels are related to employees' wages, the level and cost of these benefits increase as wages increase; when benefit levels are stated as fixed amounts, inflation results in employee pressure for increases. For most employers, the cost of group benefits has increased at a rate faster than wages, primarily because of the skyrocketing increase in the cost of providing medical expense benefits.

Legislation

Most states traditionally limited the types of groups that are eligible for group insurance coverage as well as the types, and in some cases the amounts, of coverage that could be written. In recent years, the majority of these states have liberalized their laws and allowed more group insurance products to be available to an increasing variety of groups.

Furthermore, historically the federal government and many states passed legislation mandating that certain benefits be included in group insurance contracts or that existing benefits be broadened. Examples include legislation requiring benefits for maternity, alcoholism, and drug abuse. These added benefits also increased the cost of providing group insurance coverage.

In its major redesign of the medical expense insurance industry, the Affordable Care Act broadened access to health care benefits, increased the scope of benefits provided, and increased the efficiency of providing health care to all Americans.

Many employers must provide other benefits, such as family leave. In addition, many proposals for national health insurance would require most employers to provide medical expense coverage to employees and their families.

IMPORTANCE OF BENEFIT PLANNING

The significant growth in employee benefits and the onset of the Affordable Care Act have called for increasingly complex decisions. Whether these decisions are made by employers providing benefits, unions negotiating for benefits, or employees selecting benefit options, proper benefit planning is crucial. Benefit planning is much more than a description of the many types of plans and provisions. The following is a brief overview of this process.

Benefit Planning Process

Employee benefit planning is a dynamic process that must continually be reviewed and modified if an overall benefit plan is to meet the changing needs of a changing environment. The first step in this process is to determine the employer's objectives. Is the benefit package to be in line with the competition? Or is it to be viewed as a leader, better enabling the firm to attract employees?

Once the employer's objectives are determined, a plan should be designed to meet these objectives. The employer should seek advice from a broker or consultant who is knowledgeable in the products available in both the private sector and through the future state exchanges. The broker or consultant should also be knowledgeable of the tax advantages and penalties associated with the Affordable Care Act. The plan design process requires an analysis of plan costs from both a short-term and a long-term standpoint. If the costs are excessive even though the plan has been designed in the most cost-effective manner, the employer's objectives will need revision. A major determinant of a benefit plan's cost is the method of funding. Should employers, employees, or both pay the plan's cost? Should the plan be insured, funded from current revenues, or funded by some combination of the two approaches? Employers often use alternatives to traditional funding arrangements in an effort to reduce costs.

The third step in the process is to implement the plan. This may be as simple as adding an additional vacation day or as complex as taking competitive proposals for a pension plan from insurance companies, trust departments of banks, and other providers of services.

A crucial step in the employee benefit planning process is to communicate the plan properly to participating employees. Without good communication, it is often difficult for an employer's objectives to be realized effectively. Communication has become more than merely describing benefits; it also involves letting employees know the value of the benefits.

Finally, employers should monitor the plan's performance and make any necessary changes. As new benefits or funding arrangements appear on the scene, should they be considered? Has the character of the work force changed so that a different benefit package would better meet the needs of employees?

Throughout this book, the discussion looks at the issues and decisions that are part of this process.

CHAPTER REVIEW

Key Terms and Concepts

employee benefits
group benefits

welfare benefits
nondiscrimination rules

Review Questions

Review questions are based on the learning objectives in this chapter. For example, a [3] at the end of a questions means that the question is based on learning objective 3. If there are multiple objectives, they are all listed.

1. What categories of benefits are included in a broad definition of employee benefits? [1]

2. How has organized labor influenced the growth of employee benefit plans? [2]

3. Briefly explain how favorable tax laws have contributed to the growth of many types of group insurance. [2]

4. How has legislation affected the growth of employee benefits? [2]

5. Identify and briefly describe the steps in the benefit planning process. [3]

Review Question Answers

1. A broad definition of employee benefits includes the following five categories:

- legally required payments for government programs. These include employer contributions to such programs as Social Security.

- payments for private insurance and retirement plans. These include the cost of establishing such plans, as well as contributions in the form of insurance premiums or payments through alternative funding arrangements.

- payments or other benefits for time not worked, such as vacations, holidays, and jury duty

- extra cash payments, other than wages and bonuses based on performance, to employees, such as educational assistance and Christmas bonuses

- cost of services to employees, such as subsidized cafeterias, wellness programs, day care, and free parking

2. A Supreme Court ruling in 1949 about the right of labor unions to legally negotiate for employee benefits strengthened the influence of labor unions. Labor unions have also affected benefits for nonunion employees because some employers provide generous benefit plans in an effort to discourage their employees from unionizing. In addition, employers with both union and nonunion employees often provide the same benefits for the nonunion employees as those stipulated in the union contracts.

3. The Internal Revenue Code provides favorable tax treatment to employer contributions for certain types of group benefits. The employer may deduct most group benefit contributions as usual business expenses, and employees often have no taxable income as a result of employer contributions on their behalf. In addition, employees may receive tax-free benefits from certain types of group benefit plans and payments or services from many other types of group benefit programs, even if provided by employer contributions.

4. In recent years, the majority of states have liberalized their laws and allowed more group insurance products to be available to an increasing variety of groups. Furthermore, the federal government and many states have passed legislation mandating that certain benefits be included in group insurance contracts or that existing benefits be broadened. Examples include legislation requiring benefits for maternity, alcoholism, and drug abuse. Many employers must provide other benefits, such as family leave.

5. The first step in the process is to determine the employer's objectives. Is the benefit package to be in line with the competition? Or is it to be viewed as a leader? The second step is the design of a plan to meet these objectives. This process requires an analysis of plan costs. A major determinant of a benefit plan's cost is the method of funding. Should employers, employees, or both pay the plan's cost? Should the plan

be insured, funded from current revenues, or funded by some combination of the two approaches? The third step in the process is to implement the plan. This may be as simple as adding an additional vacation day or as complex as taking competitive proposals for a pension plan from insurance companies, trust departments of banks, and other providers of services.

Chapter 2

Basic Concepts of Group Benefits

Learning Objectives

An understanding of the material in this chapter should enable the student to

1. **Describe the ways an employer can structure a benefit plan.**

2. **Identify the characteristics that distinguish group insurance from individual insurance.**

3. **Explain why voluntary benefits have grown in popularity, and describe their characteristics.**

To best understand the field of group benefits, it is first necessary to comprehend certain basic concepts. These include the structure of benefits plans, basic characteristics of group insurance, an introduction to alternative funding methods for group benefits, and the nature of voluntary benefit plans.

STRUCTURE OF BENEFIT PLANS

Many types of benefits are available to employees through the workplace. In some cases, the employer pays the entire cost or part of the cost of a benefit. In other cases, the employer merely sets up a benefit plan under which an employee can elect to participate by paying the full cost of his or her coverage. The actual structure of any single benefit plan may take many forms, including group insurance arrangements, alternative funding, and policies of individual insurance.

Group Insurance Arrangements

group insurance

Group insurance is a policy under which many individuals and possibly their dependents are insured under a single policy issued to another entity. In most situations, the entity is an employer, and the individuals are employees. The employer may pay all, some, or none of the cost of the coverage provided. The insurer administers many aspects of the benefit plan, and bears the risk that benefit payments will exceed those expected. Group insurance is the predominant method that employers use to provide their employees with life insurance, disability income expense insurance, medical expense insurance, dental insurance, and others.

The term group insurance is used in a very broad sense in this book. It encompasses the products of traditional insurance companies as well as products of such organizations as

Basic Concepts of Group Benefits   2.3

Blue Cross and Blue Shield plans, health maintenance organizations (HMOs), preferred-provider organizations (PPOs), and other types of organizations from which employers obtain benefits for their employees.

Alternative Funding

As the cost of providing insurance benefits to employees has risen, employers have increasingly turned from fully insured plans to alternative funding methods to minimize this cost. In some cases, these alternative methods consist of variations in group insurance contracts, such as premium-payment delays and reserve-reduction arrangements. At the opposite end of the spectrum are totally self-funded (self-insured) plans, in which no insurance is purchased and benefits are paid from either current revenue or a trust to which periodic payments have been made. Between these two extremes are such programs as minimum-premium plans, stop-loss arrangements, and big-deductible plans that combine various aspects of traditionally insured plans with those of self-funding. Even when employers use self-funding, they often contract with an insurance company or other organization for administrative services.

self-funding

In its purest sense, **self-funding** is a method by which an employer pays benefit costs from current revenue, administers all aspects of a benefit plan, and bears the risk that benefit payments will exceed those expected. Self-funding is the typical form for benefits such as vacations, educational assistance, sick leave/short term disability, and wellness programs. It has always been a common method for some large employers to finance benefits such as medical expense coverage. In recent years, smaller employers are increasingly using some degree of self-funding for some benefits that were once fully insured.

These alternative funding methods are the subject of later discussion. At this point, however, it should be noted that the use of alternative funding methods does not eliminate the need for making decisions regarding such factors as eligibility, benefit levels, and claims handling. In most cases, provisions for these factors are similar, if not identical, to the provisions found in the types of group insurance contracts discussed throughout this book.

Policies of Individual Insurance

voluntary benefit

Individual insurance policies are used to fund many employee benefits. In most situations, these policies are part of a **voluntary benefit**, which is usually defined as a benefit plan made available by an employer, but for which employees voluntarily elect to participate and pay the entire cost of the coverage they receive. Voluntary benefit plans often use individual insurance policies for each participant but may also use group insurance contracts. Many supplemental life insurance plans and most long-term care insurance plans are structured as voluntary plans of individual insurance.

Employers may also use individual polices to provide benefits to top executives. In most cases, these benefits are limited to the top executives only, and the employer pays the premium for the insurance policies.

GROUP INSURANCE CHARACTERISTICS

Group insurance is characterized by a group contract, experience rating of larger groups, and group underwriting. Perhaps the best way to define group insurance is to compare its characteristics with those of individual insurance, which insurers underwrite on an individual basis. The following sections represent group insurance in general. Any product-specific variances will be discussed with those products in later chapter.

The Group Contract

master contract

In contrast to most individual insurance contracts, the group insurance contract provides coverage to a number of persons under a single contract issued to someone other than the persons insured. The contract, referred to as a **master contract**, provides benefits to a group of individuals who have a specific relationship to the policyowner. Group contracts usually cover individuals who are full-time employees, and the policyowner is either their employer or a trust established to provide benefits for the employees. Although the employees are not actual parties to the master contract, they can legally enforce their rights. Consequently, employees are often referred to as third-party beneficiaries of the insurance contract.

certificate of insurance

Each employee covered under the contract receives a **certificate of insurance** as evidence of his or her coverage. A certificate is merely a description of the coverage provided and is not part of the master contract. In general, a certificate of insurance is not even considered a contract and usually contains a disclaimer to that effect. However, some courts have held the contrary to be true when the provisions of the certificate or even the explanatory booklet of a group insurance plan varies materially from the master contract.

In individual insurance, the insured's coverage normally begins with the inception of the insurance contract and ceases with its termination. However, in group insurance, individual members of the group may become eligible for coverage long after the inception of the group contract, or they may lose their eligibility status long before the contract terminates.

Experience Rating

A second distinguishing characteristic of group insurance is the use of experience rating. If a group is sufficiently large, the actual claims experience of that particular group is a factor in determining the premium the policyowner is charged. The experience of an insurance company is also reflected in the dividends and future premiums associated with individual insurance. However, such experience is determined on a class basis and applies to all insureds in that class. This is also true for group insurance contracts when the group's membership is small.

VOLUNTARY BENEFITS

voluntary benefits

A major area of growth for insurance companies in recent years has been through the marketing of voluntary benefits for employees, many of which are discussed later in this book. These products—which can be either group insurance or individual insurance—vary considerably among insurance companies. Even the names used to describe these products are not uniform, with terminology like payroll deduction plans and worksite marketing often being used. **Voluntary benefits** are defined as products provided by the employer that the employee chooses to purchase and for which he or she pays 100 percent of the premium, usually through payroll deduction.

A recent LIMRA survey[1] found that 70 percent of employers improve the morale for their existing employees and attract and retain new employees through offering voluntary benefits.

---

1.   LIMRA, *LIMRA Study Finds Employers Interested in Offering Voluntary Benefits*, 9-15-14.

Reasons for Popularity

portability

Voluntary benefits, although their growth has slowed in recent periods, experienced significantly increased popularity over recent decades. Employer attempts to contain the rising costs of employee benefits—particularly the cost for medical expense coverage—have been a primary reason. For example, an employer may determine that it cannot afford to institute a new group insurance program and pay any portion of the cost of coverage. Even though employees would naturally like to have the employer share in the cost, the ease of payroll deduction and more liberal underwriting still make a payroll deduction plan attractive to them. In addition, **portability** of the coverage is often appealing. Portability allows an employee to continue coverage under an employer-sponsored plan after termination of employment by paying premiums directly to the insurance company.

Voluntary benefits have also grown in popularity as a method of supplementing the benefits provided under a group plan financed by the employer. For example, an employer may pay for a group long-term disability income plan that provides benefits equal to 50 percent of salary. Voluntary benefits then allow employees to purchase additional protection. Or the employer may pay for short-term disability income protection only and make long-term protection available under a voluntary benefit plan.

Changes in demographics make it increasingly difficult for employers to offer an overall benefit plan that meets the needs of all employees. One alternative is to offer a cafeteria plan, under which an employee can allocate the benefit dollars spent by his or her employer among a variety of benefits. Another option is to provide a basic core of benefits that all employees want. Additional benefits, such as long-term care insurance, can be offered on a voluntary basis.

Another reason for the increase in the popularity of voluntary benefits is the increased availability of products. More insurance companies have entered the market to obtain additional revenue at a time when revenue from other sources has been decreasing. As is often the case, this has sometimes resulted in more competitive premiums and more liberal underwriting.

Market Characteristics

The voluntary benefit market is very diverse. The remainder of this section briefly describes some of the variations.

Insurance Company Involvement

Estimates suggest that up to 100 insurance companies offer voluntary benefits. Some carriers specialize in individual products while other specialize in group products. Some companies offer both.

As a rule, individual insurers target employers with fewer employees than do group insurers. However, many insurance companies provide coverage for the employees of almost any size employer. Most companies target employees in the middle-income range.

Types of Products Available

A major goal of many insurance companies in the voluntary market is to sell life insurance to employees and their dependents. Individual insurers are heavily concentrated in this market. Life insurance is also a popular product of group insurers, but they are more likely to offer health insurance products as well. Life insurance runs the gamut from basic term insurance to whole life and variable universal life insurance and includes accidental death and dismemberment insurance.

Short-term and long-term disability income insurance is a prominent health product. Major medical coverage is seldom offered, but insurers sell supplemental medical plans that also represent significant shares of total voluntary premiums. These products include accident insurance, specified-disease and critical illness policies, and hospital-indemnity and other supplemental medical coverage. Dental insurance and vision coverage are common products as well. An increasingly common product is long-term care insurance. All these types of benefits are discussed later in this book.

Depending on the size of the employer, insurance companies can tailor group products to the employer's needs. The five voluntary benefits most commonly offered by employers to their employees are:[2]

- life Insurance (94%)
- vision coverage (84%)
- disability Income (80%)
- dental coverage (80%)
- accident coverage (68%)

---

2. www.benefitspro.com; *5 most popular voluntary benefits;* August 14, 2013.

Target Markets

The spectrum of organizations sponsoring voluntary benefit plans has broadened, as reflected in expanding employer markets and special markets that include membership organizations and affinity groups. New voluntary benefit sales in 2013 totaled over $6.6 billion.[3]

Expanding Employer Markets. Insurer targets within the employer market that had focused on larger employee group sizes and higher-income white-collar workers have broadened over the last 25 years. Small and even some medium-sized firms, which are less likely to have traditional employer-funded group benefits, offer the most potential for strong voluntary program growth. Despite recent declines, this strategy has shown longer-term success. Total new voluntary plan premiums sold for the first quarter of 2015 were 14 percent higher than the same time frame in 2014. The total worksite premium was over $1.8 billion with voluntary life insurance sales of almost $700 million and voluntary health sales topping $1 billion.[4]

Special Markets. A wide variety of member organizations, such as credit unions and associations, may sponsor voluntary programs. These organizations often view voluntary programs as valuable, cost-effective services that reinforce the value of membership. For example, the voluntary products for a professional association could include malpractice, errors and omissions, or directors and officers liability insurance. By contrast, life, Medicare supplement, long-term care, and specified disease coverages would be attractive to an employee retiree association.

Banks are also a special target market that can establish affinity relationships with insurers. A voluntary program successfully established with a bank's employees can lead an insurer to suggest solicitation of a bank's clients, such as commercial accounts as well as depositors, borrowers, and credit card holders. Indeed, some of these relationships produce reciprocal agreements whereby the insurance company offers certificates of deposit, mortgages, and other financial services at the worksite.

3.   www.businesswire.com, *Voluntary Industry Growth Continues in 2013, According to Eastbridge's Annual Sales Study,* April 29, 2014

4.   LIMRA, *U.S. Worksite Sales: 2015 First Quarter Review, 2015*

Underwriting

guaranteed issue

simplified issue

modified guaranteed issue

Surveys of both employers and employees indicate that insurance company underwriting affects the success of a voluntary benefit plan. Although some voluntary benefits are fully underwritten on an individual basis, most plans are responsive to market demands and use either simplified underwriting or guaranteed issue, with group coverage being more likely than individual coverage to have the latter. **Guaranteed issue** means that the insurer issues coverage without an employee having to provide evidence of insurability. **Simplified issue** means that the insurer issues coverage with satisfactory responses to questions on an abbreviated application form. Some insurers have a category of underwriting—called **modified guaranteed issue**—that falls somewhere between guaranteed issue and simplified issue. In this case, the insurer accepts most applicants but asks a few medically related questions that may result in the declination of a small number of applicants.

As a rule, employers want guaranteed-issue coverage unless simplified-issue underwriting results in significant cost savings to employees. Several factors affect the underwriting policy of an insurance company, including size, participation level, and issue limits. For example, an insurance company might use simplified-issue underwriting for its universal life product if there is a minimum 8 percent participation rate among employers with 500 employees and the issue limit is $100,000. For a group of 50 employees, the percentage might be 15 and the issue limit $85,000. For guaranteed issue, the figures might be 35 percent and $80,000 for employers with 500 employees and 55 percent and $50,000 for employers with 50 employees.

Cost

Estimates indicate that voluntary benefits are about 10 percent less expensive than coverage purchased in the individual marketplace outside the employment relationship. However, significant variations exist. Even when there is no cost differential, the ease of payroll deduction is appealing to employees.

Because both employers and employees have considerable interest in voluntary products being offered on a tax-favored basis, an employer may provide benefits under a cafeteria plan. However, the use of a cafeteria plan might pose problems, and some benefit consultants feel that voluntary benefits should be kept separate from a firm's cafeteria plan.

Methods of Premium Payment

The vast majority of voluntary benefits use payroll deduction as the method for premium payments, with the employer remitting the premiums to the insurance company. Some insurers bill employees directly if an employer is unwilling to participate in a payroll deduction arrangement. However, payroll deduction is very popular with employees, and direct billing probably has an adverse effect on plan participation, although it may also reduce the rate at which coverage lapses when employment terminates.

Premiums are usually a function of the benefits purchased and the frequency of payroll deductions. However, insurers sometimes sell life insurance on the basis of the amount of coverage that an employee can purchase with a given premium, such as $1, $2, or $5 per week (or other period). Because the amount of coverage is a function of the employee's attained age, larger amounts of coverage are available to younger employees than to older employees.

Portability

Individual insurance products are automatically portable when an employee terminates employment. However, there are several possibilities with group coverage. In a few cases, coverage ceases; in some cases, the employee must convert to an individual policy. In most cases, the employee can continue the group coverage on a direct-bill basis.

Premiums often remain the same after termination of employment, but the insured may have to pay them less frequently. For example, instead of paying a monthly periodic deduction, the insurer might bill an individual quarterly. Under some plans, the insurer makes an extra administrative charge for the cost of direct billing.

CHAPTER REVIEW

Key Terms and Concepts

group insurance   voluntary benefits
self-funding   portability
voluntary benefit   guaranteed issue
master contract   simplified issue
certificate of insurance   modified guaranteed issue

Review Questions

Review questions are based on the learning objectives in this chapter. For example, a [3] at the end of a questions means that the question is based on learning objective 3. If there are multiple objectives, they are all listed.

1. Briefly describe each of the following structural forms for a benefit plan: [1]

    a. group insurance arrangements

    b. alternative funding

    c. individual policies

2. Regarding alternative funding methods: [1]

    a. Why have employers turned to alternative funding methods for group benefits?

    b. What effect does an alternative funding method have on such factors as eligibility and benefit levels?

3. What general characteristics distinguish group insurance from individual insurance? [2]

4. Regarding the popularity of voluntary benefits: [3]

    a. What is the primary reason for the increase in popularity of voluntary benefits?

    b. What are the other reasons for its increase in popularity?

5. Regarding the voluntary market: [3]

    a. What are the target markets for voluntary benefit plans?

    b. What types of products are often available in the voluntary market?

6. Explain the difference between each of the following underwriting methods: [3]

    a. guaranteed issue

    b. simplified issue

    c. modified guaranteed issue

7. What is the method of premium payment used for most voluntary benefit plans? [3]

8. To what extent are voluntary benefits portable? [3]

Review Question Answers

1. a.   Group insurance is a technique under which many individuals and possibly their dependents are insured under a single policy issued to another entity. In most situations, the entity is an employer, and the individuals are employees. The employer may pay all, some, or none of the cost of the coverage provided. The insurer administers many aspects of the benefit plan, and bears the uncertainty that benefit payments will exceed those expected.

    b.   In its purest sense, self-funding is a method by which an employer pays benefit costs from current revenue, administers all aspects of a benefit plan, and bears the uncertainty that benefit payments will exceed those expected. Employers have increasingly turned from fully insured plans to alternative funding methods to minimize the cost of providing benefits. There are several alternative funding methods including premium payment delays, reserve reduction arrangements as well as minimum premium plans and large deductible plans. The ultimate alternative funding method is self-funding.

    c.   Voluntary benefits are usually policies of individual insurance that employers make available to employees as a benefit plan. The employees voluntarily elect to participate in the plan and pay the entire cost of the coverage they receive. Many supplemental life insurance plans and most long-term care insurance plans are structured as voluntary plans of individual insurance.

2. a.   As the cost of providing insurance benefits to employees has risen, employers have increasingly turned from fully insured plans to alternative funding methods to minimize this cost.

    b.   The use of alternative funding methods does not eliminate the need for making decisions regarding such factors as eligibility, benefit levels, and claims handling. In most cases, provisions for these factors are similar, if not identical, to the provisions found in the types of group insurance contracts.

3. First, in contrast to most individual insurance contracts, the group insurance contract provides coverage to a number of persons under a single contract issued to someone other than the persons insured. Group contracts usually cover individuals who are full-time employees, and the policyowner is either their employer or a trust established to provide benefits for the employees.

    Each employee covered under the contract receives a certificate of insurance as evidence of his or her coverage. A certificate is merely a description of the coverage provided and is not part of the master contract.

In individual insurance, the insured's coverage normally begins with the inception of the insurance contract and ceases with its termination. However, in group insurance, individual members of the group may become eligible for coverage long after the inception of the group contract, or they may lose their eligibility status long before the contract terminates.

A second distinguishing characteristic of group insurance is the use of experience rating. If a group is sufficiently large, the actual claims experience of that particular group is a factor in determining the premium the policyowner is charged. However, such experience is determined on a class basis and applies to all insureds in that class.

Finally, for group insurance, individual members of the group are usually not required to show any evidence of insurability when initially eligible for coverage. This is not to say that there is no underwriting, but rather that underwriting is focused on the characteristics of the group instead of on the insurability of each person as in the case of individual insurance.

4. a. Voluntary benefits have increased in popularity in recent years, primarily because of employers' attempts to contain the rising costs of employee benefits—particularly the cost for medical expense coverage. In addition, portability of this type of coverage is often appealing. This feature allows an employee to continue coverage under an employer-sponsored plan after termination of employment by paying premiums directly to the insurance company.

    b. Voluntary benefits have also grown in popularity as a method of supplementing the benefits provided under a group plan financed by the employer because they allow employees to purchase additional protection.

5. a. The target market is broad and includes not only large employer groups but also small- and medium-size groups as well. Special markets for voluntary benefits also include membership organizations and affinity groups.

    b. A major goal of many insurance companies in the voluntary market is to sell life insurance to employees and their dependents. Life insurance products run the gamut from basic term insurance to variable universal life insurance and include accidental death and dismemberment insurance. The most prevalent health insurance products are short-term and long-term disability income. Major medical coverage is seldom offered, but insurers sell supplemental medical plans that also represent significant shares of total voluntary premiums. These products include accident insurance (16 percent), specified-disease and critical illness policies (13 percent) and hospital-indemnity and other medical coverage (15 percent). More recently, limited-benefit medical plans, known as mini-med plans, are becoming increasingly available as part of this last category. Dental insurance is common with 7 percent of voluntary market premiums. Prescription drug coverage and vision coverage are less common, but are also found. An increasingly common product is long-term care insurance. A few companies also write property and liability insurance.

6.   a.   Guaranteed issue means that coverage is issued without an employee having to provide evidence of insurability.

    b.   Simplified issue means that coverage is issued with satisfactory responses to questions on an abbreviated application form.

    c.   Some insurers have a category of underwriting—called modified guaranteed issue—that falls somewhere between guaranteed issue and simplified issue. In this case, the insurer accepts most applicants but asks a few medically related questions that may result in the declination of a small number of applicants.

7.   The vast majority of voluntary benefits use payroll deduction as the method for premium payments, with the employer remitting the premiums to the insurance company.

8.   Individual insurance products that provide voluntary benefits are automatically portable when an employee terminates employment. However, there are several possibilities with group voluntary benefits. In a few cases, coverage ceases; in some cases, the employee must convert to an individual policy. In most cases, the employee can continue the group coverage on a direct-bill basis.

Chapter 3

The Governmental Environment for Group Benefits

Learning Objectives

An understanding of the material in this chapter should enable the student to

1.   **Describe the nature of the major social insurance programs.**

2.   **Identify the types of groups eligible for coverage under the laws of most states, and explain the significant characteristics and regulations pertaining to each.**

3.   **Describe the major aspects of state regulation that apply to group insurance.**

4.   **Explain the major provisions of the Affordable Care Act and the effect the mandates have on medical expense coverages.**

5.   **Explain the effect of other federal legislation on employee benefit plans.**

The character of group benefits is greatly influenced by social insurance programs and the numerous other laws and regulations that both the state and federal governments impose. The major impact of state regulation is felt through the insurance laws governing insurance companies and the products they sell. Traditionally, these laws have affected only those benefit plans funded with insurance contracts. The federal laws affecting group benefits, on the other hand, generally are directed toward any plans that employers establish for their employees, regardless of the funding method used.

SOCIAL INSURANCE

social insurance

Federal and state insurance programs provide most Americans with some coverage for losses arising from death, old age, disability, and sickness. These **social insurance** programs are government run or regulated and are designed to solve social problems that affect a large portion of society. They are distinguished by compulsory employment-related coverage, partial or total employer financing, benefits prescribed by law, benefits as a matter of right, and an emphasis on social adequacy rather than on individual equity.

Social insurance programs form the foundation for many employer-designed benefit plans. Some benefit plans apply only to those employees who are not adequately covered under comparable social insurance programs; other benefit plans may cover all employees but provide reduced benefits in those areas where similar social insurance benefits are available. The five major social insurance programs are

- Social Security
- Medicare
- unemployment insurance
- temporary disability insurance
- worker's compensation insurance

Social Security

Social Security

Many social insurance and public assistance programs are the result of the Social Security Act and its many amendments over the years. Although all these programs can broadly be described as **Social Security**, the term is almost universally used to describe the federal old-age, survivors, and disability insurance (OASDI) program established by the act. In addition to providing retirement income for most older workers, Social Security provides income benefits to dependent, unmarried children of deceased workers and the spouses who care for these children.

Social Security also provides disability income benefits to disabled workers, generally after 6 months of disability, if a very stringent definition of disability is satisfied. Employer-provided disability income plans take these benefits into account in a variety of ways.

Detailed information on Social Security can be found on the Web site of the Social Security Administration: socialsecurity.gov.

Medicare

Medicare

Most Americans aged 65 or older and certain younger, disabled workers are eligible for medical expense benefits under **Medicare**, another federal program established by the Social Security Act. Medicare Part A, which provides benefits for hospital expenses, is funded through payroll taxes for Medicare beneficiaries. Medicare Part B includes benefits for many other types of medical expenses. Beneficiaries must pay a monthly premium for Part B. Parts A and B, collectively referred to as original Medicare, are government-run programs.

There are also two parts of Medicare that are voluntary private insurance programs. These are Parts C and D. Part C, called Medicare Advantage, provides alternative plans to original Medicare. Part D provides prescription drug coverage. Parts C and D are subject to federal regulations.

The Medicare Web site (medicare.gov) contains detailed information about Medicare.

Unemployment Insurance

unemployment insurance

Most workers in the United States are covered by **unemployment insurance** programs that provide them with a portion of their former income when they lose their jobs but are still able and willing to work. These programs are established and administered by the states under federal guidelines. The federal government provides the financing for a large portion of the benefits paid. Employers often take the benefits under unemployment insurance programs into consideration when they design severance packages and supplemental unemployment insurance programs.

Temporary Disability Laws

temporary disability law

Five states—California, Hawaii, New Jersey, New York, and Rhode Island—require that employers provide short-term disability income coverage to their employees. Under such a **temporary disability law**, the coverage must provide benefit levels of at least a specified amount, and the employer may be required to pay all or at least a portion of the cost of the coverage.

Workers' Compensation Insurance

workers' compensation insurance

Every state has a law that requires an employer to provide **workers' compensation insurance** for most employees. This type of insurance provides specified levels of medical expense and disability income benefits to employees who suffer injury or illness because of work-related accidents or diseases. Survivors also receive death benefits if these injuries or illnesses result in death. Most of the disability, medical expense, and dental plans described in this book exclude coverage to the extent that benefits are payable under workers' compensation laws.

STATE REGULATION

McCarran-Ferguson Act

Even though the United States Supreme Court has declared insurance to be commerce and thus subject to federal regulation when conducted on an interstate basis, Congress gave the states substantial regulatory authority by the passage of the **McCarran-Ferguson Act** (Public Law 15) in 1945. The act exempts insurance from certain federal regulations to the extent that individual states actually regulate insurance. In addition, it stipulates that most other federal laws are not applicable to insurance unless they are specifically directed at the business of insurance.

National Association of Insurance Commissioners (NAIC)

Because of the McCarran-Ferguson Act, a substantial body of laws and regulations has been enacted in every state. Since no two states have identical laws and regulations, there have been attempts to encourage uniformity among the states. The most significant influence in this regard has been the **National Association of Insurance Commissioners (NAIC)**, which is composed of state regulatory officials. Because the National Association of Insurance Commissioners promotes uniformity in legislation and administrative rules affecting insurance, it has developed numerous model laws. Although states are not bound to adopt NAIC model laws, numerous states have enacted many of them in whole or in part.

Some of the more significant state laws and regulations affecting group insurance pertain to the types of groups eligible for coverage, benefit limitations, contractual provisions, and tax treatment. Moreover, because many employers have employees in several states, the extent of each state's regulatory jurisdiction is a matter of some concern.

Eligible Groups

Most states do not allow insurance companies to write group insurance contracts unless a minimum number of persons are insured under the contract. This requirement may vary by type of coverage and type of group. The minimum number required for plans established by individual employers may be as few as 2.

Most states also have insurance laws concerning the types of groups for which insurance companies may write group insurance. Most of these laws specify that an insurer cannot deliver a group insurance contract to a policyowner in the state unless the group meets certain statutory eligibility requirements for its type of group. In some states, these eligibility requirements even vary by type of coverage. Although the categories of eligible groups may differ, at least five types of groups are acceptable in virtually all states: individual employer groups, negotiated trusteeships, trade associations, creditor-debtor groups, and labor union groups.

Individual Employer Groups

individual employer group

The most common type of eligible group is the **individual employer group**, in which the employer may be a corporation, a partnership, or a sole proprietorship. Many state laws are very specific about what constitutes an employee for group insurance purposes. In addition to those usually considered employees of a firm, insurers generally write coverage for retired employees and employees of subsidiary and affiliated firms. Furthermore, individual proprietors or partners are usually eligible for coverage as long as they actively engage in and devote a substantial part of their time to the organization. Similarly, directors of a corporation may be eligible for coverage if they are also employees of the corporation.

Negotiated Trusteeships (Taft-Hartley Trusts)

negotiated trusteeship

A **negotiated trusteeship** is formed as a result of collective bargaining over benefits between a union and the employers of the union members. Generally, the union employees are in the same industry or related ones. For the most part, frequent movement of union members among employers characterizes these industries (such as trucking or construction). The Taft-Hartley Act prohibits employers from paying funds directly to a labor union for the purpose of providing group insurance coverage to members. They must make payments to a trust fund established for the purpose of providing benefits to employees. The trustees of the fund, who must consist of equal numbers of representatives from both the employers and the union, can elect either to self-fund benefits or to purchase insurance contracts with themselves as the policyowners. Because eligible employees include only members of the collective-bargaining unit (which may include some nonunion members), benefits for other employees must be provided in some other manner.

Negotiated trusteeships differ from other types of groups in how they finance benefits and determine eligibility for benefits. Employers often make contributions based on the number of hours worked by the employees covered under the collective-bargaining agreement, regardless of whether these employees are eligible for benefits. Eligibility for benefits during a given period is usually based only on some minimum number of hours worked during a previous period. For example, a union member might receive coverage during a calendar quarter (even when unemployed) if he or she worked at least 300 hours in the previous calendar quarter. This situation, where the employees for whom the employer makes contributions may differ from those who are eligible for benefits, presents a unique problem for the underwriter. Rates must be adequate to build up the contingency reserves necessary to pay benefits in periods of heavy layoffs, during which a large portion of contributions ceases but eligibility for benefits continues.

Although negotiated trusteeships normally provide benefits for the employees of several employers, they can also be established for the employees of a single employer. However, situations involving collective bargaining with a single employer usually result in the employer being required to provide benefits for the employees under a group insurance contract purchased by the employer. Although the bargaining unit specifies benefits, the employer is the policyowner and the group is an individual employer group rather than a negotiated trusteeship. This approach also enables the employer to provide benefits for nonunion employees under the same contract.

Trade Associations

trade association

For eligibility purposes, a **trade association** is an association of employers that has been formed for reasons other than obtaining insurance, such as lobbying, providing education, or setting industry standards for its members. In most cases, these employers are in the same industry or type of business—for example, travel planning, interior decorating, or manufacturing of a specific type of product. Many such associations frequently have a large number of employers without the minimum number of employees necessary to qualify for an individual employer group insurance contract. In some states, insurers issue the master contract directly to the trade association; most states, however, require the establishment of a trust. Individual employers may provide coverage for their employees through payment of premiums to the association or trust.

Labor Union Groups

Labor unions may establish group insurance plans to provide benefits for their members, with the master contract issued to the union. In addition to the prohibition by the Taft-Hartley Act of employer payments to labor unions for insurance premiums, state laws generally prohibit plans in which union members pay the entire cost from their own pockets.

Creditor-Debtor Groups

creditor-debtor group

A **creditor-debtor group** arises out of a creditor-debtor relationship. Such groups are often eligible for group term life insurance and group disability income insurance. Although the types of creditors and debtors may vary, insurers normally make coverage available for such organizations as banks, finance companies, and retailers with respect to time-payment purchases, personal loans, or charge accounts. A unique feature of group credit insurance is that the creditor must be the beneficiary of the coverage in addition to being the policyowner, even though the debtors are the insured. In group credit life insurance, the creditor must use any payments to cancel the insured portion of the debt; in group credit disability income insurance, the creditor must use any payments to relieve the debtor of making periodic payments during the insured period of disability. Premiums for group credit insurance may be shared by the creditor and the debtor or may be totally paid by either party.

Although this book concentrates on the use of group insurance as an employee benefit, it should be noted that group credit insurance, particularly credit life insurance, is a significant form of group insurance. According to the American Council of Life Insurance, $81 billion of credit life insurance was in force at the end of 2013, under approximately 17 million individual policies or certificates of group insurance.

Other Groups

Numerous other types of groups, such as alumni associations, professional associations, veterans' groups, savings account depositors, and credit card holders, may be eligible for group insurance under the regulations of many states. Insurance company underwriting practices and state regulation may impose more stringent requirements on these types of groups than on those involving an employer-employee relationship. Insurers frequently require individual evidence of insurability for other than small amounts of coverage. In addition, they generally impose a larger minimum size upon the group.

State Regulation of Group Insurance Plans

Contractual Provisions

Every state regulates contractual provisions through its insurance laws. In many instances, certain contractual provisions must be included in group insurance policies. The insurer may alter these mandatory provisions only if such changes result in more favorable treatment of the policyowner. Because of state regulation, coupled with industry practices, the provisions of most group life and health insurance policies are relatively uniform from company to company. Although an insurance company's policy forms can usually be used in all states, riders may be necessary to bring certain provisions into compliance with the regulations of some states.

Traditionally, the regulation of contractual provisions has focused on provisions pertaining to such factors as the grace period, conversion, and incontestability rather than on those applicable to the types or levels of benefits. These latter provisions have been a matter between the policyowner and the insurance company.

With few exceptions, the regulation of contractual provisions affects only those employee benefit plans funded with insurance contracts because provisions of ERISA exempts employee benefit plans from most types of state regulation. However, there are exceptions to this exemption, including insurance regulation and therefore the provisions in insurance contracts. Because of ERISA exemption, states have few laws and regulations applying to the provisions of uninsured benefit plans.

Benefit Levels

The level of benefits that an insurer can provide under group insurance contracts issued to certain types of eligible groups may be subject to statutory limitations. Medical expense benefit levels are regulated by the Affordable Care Act. Benefit levels will be discussed more by line of business throughout the chapters of this book.

Tax Treatment

Every state levies a premium tax on foreign (out-of-state) insurance companies licensed to do business in its state, and most states tax the premiums of insurance companies domiciled in their state. These taxes, which are applicable to premiums written within a state, average about 2 percent.

The imposition of the premium tax has placed insurance companies at a competitive disadvantage with alternative methods of providing benefits. In some states, premiums paid to health maintenance organizations and Blue Cross and Blue Shield plans are not subject to the tax. The elimination of this tax is one cost saving under self-funded plans. Because the trend toward self-funding of benefits by large corporations has resulted in the loss of substantial premium tax revenue to the states, there have been suggestions that all premiums paid to any type of organization or fund for the purpose of providing insurance benefits to employees be subject to the premium tax.

Regulatory Jurisdiction

A group insurance contract often insures individuals living in more than one state—a situation that raises the question of which state or states have regulatory jurisdiction over the contract. This issue is a crucial one because such factors as minimum enrollment percentages, maximum amounts of life insurance, and required contract provisions vary among the states.

doctrine of comity

Few problems arise if the insured group qualifies as an eligible group in all the states where insured individuals reside. Under the **doctrine of comity**, by which states recognize within their own territory the laws of other states, it is generally accepted that the state in which the group insurance contract is delivered to the policyowner has governing jurisdiction. Therefore, the contract must conform only to the laws and regulations of this one state, even though certificates of insurance may be delivered in other states. A few states have statutes that prohibit insurance issued in other states from covering residents of their state unless the contract conforms to their laws and regulations.

Most insurers are reluctant to issue a group contract in any state unless a corporate officer or trustee who can execute acceptance of the contract is located in that state. The principal functions related to the administration of the group contract must also be performed there.

HEALTH CARE REFORM

Overview of Health Care Reform

Affordable Care Act (ACA)

On March 23, 2010, the Patient Protection and Affordable Care Act was passed. It was followed by the Health Care and Education Reconciliation Act on March 30, 2010. Together, these two laws are referred to as the **Affordable Care Act (ACA)**.

The Affordable Care Act created a massive overhaul of the health care system in the United States. Changes are being implemented through changes in the Social Security

Administration, the Internal Revenue Service, the Public Health Service Act, the Fair Labor Standards Act, ERISA, and HIPAA among others. There are no changes to COBRA included in ACA.

The Affordable Care Act has four main goals:

- To increase access to preventive care
- To increase access to wellness care
- To create transparency for consumers
- To eliminate waste and fraud within the healthcare system

There are several federal agencies responsible for monitoring the implementation of ACA and ensuring compliance with the laws. They include the Department of Health and Human Services, the Department of Labor and the Internal Revenue Service.

essential health benefits

ACA introduced the concept of **essential health benefits** which include ambulatory patient services, hospitalization, emergency services, maternity and newborn care, mental health and substance abuse disorders including behavioral health treatment, rehabilitative services, laboratory services, preventive care and wellness services, chronic disease management, pediatric services including oral and vision care, and prescription drugs. ACA compliant plans must provide these benefits. The Department of Health and Human Services reserves the right to add benefits to the definition.

The Affordable Care Act increases the access to affordable health care provided through individual coverage, group health coverage, Medicaid, Medicare, and the state health benefit exchanges. The definition of a group health plan is an employee welfare benefit plan (as defined in ERISA) to the extent that the plan provides medical care (including items and services paid for as medical care) to employees or their dependents (as defined under the terms of the plan) directly or through insurance, reimbursement, or otherwise.

Summary of Affordable Care Act Changes

The following are high level summaries of the main ACA mandates.

Dependent coverage to age 26—Any dependents who were dropped from coverage due to aging out of eligibility must be re-enrolled with no medical underwriting. To continue to be covered as an adult dependent there is no requirement for tax dependence, residency, student status, marital status, employment status, or eligibility for other coverage.

Prohibition of lifetime maximum limits and annual dollar restrictions on essential health benefits—Anyone who exceeded an established maximum lifetime limit can be reenrolled. There are no waivers allowed for the prohibition of lifetime maximum limits.

Rescission prohibition —Retroactive rescissions due to unintentional errors on the application information are prohibited. Rescission can still occur due to fraud, intentional misrepresentations, etc. Retroactive terminations are allowed for (1) course of business reporting delays such as an employer reconciliation of employee eligibility and (2) failure to notify a plan administrator of a divorce. For other reasons, the rescission is prospective only.

Preventive care cost-sharing elimination —Preventive care and wellness cost-sharing provisions are prohibited.

Expansion of Medicaid eligibility to adults without children with incomes up to 133 percent of the federal poverty level—The requirement to have dependent children for eligibility for Medicaid coverage has been removed. Federal funding has also been adjusted in that from 2014 to 2016, newly eligible adults will be funded 100 percent by the federal government. The federal funding will be phased downward to 90 percent for 2020 and thereafter.

medical loss ratio (MLR)

Medical loss ratio regulations —This mandate states that for large groups, the insurance carriers or health plans are required to spend 85 percent of the premium on medical care services. For the small group and individual products, they are required to spend 80 percent of the premium on medical care services. If this medical loss ratio is not met, the insurance carrier or health plan must rebate the excess to the purchaser. There can be exceptions granted for individual plans only by the Department of Health and Human Services in areas where the medical loss ratio requirements are causing health plans to exit the marketplace. There have been some exceptions granted.

state health benefit exchanges

navigator

State health benefit exchanges established— The exchanges function as an insurance marketplace in each state for individuals and small employers. Small group may be defined as 50 and under employees or 100 and under employees at the state's discretion. There are four levels of plans offered with varying actuarial equivalent benefit levels: bronze (60 percent), silver (70 percent), gold (80 percent), and platinum (90 percent). Participants may choose the desired level of benefits. A new role called a **navigator** advises employers and individuals regarding plans and coverages available in the exchanges. There will be premium subsidies available for those persons who qualify.

individual mandate

Individual mandate—This mandate says that everyone will be required to obtain health care coverage or pay a penalty tax (generally $325 per adult, $162.50 per child, with a family maximum of $975 for 2015). The tax will increase over time.

Preexisting condition exclusion total prohibition—This mandate established a preexisting condition exclusion for all persons regardless of age. There will be no more medical underwriting for health care coverage. Underwriting may be continued based on age, gender, geographic location, and smoking status only. Premiums cannot be rated up for medical reasons.

Grandfathered Plans

grandfathered plan

If medical coverage existed on March 23, 2010, ACA offered exemptions from compliance with some of its mandates. This allowed consumers to keep most of the coverage they already had before the law was enacted.

Grandfathered plans are not required to:

- provide recommended preventive services with no cost-sharing
- limit overall cost-sharing for essential health benefits
- provide essential health benefits
- offer new protections for consumers appealing claims and coverage denials
- protect the choice of health care providers and access to emergency care
- prohibit using health status in setting premium rates

In addition, grandfathered individual health plans are not required to:

- phase out annual dollar limits on key benefits
- eliminate preexisting condition exclusions for children under 19 years old

Depending on the reasons for making changes to a grandfathered plan, the plan may or may not lose its grandfathered status. If you lose grandfathered status, all provisions of ACA apply upon renewal.

Excepted Plans

excepted plan

There are certain benefits which are considered to be "excepted" from the healthcare reform Public Health Services Act (PHSA) portion of the mandates. Some examples of these benefits include:

- accident-only coverage
- dental plans
- worker's compensation coverage
- specific disease coverage
- hospital indemnity or other fixed indemnity coverage
- separate policies for Medicare or Armed Forces supplements
- credit coverage
- coverage for on-site medical clinics
- disability income coverage
- medical coverage issued to groups with less than 2 employees
- health savings accounts
- long-term care plans
- retiree-only plans
- tribal plans
- vision plans

The official government website for additional information on healthcare reform is health-care.gov. The American College offers two courses which focus on the Affordable Care Act: HS 345 Healthcare Reform for Employers and Advisors and HS 346 The Healthcare Consultant.

OTHER FEDERAL REGULATION

Many pieces of federal regulation besides ACA affect the establishment and character of group insurance. The following acts affect several types of group benefits and are discussed in this chapter:

- Age Discrimination in Employment Act
- Employee Retirement Income Security Act

The income tax implications of the Internal Revenue Code are also significant and often vary for different types of group insurance coverage.

Age Discrimination in Employment Act

Age Discrimination in Employment Act

The **Age Discrimination in Employment Act (ADEA)** applies to employers with 20 or more employees and affects employees aged 40 and older. The act, passed in 1967, prohibits discrimination against these workers in terms, conditions, or privileges of employment—including wages and benefits. With some exceptions, such as individuals in executive or high policymaking positions, compulsory retirement is not allowed. Employee benefits, which traditionally ceased or were severely limited at age 65, must be continued for older workers. However, some reductions in benefits are allowed.

The act permits a reduction in the level of some benefits for older workers so that the cost of providing benefits for older workers is no greater than the cost of providing them for younger workers. However, the most expensive benefit—medical expense coverage—cannot be reduced. The following discussion is limited to reductions after age 65—by far the most common age for reducing benefits, even though reductions can start at an earlier age if they are justified on a cost basis. It should be emphasized that these restrictions apply to benefits for active employees only; there are no requirements under the act that an employer continue any benefits for retired workers.

In cases where benefits are reduced, the act allows an employer to use one of two approaches: a benefit-by-benefit approach or a benefit-package approach. Under the more common benefit-by-benefit approach, the employer may reduce each employee benefit to a lesser amount as long as each reduction can be justified on a cost basis. Under a benefit-package approach, the employer may alter the overall benefit package. Some benefits may be eliminated or reduced to a lesser amount than can be justified on a cost basis, as long as other existing benefits are not reduced or the benefit package is increased by adding new benefits for older workers. The only cost restriction is that the cost of the revised benefit package may be no less than if a benefit-by-benefit reduction had been used. The act also places two other restrictions on the benefit-package approach by prohibiting any reduction in medical expense benefits or retirement benefits.

Although reductions in group insurance benefits for older employees are permissible, they are not required. Some employers make no reductions for older employees, but most employers reduce life insurance benefits at age 65 and long-term disability benefits at age 60 or 65.

Group Term Life Insurance Benefits

Basing their conclusions on mortality statistics, most insurance companies feel that group term life insurance benefits can be reduced to certain percentages of the amount of coverage provided immediately prior to age 65 (see table below). However, some insurers recommend different percentage reductions.

Table 3-1 Group Term Life Insurance Benefit Reductions	
Age	Percentage
65–69	65
70–74	45
75–79	30
over 79	20

For this example, if employees normally receive $40,000 of group term life insurance, then employees between the ages of 65 and 69 can receive only 45 percent of that amount ($26,000), employees between the ages of 70 and 74 can receive 30 percent ($18,000), and so forth. Similarly, if employees normally receive coverage equal to 200 percent of salary, this coverage may be reduced by 35 percent to 130 percent of salary at age 65, with additional reductions at later ages. Reductions may also be made on an annual basis rather than an age-banded basis.

Group Disability Income Benefits

The act allows reductions in insured short-term disability income plans. However, no reductions are allowed in uninsured sick-leave plans. Some insurance companies feel a benefit reduction of approximately 20 percent is appropriate for employees between 65 and 69, with additional decreases of 20 percent of the previous benefit for each consecutive 5-year period. However, the laws of the few states that require short-term disability income benefits to be provided allow neither a reduction in benefits nor an increase in any contribution rate for older employees.

Under the act, two methods are allowed for reducing long-term disability income benefits for employees who become disabled at older ages. Either the level of benefits may be reduced without altering benefit eligibility or duration, or the benefit duration may be reduced without altering the level of benefits. Again, these reductions must be justified on a cost basis. Unfortunately, no rough guidelines can be given because any possible reductions vary considerably, depending on the eligibility requirements and the duration of benefits under a long-term disability plan. For example, one insurance company suggests that if a plan previously provided full benefits until age 70, then the duration of the benefits could be reduced to 12 months for disabilities occurring between the ages of 70 and 74 and 6 months for disabilities occurring after age 74.

Group Medical Expense Benefits

The Age Discrimination in Employment Act requires that employers offer all employees over age 65 (and any employees' spouses who are also over age 65) the same medical coverage they provide for younger employees (and their spouses). Consequently, benefits cannot be reduced for older employees because of increasing cost to the employer. In addition, older employees cannot be required to contribute more than younger employees contribute.

For employers with 20 or more employees, the employer's plan is the primary payer of benefits, with Medicare assuming the secondary-payer role. Although employees may reject the employer's plan and elect Medicare as the primary payer of benefits, federal regulations prevent an employer from offering a health plan or option designed to induce such a rejection. This effectively prohibits an employer from paying the Part B premium or offering any type of supplemental plan to employees who elect Medicare as primary. When Medicare is secondary, the employer may pay the Part B premium for those employees who elect Medicare, but the employer has no legal responsibility to do so.

Employee Retirement Income Security Act

Employee Retirement Income Security Act (ERISA)

Congress enacted the **Employee Retirement Income Security Act (ERISA)** in 1974 to protect the interests of participants in employee benefit plans as well as the interests of participants' beneficiaries. The most significant sections dealing with employee welfare benefit plans are those pertaining to (1) fiduciary responsibility and (2) reporting and disclosure. Because the act and its accompanying regulations are lengthy and extremely complex, the discussion below only addresses the highlights of ERISA and its effect on employee welfare benefit plans. Other references to the act are mentioned throughout the book.

Employee Welfare Benefit Plans

employee welfare benefit plan

An **employee welfare benefit plan** to which ERISA applies is defined as including any plan, fund, or program established or maintained by an employer (or an employee organization) for the purpose of providing for its participants or their beneficiaries any of the following benefits:

- medical, surgical, or hospital care or benefits
- benefits in the event of sickness, accident, disability, death, or unemployment
- vacation benefits
- apprenticeship or other training programs
- day-care centers
- scholarship funds
- prepaid legal services
- any benefit described in Sec. 302(c) of the Labor Management Relations Act of 1947 (such as holiday pay and severance pay)

There are some exceptions, however, to this general rule. Certain types of employee welfare benefit plans are specifically exempt from regulation under ERISA. Among these are

- government plans
- church plans (unless they elect to be covered)
- plans maintained solely to comply with workers' compensation, unemployment compensation, or disability insurance laws

Requirement of a Written Instrument

One of the requirements of ERISA is that every employee welfare benefit plan that is subject to the act's regulations be established and maintained pursuant to a written instrument. This instrument must provide for one or more named fiduciaries who have the authority to control and manage the plan's operation and administration. In the case of an insured plan, the fiduciary (or fiduciaries) has the responsibility for selecting the insurance carrier. In addition, a plan administrator is usually named. The plan administrator, who has the responsibility for complying with the reporting and disclosure requirements under ERISA, may be the employer (that is, the corporation, partnership, or sole proprietorship). But it usually is a benefits committee or a specific person, such as the benefits manager or, in the case of a small firm, the owner. If no plan administrator is named, the plan sponsor is considered the plan administrator. In the case of an employee welfare benefit plan established or maintained by a single employer, the employer is considered to be the plan's sponsor.

In addition to naming a fiduciary, the plan instrument must accomplish the following:

- provide a procedure for establishing and carrying out a funding policy and method consistent with the plan's objectives

- provide a procedure for amending the plan and for identifying the persons who have the authority to amend it

- specify the basis on which payments are made to and from the plan

Establishment of a Trust

Unless the assets of an employee welfare benefit plan consist of insurance contracts or are held by an insurance company, ERISA requires that one of more trustees hold all assets of an employee welfare benefit plan in trust. The trustee (or trustees) may be named in either the trust instrument or in the written plan instrument or may be appointed by the named fiduciary. The trustee has the exclusive authority and discretion to manage and control the plan's assets except where the trustee is subject to the direction of the named fiduciary or where the authority to manage, acquire, or dispose of plan assets is delegated to one or more investment managers.

Fiduciary Responsibility

fiduciary

ERISA prescribes very detailed standards for fiduciaries and other parties-in-interest of employee welfare benefit plans. In addition to the named fiduciary (or fiduciaries) in a plan instrument, a **fiduciary** is defined as any person who

- exercises discretionary authority or control over plan management or assets

- provides investment advice to a plan for a fee or other compensation

- has discretionary authority or responsibility in the administration of a plan

ERISA requires that a fiduciary discharge his or her duties regarding a plan solely in the interest of the participants and their beneficiaries and that the fiduciary do so

- for the exclusive purpose of (1) providing benefits to participants and their beneficiaries and (2) defraying reasonable expenses of administering the plan

- with the same care, skill, prudence, and diligence under the given circumstances that a prudent person acting in a like capacity and familiar with such matters would use in a similar situation

- by diversifying the investments of the plan to minimize the risk of large losses, unless under the circumstances it is clearly prudent not to do so

- in accordance with the documents and instruments governing the plan insofar as such documents and instruments are consistent with the fiduciary provisions of ERISA

Any fiduciary who breaches any of these duties is personally liable for the full amount of any loss resulting from such actions. Furthermore, a fiduciary is also personally liable for similar breaches by another fiduciary to the extent that his or her actions contributed to the other fiduciary's breach. A breach of fiduciary responsibilities can also result in civil penalties and, if the breach is willful, in criminal penalties as well.

party-in-interest

ERISA also contains a list of prohibited transactions for parties-in-interest to an employee welfare benefit plan. In addition to fiduciaries, a **party-in-interest** is defined as including

- any counsel or employee of the plan

- any person providing services to the plan

- an employer of any covered employees of the plan

- an employee organization, any of whose members are covered under the plan

- any owner, direct or indirect, of 50 percent or more of the firm sponsoring the plan

- any relative of a party-in-interest

- certain other related corporations, employees, officers, directors, partners, and joint venturers

The results of the prohibited-transactions provision are that a party-in-interest may not

- cause the plan to engage in any transaction with a party-in-interest that constitutes a direct or indirect (1) sale, exchange, or leasing of property; (2) lending of money; (3) extension of credit; (4) furnishing of goods, services, or facilities; or (5)

transfer of any plan assets to a party-in-interest or use of any plan assets by or for the benefit of a party-in-interest

- acquire or hold more than 10 percent of the plan assets in employer securities or real estate

- deal with the assets of the plan in his or her own interest or for his or her own account

- act in any capacity in any transaction involving the plan on behalf of a party whose interests are adverse to the interests of the plan, its participants, or its beneficiaries

- receive any consideration for his or her own personal account from any party dealing with the plan in connection with a transaction involving plan assets

- be paid for his or her services, if already receiving full-time pay from an employer whose employees are participants in the plan, except for reimbursement of expenses incurred

Reporting and Disclosure—General Requirements

ERISA requires a plan administrator to make available certain information concerning any employee welfare benefit plan to some or all of the following: (1) plan participants (including beneficiaries of plan participants who are receiving benefits), (2) the Department of Labor, and (3) the Internal Revenue Service (IRS). This information must consist of all the following for employers with more than 100 employees. As discussed later, there are slightly different rules for smaller employers.

- a summary plan description

- a summary of material modifications

- an annual return/report—Form 5500 (or one of its variations)

- a summary annual report

- other reports

ERISA imposes significant monetary penalties for failure to comply with the reporting and disclosure requirements within the prescribed time periods. For example, a fine of up to $1,100 per day can be imposed from the date of failure or refusal to file Form 5500. A fine of up to $110 per day can also be imposed for failure to provide certain requested information to plan participants within 30 days of request. In addition, civil and criminal action can be taken against any plan administrator who willfully violates any of the requirements or who knowingly falsifies or conceals ERISA disclosure information.

summary plan description (SPD)

Summary Plan Description. The plan administrator must automatically provide a **summary plan description (SPD)** to each plan participant within 120 days after the adoption of an employee welfare benefit plan and forward it to the Department of Labor upon request. Copies must be provided to new participants within 90 days of first becoming eligible to participate, and an updated SPD must be provided once every 5 years if a plan has been materially modified, otherwise once every 10 years. The SPD must be written in language that is understandable to the average plan participant and must contain information regarding the plan: plan administration, plan sponsor, plan being offered, plan funding, eligibility and disqualification guidelines, plan changes, claims processes, COBRA rights, ERISA rights, and other information.

ERISA does not require that an SPD be provided on a specific form, only that certain information be provided. Some employers use a single document; other employers incorporate much of the required information into the employee benefits handbook that their employees receive. Electronic transmissions of SPDs and other required information for participants is acceptable as long as the transmissions meet certain conditions.

summary of material modification

Summary of Material Modification. For most welfare benefit plans, the **summary of material modification** must be automatically provided to each plan participant and the Department of Labor within 210 days after the end of a plan year (that is, the plan's fiscal year) in which a material change has been made in the plan. This summary covers the same information as in the summary plan description and is essentially an annual update of any information that has changed.

annual return/report

Annual Return/Report (Form 5500). The **annual return/report** must be filed with the IRS within 210 days after the end of a plan year. This form, which includes financial information about the plan, must be furnished to any plan participant upon written request to the plan administrator.

summary annual report

Summary Annual Report. A **summary annual report** must be automatically provided to each plan participant within 9 months after the end of a plan year. The information provided in this form is a relatively brief summary of some of the information in the annual return/report and consists of a list of the plan's assets and liabilities (or a description of the insurance contract used) and a schedule of the plan's receipts and disbursements.

Reporting and Disclosure—Small Groups

Employee welfare benefit plans that cover fewer than 100 participants at the beginning of a plan year are exempt from certain reporting and disclosure requirements if they meet either of the following conditions:

- The plan pays benefits as needed solely from the general assets of the employer or employee organization maintaining the plan.

- The plan provides benefits exclusively through insurance contracts or policies or through health maintenance organizations (HMOs). The employer (or employee organization) must pay premiums directly from its general assets or partly from its general assets and partly from participants' contributions (provided that the employer forwards participants' contributions to the insurance company within 3 months of receipt). The plan must inform contributing participants of the provisions for the allocation of refunds.

If these requirements are met, the plan administrator does not have to furnish a summary annual report to participants or furnish an annual return/report (Form 5500).

Note that a plan administrator must still furnish a summary plan description and a summary of material modifications to plan participants. In addition, certain underlying documents must be furnished to a participant upon the participant's request.

CHAPTER REVIEW

Key Terms and Concepts

social insurance
Social Security
Medicare
unemployment insurance
temporary disability law
workers' compensation insurance
McCarran-Ferguson Act
National Association of Insurance
   Commissioners (NAIC)
individual employer group

negotiated trusteeship
trade association
creditor-debtor group
doctrine of comity
Affordable Care Act (ACA)
essential health benefits
medical loss ratio (MLR)
state health benefit exchanges
navigator
individual mandate

grandfathered plan
excepted plan
Age Discrimination in Employment
   Act
Employee Retirement Income Security
   Act (ERISA)
employee welfare benefit plan

fiduciary
party-in-interest
summary plan description (SPD)
summary of material modification
annual return/report
summary annual report

Review Questions

Review questions are based on the learning objectives in this chapter. For example, a [3] at the end of a questions means that the question is based on learning objective 3. If there are multiple objectives, they are all listed.

1. How do social insurance programs form the foundation for many employer-designed benefit plans? [1]

2. Briefly describe the benefits available under each of the following social insurance programs: [1]

    a. Social Security

    b. Medicare

    c. unemployment insurance

    d. temporary disability laws

    e. workers' compensation insurance

3. What categories of persons are generally eligible for coverage under group insurance contracts issued to individual employer groups? [2]

4. How do negotiated trusteeships (Taft-Hartley trusts) differ from other types of groups with respect to [2]

    a. the financing of benefits?

    b. the determination of eligibility?

5. How do labor union groups differ from negotiated trusteeships? [2]

6. Regarding creditor-debtor group plans: [2]

    a. What is the coverage designed to do?

    b. Who is the beneficiary?

7. Explain the extent to which the states regulate the provisions found in group insurance contracts. [3]

8. How do state premium taxes put insurance companies at a competitive disadvantage with alternative methods of providing benefits? [3]

9. The Hatton Corporation is incorporated in the state of Washington, where it was established. However, its principal office is now located in Portland, Oregon, where all administrative functions are performed. While it has some employees in these two states, the majority of its workforce of 500 are employed in Idaho. The corporation has been told by its insurance agent that most insurance companies will deliver the group insurance contracts for its employees in any of these three states. [3]

    a. Is the agent correct? Explain.

    b. From a practical standpoint, why might the corporation prefer a situs other than the state where its administrative functions are performed?

10. What are the four main goals of ACA? [4]

11. Which federal agencies are responsible for the implementation and regulation of the Affordable Care Act? [4]

12. Describe the benefits included in the category "essential health benefits." [4]

13. Affordable Care Act affects which types of medical coverage? [4]

14. Describe the following ACA mandates: [4]

    a. dependent coverage extension to age 26

    b. prohibition of lifetime maximum limits on essential health benefits

    c. rescission prohibition

    d. preventive care cost-sharing elimination

    e. preexisting condition exclusion total prohibition

    f. Medicaid expansion

    g. medical loss ratio

15. What are the Affordable Care Act medical loss ratio requirements for: [4]

    a. large group?

    b. small group?

    c. individual plans?

Group Benefits: Basic Concepts and Alternatives

    d. Medicare?

16. Regarding the state health benefit exchange program: [4]

    a. Describe the state health benefit exchange program.

    b. What is the role of the navigator in the exchanges?

    c. When will large group begin to participate in the exchanges?

17. Regarding the individual mandate: [4]

    a. What is the individual mandate?

    b. What will the penalty be for noncompliance?

18. Regarding grandfathered plans: [4]

    a. What is a grandfathered plan?

    b. Compliance with which mandates are not required for grandfathered plans?

    c. Grandfathered individual plans are not required to comply with which additional mandates?

19. What types of benefits are considered "excepted benefits" under ACA? [4]

20. What employees and employers are subject to the Age Discrimination in Employment Act? [5]

21. Describe the general approaches that an employer may use to reduce benefits under the Age Discrimination in Employment Act. [5]

22. Explain the extent to which reductions in each of the following appear justified (using a benefit-by-benefit approach) under the Age Discrimination in Employment Act. [5]

    a. group term life insurance

    b. group disability income insurance

23. Explain the effect of the Age Discrimination in Employment Act on medical expense benefits. [5]

24. What specific provisions does ERISA require in a written plan instrument? [5]

25. Explain how a fiduciary under a plan subject to ERISA must discharge his or her duties. [5]

26. Regarding a party-in-interest: [5]

    a.   Who is a party-in-interest according to ERISA?

    b.   What types of transactions does ERISA prohibit for a party-in-interest?

27. For welfare benefit plans with 100 or more employees, identify the information that must be provided under ERISA to: [5]

    a.   plan participants

    b.   the Department of Labor

    c.   the Internal Revenue Service

28. What type of information must be contained in a summary plan description for a welfare benefit plan? [5]

Review Question Answers

1. Some employer-designed benefit plans apply only to those employees who are not adequately covered under comparable social insurance programs; other benefit plans may cover all employees but provide reduced benefits in those areas where similar social insurance benefits are available.

2. a.   In addition to providing retirement income for most older workers, Social Security provides income benefits to dependent, unmarried children of deceased workers and the spouses who care for these children. Social Security also provides disability income benefits to disabled workers, generally after 6 months of disability, if a very stringent definition of disability is satisfied.

    b.   Most Americans aged 65 or older and certain younger, disabled workers are eligible for medical expense benefits under Medicare. Medicare Part A covers benefits for hospital expenses at no charge to Medicare beneficiaries. Medicare Part B includes benefits for many other types of medical expenses. However, beneficiaries must pay a monthly premium for Part B. Medicare also provides a few benefits, such as kidney dialysis, for younger workers and their dependents. Parts A and B, collectively referred to as original Medicare, are government-run programs. There are also two parts of Medicare that are voluntary private insurance programs, but which are subject to federal requirements. These are Parts C and D. Part C, called Medicare Advantage, provides alternative plans to original Medicare. Part D provides prescription drug coverage. The federal government heavily subsidizes both Parts A and B, and participants usually also pay a premium.

    c.   Unemployment insurance programs provide most workers in the United States with a portion of their former income when they lose their jobs but are still able and willing to work. These programs are established and administered by the states under federal guidelines and the federal government provides the financing for a large portion of the benefits paid.

    d.   Five states—California, Hawaii, New Jersey, New York, and Rhode Island—and Puerto Rico require that employers provide short-term disability income coverage to their employees. Under such a temporary disability law, the coverage must provide benefit levels of at least a specified amount, and the employer may be required to pay all or at least a portion of the cost of the coverage.

    e.   Every state has a law that requires an employer to provide workers' compensation insurance for most employees. This type of insurance provides specified levels of medical expense and disability income benefits to employees who suffer injury because of work-related accidents or diseases. Death benefits are also paid to survivors if these injuries result in death.

3.   The most common type of eligible persons are employees and many state laws are very specific about what constitutes an employee for group insurance purposes. In addition to those usually considered to be employees of a firm, insurers generally write coverage for retired employees and employees of subsidiary and affiliated firms. Furthermore, individual proprietors or partners are usually eligible for coverage as long as they are actively engaged in and devote a substantial part of their time to the conduct of the organization. Similarly, directors of a corporation may be eligible for coverage if they are also employees of the corporation.

4.   a.   Under negotiated trusteeships, employers often make contributions based on the number of hours worked by the employees covered under the collective-bargaining agreement, regardless of whether these employees are eligible for benefits.

    b.   Eligibility for benefits during a given period is usually based only on some minimum number of hours worked during a previous period.

5.   Unlike the arrangements required by the Taft-Hartley Act for negotiated trusteeships, labor union groups may establish group insurance plans to provide benefits for their members, with the master contract issued to the union. In addition to the prohibition of employer payments to labor unions for insurance premiums, state laws generally prohibit plans in which union members pay the entire cost from their own pockets. Consequently, the premiums come solely from union funds or partially from union funds and partially from members' contributions.

6. a. A creditor-debtor group is designed to protect loan balances for the institution who issued the loans. If the insured becomes disabled or dies, the loan is paid off.

    b. The lending institution is automatically the beneficiary on the contract to the level of the loan balance.

7. Traditionally, the regulation of contractual provisions has focused on provisions pertaining to such factors as the grace period, conversion, and incontestability rather than on those applicable to the types or levels of benefits. More recently, some states, now require that certain benefits, such as well-baby care, treatment for alcoholism or drug abuse, and mental health parity be included in any group insurance contract. In other states, however, these benefits must be offered to group policyowners but are optional. Still other state laws and regulations specify minimum levels for certain benefits if those benefits are included.

8. In some states, premiums paid to health maintenance organizations and Blue Cross and Blue Shield plans are not subject to tax. In addition, the elimination of this tax is one cost saving under self-funded plans.

9. a. The agent is probably incorrect. Most insurance companies hesitate to deliver a group insurance contract in any state unless the principal administrative functions pertaining to the contract will be performed there and unless a corporate officer who can accept the contract is also located in the state.

    However, all three states have a significant relationship to the insurance transaction—Oregon having the principal office, Washington being the state of incorporation, and Idaho having the majority of the employees. Consequently some insurance companies will consider any of the three states to be an acceptable situs for the contract and deliver it where the corporation desires.

    b. The major reason for choosing one state over another is that the state of delivery will have regulatory jurisdiction over the contract. Thus the insurance laws of that state, which the corporation might find more favorable, will be applicable.

10. The four main goals for the Affordable Care Act are:

    a. to increase access to preventive care

    b. to increase access to wellness care

    c. to create transparency for consumers

    d. to eliminate waste and fraud within the health care system

11. The Affordable Care Act will be regulated and implemented by the Department of Health and Human Services, the Department of Labor and the Internal Revenue Service.

12. Essential health benefits include ambulatory patient services; hospitalization; emergency services; maternity and newborn care; treatment for mental health and substance abuse disorders including behavioral health treatment; rehabilitative services; laboratory services; preventive care and wellness services; chronic disease management; pediatric services including oral and vision care; and prescription drugs.

13. The Affordable Care Act affects health care provided through individual coverage, group health coverage, Medicaid, Medicare, and the state health benefit exchanges.

14. a. Any dependents who were dropped from coverage due to aging out of eligibility must be reenrolled with no medical underwriting. Tax dependence, residency, student status, marital status, employment status, or eligibility for other coverage does not come into play with eligibility.

    b. Anyone who exceeded an established maximum lifetime limit can be reenrolled on their plan. Maximum benefits were eliminated.

    c. Retroactive rescission of medical expense coverage is only allowed for fraud or intentional misrepresentations and a few other administrative reasons.

    d. Preventive care and wellness cost-sharing provisions have been eliminated.

    e. The preexisting condition exclusion applies to all persons regardless of age.

    f. The Medicaid expansion to those up to 133% of the federal poverty level with no dependent requirement allows millions to be eligible for coverage.

    g. The medical loss ratio requirements require health plans to spend a designated portion of the premium dollars on medical care services. It enforces the affordability goal of the ACA.

15. a. The medical loss ratio requirement for large groups is 85 percent.

    b. The medical loss ratio requirement for small group is 80 percent.

    c. The medical loss ratio requirement for individual plans is 80 percent.

    d. The medical loss ratio requirement for Medicare plans is 85 percent.

16. a. The state health benefit exchanges function as an insurance marketplace in each state for individuals and small employers. There are four levels of plans with

varying actuarial equivalent benefit levels offered: bronze (60 percent), silver (70 percent), gold (80 percent), and platinum (90 percent).

b. The navigator advises employers and individuals regarding plans and coverages available in the exchanges. It will be a role similar to a broker role outside of the exchanges.

c. Large groups can join the exchange marketplace in 2017 per the current implementation schedule.

17. a. The Individual mandate requires everyone to obtain some form of health care coverage.

b. If someone does not obtain health coverage, (s)he will be required to pay a penalty tax ($325 in 2015). The penalty tax will increase over time.

18. a. A grandfathered plan is one which existed on March 23, 2010, which the employer has designated as participating in exemptions from compliance with some of the new mandates.

b. Grandfathered plans are not required to provide recommended preventive services with no cost-sharing; limit overall cost-sharing for essential health benefits; provide essential health benefits; offer new protections for consumers appealing claims and coverage denials; protect the choice of health care providers and access to emergency care; and prohibit using health status in setting premium rates.

c. Grandfathered individual health plans are also not required to phase out annual dollar limits on key benefits and eliminate preexisting condition exclusions for children under age 19.

19. Excepted plans include: accident only coverage, dental plans, worker's compensation coverage; specific disease coverage; hospital indemnity plans; separate policies for Medicare or Armed Forces supplements; credit coverage; coverage for on-site medical clinics; disability income coverage; medical coverage issued to groups with less than 2 employees; health savings accounts, long term care plans; retiree only plans, tribal plans, and vision plans.

20. The Age Discrimination in Employment Act applies to employers with 20 or more employees and affects employees aged 40 and older.

21. Under the more common benefit-by-benefit approach, the employer may reduce each employee benefit to a lesser amount as long as each reduction can be justified on a cost basis. Under a benefit-package approach, the employer may alter the overall

benefit package. Some benefits may be eliminated or reduced to a lesser amount than can be justified on a cost basis, as long as other existing benefits are not reduced or the benefit package is increased by adding new benefits for older workers. The only cost restriction is that the cost of the revised benefit package may be no less than if a benefit-by-benefit reduction had been used. The act also places two other restrictions on the benefit-package approach by prohibiting any reduction in medical expense benefits or retirement benefits.

22. a. Basing their conclusions on mortality statistics, most insurance companies feel they can reduce group term life insurance benefits to certain percentages of the amount of coverage provided immediately prior to age 65. Reductions may also occur on an annual basis.

   b. The act allows reductions in insured short-term disability income plans. However, no reductions are allowed in uninsured sick-leave plans. Although disability statistics for those aged 65 and older are limited, some insurance companies feel a benefit reduction of approximately 20 percent is appropriate for employees between 65 and 69, with additional decreases of 20 percent of the previous benefit for each consecutive 5-year period.

      Under the act, two methods are allowed for reducing long-term disability income benefits for employees who become disabled at older ages. Either the level of benefits may be reduced without altering benefit eligibility or duration, or the benefit duration may be reduced without altering the level of benefits.

23. The Age Discrimination in Employment Act requires that employers offer all employees over age 65 (and any employees' spouses who are also over age 65) the same medical coverage they provide for younger employees (and their spouses). Consequently, benefits cannot be reduced for older employees because of increasing cost to the employer. In addition, older employees cannot be required to contribute more than younger employees contribute.

24. The written plan instrument must provide for one or more named fiduciaries who have the authority to control and manage the plan's operation and administration. In addition, a plan administrator is usually named. If no plan administrator is named, the plan sponsor is considered the plan administrator. In the case of an employee welfare benefit plan established or maintained by a single employer (including those situations where coverage is arranged through a multiple-employer welfare arrangement), the employer is considered to be the plan's sponsor. There is no prohibition against the administrator of a plan also being its named fiduciary.

In addition to naming a fiduciary, the plan instrument must accomplish the following:

- provide a procedure for establishing and carrying out a funding policy and method consistent with the plan's objectives

- provide a procedure for amending the plan and for identifying the persons who have the authority to amend it

- specify the basis on which payments are made to and from the plan

25. ERISA requires that a fiduciary discharge his or her duties regarding a plan solely in the interest of the participants and their beneficiaries and that the fiduciary do so

- for the exclusive purpose of (1) providing benefits to participants and their beneficiaries and (2) defraying reasonable expenses of administering the plan

- with the same care, skill, prudence, and diligence under the given circumstances that a prudent person acting in a like capacity and familiar with such matters would use in a similar situation

- by diversifying the investments of the plan to minimize the risk of large losses, unless under the circumstances it is clearly prudent not to do so

- in accordance with the documents and instruments governing the plan insofar as such documents and instruments are consistent with the fiduciary provisions of ERISA

26. a. A party-in-interest is defined as including

- any counsel or employee of the plan

- any person providing services to the plan

- an employer of any covered employees of the plan

- an employee organization, any of whose members the plan covers

- any owner, direct or indirect, of 50 percent or more of the firm sponsoring the plan

- any relative of a party-in-interest

- certain other related corporations, employees, officers, directors, partners, and joint venturers

b. A party-in-interest may not

- cause the plan to engage in any transaction with a party-in-interest that constitutes a direct or indirect (1) sale, exchange, or leasing of property; (2) lending of money; (3) extension of credit; (4) furnishing of goods, services, or facilities; or (5) transfer of any plan assets to a party-in-interest or use of any plan assets by or for the benefit of a party-in-interest

- acquire or hold more than 10 percent of the plan assets in employer securities or real estate

- deal with the assets of the plan in his or her own interest or for his or her own account

- act in any capacity in any transaction involving the plan on behalf of a party whose interests are adverse to the interests of the plan, its participants, or its beneficiaries

- receive any consideration for his or her own personal account from any party dealing with the plan in connection with a transaction involving plan assets

- be paid for his or her services, if already receiving full-time pay from an employer whose employees are participants in the plan, except for reimbursement of expenses incurred

27. a. The plan administrator must automatically provide a summary plan description (SPD) to each plan participant within 120 days after the adoption of an employee welfare benefit plan. Copies must be provided to new participants within 90 days of first becoming eligible to participate, and an updated SPD must be provided once every 5 years if a plan has been materially modified, otherwise once every 10 years.

For most welfare benefit plans, the summary of material modification must be automatically provided to each plan participant within 210 days after the end of a plan year (that is, the plan's fiscal year) in which a material change has been made in the plan.

A summary annual report must be automatically provided to each plan participant within 9 months after the end of a plan year. The information provided in this form is a relatively brief summary of some of the information in the annual return/report and consists of a list of the plan's assets and liabilities (or a description of the insurance contract used) and a schedule of the plan's receipts and disbursements.

b. A copy of SPD must be forwarded to the Department of Labor upon its request. However, a summary of material modification must be sent to the Department of Labor within the same period it is sent to participants. In addition, the plan administrator must file underlying documents with the Department of Labor, if so requested. These are documents under which the plan was established or is operated, such as a trust agreement or a collective-bargaining agreement. Finally, certain other records must be provided if requested by the Department of Labor and must also be available to plan participants under certain circumstances.

c. The annual return/report must be filed with the IRS within 210 days after the end of a plan year. This form, which includes financial information about the plan, must be furnished to any plan participant upon written request to the plan administrator. A terminal report must be filed with the IRS for a plan that has been terminated. The filing of the annual return/report for the final plan year will satisfy this requirement. The terminal report must be furnished to plan participants upon request.

28. The summary plan description must contain information regarding the plan, plan administration, plan sponsor, plan being offered, plan funding, eligibility and disqualification guidelines, plan changes, claims processing, COBRA rights, ERISA rights, and other information.

Chapter 4

Group Life Insurance

Learning Objectives

An understanding of the material in this chapter should enable the student to

1. **Describe the nature and significance of group term insurance.**

2. **Explain how the benefit schedules under group term life insurance plans might be determined.**

3. **Describe the eligibility requirements and other contract provisions usually found in group term life insurance plans.**

4. **Describe the added coverages that are often written in conjunction with group term life insurance for employees.**

5. **Explain the tax treatment of group term insurance to both employers and employees.**

6. **Describe postretirement life insurance plans.**

life insurance

Life insurance is the transfer of part of the financial loss due to the death of an insured person. Upon the insured's death, the insurance company agrees to pay a stated amount or income to the insured's beneficiary. Traditionally, most group life insurance plans were designed to provide coverage during an employee's working years, with coverage usually ceasing upon termination of employment for any reason. Today, the majority of employees have coverage that continues, often at a reduced amount, when termination is a result of retirement.

SIGNIFICANCE OF GROUP LIFE INSURANCE

Before proceeding further, here are a few statistics that show the significance of group life insurance:

- Coverage amounting to $8.2 trillion was in force at the end of 2013 under 114 million certificates of insurance.[1]

- Group insurance amounts to 41 percent of total life insurance coverage in force.[2]

---

1. American Council of Life Insurance, *Life Insurance Fact Book 2014,* pp. 65–66.
2. Ibid, p. 65.

• Ninety-six percent of the coverage in force is term insurance.[3]

NATURE OF GROUP TERM INSURANCE

term insurance

yearly renewable term insurance

The oldest and most common form of group life insurance is **term insurance**, which provides death benefits for a limited period of time. The protection expires at the end of the period without value (that is, it has no cash value) if the insured survives that length of time. Group term insurance consists primarily of **yearly renewable term insurance**, which means that coverage is renewed annually with each successive policy period being for one year. The group insurance marketplace with its widespread use of yearly renewable term contrasts with the individual marketplace, in which term insurance accounts for about 36 percent of newly issued policies[4]. This lower prevalence of term insurance in the individual marketplace is primarily due to its increasing annual premiums, which become prohibitive for many insureds at older ages. In group life insurance plans, the overall premium, in addition to other factors, is a function of the age distribution of the group's members. Although the premium for any individual employee increases with age, the flow of younger workers into the plan and the retirement of older workers tend to result in a relatively stable age distribution and thus an average group insurance rate that remains constant or rises only slightly.

The following discussion of group term insurance focuses largely on common contract provisions, other coverages that are often added to the basic contract, and relevant federal tax laws.

CONTRACT PROVISIONS

The provisions contained in group term insurance contracts are more uniform than those found in other types of group insurance. Much of this uniformity is a result of the adoption by most states of the NAIC Group Life Insurance Standard Provisions Model Bill. This bill, coupled with the insurance industry's attempts at uniformity, has resulted in provisions that are virtually identical among insurance companies. Although the following contract

3. LIMRA, *U.S. Group Life Insurance Sales Survey: 2012 Third Quarter Review,* 2012.
4. *Life Insurers Fact Book, 2014,* p. 64.

provisions represent the norm and are consistent with the practices of most insurance companies, some states may require slightly different provisions, and some companies may vary their contract provisions. In addition, negotiations between a policyowner and an insurance company may result in the modification of contract provisions.

Benefit Schedules

benefit schedule

A **benefit schedule** classifies the employees who are eligible for coverage, and it specifies the amount of life insurance that is provided to the members of each class. A benefit schedule can be as simple as providing a single amount of life insurance for all employees or as complex as providing different amounts of insurance for different classes of employees. For most individual employer groups, the benefit schedules are those in which the amount of life insurance is based on either a multiple of earnings or a specified dollar amount. Benefit schedules may also combine these two approaches.

Benefit schedules usually provide for a change in the amount of an employee's coverage when the employee moves into a different classification or has a change of earnings if a multiple-of-earnings schedule is used, even if this does not occur on the policy anniversary date. Some schedules, however, specify that adjustments in amounts of coverage are only made annually or on monthly premium due dates.

Multiple-of-Earnings Schedules

The most common type of benefit schedule is an earnings schedule under which the amount of life insurance is determined as a multiple (or percentage) of each employee's earnings. For example, the amount of life insurance for each employee may be twice (200 percent of) the employee's annual earnings. Most plans use a multiple between one and two, but higher and lower multiples are occasionally used. The amount of insurance is often rounded to the next higher $1,000. Some plans have no maximum benefit amount for individual employees, but the majority of plans do because of underwriting and cost considerations. Depending on the plan, this maximum may vary from less than $50,000 to $1 million or more. For purposes of the benefit schedule, an employee's earnings usually consist of base salary only and do not include additional compensation like overtime pay or bonuses.

Specified-Dollar-Amount Schedules

There are numerous types of benefit schedules that base benefits on specified dollar amounts: flat-benefit schedules and schedules that vary by earnings, position, or length of service.

Flat-Benefit Schedules. By far the most common type of specified-dollar-amount schedule is the flat-benefit schedule, under which the same amount of life insurance is provided for all employees regardless of salary or position. This type of benefit schedule is commonly used in group insurance plans covering hourly paid employees, particularly when benefits are negotiated with a union. In many cases, the amount of life insurance under a flat-benefit schedule is relatively small, such as $10,000 or $20,000; however, it may be as much as $50,000 or higher. When an employer wants to provide only a minimum amount of life insurance for all employees, a flat-benefit schedule is often used.

Dollar-Amount-By-Earnings Schedules. Some benefit schedules provide a specified amount of coverage that varies by earnings, with higher-paid employees typically receiving a proportionally larger benefit than lower-paid employees. The following table is an example of one such schedule.

Table 4-1 Dollar-Amount-By-Earnings Schedule	
Annual Earnings	Amount of Life Insurance
Less than $20,000	$ 20,000
$20,000 to $29,999	40,000
$30,000 to $39,999	75,000
$40,000 to $49,999	100,000
$50,000 and over	150,000

Position Schedules. Under position schedules, as the following table shows, the amount of life insurance is based on an employee's position within the firm.

Table 4-2 Position Schedule	
Position	Amount of Life Insurance
President	$300,000
Vice presidents	150,000
Managers	90,000
Salespersons	60,000
Other employees	30,000

Because individuals in high positions are often involved in designing the benefit schedule, underwriters are concerned that the benefits for these individuals be reasonable in relation to the overall plan benefits. Position schedules may also pose problems in meeting nondiscrimination rules if excessively large amounts of coverage are provided to persons in high positions.

Even though position schedules are often used when annual earnings can be easily determined, they are particularly useful when it is difficult to determine an employee's annual income. This is the situation when income is materially affected by such factors as commissions earned, number of hours worked, or bonuses based on either the employee's performance or the firm's profits.

Length-of-Service Schedules. In the early days of group life insurance, length-of-service schedules were relatively common and viewed as a method for rewarding longtime employees. However, because of the current view that the primary purpose of group life insurance is to replace income, such schedules are not extensively used. These schedules may also be considered discriminatory if a disproportionate number of the persons with longer service records are also the most highly paid employees. The following is an example of a length-of-service schedule.

Table 4-3 Length-of-Service Schedule	
Length of Service	**Amount of Life Insurance**
Less than 2 years	$ 8,000
2 years or more but less than 5 years	16,000
5 years or more but less than 10 years	24,000
10 years or more but less than 15 years	32,000
15 years or more but less than 20 years	40,000
20 years or more	50,000

Reduction in Benefits

Group life insurance plans often provide for a reduction in benefits for active employees who reach a certain age, commonly 65 to 70. Such a reduction, which is due to the high cost of providing benefits for older employees, is specified in the plan's benefit schedule. Any reduction in the amount of life insurance for active employees is subject to the provisions of the Age Discrimination in Employment Act.

Benefit reductions fall into three categories: (1) a reduction to a flat amount of insurance; (2) a percentage reduction, such as to 65 percent of the amount of insurance that was previously provided; or (3) a gradual reduction over a period of years (for example, a 10 percent reduction in coverage each year until a minimum benefit amount is reached).

Eligibility

Group insurance contracts are very precise in their definition of what constitutes an eligible person for coverage purposes. For group life insurance, an employee generally must be in a covered classification, work full-time, and be actively at work. In addition, any requirements concerning probationary periods, insurability, or premium contributions must be satisfied.

Covered Classifications

covered classifications

All group insurance contracts specify that an employee must fall into one of the categories of employees contained in the benefit schedule. Called **covered classifications**, these categories may be broad enough to include all employees of the organization, or they may be so limited as to exclude many employees from coverage. In some cases, these excluded employees may have coverage through a negotiated trusteeship or under other group insurance contracts provided by the employer; in other cases, they may have no coverage because the employer wishes to limit benefits to certain groups of employees. No employee may be in more than one covered classification, and the responsibility for determining the appropriate covered classification for each employee falls on the policyowner.

Other Contract Provisions

Full-Time Employment

full-time employee

Most group insurance contracts limit eligibility to full-time employees. A **full-time employee** is generally defined as one who works no fewer than the number of hours in the normal workweek established by the employer, which must be at least 30 hours.

Subject to insurance company underwriting practices, an employer can provide coverage for part-time employees. When this is done, part-time is generally defined as less than full-time but more than some minimum number of hours per week.

Actively-at-Work Provision

actively-at-work provision

Most group insurance contracts contain an **actively-at-work provision**, whereby an employee is not covered if absent from work because of sickness, injury, or other reasons on the otherwise effective date of coverage under the contract. Coverage commences when the employee returns to work. Insurers often waive this provision for employers with a large number of employees when coverage is transferred to a different insurance company and the employees involved were insured under the previous insurance company's contract.

Probationary Periods

Group insurance contracts may contain a probationary period, which is a specified length of time that must be satisfied before an employee is eligible for coverage. Such probationary periods are usually either 1 or 3 months and rarely exceed 6 months. An employee is eligible for coverage either on the first day after the probationary period or on the first day of the month following the end of the probationary period.

Insurability

Although insurers issue most group insurance contracts without individual evidence of insurability, underwriting practices require evidence of insurability in some instances. This commonly occurs when an employee fails to elect coverage under a contributory plan and later wants coverage or when an employee is eligible for a large amount of coverage. In these cases, an employee is not eligible for coverage until he or she submits the proper evidence of insurability and the insurance company determines that the evidence is satisfactory.

Beneficiary Designation

beneficiary

With few exceptions, an insured person has the right to name the **beneficiary**, who is the person who will receive the death benefits under the group life insurance coverage. These exceptions include credit life insurance, where the creditor is the beneficiary, and dependent life insurance, where the employee is the beneficiary. In addition, the laws and regulations of some states prohibit naming the employer as beneficiary. All insurance contracts require that the insurance company be notified of any beneficiary change in writing, but the effective date of the change may vary, depending on contract provisions. Some contracts specify that a change is effective on the date it is received by the insurance company; others make it effective on the date the change is requested by the employee.

successive beneficiary provision

Under individual life insurance policies, the insurer pays death benefits to an insured person's estate if no beneficiary is named or if all beneficiaries died before the insured. Some group term insurance contracts contain an identical provision; others stipulate that the insurer will pay the death benefits through a **successive beneficiary provision**. Under the successive beneficiary provision, the insurer pays the proceeds (at the option of the insurance company) to any one or more of the following survivors of the insured person: spouse, children, parents, brothers and sisters, or executor of the employee's estate. In most cases, insurance companies pay the proceeds to the person or persons in the first category that includes eligible survivors.

Claims

The provision concerning death claims under group life insurance policies is very simple. It states that the amount of insurance under the contract is payable when the insurance company receives written proof of death. There is no specified time in which a beneficiary must file a claim. However, most companies require that the policyowner and the beneficiary complete a brief form before a claim is processed.

Settlement Options

settlement options

Settlement options are the various methods by which an employee or beneficiary may elect to have life insurance proceeds paid. With the exception of survivor income benefit insurance plans, group term insurance contracts provide that death benefits are payable in a lump sum unless an optional mode of settlement is selected. Each employee insured under the contract has the right to select and change any available mode of settlement during his or her lifetime.

If no optional mode of settlement is in force at the employee's death, the beneficiary generally has the right to elect any of the available options. The most common provision in group term insurance contracts is that the available modes of settlement are those that the insurance company customarily offers at the time the selection is made. The insurer does not generally specify the available options in the contract, but information about them is usually given to the group policyowner. In addition, many insurance companies have brochures that describe either all or the most common options available to employees. Any guarantees associated with these options are the guarantees in effect when the option is selected.

In addition to a lump-sum option, most insurance companies offer all the following options and possibly other options as well:

- an interest option. The proceeds are left on deposit with the insurance company, and the interest on the proceeds is paid to the beneficiary. The beneficiary can usually withdraw the proceeds at any time. The amount of any periodic install- ment is a function of the interest rate paid by the insurance company.

- an installment option for a fixed period. The proceeds are paid in equal install- ments for a specified period of time. The amount of any periodic installment is a function of the time period and the amount of the death proceeds.

- an installment option for a fixed amount. The proceeds are paid in equal install- ments of a specified amount until the proceeds and any interest earnings are exhausted.

- a life income option. The proceeds are payable in installments during the lifetime of the beneficiary. A choice of guarantee periods is usually available, during which a secondary beneficiary or the beneficiary's estate continues to receive benefits even if the beneficiary dies. The amount of any periodic installment is a function of the age and gender of the beneficiary, the period for which payments are guaran- teed, and the amount of the death proceeds.

Premiums

Group insurance contracts stipulate that it is the policyowner's responsibility to pay all premiums to the insurance company, even if the group insurance plan is contributory. Any required contributions from employees are incorporated into the employer's group insur- ance plan, but they are not part of the insurance contract and therefore do not constitute an obligation to the insurance company by the employees. Rather, these contributions rep- resent an obligation to the employer by the employees and are commonly paid by payroll deduction. Subject to certain limitations, any employee contributions are determined by the employer or as a result of labor negotiations.

Most states require that the employer pay at least a portion of the premium for group term insurance (but not for other group insurance coverage), and a few states limit the amounts that may be paid by any employee.

Premiums are payable in advance to the insurance company or any authorized agent for the time period specified in the contract. In most cases, premiums are payable monthly but may be paid less frequently. The rates used to determine the premium for any policyowner are guaranteed for a certain length of time, usually one year. The periodic premium is determined by applying these rates to the amount of life insurance in force. Consequently, the premium actually payable changes each month as the total amount of life insurance in force under the group insurance plan varies.

Incontestability

incontestability provision

Like individual life insurance contracts, group insurance contracts contain an **incontestability provision**. Except for the nonpayment of premiums, the insurer cannot contest the validity of the contract after it has been in force for a specified period, generally either 1 or 2 years. During this time, the insurance company can contest the contract on the basis of policyowner statements in the application attached to the contract that are considered to be material misrepresentations. Statements by any insured person can be used as the basis for denying claims during the first 2 years that coverage is in force on the insured but only if such statements relate to the individual's insurability. In addition, the statements must have been made in a written application signed by the individual, and a copy of the application must have been furnished to either the individual or his or her beneficiary. It should be pointed out that the incontestability clause does not concern most covered persons, because evidence of insurability is not usually required and thus no statements about individual insurability are made.

Misstatement of Age

misstatement of age provision

Group insurance contracts contain a **misstatement of age provision**. If the age of any person covered under a policy is misstated, the benefit payable is the amount that is specified under the benefit schedule. However, the insurer adjusts the premium to reflect the true age of the individual. Under a group insurance contract, the responsibility for paying any additional premium or the right to receive a refund belongs to the policyowner and not to the individual employee whose age is misstated, even if the plan is contributory. If the misstated age would have affected the employee's contribution, this is a matter to be resolved between the employer and the employee.

Termination

All group insurance contracts stipulate the conditions under which the insurance company or the policyowner may terminate the contract and under which the coverage for a particular insured person terminates.

The insurer can terminate a group term insurance contract for nonpayment of premium at the end of the grace period. Insurance companies may also terminate coverage for an individual employer group on any premium due date if certain conditions exist and notice of termination has been given to the policyowner at least 31 days in advance. These conditions include the failure to maintain a stated minimum number of participants in the plan and, in contributory plans, the failure to maintain a stated minimum percentage participation. The policyowner may also terminate the contract at any time by giving the insurance company 31 days' advance written notice. Moreover, the policyowner has the right to request the amendment of the contract at any time by notifying the insurance company.

The coverage for any insured person terminates automatically (subject to any provisions for a continuation or conversion of coverage) when

- the employee terminates employment
- the employee ceases to be eligible (for example, if the employee no longer satisfies the full-time work requirement or no longer falls into a covered classification)
- the policyowner or insurance company terminates the master contract
- any required contribution by the employee has not been made (generally because the employee has notified the policyowner to cease the required payroll deduction)

Continuation of Coverage for Disabled Employees

waiver-of-premium provision

Most group term insurance contracts make some provision for the continuation of coverage on employees whose active employment terminates due to disability. By far the most common provision in use today is the **waiver-of-premium provision**. Under this provision, the contract continues the life insurance coverage without the payment of premium as long as the employee is totally disabled, even if the master contract is terminated. However, certain requirements must be met:

- The disability must commence while the employee is insured under the master contract.

- The disability must begin prior to a specified age, commonly age 60.

- The employee must be totally disabled. Total disability is normally defined as the employee's complete inability to engage in any gainful occupation for which he or she is or becomes qualified by reason of education, training, or experience.

- The disability must have lasted continuously for a specified time, often 6 or 9 months.

- The employee must file a claim within a prescribed period (normally 12 months) and must submit annual evidence of continuing disability.

If an employee no longer meets the definition of disability and returns to work, the employee may again be insured under the group insurance contract on a premium-paying basis as long as the employee meets the contract's eligibility requirements. If for any reason the employee is not eligible for insurance under the group insurance contract, he or she can exercise the conversion privilege.

Conversion

conversion provision

All group term insurance contracts covering employees contain a **conversion provision** that gives any employee whose coverage ceases the right to convert to an individual insurance policy. The terms of the conversion privilege vary, depending upon the reason for the termination of coverage under the group contract. The most generous conversion rights are available to those employees who either have terminated employment or no longer fall into one of the eligible classifications still covered by the master contract. These employees have the right to purchase an individual life insurance policy from the insurance company without evidence of insurability, but it is often one without accidental death and dismemberment or other supplementary benefits. However, this right is subject to the following conditions:

- The employee must apply for conversion within 31 days after the termination of employment or membership in an eligible classification. During this 31-day period, the employee's death benefit is equal to the amount of life insurance that is available under the conversion privilege, even if the employee does not apply for conversion. Disability and supplementary benefits are not extended during this period unless they are also subject to conversion. The premium for the individual policy must accompany the conversion application, and coverage is effective at the end of the conversion period.

- The individual policy the employee selects may generally be any form, except term insurance, that the insurance company customarily issues at the age and amount applied for.

- The face amount of the individual policy may not exceed the amount of life insurance that terminated under the group insurance contract.

- The premium for the individual policy is determined using the insurance company's current rate applicable to the type and amount of the individual policy for the employee's attained age on the date of conversion and for the class of risk to which the employee belongs.

Estimates are that only one or two percent of eligible employees actually take advantage of the conversion privilege. Several factors account for this. Many employees obtain coverage with new employers; others are discouraged by the high cost of the permanent insurance to which they must convert. Still others, if they are insurable at standard rates, may find coverage at a lower cost with other insurers and be able to purchase supplementary coverage (such as disability benefits) that are not available under conversion policies.

There may be a more restrictive conversion privilege if an employee's coverage ceases because the master contract is terminated for all employees or is amended to eliminate eligible classifications. Under these circumstances, the employee is generally given a conversion right only if he or she was insured under the contract for a period of time (usually 5 years) immediately preceding the date on which coverage was terminated. In addition, the amount of insurance that can be converted may be limited.

Portability of Term Coverage

Some insurers issue contracts with a portability provision that allows employees whose coverage terminates to continue coverage at group rates. The rates are age based and continue to increase as an insured person ages. The insurer then bills these employees directly.

Significant variations exist among the insurers that offer portable coverage. Some of these variations include the following:

- Some insurers automatically include a portability provision in their contracts; other insurers make it available as an optional provision that the employer can select.

- Most insurers allow portability if employment is terminated, and some insurers make it available to retiring employees. Most insurers do no make it available upon termination of a master contract.

- Some insurers allow portability only if the group contract covers a minimum number of persons, such as 200; other insurers have no minimum size for the group.

- Some insurers allow the period of coverage to run indefinitely; other insurers terminate the converted coverage after some duration of time or after some age, such as 65 or 70. When coverage continues past age 65, it usually reduces in face amount.

- Most insurers have some minimum and maximum amount of coverage that can be continued on a portability basis. For employees, the minimum amount is most commonly either $5,000 or $10,000. Maximum amounts vary significantly among insurers, but $300,000 and $500,000 are not unusual. However, amounts in excess of some limit, such as $100,000, are often subject to evidence of insurability.

- Some insurers charge an additional transaction fee for coverage portability. This might be a one-time charge, such as $25 or $50, or a charge per billing, such as $2 or $3.

Accelerated Benefits

Often what becomes popular in the individual marketplace starts to show up in the group insurance marketplace. Such is the case with accelerated benefits, which most insurers now offer.

accelerated-benefits provision

Under an **accelerated-benefits provision** (sometimes called a critical-illness rider), an insured is entitled to receive a portion of his or her death benefit while still living if one or more specified events occur. These events might include

- a terminal illness that is expected to result in death within 6 or 12 months

- a specified catastrophic illness, such as cancer, renal failure, AIDS, a stroke, or Alzheimer's disease

- the incurring of nursing home and possibly other long-term-care expenses

The categories of triggering events and the specific definitions of each vary among insurers. However, most group insurers allow accelerated benefits for terminal illnesses only. Some insurers use a life expectancy of 6 months or less; most use a life expectancy of 12 months or less. In either case, a doctor must certify the life expectancy.

The amount of the accelerated benefit is expressed as a percentage of the basic life insurance coverage and may range from 25 percent to 100 percent. In addition, many insurers limit the maximum benefit to a specified dollar amount. This amount varies widely among insurers and can be as low as $25,000 or as high as $500,000 or more. The insurer pays any amount not accelerated to the beneficiary upon the insured's death.

A few insurers charge the policyowner an additional premium for the inclusion of accelerated death benefit coverage and make no additional charge when a benefit is accelerated. The majority of insurers, however, follow one of two alternative approaches. Some insurers charge no additional premium but often levy a transaction charge each time a benefit is accelerated. Other insurers also charge no additional premium but shift the cost of the benefit to the insured by either (1) discounting the accelerated benefit to reflect lost interest or (2) treating the advance payment as a lien against the coverage and charge interest on the amount advanced. A few insurers allow the insured to select whether the discounting or lien approach is used.

There are no limitations on how the accelerated benefit can be used. It might be used to pay medical expenses and nursing home care not covered by other insurance, or it could even be used to prepay funeral expenses.

ADDED COVERAGES

rider

Group term insurance contracts often provide additional insurance benefits. Historically, these benefits have been obtained through the use of a **rider**, which is an endorsement to an insurance policy for the purpose of adding, deleting, or classifying coverage. Many companies, however, now incorporate some or all of the benefits into their basic term insurance contracts. These benefits are also forms of group term insurance and consist of (1) supplemental life insurance, (2) accidental death and dismemberment insurance, and (3) dependent life insurance. These added benefits can be provided for all employees insured under the basic group term contract or may be limited to certain classes of employees. With the exception of dependent life insurance, these coverages may also be written as separate contracts.

Supplemental Life Insurance

supplemental life insurance

The majority of group life insurance plans enable all or certain classes of employees to purchase additional amounts of life insurance, commonly referred to as **supplemental life insurance**. Generally, the employer provides a basic amount of life insurance to all eligible employees on a noncontributory basis. This is commonly a flat amount of coverage or a multiple of annual earnings. The supplemental coverage is contributory and may be either incorporated into the basic group life insurance contract or contained in a separate contract. The latter method tends to be more common when the supplemental coverage is available to only a select group of employees. Although the employee may pay the entire cost of the supplemental coverage, either state laws that require employer contributions or insurance company underwriting practices may result in the employer's paying a portion of the cost. It is not unusual for there to be two sets of rates—one for smokers and another for nonsmokers.

A benefit schedule specifies the amount of supplemental coverage available. Under some plans, an employee must purchase the full amount of coverage; under other plans, an employee may purchase a portion of the coverage. The following tables are two examples of benefit schedules for a basic-plus-supplemental life insurance plan.

Table 4-4 Supplemental Life Insurance: Example 1	
Type of Coverage	**Amount of Life Insurance**
Basic insurance	$25,000
Supplemental insurance	50,000

Table 4-5 Supplemental Life Insurance: Example 2	
Type of Coverage	**Amount of Life Insurance**
Basic insurance	1 times salary
Supplemental insurance	½, 1, 1½, or 2 times salary, subject to a maximum (including basic insurance) of $250,000

Because giving employees the right to choose their benefit amounts leads to adverse selection, more stringent underwriting requirements usually accompany supplemental coverage. These may include requiring individual evidence of insurability for the full amount of coverage. However, many insurers will issue a specific amount of supplemental coverage on a guaranteed-issue basis, with the guaranteed amount based on the size of the group and the amount of basic coverage. Larger amounts of supplemental coverage are subject to individual underwriting. The insurer may charge higher rates for the supplemental insurance than for the basic coverage.

Accidental Death and Dismemberment Insurance

accidental death and dismemberment (AD&D)

voluntary accidental death and dismemberment insurance

Many group life insurance contracts contain an **accidental death and dismemberment (AD&D)** provision that gives additional benefits if an employee dies accidentally or suffers certain types of injuries. Traditionally, this group coverage was available only as a rider to a group life insurance contract. Now, however, it is common to find these benefits in separate group insurance contracts in which coverage is usually contributory on the part of employees. Such contracts are referred to as **voluntary accidental death and dismemberment insurance**. There are also separate contracts that employers can purchase to replace the employer-paid coverage available from their group term life insurance carrier.

Traditional Coverage

Under the usual traditional form of accidental death and dismemberment insurance, an employee eligible for group life insurance coverage (and electing the life insurance coverage if it is contributory) automatically has the accidental death and dismemberment coverage if the employer adds it or if the insurer includes it as a standard part of its group term life insurance contract. Under the typical accidental death and dismemberment rider, the insurance company pays an additional amount of insurance that is equal to the amount of coverage under the basic group life insurance contract (referred to as the principal sum) if an employee dies as a result of accidental bodily injuries while he or she is covered under the policy. Most riders specify that death must occur within a certain time, often 90 days, following the date that injuries are sustained, but some courts have ruled this period is invalid and have required insurance companies to pay claims when longer periods have been involved. In addition to an accidental death benefit, a benefit schedule like the one shown in the first table below is provided for certain specific types of injuries.

In some cases, the accidental death and dismemberment rider provides the same benefits for any accident covered under the contract. However, it is not unusual to have a higher level of benefits for accidents that occur while the employee is traveling on business for the employer. These larger travel benefits may apply to death benefits only. They may also be limited to accidents that occur while the employee is occupying (or entering, alighting from, or struck by) a public conveyance and possibly a company-owned or personally owned vehicle. The second table below is an example of a benefit schedule reflecting some of these variations.

Table 4-6 AD&D Schedule of Benefits: Example 1	
Type of Injury	**Benefit Amount**
Loss of (including loss of use of):	
Both hands or both feet	The principal sum
The sight of both eyes	The principal sum
One hand and sight of one eye	The principal sum
One foot and sight of one eye	The principal sum
One foot and one hand	The principal sum
One hand	One-half the principal sum
One foot	One-half the principal sum
The sight of one eye	One-half the principal sum

Table 4-7 AD&D Schedule of Benefits: Example 2	
Type of Loss	**Benefit Amount**
Death while traveling on business when occupying, boarding, alighting from, or struck by any motor vehicle, airplane, or other conveyance, including company-owned or personally owned vehicles	3 times the principal sum
Death at all other times	2 times the principal sum
Dismemberment	Up to the principal sum (as shown in the previous schedule)

The insurer pays death benefits in accordance with the beneficiary provision of the group life insurance contract and pays dismemberment benefits to the employee. Coverage is usually written to cover both occupational and nonoccupational accidents. However, when employees are in hazardous occupations, coverage may apply only to nonoccupational accidents, in which case employees still have workers' compensation coverage for any occupational accidents.

Some insurers also pay an additional benefit if an insured suffers a covered loss as the result of an automobile accident as long as the insured is wearing a properly fastened seat belt and is not under the influence of alcohol.

Coverage is usually not subject to a conversion privilege. However, an increasing number of insurers are allowing conversion, but possibly only up to specified limits that are lower than the former group coverage. When life insurance coverage continues after retirement, accidental death and dismemberment benefits are normally no longer available. As with the life insurance coverage, however, the employer may continue this coverage during temporary periods of unemployment. In contrast to the group term insurance policy to which it is attached, group accidental death and dismemberment insurance does contain some exclusions. These exclusions include losses resulting from the following situation and events:

- suicide at any time (It is interesting to note that, except for a few multiple-employer trusts, group term insurance does not contain a suicide provision.)

- disease or bodily or mental infirmity, or medical or surgical treatment thereof

- ptomaine or any infection other than one occurring simultaneously with and through an accidental cut or wound

- war

- travel or flight in any type of aircraft either as a pilot, as a student pilot, or as an officer or member of the crew (However, there is a trend toward eliminating this exclusion, particularly when coverage is written on large groups.)

Voluntary AD&D Coverage

The provisions of voluntary group accidental death and dismemberment insurance are practically identical to those in a group life insurance contract with an accidental death and dismemberment insurance rider. However, there are a few differences. Voluntary plans usually require that the employee pay the entire cost of coverage, and they virtually always provide both occupational and nonoccupational coverage. Subject to limitations, the employee may select the amount of coverage desired, and the maximum amount of coverage available tends to be larger than when a rider provides coverage. For example, one plan allows an employer to purchase coverage at the following levels: $50,000, $75,000, $100,000, $200,000, $300,000 or $500,000, as long as the amount selected does not exceed 10 times annual salary. The amount of coverage often decreases after age 65 or 70, just as the amount of traditional coverage decreases when it is a function of a life insurance benefit that reduces at older ages.

Another difference is the frequent use in voluntary plans of a common accident provision, whereby the amount payable by the insurance company is limited to a stipulated maximum for all employees killed or injured in any single accident. If this exceeds the sum of the benefits otherwise payable for each employee, insurers prorate benefits.

A final difference is that some voluntary plans allow an employee to purchase accidental death and dismemberment coverage on dependents.

Dependent Life Insurance

dependent life insurance

Some group life insurance contracts provide insurance coverage on the lives of employees' dependents. **Dependent life insurance** is a method of giving the employee resources to meet the funeral and burial expenses associated with a dependent's death. Consequently, the employee is automatically the beneficiary. The employee also elects and pays for this coverage if it is contributory. Coverage for dependents is almost always limited to employees who themselves have coverage under the group contract. Thus, if an employee's coverage is contributory, the employee must elect coverage for himself or herself in order to be eligible to elect dependent coverage.

For purposes of dependent life insurance coverage, dependents are usually defined as an employee's spouse who is not legally separated from the employee and an employee's unmarried dependent children (including stepchildren and adopted children) who are over 14 days of age and younger than some specified age, commonly 19 or 21. The plan sometimes extends this to a later age, such as 23 or 25, if the dependent is a full-time student. To prevent adverse selection, an employee usually cannot select coverage on individual dependents. A few policies do allow an employee to elect coverage for the spouse only or for children only. If dependent coverage is selected, all dependents fitting the definition have insurance. When dependent coverage is in effect for an employee, any new eligible dependents are automatically insured.

The amount of coverage for each dependent is usually quite modest. Some states limit the maximum amount of life insurance that an insurance company can write, and a few states actually prohibit writing any coverage on dependents. Employer contributions used to purchase more than $2,000 of coverage on each dependent result in income to the employee for purposes of federal taxation. However, amounts in excess of $2,000 may be purchased with employee contributions without adverse tax consequences. In some cases, the plan provides the same amount of coverage for all dependents; in other cases, the plan provides a larger amount for the spouse than for the children. It is also not unusual for the amount of coverage on children to be less until the children attain some specified age, such as 6 months. The following tables are examples of benefit schedules under dependent coverage.

Table 4-8	
Dependent Life Insurance Benefit Schedule: Example 1	
Class	**Amount of Insurance**
Each dependent	$2,000

Table 4-9	
Dependent Life Insurance Benefit Schedule: Example 2	
Class	**Amount of Insurance**
Spouse	50% of the employee's insured amount, subject to a maximum of $5,000
Dependent children: at least 14 days old but less than 6 months	$ 500
6 months or older	$1,000

A single premium applies to the dependent coverage for each employee and is unrelated to the number of dependents. In some cases, the premium may vary, depending on the age of the employee (but not the dependents), but more commonly it is the same amount for all employees regardless of age. Dependent coverage usually contains a conversion privilege that applies only to the coverage on the spouse. However, some states require that the conversion privilege apply to the coverage on all dependents. Some insurers also have portability provisions so that the group coverage can continue on a direct-bill basis.

Assignment is almost never permitted, and no waiver of premium is available if a dependent becomes disabled. However, if the basic life insurance contract contains a waiver-of-premium provision applicable to the employee, the employee's disability sometimes results in a waiver of premium for the dependent coverage. A provision similar to the actively-at-work provision pertaining to employees is often included for dependents. It specifies that dependents have no coverage when otherwise eligible if they are confined in a hospital (except for newborn children, who are covered after 14 days). Coverage commences when the hospital discharges the dependent.

TAX TREATMENT

A discussion of group term life insurance is incomplete without an explanation of the tax laws affecting its use. Although discussions of these laws are often limited to federal income and estate taxation, federal gift taxation and taxation by the states are also important considerations.

Federal Tax Treatment

The growth of group term insurance has been greatly influenced by the favorable tax treatment afforded it under federal tax laws. This section looks at the effects of these tax laws on basic group term insurance and on coverages that may be added to a basic group term insurance contract. A complete explanation of the federal tax laws pertaining to group term insurance and their interpretation by the Internal Revenue Service (IRS) is lengthy and beyond the scope of this book. Consequently, this discussion and subsequent discussions of federal tax laws only highlight these laws.

Deductibility of Premiums

In general, employer contributions for an employee's group term insurance coverage (as well as for most other types of employee benefits) are fully deductible to the employer as an ordinary and necessary business expense as long as the employee's overall compensation is reasonable. However, the IRS considers the following persons self-employed persons for income tax purposes and allows no deduction: sole proprietors, partners, members of limited liability companies (LLCs), and more-than-2-percent shareholders of S corporations. The reasonableness of compensation (which includes wages, salary, and other fringe benefits) is usually only a potential issue for the owners of small businesses or the stockholder-employees of closely held corporations. For income tax purposes, a firm may not deduct any compensation that the IRS determines to be unreasonable. In addition, the Internal Revenue Code does not allow a firm to take an income tax deduction for contributions that are made in behalf of stockholders unless they are providing substantive services to the corporation. Finally, no deduction is allowed if the employer is named as beneficiary of an employee's life insurance coverage.

Contributions by any individual employee are considered payments for personal life insurance and are not deductible for income tax purposes by that employee. Thus, the amount of any payroll deductions authorized by an employee for group term insurance purposes is included in the employee's taxable income.

Employees' Income Tax Liability

Sec. 79

In the absence of tax laws to the contrary, the amount of any compensation for which an employer receives an income tax deduction (including the payment of group insurance premiums) represents taxable income to the employee. However, **Sec. 79** of the Internal Revenue Code gives favorable tax treatment to employer contributions for life insurance that qualifies as group term insurance.

Sec. 79 Requirements. In order to qualify as group term insurance under Sec. 79, life insurance must meet the following conditions:

- It must provide a death benefit excludible from federal income tax.

- It must be given to a group of employees, defined to include all employees of an employer. If all employees are not covered, membership must be determined on the basis of age, marital status, or factors relating to employment.

- It must be provided under a policy carried directly or indirectly by the employer. This includes any policy for which the employer pays any part of the cost. If the employer pays no part of the cost, it also includes any policy arranged by the employer if at least one employee is charged less than his or her cost (using Uniform Premium Table I, which is discussed later) and at least one other employee is charged more than his or her cost. A policy is defined to include a master contract or a group of individual policies. The term carried indirectly refers to those situations when the employer is not the policyowner but rather provides coverage to employees through master contracts issued to organizations, such as negotiated trusteeships or multiple-employer welfare arrangements.

- The plan must be arranged to preclude individual selection of coverage amounts. However, it is acceptable to have alternative benefit schedules based on the amount an employee elects to contribute. Supplemental plans that give an employee a choice, such as 1, 1 1/2, or 2 times salary, fall within this category. A plan can allow an employee to reject coverage in excess of $50,000 if he or she does not want any imputed income.

All life insurance that qualifies under Sec. 79 as group term insurance is considered to be a single plan of insurance, regardless of the number of insurance contracts used.

Example

The Grant Corporation provides coverage for its union employees under a negotiated trusteeship, coverage for its other employees under an individual employer group insurance contract, and additional coverage for its top executives under a group of individual life insurance policies. Under Sec. 79, these all constitute a single plan.

This plan must be provided for at least 10 full-time employees at some time during the calendar year. For purposes of meeting the 10-life requirement, employees who have not satisfied any required waiting periods may be counted as participants. Employees who have elected not to participate are also counted as participants—but only if they would not have been required to contribute to the cost of other benefits besides group term insurance if they had participated. As described later, a plan with fewer than 10 full-time employees may still qualify for favorable tax treatment under Sec. 79 if it meets more restrictive requirements.

Exceptions to Sec. 79. Even when a plan meets all the previous requirements, there are some situations in which Sec. 79 does not apply. In some cases, different sections of the Internal Revenue Code provide alternative tax treatment. For example, when group term insurance is issued to the trustees of a qualified pension plan and is used to provide a death benefit under the plan, the full amount of any life insurance paid for by employer contributions results in taxable income to the employee.

There are three situations in which employer contributions for group term insurance do not result in taxable income to an employee, regardless of the amount of insurance:

- if an employee has terminated employment because of disability
- if a qualified charity (as determined by the Internal Revenue Code) has been named as beneficiary for the entire year
- if the employer has been named as beneficiary for the entire year

Coverage on retired employees is subject to Sec. 79, and these persons are treated in the same manner as active employees. In general, they have taxable income in any year in which the amount of coverage received exceeds $50,000.

General Tax Rules. Under Sec. 79, the cost of the first $50,000 of coverage is not taxed to the employee. Because all group term insurance provided by an employer that qualifies under Sec. 79 is considered to be one plan, this exclusion applies only once to each employee.

Example

John has $5,000 of coverage that is provided to all nonunion employees under a group insurance policy of the Grant Corporations. He also has $200,000 of coverage provided to executives under a separate insurance policy. For purpose of Sec. 79, John has a single $50,000 exclusion.

Uniform Premium Table I

The cost of coverage in excess of $50,000, minus any employee contributions for the entire amount of coverage, represents taxable income to the employee. For purposes of Sec. 79, the cost of this excess coverage is determined by a government table called the **Uniform Premium Table I** (see the table below).

Table 4-10 Uniform Premium Table I	
Age	**Cost per Month per $1,000 of Coverage**
24 and under	$ .05
25–29	.06
30–34	.08
35–39	.09
40–44	.10
45–49	.15
50–54	.23
55–59	.43
60–64	.66
65–69	1.27
70 and over	2.06

To calculate the cost of an employee's coverage for one month of protection under a group term insurance plan, the Uniform Premium Table I cost shown for the employee's age bracket (based on the employee's attained age at the end of the tax year) is multiplied by the number of thousands in excess of 50 of group term insurance on the employee. The monthly costs are then totaled to obtain an annual cost.

Example

Theresa, aged 57, is provided with $150,000 of group term insurance by her employer. She is not a key employee and the employer's plan is not discriminatory. The Table I monthly cost for someone her age is $43 per $1,000 of coverage. The monthly cost of her coverage (assuming no employee contributions) is calculated as follows:

Coverage provided	**$150,000**
Minus Sec. 79 exclusion	**–50,000**
Amount subject to taxation	**$100,000**

Monthly cost = $.43/$1,000 × $100,000 = $43

Annual cost (assuming no change in the amount of coverage during the year) = $516

Finally, any employee contributions for the entire amount of coverage are deducted from the annual cost to determine the taxable income that an employee must report. If Theresa contributes $.25 per month ($3 per year) per $1,000 of coverage, her total annual contribution for $150,000 of coverage is $450. This reduces the amount reportable as taxable income from $516 to $66. If her employee contribution is $.30 rather than $.25 per month, the annual contribution is $540. Because $540 exceeds the Table I cost, there is no imputed income.

One final point is worthy of attention. The use of Uniform Premium Table I results in favorable tax treatment for the cost of group term insurance when the monthly costs in the table are lower than the actual cost of coverage in the marketplace. However, group term insurance coverage can often be purchased at a lower cost than Table I rates. There are some who argue that in these instances the actual cost of coverage can be used in place of the Table I cost for determining an employee's taxable income. From the standpoint of logic and consistency with the tax laws, this view makes sense. However, the regulations for Sec. 79 are very specific: Only Table I costs are to be used.

Nondiscrimination Rules. Any plan that qualifies as group term insurance under Sec. 79 is subject to nondiscrimination rules, and the $50,000 exclusion is not available to key employees if a plan is discriminatory. Such a plan favors key employees in either eligibility or benefits. In addition, the value of the full amount of coverage for key employees, minus their own contributions, is considered taxable income, based on the greater of actual or Table I costs. (The actual cost of discriminatory coverage is determined by a complex process that is not covered in this book. See Internal Revenue Code Reg. 1.79-4T.)

key employee

A **key employee** of a firm is defined as any person (either active or retired) who at any time during the plan year containing the discrimination date is any of the following:

- an officer of the firm who earns more than $170,000 (in 2015) in annual compensation from the firm. This amount is subject to periodic indexing. For purposes of this rule, the number of employees treated as officers is the greater of 3 employees or 10 percent of the firm's employees, subject to a maximum of 50. In applying the rule, the following employees can be excluded: persons who are part-time, persons who are under 21, and persons with less than 6 months of service with the firm.

- a 5 percent owner of the firm. For a corporation, a 5 percent owner is a person who owns (1) more than 5 percent of the firm's outstanding stock or (2) stock that has more than 5 percent of the combined voting power of all the firm's stock. For a noncorporate entity, it is any person who owns more than 5 percent of the firm's capital or profits.

- a 1 percent owner of the firm who earns over $150,000 in annual compensation from the firm. The definition of a 1 percent owner is the same as that of a 5 percent owner with 1 percent substituted for 5 percent.

Eligibility requirements are not discriminatory if (1) at least 70 percent of all employees are eligible, (2) at least 85 percent of all employees who are participants are not key employees, (3) participants constitute a classification that the IRS determines is nondiscriminatory, or (4) the group term insurance plan is part of a cafeteria plan and Sec. 125 requirements are satisfied. For purposes of the 70 percent test, employees with less than 3 years' service, part-time employees, and seasonal employees may be excluded. Employees covered by collective-bargaining agreements may also be excluded if plan benefits were the subject of good-faith bargaining.

Benefits are not discriminatory if neither the type nor amount of benefits discriminates in favor of key employees. It is permissible to base benefits on a uniform percentage of salary.

Groups with Fewer than 10 Full-Time Employees. A group insurance plan that covers fewer than 10 employees must satisfy an additional set of requirements before it is eligible for favorable tax treatment under Sec. 79. Again, note that Sec. 79 applies to an employer's overall plan of group insurance, not to separate group insurance contracts. For example, an employer providing group insurance coverage for its 50 hourly employees under one group insurance contract and for its six executives under a separate contract is considered to have a single plan covering 56 employees and thus is exempt from the under-10 requirements. Although the stated purpose of the under-10 requirements is to preclude individual selection, their effect is to prevent the group insurance plan from discriminating in favor of the owners or stockholder-employees of small businesses.

With some exceptions, plans covering fewer than 10 employees must provide coverage for all full-time employees. For purposes of this requirement, employees who are not customarily employed for more than 20 hours in any one week or 5 months in any calendar year are considered part-time employees. It is permissible to exclude full-time employees from coverage under the following circumstances:

- The employee has reached age 65.

- The employee has not satisfied the probationary period under the plan, which may not exceed 6 months.

- The employee has elected not to participate in the plan, but only if the employee would not have been required to contribute to the cost of other benefits besides group term life insurance if he or she had participated.

- The employee has not satisfied the evidence of insurability required under the plan. An employee's eligibility for insurance (or the amount of insurance on the employee's life) may be subject to evidence of insurability. However, this evidence of insurability must be determined solely on the basis of a medical questionnaire completed by the employee and not by a medical examination.

The amount of coverage must be a flat amount, a uniform percentage of compensation, or an amount based on different employee classifications. These employee classifications are referred to as coverage brackets in Sec. 79. The amount of coverage for each employee in any classification may be no greater than 2 1/2 times the amount of coverage provided to each employee in the next lower classification. In addition, each employee in the lowest classification must be provided with an amount of coverage that is equal to at least 10 percent of the amount for each employee in the highest classification. There must also be a reasonable expectation that there will be at least one employee in each classification.

Example

The Lindsay Corporation has nine employees—a president, two salaried supervisors and six hourly employees. It has the following benefit schedule for its group term life insurance plan:

• **President**	**$100,000**
• **Supervisor**	**40,000**
• **Hourly employees**	**5,000**

This schedule is unacceptable for favorable tax treatment under Sec. 79 for two reasons. First, the amount of coverage provided for the hourly employees is only 5 percent of the amount of coverage provided for the president. Second, the amount of coverage on the supervisor is more than 2 1/2 times the amount of coverage provided for the hourly employees.

The following schedule, however, would be acceptable:

- President $100,000
- Supervisor   40,000
- Hourly employees   20,000

If a group insurance plan that covers fewer than 10 employees does not qualify for favorable tax treatment under Sec. 79, any premiums paid by the employer for such coverage represents taxable income to the employees. The employer, however, still receives an income tax deduction for any premiums paid on behalf of the employees as long as overall compensation is reasonable.

Tax Treatment of Proceeds

In most instances, the death proceeds under a group term insurance contract do not result in any taxable income to the beneficiary if they are paid in a lump sum. If the proceeds are payable in installments over more than one taxable year, only the interest earnings attributable to the proceeds are included in the beneficiary's income for tax purposes.

Under certain circumstances, the proceeds are not exempt from income taxation if the coverage was transferred (either in whole or in part) for a valuable consideration. Such a situation arises when the stockholder-employees of a corporation name each other as beneficiaries under their group term insurance coverage as a method of funding a buy-sell agreement. The mutual agreement to name each other as beneficiaries is the valuable consideration. Under these circumstances, any proceeds paid to a beneficiary constitute ordinary income to the extent that the proceeds exceed the beneficiary's tax basis, as determined by the Internal Revenue Code.

In many cases, benefits paid by an employer to employees or their beneficiaries from the firm's assets receive the same tax treatment as benefits provided under an insurance contract. This is not true for death benefits. If they are provided other than through an insurance contract, the amount of the proceeds represents taxable income to the beneficiary. For this reason, employers are less likely to use alternative funding arrangements for death benefits than for disability and medical expense benefits.

Proceeds of a group term insurance contract, even if paid to a named beneficiary, are included in an employee's gross estate for federal estate tax purposes as long as the employee possessed incidents of ownership in the coverage at the time of death. However, no estate tax is levied on any amounts, including life insurance proceeds, left to a surviving spouse. In addition, taxable estates of $5.43 million or less in 2015 are generally free of estate taxation regardless of the beneficiary.

When an estate is otherwise subject to estate taxation, an employee may remove the proceeds of group term insurance from his or her taxable estate by absolutely assigning all incidents of ownership to another person, usually the beneficiary of the coverage. Incidents of ownership include the right to change the beneficiary, to terminate coverage, to assign coverage, or to exercise the conversion privilege. For this favorable treatment, however, the Internal Revenue Code requires that such an assignment be permissible under both the group term insurance master contract and the laws of the state having jurisdiction. The absolute assignment is usually in the form of a gift, which has its own tax implications. The amount of insurance is considered a gift made each year by the employee to the person to whom the absolute assignment was granted. Consequently, if the value of the gift is of sufficient size, federal gift taxes are payable. Because the Code and the IRS regulations are silent on the specific gift tax consequences of assigned group term insurance, there is disagreement about whether the gift is valued at Table I costs or at the actual premium for the coverage.

If certain requirements are satisfied, accelerated death benefits paid to persons who are either terminally or chronically ill receive favorable tax treatment. Benefits received because of a terminal illness are treated as income-tax-free death benefits as long as a physician has certified that the insured has an illness or physical condition that can reasonably be expected to result in death within 24 months or less after the date of certification. If a group contract provides accelerated death benefits to other categories of individuals, benefits can also be received with favorable tax treatment if a person is chronically ill and the coverage qualifies as a long-term care insurance contract.

Tax Treatment of Added Coverages

It is also important to discuss the tax treatment of supplemental life insurance, accidental death and dismemberment insurance, and dependent life insurance.

Supplemental Life Insurance. Supplemental life insurance can be written either as a separate contract or as part of the contract providing basic group term life insurance coverage. If it is a separate contract and if the supplemental group life insurance meets the conditions of qualifying as group term insurance under Sec. 79, the amount of coverage provided is added to all other group term insurance for purposes of calculating the Uniform Premium Table I cost. Any premiums the employee pays for the supplemental coverage are included in the deduction used to determine the final taxable income. In all other ways, supplemental life insurance is treated the same as group term insurance.

Many separate supplemental contracts are fully contributory and do not qualify as group term insurance under Sec. 79. This occurs only if all employees are charged rates that are either (1) equal to or lower than Table I costs or (2) equal to or greater than Table I costs. In either of these cases, the value of the coverage is not included in an employee's income.

When supplemental life insurance coverage is written in conjunction with a basic group life insurance plan, employers have the option of treating the supplemental coverage as a separate policy of insurance as long as the premiums are properly allocated between the two portions of the coverage. There is no advantage in treating the supplemental coverage as a separate policy if it would still qualify by itself as group term insurance under Sec. 79. However, this election minimizes taxable income to employees if the cost of the supplemental coverage is paid totally by the employees and all employees are charged rates at or below Table I costs.

Accidental Death and Dismemberment Insurance. Premiums paid for AD&D insurance are considered to be health insurance premiums rather than group term insurance premiums. However, these are also deductible to the employer as an ordinary and necessary business expense, just like group term insurance. Benefits paid to an employee under the dismemberment portion of the coverage are treated as benefits received under a health insurance contract and are income tax free. Death benefits received under the coverage are treated like death benefits received under group term life insurance.

Dependent Life Insurance. Employer contributions for dependent life insurance coverage are fully deductible by the employer as an ordinary and necessary business expense if the employee's overall compensation is reasonable. Employer contributions do not result in taxable income to an employee as long as the value of the benefit is *de minimis*. This means that the value is so small that it is administratively impractical for the employer to account for the cost on a per-person basis. Dependent coverage of $2,000 or less on any person falls into this category. The IRS considers amounts of coverage in excess of $2,000 on any dependent to be more than *de minimis*. If more than $2,000 of coverage is provided for any dependent from employer contributions, the cost of the entire amount of coverage for that dependent (as determined by Uniform Premium Table I costs) is considered taxable income to the employee.

Death benefits are free of income taxation and are not included in the dependent's taxable estate for estate tax purposes.

State Tax Treatment

In most instances, state tax laws affecting group term insurance are similar to the federal laws. However, two major differences do exist. In most states, the payment of group term insurance premiums by the employer does not result in any taxable income to the employee, even if the amount of coverage exceeds $50,000. In addition, death proceeds receive favorable tax treatment under the estate and inheritance tax laws of most states. Generally, the proceeds are at least partially, if not totally, exempt from such taxation.

CONTINUATION OF GROUP LIFE INSURANCE AFTER RETIREMENT

Group term insurance plans were traditionally designed to provide employees with preretirement life insurance coverage. At retirement, an employee was faced with the decision of whether to let coverage terminate or to convert to an individual policy at an extremely high premium rate. In recent years, however, an increasing number of group life insurance plans have been designed to provide postretirement as well as preretirement life insurance coverage. In some cases, this is accomplished by continuing group term insurance coverage, often at a reduced amount, after retirement. In other cases, it is done through life insurance that provides permanent benefits funded during employees' working years.

The popularity of various approaches for providing postretirement life insurance coverage has changed over time, primarily because of changes in tax laws. Older and once-popular products, such as group paid-up insurance and group ordinary insurance, are no longer written. Newer products like group universal life insurance and group variable universal life insurance have come on the scene and had modest success. Four approaches are currently used:

- continuation of group term insurance
- group universal life insurance
- group variable universal life insurance
- group term carve-outs

Most postretirement life insurance coverage consists of the continuation of group term insurance. This requires the employer to make two important decisions: the amount of coverage to be continued and the method of paying for the continued coverage. Although the full amount of coverage prior to retirement may be continued, the high cost of group term insurance coverage for older employees frequently results in a reduction in the amount of coverage.

Current Revenue Funding

current revenue funding

Current revenue funding is the most common method to provide post-retirement life insurance. Each periodic premium to the insurance company is paid from the employer's current revenue and is based on the lives of all employees covered, both active and retired. Because retired employees have no salary or wages from which payroll deductions can be made, most postretirement life insurance coverage is noncontributory.

The tax implications of providing postretirement group term insurance on a current-revenue basis are the same for both the employer and the employee as those for active employees.

Retired Lives Reserves

In the late 1970s and early 1980s, there was increasing interest in prefunding the cost of postretirement group term insurance coverage through retired-lives-reserve arrangements. Much of this interest stemmed from the IRS changing Sec. 79 regulations and making previously popular products less attractive. The concept was not new. Retired lives reserves, although not extensively used prior to that time, had been in existence for many years, primarily for very large employers. However, the trend in the 1970s was to establish them for smaller employers because the tax laws allowed the plans to be designed so that they often provided significant benefits to the firm's owners or key employees. Because the Tax Reform Act of 1984 imposed more stringent requirements on retired lives reserves and because of the availability of newer products for postretirement coverage, there is little interest in establishing new plans. Nevertheless, plans still exist, primarily in heavily unionized industries and usually for employers with 2,000 to 5,000 employees. In addition, other plans still exist for employees and retirees previously covered under them, but other arrangements are used for newer employees.

retired lives reserve

A **retired lives reserve** is best defined as a fund established during employees' working years to pay all or a part of the cost of their group term insurance after retirement. The fund may be established and maintained through a trust or with an insurance company. If properly designed, a retired lives reserve (1) enables an employer to make currently tax-deductible contributions to the fund during employees' working years and (2) does not result in any taxable income to employees before retirement. However, an employer may take current deductions only for prefunding coverage that is received tax free by retired employees under Sec. 79. This amount is generally $50,000 but may be higher for certain employees, subject to a grandfather clause. In addition, an employer cannot deduct contributions on behalf of key employees if the plan is discriminatory under Sec. 79.

At retirement, the employer can use the assets of the fund can to pay the cost of maintaining the postretirement coverage. If the employer withdraws assets from a trust, there is the possibility of the fund being inadequate in the long run because of higher premiums and/or shorter life expectancies than anticipated. However, insurance company products typically assume this uncertainty and guarantee that the fund will be adequate to maintain the promised benefits as long as the employer has deposited the prescribed contributions.

As long as an employee has no rights in a retired lives reserve except to receive postretirement group term insurance coverage until his or her death, the employee incurs no income taxation as a result of either employer contributions to the reserve or investment earnings on the reserve. In addition, up to $50,000 can be received income tax free by beneficiaries.

In those instances when death benefits are paid directly from trust assets, the tax consequences to the employee are the same as if death benefits are provided through group term insurance contracts, except that death proceeds represent taxable income to the beneficiary.

Group Universal Life Insurance

group universal life insurance

Group universal life insurance is a flexible-premium policy that, unlike traditional cash value life insurance, divides the pure insurance protection and the cash value accumulation into separate and distinct components. The employee is required to pay a specified initial premium, from which a charge is subtracted for one month's insurance protection. This mortality charge in effect is used to purchase the required amount of pure or term insurance (often referred to as the amount at risk) at a cost based on the insured's current age. Under some policies, an additional deduction is made for expenses. The balance of the initial premium becomes the initial cash value of the policy, which, when credited with interest, becomes the cash value at the end of the period. The process continues in succeeding periods. New premiums are added to the cash value, charges are made for expenses and mortality, and interest is credited to the remaining cash value. Employees receive periodic disclosure statements showing all charges made for the period as well as any interest earnings.

Group universal life insurance offers an employee considerable flexibility to meet several life-cycle financial needs with a single type of insurance coverage. The death benefit can be increased because of marriage, the birth of a child, or an increase in income. The death benefit can be reduced later if the need for life insurance decreases. Cash withdrawals can be made for the down payment on a home or to pay college tuition. Premium payments can be reduced during those periods when a young family has pressing financial needs. As financial circumstances improve, premiums can be increased so that an adequate retirement fund can be accumulated. The usual settlement options found in traditional cash value life insurance are available, so an employee can periodically elect to liquidate the cash accumulation as a source of retirement income.

Marketing efforts tout group universal life insurance as having the following advantages to the employer:

- no direct cost other than that associated with payroll deductions and possibly enrollment, because the entire premium cost is borne by the employee. In this sense, group universal life insurance plans are much like voluntary benefit plans that offer individual universal life insurance policies.

- no ERISA filing and reporting requirement if the master contract is issued to a trust and there are no employer contributions for the cost of coverage. The current products are marketed through multiple-employer trusts, with the trust being the policyowner.

- the ability of employees to continue "permanent" life coverage into retirement, alleviating pressure for the employer to provide postretirement life insurance benefits

The following advantages are being claimed for employees:

- the availability of permanent life insurance at group rates

- the opportunity to continue insurance coverage after retirement, possibly without any postretirement contributions

- flexibility in designing coverage to best meet the needs of the individual employee

Underwriting

Insurers that write group universal life insurance have underwriting standards concerning group size, the amounts of coverage available, and insurability.

Currently, most group universal life insurance products are limited primarily to employers who have at least 100 or 200 employees. However, a few insurers write coverage for smaller groups. Some insurance companies also have an employee percentage-participation requirement, such as 20 or 25 percent, that must be satisfied before a group can be installed. Other insurance companies feel their marketing approach is designed so that adequate participation results and therefore have no participation requirements.

The extent to which evidence of insurability is required of individual employees is also similar to that found under most supplemental group term life insurance plans. When an employee is initially eligible, coverage is usually issued on a guaranteed-issue basis up to specified limits, which again are influenced by the size of the group, the amount of coverage provided under the employer's basic group term insurance plan, and the degree of participation in the plan. If an employee chooses a larger death benefit, simplified-issue underwriting is used up to a second amount, after which regular underwriting is used. Guaranteed-issue underwriting is often unavailable for small groups, in which case underwriting on the basis of a simplified questionnaire is used up to a specific amount of death benefit, after which regular underwriting is used.

Death Benefit

The policyowner under an individual group universal life insurance policy typically has a choice of two death benefit options. Option A provides a level death benefit in the early policy years. As the cash value increases, the amount of pure insurance decreases so that the total amount paid to a beneficiary upon the insured's death remains constant. Without any provision to the contrary, the cash value would eventually approach the amount of the total death benefit. To prevent this from occurring, and also to keep the policy from failing to qualify as a life insurance policy under existing tax regulations, the amount of pure insurance does not decrease further once the cash value reaches a predetermined level. Thereafter, the total death benefit increases unless the cash value decreases. The first figure below graphically demonstrates option A. Note that this and the following figure are for illustrative purposes only. The actual death benefit for a particular individual varies by such factors as the amount of interest credited, premiums paid, loans, and withdrawals.

Figure 4-1

Universal Life Insurance—Death Benefit Option A

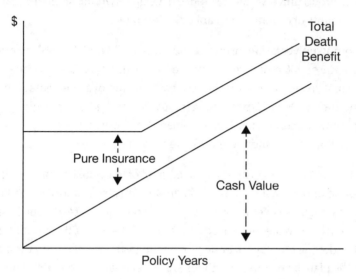

Under option B, the amount of pure insurance is constant, and the death benefit increases each period by the change in the policy cash value. The following figure shows this.

Figure 4-2

Universal Life Insurance—Death Benefit Option B

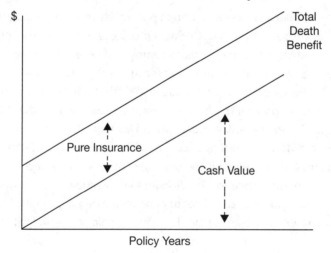

With group universal life insurance products, an employee usually has only one death benefit option available, and whether it is option A or option B depends on which one the employer has selected. In general, there seems to be a feeling that the availability of both options makes a plan more difficult to explain to employees and more costly to administer. Most employers have selected option B, which is usually easier to market to employees because the increasing total death benefit is a visible sign of any increase in their cash value or "investment." As a result, several insurers now make only option B available with their group products.

Universal life insurance products give the insured the right to increase or decrease the death benefit from the level originally selected as circumstances change. For example, the policyowner might have initially selected a pure death benefit of $100,000 under option B. Because of the birth of a child, this amount might be increased to $150,000. Increases, but not decreases, typically require that the insured provide evidence of insurability.

Mortality Charges

Most products have a guaranteed mortality charge for 3 years, after which the insurer bases the mortality charge on the experience of each particular group. As with experience rating in general, the credibility given to a group's actual experience is greater for larger groups. Most insurance companies guarantee that any future increases in the mortality charge will not exceed a stated maximum.

The products designed for small groups typically use pooled rates that apply to all groups insured through a particular trust. Therefore, the mortality charge for any employer varies, not with the employer's overall experience but rather with the overall experience of the trust.

Expense Charges

Probably the greatest variations among group life insurance products occur in the expense charges that insurers levy. Typically, a percentage of each premium, such as 2 percent, is deducted for expenses. In addition, there is a flat monthly charge, which normally ranges from $1 to $3, to maintain the accumulation account. Some insurance companies levy this charge against all certificate holders, even those who are contributing only enough to have the pure insurance coverage. Other insurance companies levy the charge only against those accounts that have a positive cash value accumulation. A few insurance companies also load their mortality charges for expenses.

Interest Rates

Insurance companies guarantee that the initial interest rate credited to cash value accumulations will remain in effect for a minimum period, often one year. After that time, the rate is typically adjusted quarterly or semiannually but cannot fall below some contractual minimum, typically in the range of 2½ to 3½ percent for newer policies. The interest rate credited is usually determined on a discretionary basis but is influenced by the insurance company's investment income and competitive factors. However, some insurers stipulate that it is linked to some money market instrument, such as 3-month Treasury bills. In general, the same interest is credited to all groups that an insurance company has underwritten.

Premium Adjustments

Employees have considerable flexibility in the amount and timing of premium payments. Premiums can be raised or lowered and even suspended. In the latter case, the contract terminates if an employee's cash value accumulation is inadequate to pay current mortality and expense charges. Of course, premium payments could be reinstated to prevent this from happening. Additional lump-sum contributions may also be made to the accumulation account.

Insurers place two restrictions on premium adjustments. First, the premium payment cannot be such that the size of the cash value accumulation becomes so large in relationship to the pure protection that an employee's coverage fails to qualify as a policy of insurance under IRS regulations. Second, because changes in premium payments through payroll deductions are costly to administer, many employers limit the frequency with which adjustments are allowed.

Loans and Withdrawals

Employees are allowed to make loans and withdrawals from their accumulated cash values, but for administrative reasons the frequency of loans and withdrawals may be limited. There are also minimum loan and withdrawal amounts, such as $250 or $500. In addition, an employee is usually required to leave a minimum balance in the cash value account sufficient to pay mortality and expense charges for some time period, possibly as long as one year. The interest rate charged on policy loans is now usually set on a discretionary basis by each insurer and subject to change.

An employee can withdraw his or her entire cash value accumulation and terminate coverage. Total withdrawals are subject to a surrender charge during early policy years. The charge decreases with policy duration and is usually in addition to any transaction charge that the insurer might levy.

Dependent Coverage

Most products allow an employee to purchase a rider that provides term insurance coverage on his or her spouse and children. For example, one insurance company allows an employee to elect spousal coverage of $10,000 to $50,000 in $10,000 increments and coverage on children in the amount of either $5,000 or $10,000. Other insurers make varying amounts available.

Accidental Death and Waiver of Premium

A group universal life insurance plan may provide accidental death benefits and a disability waiver of premium. These benefits are not optional for each employee; they are part of the coverage only if the employer has elected to include them in the plan. When a waiver of premium is included, all that the insurer waives in case of disability is the portion of the premium necessary to pay the cost of the pure insurance protection for the employee and any dependents.

Tax Treatment

Group universal life insurance products are not designed to be policies of insurance under Sec. 79. In addition, each employee pays the full cost of his or her coverage. Therefore, the tax treatment is the same to employees as if they had purchased a universal life insurance policy in the individual insurance marketplace.

Group Variable Universal Life Insurance

group variable universal life insurance

In the mid-1990s, most major insurers that wrote group universal life insurance introduced a variable product usually called **group variable universal life insurance**. It has the same basic characteristics that were previously described for group universal life with one major difference—employees have a series of investment accounts to which they may allocate their net premiums. Once an employee elects the initial allocation, all future net premiums are allocated in the same proportion unless the employee makes a written request for a change. With the one exception described below, there are no minimum guarantees, and the full investment risk rests solely with the employee.

Group variable universal life insurance plans may offer up to 20 or more differing types of investment funds. These typically include at least one and possibly more of the following: growth funds, bond funds, money market funds, index funds, international stock funds, mortgage securities funds, and small company stock funds. Employers can choose the investment options that are made available to employees. For ease of administration and communication, this number is often in the range of four to six.

Group Term Carve-Outs

Prior to 1984, employees had no taxable income if they were provided with postretirement coverage under a group term life insurance plan. At that time, coverage in excess of $50,000 became subject to the imputed income rules of Sec. 79, based on Table I costs, which are relatively high at older ages. As a result, many employers turned to group term carve-outs. Although carve-outs can be used for any employee with more than $50,000 of group term coverage, they typically apply only to shareholders and key executives.

Bonus Plans

In the simplest sense, a group term carve-out works like this: The employer decides which employees are covered under the carve-out plan and limits coverage for these employees under its group term plan to the $50,000 that is received tax free. The employer then gives any premium savings to each "carved-out" employee in the form of a bonus, which is fully deductible to the employer as long as the employee's overall compensation is reasonable. The bonus amounts are either paid directly to an insurance company for individual coverage on the lives of the participants in the carve-out plan or in some cases provided to the employees as compensation to pay life insurance premiums. In most cases, the coverage purchased under the carve-out plan is some form of permanent life insurance protection that provides paid-up coverage at retirement. Traditional whole life insurance, universal life insurance, variable universal life insurance, and variable life insurance are all viable alternatives. At retirement, the employee can either keep the coverage in force (possibly at a reduced paid-up amount) or surrender the policy for its cash value.

The popularity of carve-out plans lies in the fact that the employer can provide a comparable or greater amount of life insurance coverage to participants at a lower cost than if the participants receive all their coverage under the group term life insurance plan. Because the carve-out plan does not qualify as a plan of insurance under Sec. 79, each participant has taxable income in the amount of the bonus. However, the absence of any imputed income from Table I offsets this income.

In reality, carve-out plans are more complex. In many cases, the cost of permanent coverage for an employee may actually be greater than the cost of group term coverage during the working years. However, this high cost is often more than compensated for by the cash value at retirement and the absence of imputed income after retirement. Under some carve-out plans, participants must pay this increased premium cost with after-tax dollars. Under other plans, the employer increases the bonus amount. In effect, the employer is now paying more than if the carve-out plan did not exist, but this arrangement is often acceptable to the employer as a way of providing shareholders and key executives with a benefit that is not available to other employees. In many plans, the bonus is also increased to compensate the employee for any additional income taxes that must be paid because of the carve-out plan. Such an arrangement is commonly referred to as a *zero-tax approach*.

A carve-out plan can pose a potential problem if there are rated or uninsurable employees, but the problem is ameliorated if the plan has enough participants that the insurance company will use simplified-issue underwriting or grant concessions on impaired risks. Any employee who is still uninsurable can be continued in the group term plan.

Other Types of Carve-Out Plans

death-benefit-only plan

A bonus arrangement is the most common type of carve-out plan, but other alternatives are available. A carve-out plan is sometimes designed as a **death-benefit-only plan**, under which the employer agrees only to pay a death benefit to the employee's beneficiary out of corporate assets. The employer often funds the plan with corporate-owned life insurance on the employee's life. With this approach, the employee has no taxable income, but death benefits result in taxable income to the beneficiary. In addition, the employer is unable to deduct the premiums as a business expense but does receive the death proceeds tax-free.

Some firms also use split-dollar life insurance in carve-out plans. The most common approach is to use a collateral assignment arrangement under which the employer pays most of the premium, and the employee collaterally assigns a portion of the cash value and death benefit to the employer equal to the employer's premium payments. At retirement (or any other predetermined time), the employee withdraws the cash value necessary to repay the employer, who then removes the collateral assignment. At that time, the employee has full control of the policy, and the remaining cash value can be used to keep coverage in force. Many split-dollar arrangements are also used to provide nonqualified retirement benefits to key employees as a supplement to the benefits under the employer's qualified retirement plan.

Determining the Best Plan

In many instances, carve-out plans are the most cost-effective approach for providing benefits to key employees. The best plan depends on the employer's overall benefit objectives. A proper analysis of alternatives involves a complex consideration of many factors, including the employer's tax bracket, the effect on the employer's financial statements, the employee's tax bracket, premium costs, and the time value of money.

CHAPTER REVIEW

Key Terms and Concepts

life insurance
term insurance
yearly renewable term insurance
benefit schedule
covered classifications
full-time employee
actively-at-work provision
beneficiary
successive beneficiary provision
settlement options
grace period
incontestability provision
misstatement of age provision
waiver-of-premium provision
conversion provision
accelerated-benefits provision

rider
supplemental life insurance
accidental death and dismemberment (AD&D)
voluntary accidental death and dismemberment insurance
dependent life insurance
Sec. 79
Uniform Premium Table I
key employee
current revenue funding
retired lives reserves
group universal life insurance
group variable universal life insurance
death-benefit-only plan

Review Questions

Review questions are based on the learning objectives in this chapter. For example, a [3] at the end of a questions means that the question is based on learning objective 3. If there are multiple objectives, they are all listed.

1. Why has yearly renewable term insurance been more popular in the group insurance marketplace than in the individual insurance marketplace? [1]

2. Describe the following types of benefit schedules: [2]

a. multiple-of-earnings schedules

b. flat-benefit schedules

c. dollar-amount-by-earnings schedules

d. position schedules

e. length-of-service schedules

3. Regarding benefit reduction for older employees: [2]

    a. Why are life insurance benefits often reduced for older employees?

    b. What are the approaches used to reduce benefits for older employees?

4. What criteria generally must be satisfied before an employee is eligible for group term insurance coverage? [3]

5. For what reasons are the covered classifications for group insurance contracts often designed to exclude certain employees? [3]

6. Explain the alternative approaches used in group term contracts for paying benefits if no beneficiary has been named or if there is no surviving beneficiary. [3]

7. Describe the settlement options offered by most insurance companies for death benefits under group term insurance contracts. [3]

8. For contributory group term insurance plans, describe the following: [3]

    a. the employee's responsibility to make premium payments to the insurance company

    b. the extent to which state laws may limit the amount of employee contributions

    c. the use of dividends or experience refunds

9. For what reasons might group term insurance coverage terminate on an active employee? [3]

10. Describe the methods for continuing coverage on disabled employees. [3]

11. Because of severe business difficulties, the Newtown Manufacturing Company permanently laid off 20 percent of its employees last March. All had been employed by the company for less than 3 years. In June salaries and fringe benefits were reduced for the remaining employees. This included the amending of the company's group term insurance contract to eliminate all eligible classifications except those pertaining to 4 executives and 14 managers, with the amount of coverage for these two groups being

reduced by 50 percent. Explain the extent, if any, to which the following groups of employees would have had the right to convert any coverage that was either terminated or reduced under the plan: [3]

    a.   the employees who were laid off in March

    b.   the employees whose coverage was terminated in June

    c.   the executives and managers whose coverage was reduced

12. Regarding accelerated benefits: [3]

    a.   Under what circumstances might an employee be allowed to elect an accelerated group term life insurance benefit?

    b.   How do provisions for accelerated benefits vary among insurance companies?

    c.   What methods might insurance companies use to charge for the inclusion of an accelerated death benefit?

13. How have insurance companies handled the problem of adverse selection associated with supplemental life insurance? [4]

14. Explain how the amount of an accidental death benefit may vary depending on when and how an employee dies. [4]

15. What exclusions are often found in coverage for accidental death and dismemberment? [4]

16. How might voluntary accidental death and dismemberment coverage differ from coverage written in the form of a rider to a group life insurance contract? [4]

17. Why are amounts of dependent life insurance usually relatively small? [4]

18. How does dependent life insurance differ from group term insurance on employees with respect to each of the following? [4]

    a.   the conversion privilege

    b.   the ability to assign benefits

    c.   the availability of a waiver-of-premium provision

19. Identify the circumstances under which employer contributions for an employee's group term insurance coverage are not deductible to the employer for federal income tax purposes. [5]

20. Are employees allowed an income tax deduction for contributions made to a group term insurance plan? Explain. [5]

21. What requirements must be met in order for life insurance to qualify as group term insurance under Sec. 79 of the Internal Revenue Code? [5]

22. Under what circumstances is life insurance that otherwise meets the definition of group term insurance not subject to Sec. 79? [5]

23. Regarding Sec. 79: [5]

    a. Last year Sarah Robbins, aged 32, was provided with $75,000 of group term insurance by her employer for the full year. The employer paid the entire premium. Using Uniform Premium Table I, calculate the amount of federal taxable income Sarah had because of this coverage.

    b. How would the answer to question a. change if Sarah had contributed $3.00 per month for her coverage?

24. Regarding Sec. 79: [5]

    a. For purposes of Sec. 79, who is a key employee?

    b. What criteria must be satisfied so that a group term plan is not discriminatory with respect to eligibility?

    c. What criteria must be satisfied so that a group term plan is not discriminatory with respect to benefits?

    d. What is the effect on employees if a group term plan is discriminatory?

25. The consulting firm of Herberts, Stephans, and Edwards has nine employees consisting of three principals who are paid annual salaries of $350,000 each, two consultants who are paid $65,000 each, and four secretaries who each earn $30,000. The firm's group term insurance plan provides a benefit of two times salary for eligible employees. All employees are eligible for coverage except one secretary who is past the plan's maximum age of 65. [5]

    a. Does this plan satisfy the under-10 requirement of Sec. 79? Explain.

    b. Does the plan satisfy the provisions of the Age Discrimination in Employment Act? Explain.

26. Why are employers less likely to provide death benefits on a self-funded basis than disability or medical expense benefits? [5]

27. What are the tax implications of assigning group term insurance coverage? [5]

28. Under what circumstances do accelerated death benefits from a group term insurance contract receive favorable income tax treatment? [5]

29. Regarding supplemental group life insurance: [5]

    a.   What are the general rules for the taxation of supplemental group life insurance benefits under Sec. 79?

    b.   Under what circumstances can supplemental group life insurance be treated as a policy of insurance that is not subject to Sec. 79?

30. How does the federal income tax treatment of the following coverages differ from the treatment of group term insurance provided to employees? [5]

    a.   accidental death and dismemberment insurance

    b.   dependent life insurance

31. How do state tax laws affecting group term insurance usually differ from federal tax laws? [5]

32. Why is postretirement life insurance coverage usually noncontributory? [6]

33. To what extent can an employer prefund postretirement life insurance through a retired lives reserve and receive a current income tax deduction? [6]

34. What are the federal tax implications of a retired lives reserve to an employee and his or her beneficiaries? [6]

35. Briefly describe the general nature of group universal life insurance. [6]

36. How does group universal life insurance give an employee flexibility to meet several life-cycle financial needs with a single type of insurance coverage? [6]

37. What are the advantages of group universal life insurance for each of the following? [6]

    a.   the employer

    b.   the employee

38. What underwriting requirements are often found in group universal life insurance products with respect to each of the following? [6]

    a.   group size

    b.   insurability

39. Why is an option B death benefit usually the only one made available under a group universal life insurance plan? [6]

40. Briefly describe the typical group universal life insurance product with respect to each of the following: [6]

    a. guarantees of mortality charges

    b. types of expense charges

    c. interest rates credited

41. Briefly describe the provisions in group universal life insurance products for each of the following: [6]

    a. premium adjustments

    b. loans and withdrawals

    c. dependent coverage

    d. accidental death and waiver of premium

42. Why is group universal life insurance not treated as group term life insurance for tax purposes? [6]

43. How does group variable universal life insurance differ from group universal life insurance? [6]

44. Describe the general nature of a group term carve-out. [6]

45. Briefly describe the types of group term carve-out plans. [6]

46. What factors should be considered in designing a group term carve-out plan? [6]

Review Question Answers

1. The lower prevalence of term insurance in the individual marketplace is primarily due to its increasing annual premiums, which become prohibitive for many insureds at older ages. In group life insurance plans, the overall premium, in addition to other factors, is a function of the age distribution of the group's members. Although the premium for any individual employee increases with age, the flow of younger workers into the plan and the retirement of older workers tend to result in a relatively stable age distribution and thus an average group insurance rate that remains constant or rises only slightly.

2. a. Under a multiple-of-earnings schedule, the amount of life insurance is determined as a multiple (or percentage) of each employee's earnings. Most plans use a multiple between one and two, but higher and lower multiples are occasionally used. The amount of insurance and may be subject to a maximum benefit, such as $200,000. For purposes of the benefit schedule, an employee's earnings usually consist of base salary only and do not include additional compensation like overtime pay or bonuses.

    A few multiple-of-earnings schedules use multiples that vary by earnings, position, or length of service with larger multiples used for persons with higher salaries, in higher positions, or with longer service.

    b. Under a flat-benefit schedule, the same amount of life insurance is provided for all employees regardless of salary or position. In most cases, the amount of life insurance is relatively small, such as $10,000 or $20,000; however, it may be as much as $50,000 or higher. When an employer wants to provide only a minimum amount of life insurance for all employees, a flat-benefit schedule is often used.

    c. Some benefit schedules provide a specified amount of coverage that varies by earnings, with higher-paid employees typically receiving a proportionally larger benefit than lower-paid employees.

    d. Under a position schedule, the amount of life insurance is based on an employee's position within the firm. Position schedules are particularly useful when it is difficult to determine an employee's annual income. This is the situation when income is materially affected by such factors as commissions earned, number of hours worked, or bonuses based on either the employee's performance or the firm's profits.

    e. Length-of-service schedules are a method for progressively rewarding employees based on their years of employment with longtime employees receiving greater amounts of life insurance under the group plan.

3. a. Group life insurance plans often provide for a reduction in benefits for active employees who are older. Such a reduction is due to the high cost of providing benefits for these employees and occurs when they reach a certain age, commonly 65 to 70.

    b. Benefit reductions fall into three categories: (1) a reduction to a flat amount of insurance; (2) a percentage reduction, such as to 65 percent of the amount of insurance that was previously provided; or (3) a gradual reduction over a period of years (for example, a 10 percent reduction in coverage each year until a minimum benefit amount is reached).

4. An employee generally must be in a covered classification, work full-time, and be actively at work. In addition, any requirements concerning probationary periods, insurability, or premium contributions must be satisfied.

5. Excluded employees may have coverage through a negotiated trusteeship or under other group insurance contracts provided by the employer; in other cases, they may have no coverage because the employer wishes to limit benefits to certain groups of employees.

6. Some group term insurance contracts contain a provision whereby death benefits are paid to an insured person's estate if no beneficiary is named or if all beneficiaries died before the insured; others stipulate that the death benefits are paid through a successive beneficiary provision. Under the successive beneficiary provision, the proceeds are paid (at the option of the insurance company) to any one or more of the following survivors of the insured person: spouse, children, parents, brothers and sisters, or executor of the employee's estate.

7. In addition to a lump-sum option, most insurance companies offer all the following options:

    •   an interest option. The proceeds are left on deposit with the insurance company, and the interest on the proceeds is paid to the beneficiary. The beneficiary can usually withdraw the proceeds at any time. The amount of any periodic installment is a function of the interest rate paid by the insurance company.

    •   an installment option for a fixed period. The proceeds are paid in equal installments for a specified period of time. The amount of any periodic installment is a function of the time period and the amount of the death proceeds.

    •   an installment option for a fixed amount. The proceeds are paid in equal installments of a specified amount until the proceeds plus any interest earnings are exhausted.

    •   a life income option. The proceeds are payable in installments during the lifetime of the beneficiary.

8. a. Any required contributions from employees are incorporated into the employer's group insurance plan, but they are not part of the insurance contract and therefore do not constitute an obligation to the insurance company by the employees. Rather, these contributions represent an obligation to the employer by the employees and are commonly paid by payroll deduction.

b.   Most states require that the employer pay at least a portion of the premium for group term insurance (but not for other group insurance coverage), and a few states limit the amounts that may be paid by any employee.

c.   Any dividends or experience refunds are payable to the policyowner in cash or may be used at the policyowner's option to reduce any premium due. To the extent that these exceed the policyowner's share of the premium, they must be used for the employees' benefit. This is usually accomplished by reducing employee contributions or increasing benefits.

9.   The coverage for any insured person terminates automatically (subject to any provisions for a continuation or conversion of coverage) when

   •   the employee terminates employment

   •   the employee ceases to be eligible (for example, if the employee no longer satisfies the full-time work requirement or no longer falls into a covered classification)

   •   the policyowner or insurance company terminates the master contract

   •   any required contribution by the employee has not been made (generally because the employee has notified the policyowner to cease the required payroll deduction)

10. Coverage on disabled employees may continue with the following methods:

   •   Under a waiver-of-premium provision, life insurance coverage is continued without the payment of premium as long as the employee is totally disabled, even if the master contract is terminated.

   •   Another provision relating to disabled employees is a maturity-value benefit. Under this type of provision, the face amount of a totally disabled employee's group life insurance is paid to the employee in a lump sum or in monthly installments. This provision is no longer common.

   •   A small but growing trend is for plans to continue disabled employees as eligible employees under a group insurance contract, with the employer paying the periodic cost of their coverage just as if they were active employees.

11. a.   The employees who were permanently laid off in March would have had the right to convert the full amount of any coverage they had under the group contract. Since employment was terminated, the period of time the employees worked for the company is not relevant. However, they would have had to exercise the conversion privilege within 31 days of termination.

b. The employees whose coverage was completely terminated in June by the amendment of the contract may also have been eligible for conversion, but in a more restrictive manner. They would have been treated as if the master contract had been terminated and could have converted their coverage only if they had been insured under the contract for a minimum period of time (usually 5 years). The amount of coverage that can be converted under these circumstances is also limited to the lesser of $10,000 or the amount of coverage they had under the group contract.

c. The executives and managers do not fall into any of the categories eligible for conversion.

12. a. These circumstances might include

- a terminal illness that is expected to result in death within 6 or 12 months

- a specified catastrophic illness, such as cancer, renal failure, AIDS, a stroke, or Alzheimer's disease

- the incurring of nursing home and possibly other long-term-care expenses

b. The amount of the accelerated benefit is expressed as a percentage of the basic life insurance coverage and may range from 25 percent to 100 percent. In addition, many insurers limit the maximum benefit to a specified dollar amount. This amount varies widely among insurers and can be as low as $25,000 or as high as $500,000 or more.

c. A few insurers charge the policyowner an additional premium for the inclusion of accelerated death benefit coverage and make no additional charge when a benefit is accelerated. The majority of insurers, however, follow one of two alternative approaches. Some insurers charge no additional premium but often levy a transaction charge each time a benefit is accelerated. Other insurers also charge no additional premium but shift the cost of the benefit to the insured by either (1) discounting the accelerated benefit to reflect lost interest or (2) treating the advance payment as a lien against the coverage and charge interest on the amount advanced. A few insurers allow the insured to select whether the discounting or lien approach is used.

13. More stringent underwriting requirements usually accompany supplemental coverage. These may include requiring individual evidence of insurability for the full amount of coverage. However, many insurers will issue a specific amount of supplemental coverage on a guaranteed-issue basis, with the guaranteed amount based on the size of the group and the amount of basic coverage. Larger amounts of

supplemental coverage are subject to individual underwriting. Higher rates may be charged for the supplemental insurance than for the basic coverage.

14. Death while traveling on business when occupying, boarding, alighting from, or struck by any motor vehicle, airplane, or other conveyance, including company-owned or personally owned vehicles may be 3 times the principal sum. Death at all other times may be 2 times the principal sum.

15. Exclusions include losses resulting from the following situation and events:

   - suicide at any time

   - disease or bodily or mental infirmity, or medical or surgical treatment thereof

   - ptomaine or any infection other than one occurring simultaneously with and through an accidental cut or wound

   - war

   - travel or flight in any type of aircraft either as a pilot, as a student pilot, or as an officer or member of the crew

16. The following are a few differences.

   - Voluntary plans usually require that the employee pay the entire cost of coverage, and they virtually always provide both occupational and nonoccupational coverage.

   - Subject to limitations, the employee may select the amount of coverage desired, and the maximum amount of coverage available tends to be larger than when coverage is provided through a rider to a group contract.

   - Another difference is the frequent use in voluntary plans of a common accident provision, whereby the amount payable by the insurance company is limited to a stipulated maximum for all employees killed or injured in any single accident.

   - A final difference is that some voluntary plans allow an employee to purchase accidental death and dismemberment coverage on dependents.

17. Dependent life insurance has been viewed largely as a method of giving the employee enough resources to meet the funeral and burial expenses associated with a dependent's death. Consequently, the employee is automatically the beneficiary. In addition, some states limit the maximum amount of life insurance that can be written, and a few states actually prohibit writing any coverage on dependents. Finally, federal tax laws serve to keep amounts of dependent coverage low because employer contributions

used to purchase more than $2,000 of coverage on each dependent result in taxable income to the employee.

18. a. Dependent coverage usually contains a conversion privilege that applies only to the coverage on the spouse. However, some states require that the conversion privilege apply to the coverage on all dependents. Some insurers also have portability provisions so that the group coverage can continue on a direct-bill basis.

    b. Assignment of dependent life benefits is almost never permitted.

    c. No waiver of premium is available if a dependent becomes disabled.

19. The following persons are considered self-employed persons for income tax purposes and no deduction to an employer or firm is allowed: sole proprietors, partners, members of limited liability companies (LLCs), and more-than-2-percent shareholders of an S corporation. For income tax purposes, a firm may not deduct any compensation that the IRS determines to be unreasonable. In addition, the Internal Revenue Code does not allow a firm to take an income tax deduction for contributions that are made in behalf of stockholders unless they are providing substantive services to the corporation. Finally, no deduction is allowed if the employer is named as beneficiary of an employee's life insurance coverage.

20. No. Contributions by any individual employee are considered payments for personal life insurance and are not deductible for income tax purposes by that employee. Thus, the amount of any payroll deductions authorized by an employee for group term insurance purposes is included in the employee's taxable income.

21. To qualify as group term life insurance under Sec. 79, life insurance must meet the following requirements:

    •   It must provide a death benefit excludible from federal income tax.

    •   It must be given to a group of employees, defined to include all employees of an employer. If all employees are not covered, membership must be determined on the basis of age, marital status, or factors relating to employment.

    •   It must be provided under a policy carried directly or indirectly by the employer.

        The term carried indirectly refers to those situations when the employer is not the policyowner but rather provides coverage to employees through master contracts issued to organizations, such as negotiated trusteeships or multiple-employer welfare arrangements.

    •   The plan must be arranged to preclude individual selection of coverage amounts. However, it is acceptable to have alternative benefit schedules based on the amount an employee elects to contribute. Supplemental plans that give an employee a choice, such as 1, 1½, or 2 times salary, are considered to fall within this category.

22. In some cases, different sections of the Internal Revenue Code provide alternative tax treatment. For example, when group term insurance is issued to the trustees of a qualified pension plan and is used to provide a death benefit under the plan, the full amount of any life insurance paid for by employer contributions results in taxable income to the employee.

In addition, there are three situations in which employer contributions for group term insurance do not result in taxable income to an employee, regardless of the amount of insurance:

- if an employee has terminated employment because of disability

- if a qualified charity has been named as beneficiary for the entire year

- if the employer has been named as beneficiary for the entire year

23. a. The amount of taxable income is determined by using the Uniform Premium Table I cost for the amount of coverage in excess of $50,000.

Coverage provided	$75,000
Minus Sec. 79 exclusion	– 50,000
Amount subject to taxation	$25,000
Uniform Premium Table I monthly cost per $1,000 of coverage at age 32	.$08
Monthly cost ($.08 × 25)	$2.00
Annual cost ($2.00 × 12)	$24.00

b. If Sarah had contributed $3.00 per month, the annual contribution of $36.00 could have been deducted from the Table I annual cost of $24.00. Because the annual cost would have been less than Sarah's contribution, no income would have been reportable because of the group insurance coverage.

24. a. A key employee of a firm is defined as any person (either active or retired) who at any time during the plan year containing the discrimination date is any of the following:

- an officer of the firm who earns more than $170,000 (in 2015) in annual compensation from the firm. For purposes of this rule, the number of employees treated as officers is the greater of 3 employees or 10 percent of the firm's employees, subject to a maximum of 50.

- a 5 percent owner of the firm.

- a 1 percent owner of the firm who earns over $150,000 in annual compensation from the firm.

b. Eligibility requirements are not discriminatory if (1) at least 70 percent of all employees are eligible, (2) at least 85 percent of all employees who are participants are not key employees, (3) participants constitute a classification that the IRS determines is nondiscriminatory, or (4) the group term insurance plan is part of a cafeteria plan and Sec. 125 requirements are satisfied.

c. Benefits are not discriminatory if neither the type nor amount of benefits discriminates in favor of key employees. It is permissible to base benefits on a uniform percentage of salary.

d. In addition, the value of the full amount of coverage for key employees, minus their own contributions, is considered taxable income.

25. a. The under-10 requirements of Sec. 79 are satisfied because it is permissible to base benefits on a uniform percentage of compensation. It is irrelevant that the three owners receive more than 10 times as much coverage as the secretaries because the amount of coverage is not determined by employee classifications. The use of such classifications is only an alternative to basing benefits on a uniform percentage of salary or a flat-dollar amount. Sec. 79 also permits eligibility to be limited to employees who have not reached age 65.

b. The Age Discrimination in Employment Act does not apply to firms with fewer than 20 employees. Therefore, the maximum age of 65 is permissible.

26. When death benefits are provided by the employer on a self-funded basis, the amount of the proceeds represents taxable income to the beneficiary. For this reason, employers are less likely to use alternative funding arrangements for death benefits than for disability and medical expense benefits.

27. When an estate is otherwise subject to estate taxation, an employee may remove the proceeds of group term insurance from his or her taxable estate by absolutely assigning all incidents of ownership to another person, usually the beneficiary of the coverage.

28. Accelerated death benefits paid to persons who are either terminally or chronically ill receive favorable tax treatment as long as a physician has certified that the insured

has an illness or physical condition that can reasonably be expected to result in death within 24 months or less after the date of certification. Accelerated benefits can also be received with favorable tax treatment if a person is chronically ill and the coverage qualifies as a long-term care insurance contract.

29. a. If the insurance is written as a separate contract and meets the condition of qualifying as group term insurance under Sec. 79, the amount of coverage provided is added to all other group term insurance for purposes of calculating the Uniform Premium Table I cost. Any premium the employee pays for the supplemental coverage are included in the deduction used to determine the final taxable income.

    When supplemental coverage is written in conjunction with a basic group life insurance plan, employers have the option of treating the supplemental coverage as a separate policy of insurance as long as the premiums are properly allocated among the two portions of the coverage. This election minimizes taxable income to employees if the cost of the supplemental coverage is paid totally by the employees and all employees are charged rates at or below Table I costs.

    b. If all employees are charged rates that are either (1) equal to or lower than the Uniform Premium Table I costs or (2) equal to greater than Table I costs, the value of the coverage is not included in an employee's income.

30. a. Premiums paid for AD&D insurance are considered to be health insurance premiums and are deductible to the employer as an ordinary and necessary business expense, just like group term insurance. Benefits paid to an employee under the dismemberment portion of the coverage are treated as benefits received under a health insurance contract and are income tax free. Death benefits received under the coverage are treated like death benefits received under group term life insurance.

    b. Employer contributions do not result in taxable income to an employee as long as the value of the benefit is de minimis. This means that the value is so small that it is administratively impractical for the employer to account for the cost on a per-person basis. Dependent coverage of $2,000 or less on any person falls into this category. If more than $2,000 of coverage is provided for any dependent from employer contributions, the cost of the entire amount of coverage for that dependent (as determined by Uniform Premium Table I costs) is considered taxable income to the employee.

    Death benefits are free of income taxation and are not included in the dependent's taxable estate for estate tax purposes.

31. In most states, the payment of group term insurance premiums by the employer does not result in any taxable income to the employee, even if the amount of coverage exceeds death proceeds receive favorable tax treatment under the estate and inheritance tax laws of most states. Generally, the proceeds are at least partially, if not totally, exempt from such taxation.

32. Because retired employees have no salary or wages from which payroll deductions can be made, most postretirement life insurance coverage is noncontributory.

33. However, an employer may take current deductions only for prefunding coverage that is received tax free by retired employees under Sec. 79. This amount is generally $50,000 but may be higher for certain employees, subject to a grandfather clause. In addition, contributions on behalf of key employees cannot be deducted if the plan is discriminatory under Sec. 79.

34. As long as an employee has no rights in a retired lives reserve except to receive postretirement group term insurance coverage until his or her death, the employee incurs no income taxation as a result of either employer contributions to the reserve or investment earnings on the reserve. In addition, up to $50,000 can be received income tax free by beneficiaries.

35. Group universal life insurance is a flexible-premium policy that, unlike traditional cash value life insurance, divides the pure insurance protection and the cash value accumulation into separate and distinct components. The employee is required to pay a specified initial premium, from which a charge is subtracted for one month's insurance protection. This mortality charge in effect is used to purchase the required amount of pure or term insurance at a cost based on the insured's current age. Under some policies, an additional deduction is made for expenses. The balance of the initial premium becomes the initial cash value of the policy, which, when credited with interest, becomes the cash value at the end of the period. The process continues in succeeding periods. New premiums are added to the cash value, charges are made for expenses and mortality, and interest is credited to the remaining cash value. Employees receive periodic disclosure statements showing all charges made for the period as well as any interest earnings.

36. First, the death benefit can be increased because of marriage, the birth of a child, or an increase in income. The death benefit can be reduced later if the need for life insurance decreases. Second, cash withdrawals can be made for the down payment on a home or to pay college tuition. Third, premium payments can be reduced during those periods when a young family has pressing financial needs. As financial circumstances improve,

premiums can be increased so that an adequate retirement fund can be accumulated. Finally, the usual settlement options found in traditional cash value life insurance are available, so an employee can periodically elect to liquidate the cash accumulation as a source of retirement income.

37. a. The following are claimed as advantages of universal life to the employer:

   • no direct cost other than that associated with payroll deductions and possibly enrollment, because the entire premium cost is borne by the employee. In this sense, group universal life insurance plans are much like voluntary benefit plans that offer individual universal life insurance policies.

   • no ERISA filing and reporting requirement if the master contract is issued to a trust and there are no employer contributions for the cost of coverage. The current products are marketed through multiple-employer trusts, with the trust being the policyowner.

   • the ability of employees to continue "permanent" life coverage into retirement, alleviating pressure for the employer to provide postretirement life insurance benefits

   b. The following advantages are claimed for employees:

   • the availability of a popular life insurance product at group rates

   • the opportunity to continue insurance coverage after retirement, possibly without any postretirement contributions

   • flexibility in designing coverage to best meet the needs of the individual employee

38. a. Currently, most group universal life insurance products are being limited primarily to employers who have at least 100 or 200 employees. However, a few insurers write coverage for even smaller groups. Some insurance companies also have an employee percentage-participation requirement, such as 20 or 25 percent, that must be satisfied before a group can be installed. Other insurance companies feel their marketing approach is designed so that adequate participation results and therefore have no participation requirements.

   b. When an employee is initially eligible, coverage is usually issued on a guaranteed basis up to specified limits, which again are influenced by the size of the group, the amount of coverage provided under the employer's basic group term insurance plan, and the degree of participation in the plan. If an employee chooses a larger death benefit, simplified underwriting is used up to a second amount, after which regular underwriting is used. Guaranteed issue is often unavailable for small groups, in which case underwriting on the basis of a simplified questionnaire is used up to a specific amount of death benefit, after which regular underwriting is used.

39. Most employers have selected option B, which is usually easier to market to employees because the increasing total death benefit is a visible sign of any increase in their cash value or "investment." As a result, several insurers now make only option B available with their group products.

40. a. Most products have a guaranteed mortality charge for 3 years, after which the mortality charge is based on the experience of each particular group. The credibility given to a group's actual experience is greater for larger groups. Most insurance companies guarantee that any future increases in the mortality charge will not exceed a stated maximum.

The products designed for small groups typically use pooled rates that apply to all groups insured through a particular trust. Therefore, the mortality charge for any employer varies with the overall experience of the trust.

b. Typically, a percentage of each premium, such as 2 percent, is deducted for expenses. In addition, there is a flat monthly charge, which normally ranges from $1 to $3, to maintain the accumulation account.

c. Insurance companies guarantee that the initial interest rate credited to cash value accumulations will remain in effect for a minimum period of time, often one year. After that time, the rate is typically adjusted quarterly or semiannually but cannot fall below some contractual minimum, typically in the range of 2½ to 3½ percent for newer policies.

41. a. Premiums can be raised or lowered and even suspended. In the latter case, the contract terminates if an employee's cash value accumulation is inadequate to pay current mortality and expense charges. Two restrictions are placed on premium adjustments. First, the premium payment cannot be such that the size of the cash value accumulation becomes so large in relationship to the pure protection that an employee's coverage fails to qualify as a policy of insurance under IRS regulations. Second, because changes in premium payments through payroll deductions are costly to administer, many employers limit the frequency with which adjustments are allowed.

b. Employees are allowed to make loans and withdrawals from their accumulated cash values, but for administrative reasons the frequency of loans and withdrawals may be limited. There are also minimum loan and withdrawal amounts, such as

$250 or $500. The interest rate charged on policy loans is now usually set on a discretionary basis by each insurer and subject to change.

An employee can withdraw his or her entire cash value accumulation and terminate coverage. Total withdrawals are subject to a surrender charge during early policy years. The charge decreases with policy duration and is usually in addition to any transaction charge that might also be levied.

c. Most products allow an employee to purchase a rider that provides term insurance coverage on his or her spouse and children. For example, one insurance company allows an employee to elect spousal coverage of $10,000 to $50,000 in $10,000 increments and coverage on children in the amount of either $5,000 or $10,000. Other insurers make varying amounts available.

Some insurance companies allow separate universal life insurance coverage to be elected, but often only for the spouse. In such cases, the coverage is provided under a separate group insurance certificate rather than a rider.

d. A group universal life insurance plan may provide accidental death benefits and a disability waiver of premium only if the employer has elected to include them in the plan. When a waiver of premium is included, all that is waived in case of disability is the portion of the premium necessary to pay the cost of the pure insurance protection for the employee and any dependents.

42. Group universal life insurance products are not designed to be policies of insurance under Sec. 79. In addition, each employee pays the full cost of his or her coverage. Therefore, the tax treatment is the same to employees as if they had purchased a universal life insurance policy in the individual insurance marketplace.

43. Group variable universal life insurance has the same basic characteristics as group universal life with one major difference—employees have a series of investment accounts to which they may allocate their net premiums. Once an employee elects the initial allocation, all future net premiums are allocated in the same proportion unless the employee makes a written request for a change. With the exception of the amount the employee may allocate to an available minimum interest-rate-guarantee account, there are no minimum guarantees, and the full investment risk rests solely with the employee.

44. The employer decides which employees are covered under the carve-out plan and limits coverage for these employees under its group term plan to the $50,000 that is received tax free. The employer then gives any premium savings to each "carved-out" employee in the form of a bonus, which is fully deductible to the employer as long

as the employee's overall compensation is reasonable. The bonus amounts are either paid directly to an insurance company for individual coverage on the lives of the participants in the carve-out plan or in some cases provided to the employees as compensation to pay life insurance premiums. In most cases, the coverage purchased under the carve-out plan is some form of permanent life insurance protection that provides paid-up coverage at retirement. However, traditional whole life insurance, universal life insurance, variable universal life insurance, and variable life insurance are all viable alternatives.

45. A bonus arrangement is the most common type of carve-out plan, but other alternatives are available. A carve-out plan is sometimes designed as a death-benefit-only plan, under which the employer agrees only to pay a death benefit to the employee's beneficiary out of corporate assets. The employer often funds the plan with corporate-owned life insurance on the employee's life. With this approach, the employee has no taxable income, but death benefits result in taxable income to the beneficiary. In addition, the employer is unable to deduct the premiums as a business expense but does receive the death proceeds tax-free.

Some firms also use split-dollar life insurance in carve-out plans. The most common approach is to use a collateral assignment arrangement under which the employer pays most of the premium, and the employee collaterally assigns a portion of the cash value and death benefit to the employer equal to the employer's premium payments. At retirement (or any other predetermined time), the employee withdraws the cash value necessary to repay the employer, who then removes the collateral assignment.

46. Proper analysis of alternatives involves a complex consideration of many factors, including the employer's tax bracket, the effect on the employer's financial statements, the employee's tax bracket, premium costs, and the time value of money.

Chapter 5

Group
Disability
Income
Insurance

Learning Objectives

An understanding of the material in this chapter should enable the student to

1. **Describe the nature of disability income insurance, and explain why it is important to employees.**

2. **Describe the characteristics of sick-leave plans.**

3. **Describe the characteristics of insured disability income plans.**

4. **Explain the tax treatment of group disability income premiums and benefits for the employer and the employees.**

disability income insurance

The purpose of **disability income insurance** is to partially replace the income of employees who are unable to work because of sickness or accident.

Although an employee may miss a few days of work from time to time, there is often a tendency to underestimate both the frequency and severity of disabilities that last for longer periods. At all working ages, the probability of being disabled for at least 90 consecutive days is much greater than the chance of dying.

All too often, the importance of adequate disability income coverage is overlooked. In terms of its financial impact on the family, long-term disability is more severe than death. In both cases, income from employment ceases. In the case of long-term disability, however, family expenses—instead of decreasing because of one less family member—may actually increase because of the cost of providing care for the disabled person.

Employers are less likely to provide employees with disability income benefits than with either life insurance or medical expense benefits. Thus, many employees may need to buy individual policies on their own.   It is difficult to estimate the exact extent of disability coverage because often benefits are not insured and workers are sometimes covered under overlapping plans. However, a reasonable estimate would be that nearly three-quarters of all full-time employees have some form of short-term employer-provided protection, and only about one-third of full-time employees have employer-provided protection for long-term disabilities other than Social Security. This does not mean that almost all employees have some sort of disability income coverage, because many employees have both short-term and long-term protection and thus are included in both estimates. These estimates are also somewhat misleading because most employees have long-term disability income coverage under Social Security as well as coverage for certain types of disabilities under other government programs.

short-term disability (STD) income plans

long-term disability (LTD) income insurance

Group disability income protection consists of two distinct products:

- **short-term disability (STD) income plans**, which provide benefits for a limited period of time, usually 6 months or less. Benefits may be provided under uninsured sick-leave plans or under insured plans, often referred to as accident and sickness insurance or weekly indemnity benefits.

- **long-term disability (LTD) income insurance**, which provides extended benefits (possibly for life) after an employee has been disabled for a period of time, frequently 6 months

An important task in designing and underwriting insured group disability income plans is to coordinate them with each other (if both a short-term and a long-term plan are provided for employees). An equally important task is to coordinate them with other benefits to which employees might be entitled under social insurance programs, uninsured sick-leave plans, and employer-sponsored retirement plans. A lack of coordination can lead to such a generous level of benefits for employees that absences from work because of disability might be either falsified or unnecessarily prolonged. Alternatively, a lack of coordination can lead to an employee having a gap in coverage from the time a short-term plan ends until a long-term plan or Social Security benefits begin.

SICK-LEAVE PLANS

sick-leave plan

Employers use two approaches to provide short-term disability benefits to employees: sick-leave plans and short-term disability income insurance plans. A **sick-leave plan** (often called a salary continuation plan) is uninsured and generally fully replaces lost income for a limited period, starting on the first day of disability or a short time later. In contrast, a short-term disability income insurance plan usually provides benefits that replace only a portion of an employee's lost income and often contains a period of time before benefits start, particularly for sickness. It is impossible to obtain precise statistics, but surveys indicate that about half of the employees with short-term coverage obtain benefits under sick-leave plans, about one-quarter under insured plans, and about one-quarter under plans that combine the two approaches.

Traditionally, many sick-leave plans were informal, with the availability, amount, and duration of benefits for an employee being discretionary on the part of the employer. Although some plans used by small firms or for a limited number of executives still operate this way, informal plans are generally inappropriate. There is a possibility that the IRS will consider benefit payments to be either a gift or a dividend and therefore not tax deductible by the employer. In addition, an informal plan increases the likelihood of suits brought by persons who are disabled but who do not receive benefits. As a result, most sick-leave plans are now formalized and have specific written rules concerning eligibility and benefits.

paid time off (PTO) program

In recent years, a few employers have combined their sick-leave plans with other types of payments for time not worked, such as vacations, holidays, and personal leave into a single **paid time off (PTO) program**. One rationale for such programs is that many employees view sick days as a right and will take the maximum number of days available, whether sick or not. With a PTO, an employee is given a specified bank of days off with full pay and can take this paid time off for any reason. The bank of days is usually slightly less than the total number of days under the prior programs, but within the range of the number of days that most employees took off.

PTO programs have generally had the effect of lowering the number of days that employees call in sick, because these days can be used for other purposes. This lowers an employer's benefit costs and minimizes other problems associated with unscheduled absences.

However, there is also a negative side of PTO plans for an employer. Some employees who should stay home may come to work when they are sick. Their productivity may be impaired, and they may sicken other employees by spreading germs.

Eligibility

Almost all sick-leave plans are limited to regular full-time employees, but benefits may also be provided for regular part-time employees. Most plans also require that an employee satisfy a short probationary period (commonly 1 to 3 months) before being eligible for benefits. Sick-leave plans may also be limited to certain classes of employees, such as top management or nonunion employees. The latter is common when the union employees are covered under a collectively bargained, but insured, plan.

Benefits

Most sick-leave plans are designed to provide benefits equal to 100 percent of an employee's regular pay. Some plans, however, provide a reduced level of benefits after an initial period of full pay.

Several approaches are used in determining the duration of benefits. The most traditional approach credits eligible employees with a certain amount of sick leave each year, such as 10 days. The majority of plans using this approach allow employees to accumulate unused sick leave up to some maximum amount, which rarely exceeds 6 months (sometimes specified as 180 days or 26 weeks). A variation of this approach is to credit employees with an amount of sick leave, such as one day, for each month of service. The following table is an example of a benefit schedule that uses this variation.

Table 5-1 Sick Leave Benefit Schedule	
Length of Service	Amount of Sick Leave*
Less than 3 months	None
3 or more months	1 day at full pay for each month of service (retroactive to date of employment)
*Maximum unused sick leave: 130 days	

Another approach, illustrated in the table below, bases the duration of benefits on an employee's length of service.

Table 5-2 Sick Leave Benefit Schedule	
Length of Service	Maximum Days of Sick Leave per Year
Less than 3 months	0
3 months to 1 year	5
2 years	10
3 years	15
5 years	20
7 years	25
10 years	30

An alternative to this approach provides benefits for a uniform length of time to all employees, except possibly those with short periods of service. However, benefits are reduced to a level less than full pay after some period of time that is related to an employee's length of service. The next table is an illustration of this increasingly common approach.

Table 5-3 Sick Leave Benefit Schedule			
	Weeks of Sick Leave per Disability		
Length of Service	100% of Pay	50% of Pay	Total Weeks
Less than 6 months	0	0	0
6 months to 1 year	2	0	2
1 year	4	22	26
2 years	8	18	26
3 years	12	14	26
4 years	16	10	26
5 years	20	6	26
6 years or more	26	0	26

In some instances, an employee is not eligible for sick-leave benefits if he or she is eligible for benefits under social insurance plans, such as workers' compensation. However, most sick-leave plans are coordinated with social insurance programs. For example, if an employee is entitled to 100 percent of pay and receives 60 percent of pay as a workers' compensation benefit, the sick-leave plan pays the remaining 40 percent.

A problem for the employer is how to verify an employee's disability. Most sick-leave plans have a provision that benefits for more than a stated number of days are paid only if the employee is under the care of a physician, who certifies that the employee is unable to work.

INSURED DISABILITY INCOME PLANS

As mentioned, insured disability income plans consist of two distinct products: short-term coverage and long-term coverage. In many respects, the contractual provisions of both short-term and long-term disability income contracts are the same or very similar. In other respects—notably, the eligibility requirements, the definition of disability, and the amount and duration of benefits—there are significant differences.

Eligibility

The eligibility requirements in group disability income insurance contracts are similar to those found in group term insurance contracts. In addition to being in a covered classification, an employee usually must work full-time and be actively at work before coverage commences. Any requirements concerning probationary periods, insurability, and premium contributions must also be satisfied.

Short-term and long-term disability income insurance plans frequently differ in both the classes of employees who are eligible for coverage and the length of the probationary period. Employers are more likely to provide short-term benefits to a wider range of employees, and it is not unusual for short-term plans to cover all full-time employees. However, these plans may be a result of collective bargaining and apply only to union employees. In this situation, other employees frequently have short-term disability benefits under uninsured sick-leave plans.

Long-term disability plans often limit benefits to salaried employees, but they may include employees with commission-based income such as stock brokers and other sales-related occupations. Claims experience has traditionally been less favorable for hourly paid employees for a number of reasons. Claims of hourly paid employees tend to be more frequent, particularly in recessionary times when the possibility of temporary layoffs or terminations increases. Such claims also tend to be of longer duration, possibly because of the likelihood that these employees hold repetitive and nonchallenging jobs. Some long-term plans also exclude employees below a certain salary level because this category of employees, like hourly paid employees, is considered to have a reasonable level of benefits under Social Security.

Long-term disability income plans usually have longer probationary periods than short-term disability income plans. Although the majority of short-term disability plans (as well as group term insurance plans and medical expense plans) either have no probationary period or have a probationary period of 3 months or less, it is common for long-term disability plans to have probationary periods ranging from 3 months to 1 year. Short-term plans only require that an employee be actively at work on the date he or she is otherwise eligible for coverage, but long-term plans sometimes require that the employee be on the job for an extended period (such as 30 days) without illness or injury before coverage becomes effective.

Definition of Disability

partial disability

Benefits are paid under disability income insurance contracts only if the employee meets the definition of disability as specified in the contract. Virtually all short-term disability income insurance contracts define disability as *the total and continuous inability of the employee to perform each and every duty of his or her regular occupation*. A small minority of contracts use a more restrictive definition, requiring that an employee be unable to engage in any occupation for compensation. Partial disabilities are usually not covered, but a few plans do provide such benefits. **Partial disability** is usually defined to mean that an employee is neither permanently nor totally disabled but can perform only some of the duties of his or her job. For example, an employee with a sprained back might work part time.

The majority of short-term contracts limit coverage to nonoccupational disabilities, because employees have workers' compensation benefits for occupational disabilities. This limitation tends to be most common when benefits under the short-term contract are comparable to or lesser in amount than those under the workers' compensation law. In those cases, where workers' compensation benefits are relatively low and the employer desires to provide additional benefits, coverage may be written for both occupational and nonoccupational disabilities.

own-occupation definition of disability

dual (split) definition of disability

A few long-term disability income contracts use the same liberal definition of disability that is commonly used in short-term contracts. However, the term material duties often replaces the term each and every duty. These often are referred to as an **own-occupation definition of disability**. Some other contracts define disability as *the total and continuous inability of the employee to engage in any and every gainful occupation for which he or she is qualified or shall reasonably become qualified by reason of training, education, or experience*. However, most long-term disability contracts use a **dual (or split) definition of disability** that combines these two. Under a dual definition, benefits are paid for some period of time (usually 24 or 36 months) as long as an employee is unable to perform his or her regular occupation. After that time, benefits are paid only if the employee is unable to engage in any occupation for which he or she is qualified by reason of training, education, or experience. The purpose of this combined definition is to require and encourage a disabled employee who becomes able after a period of time to adjust his or her lifestyle and earn a livelihood in another occupation.

Another popular definition of disability found in long-term contracts contains an occupation test and an earnings test. Under the occupation test, a person is totally disabled if he or she meets the definition of disability as described in the previous paragraph. However, if the occupation test is not satisfied, a person is still considered disabled as long as an earnings test is satisfied. This means that the person's income has dropped by at least a stated percentage, typically 20 percent, because of injury or sickness. This definition makes a group insurance contract similar to an individual disability income policy that provides residual benefits.

The definition of disability in long-term contracts may differ from that found in short-term contracts in several other respects. Long-term contracts are somewhat more likely to provide benefits for partial disabilities. However, the amount and duration of such benefits may be limited when compared with those for total disabilities, and the receipt of benefits is usually contingent upon a previous period of total disability. In addition, most long-term contracts provide coverage for both occupational and nonoccupational disabilities. Finally, short-term contracts usually have the same definition of disability for all classes of employees. Some long-term contracts use different definitions for different classes of employees—one for most employees and a more liberal definition for executives or salaried employees.

Exclusions

exclusion

An **exclusion** is a provision in an insurance contract that indicates situations that the insurer does not intend to cover. Under certain circumstances, disability income benefits are not paid even if an employee satisfies the definition of disability. Common exclusions under both short- and long-term disability income contracts specify that no benefits are paid

- for any period during which the employee is not under the care of a physician
- for any disability caused by an intentionally self-inflicted injury
- unless the period of disability commenced while the contract covered the employee. For example, an employee who previously elected not to participate under a contributory plan cannot obtain coverage for an existing disability by deciding to pay the required premium.

- if the employee is engaged in any occupation for remuneration. This exclusion applies in those situations when an employee is totally disabled with respect to his or her regular job but is engaged in other employment that can be performed despite the employee's condition.

- to the extent that benefits are payable under workers' compensation or similar laws

Long-term contracts often contain additional exclusions. These commonly deny benefits for disabilities resulting from

- war, whether declared or undeclared

- participation in an assault or felony. Some insurers have recently expanded this exclusion to include the commission of any crime.

- mental disease, alcoholism, or drug addiction. However, many contracts provide employees with benefits but limit their duration (such as for 24 months per disability); other contracts provide benefits for an employee who is confined in a hospital or institution that specializes in the care and treatment of such disorders.

- preexisting conditions

preexisting-conditions provision

The exclusion for preexisting conditions is designed to counter the adverse selection and potentially large claims that could occur if an employer established a group disability income plan or if an employee elected to participate in the plan because of some known condition that is likely to result in disability. Although variations exist, a common **preexisting-conditions provision** excludes coverage for any disability that commences during the first 12 months an employee is covered under the contract if the employee received treatment or medical advice for the disabling condition both (1) prior to the date the employee became eligible for coverage and (2) within 90 consecutive days prior to the commencement of the disability.

When coverage is transferred from one insurance company to another, it is not unusual, particularly in the case of large employers, for the new insurance company to waive the limitation for preexisting conditions for those employees who were insured under the previous contract. In some instances, the provision is modified so that benefits are limited to those that would have been provided under the previous contract, possibly for a specified period, such as one year. Note that a transfer of coverage has no effect on the responsibility of the prior insurance company to continue paying benefits for claims that have already occurred, except in rare instances in which some arrangement is made for the new contract to provide benefits.

Benefits

A discussion of the benefits under disability income contracts is more complex than a discussion of the benefits under group life insurance contracts. A similarity exists in that there are benefit schedules that classify employees and specify the amount of disability income the policy will provide. However, the relationship between an employee's earnings and the employee's potential benefits is more important in disability income insurance than in group life insurance. In addition, disability benefits are subject to several provisions not found in group life insurance contracts. These pertain to the length of time that benefits are paid and the coordination of benefits with other available types of disability income.

Benefit Schedules

As in group life insurance, there is a variety of benefit schedules found in group disability income contracts. Benefits may be available to all employees or limited to specific groups of employees. In addition, benefits may be expressed as flat-dollar amounts, varying dollar amounts by classification, or a percentage of earnings.

A major difficulty in disability insurance is determining the appropriate level of benefits to provide. Absenteeism is encouraged and the incentive to return to work is diminished if a disabled employee is given a level of income that is comparable to his or her regular earnings. In general, disability income plans are designed to provide a level of benefits that replaces between 50 and 70 percent of an employee's gross income. Although this may appear to represent a substantial reduction of regular earnings, it should be remembered that a disabled employee does not have the usual expenses associated with working, such as transportation costs. In addition, disability income benefits are not subject to Social Security and Medicare taxation after a period of time and, depending on the source and amount, may be free of income taxation. Despite the logic in providing a reduced level of income, some short-term disability income plans provide employees with 100 percent of their predisability earnings. In most cases, this level of benefits is either a result of collective bargaining or an effort by employers to provide nonunion employees with a level of benefits that is comparable to that of union employees.

Many short-term disability income plans and the majority of long-term plans base benefits on a single percentage of regular earnings (excluding bonuses, overtime, commissions, and other incentive-based income). This percentage varies widely for short-term plans, and benefits as low as 50 percent or as high as 100 percent are not unusual. However, many insurers are reluctant to underwrite plans that provide benefits higher than 70 percent of earnings. In some instances, short-term plans, like sick-leave plans, may use different percentages, such as 100 percent of earnings for 4 weeks and 70 percent of earnings for the remaining benefit period. The length of time for which the plan provides the higher level of benefits may also be a function of the length of an employee's service.

Long-term plans typically provide benefits that range from 50 to 70 percent of earnings, with 60 and 66 2/3 being the most prevalent percentages. Some plans also use a sliding scale, such as 66 2/3 percent of the first $5,000 of monthly earnings and 50 percent of earnings in excess of $5,000.

It is common for plans that determine benefits as a percentage of earnings to also place a maximum dollar amount on the benefit for any employee, regardless of earnings. For example, a short-term plan covering hourly employees may have a benefit equal to 70 percent of earnings that might be subject to a maximum of $500 per week. Similarly, a long-term plan might provide benefits equal to 66 2/3 percent of earnings, but might be subject to a monthly maximum that may vary from $3,000 or $4,000 for some small groups to as much as $6,000 to $10,000 for large groups. A few plans for large groups of well-paid executives may, however, have limits of up to $25,000. The purpose of such a maximum is to prevent the absolute benefit from being so high that an employee, by adjusting his or her lifestyle, could live comfortably on the disability income benefit and thus have no financial incentive to return to work.

Other types of benefit schedules are found in short-term disability income plans, particularly when these plans are designed for hourly paid employees. If the weekly earnings of most employees fall within a narrow range, the benefit might be expressed as a flat-dollar amount. For example, if all employees earn between $400 and $500 per week, a benefit of $270 per week might be used. If earnings vary widely, a benefit schedule like the one below might be used.

Table 5-4 Short-Term Disability Income Benefits	
Weekly Earnings	Weekly Benefit
$341 to $380	$250
$381 to $420	280
$421 to $460	310
$461 to $500	340
Over $500	370

A similar approach is occasionally used in long-term disability income plans, as shown in the benefit schedule for salaried employees earning in excess of $18,000 per year in the table below.

| Table 5-5 | |
| Short-Term Disability Income Benefits | |
Monthly Earnings	Monthly Benefit
$1,500 to $2,500	$1,200
$2,501 to $3,5001	1,800
$3,501 to $4,5002	2,400
$4,500 to $5,500	3,000
Over $5,500	4,000

Period of Benefits

To determine the period for which disability income benefits are paid, it is necessary to determine when benefits begin and how long they are paid. In both respects, there are differences between short-term and long-term plans.

waiting (elimination) period

Short-Term Plans. Short-term disability income contracts commonly contain a **waiting period** (often referred to in such contracts as an **elimination period**). The waiting period is the length of time for which an employee covered under the contract must be disabled before benefits begin. In the typical short-term contract, there is no waiting period for disabilities resulting from accidents, but a waiting period of 1 to 7 consecutive days applies to disabilities resulting from sicknesses. However, some plans have a single waiting period that applies to disabilities from either accidents or sicknesses; a few plans have no waiting periods for either. Waiting periods longer than 7 days are occasionally used, particularly when there is a sick-leave plan to provide benefits during the initial portion of a disability. Besides lowering the cost of a disability income plan, the waiting period discourages unwarranted absences from work due to sickness. In a few cases, benefits are paid retroactively to the date of disability if the disability lasts for a predetermined period. However, it is generally felt that retroactive benefits cause employees to prolong their return to work in order to receive benefits for the full period of their disability.

Once an employee begins receiving benefit payments under a short-term disability contract, the benefits continue until the end of the benefit period specified in the contract, if the employee remains disabled for that long. Although short-term contracts may provide benefits up to 2 years (with long-term contracts providing benefits for periods over 2 years), benefits rarely continue for more than a year. In fact, the majority of short-term contracts stipulate that benefits are paid for either 13 or 26 weeks, with the latter period being most prevalent. Short-term plans are often described in terms of their waiting period and their duration of benefits. For example, a "1-8-26" plan pays benefits for a maximum of 26 weeks beginning with the first day of disability in the case of an accident and with the eighth day of disability in the case of sickness.

In most plans, both the maximum benefit period and the waiting period apply to each separate disability. However, successive periods of disability caused by the same accident or the same or related sickness are generally considered to be a single disability unless they are separated by a period of continuous resumption of active employment. This provision prevents an employee from briefly returning to work in order to obtain a second maximum period of benefits for the same disability.

Although reducing short-term disability income benefits for older employees may be justifiable on a cost basis, few plans have done so.

Long-Term Plans. Waiting periods in long-term disability income plans may be as short as 30 days or as long as a year or more. Most plans use periods of 3 to 6 months, with 6 months most common. The length of the waiting period often corresponds to the length of time benefits are paid under a firm's short-term disability income plan or sick-leave plan. Unlike short-term plans, the waiting periods for sicknesses and accidents are the same.

Long-term disability income benefits may be paid for as short a period as 2 years or as long as the lifetime of the disabled employee. In a few cases, the length of the benefit period may differ, depending on whether the disability was a result of an accident or a sickness. Benefits are commonly reduced for older employees, and several different approaches are acceptable under the Age Discrimination in Employment Act. In a few cases, benefits are paid until age 70 for any disability that occurred before that age. For disabilities occurring at age 70 or later, benefits are paid for a reduced duration. A more common approach is to use a graded benefit period and give benefits to age 65 for employees who are disabled before a specified age. Employees disabled after the specified age get benefits for a limited duration, as shown in Table 5-6.

A similar approach uses a sliding level of benefit durations after a certain age. For example, a plan may provide that employees disabled prior to age 60 will receive benefits until age 65. The plan might then use the schedule shown in Table 5-7 for employees who are disabled at age 60 or older.

Table 5-6 Duration of Long-Term Disability Income Benefits	
Age at Commencement of Disability	Benefits Duration
59 and younger	To age 65
60–64	5 years
65–69	To age 70
70–74	1 year
75 and older	6 months

Table 5-7 Duration of Long-Term Disability Income Benefits	
Age at Commencement of Disability	Benefit Duration (in Years)
60	5
61	4
62	3½
63	3
64	2½
65	2
66	2
67	1
68	1
69	1

Long-term plans typically provide for successive disabilities. The majority of contracts stipulate that successive periods of disability that are separated by less than some period (usually varying from 3 to 6 months) of continuous, active full-time employment are considered a single disability, unless the subsequent disability (1) arises from an unrelated cause and (2) begins after the employee has returned to work.

Coordination with Other Benefits

To minimize the possibility that an employee will receive total benefits higher than his or her predisability earnings, disability income plans commonly stipulate that benefits be coordinated with other sources of disability income. The effect of this coordination (often referred to as integration) is to reduce the benefits payable under the disability income contract to the extent that certain other benefits are available. In general, the insurance laws or regulations of most states allow policies to have such reductions because of

benefits from social insurance programs and group insurance or retirement plans provided by the employer. Reductions because of benefits from individual disability income
contracts are not usually allowed unless the policies were purchased by the employer.
Employers and employees often resent the fact that disability income benefits that they
have "paid for" may be reduced. However, such reductions are considered in determining
the rates charged for disability income insurance. In effect, the employer is purchasing a
contract that is only a supplement to these other available sources of disability income
rather than being penalized because these resources are available.

For various reasons, including the limited duration of benefits and the desire for simplified
operating procedures, coordination with other benefits is less common for short-term
plans than in long-term plans. If a short-term plan covers only nonoccupational disabilities, there is no need for coordination with workers' compensation benefits; also, unless
benefits are provided for disabilities lasting longer than 5 months, there is no need to
coordinate benefits with Social Security. In general, benefits under short-term plans are
coordinated with the following:

- workers' compensation benefits if the plan covers occupational disabilities

- temporary disability laws, where applicable

- Social Security benefits, if the maximum benefit period is longer than 5 months

Some insurance companies sell long-term disability income coverage without any provision for coordination with other disability income benefits; however, the availability and
potential magnitude of other benefits is an underwriting factor in determining the maximum amount of coverage that is written. Usually, long-term disability income benefits are
coordinated with benefits provided under the following:

- Social Security

- workers' compensation laws

- temporary disability laws

- other insurance plans for which the employer makes a contribution or payroll
  deduction

- pension plans for which the employer has made a contribution or payroll deduction to the extent that the employee elects to receive retirement benefits because
  of disability

- sick-leave plans

- earnings from employment, either with the employer or from other sources

A few insurers also coordinate group long-term coverage with individual disability income policies.

The coordination with Social Security may be based solely on the benefit a disabled worker receives for himself or herself (referred to as the employee's primary insurance amount). It may also be based on the employee's total family benefit if the employee has eligible dependents.

Two basic approaches to Social Security coordination of disability income benefits are used: a full-coordination approach and a dual-percentage approach. Under the *full-coordination approach*, long-term disability income benefits are reduced to the extent that any benefits subject to coordination are received.

Example

Theresa earns $2,500 per month and is entitled to a disability income benefit of 60 percent, or $1,500 per month. In addition, she is entitled to a disability benefit of $900 under Social Security, as well as additional family benefits of $450 (a total of $1,350). If her long-term disability income benefit plan provides for coordination with total family benefits, she will receive $1,500 ($1,350 from Social Security and the remaining $150 from the long-term plan). However, if full coordination is provided only with respect to the primary insurance amount (in other words, the $450 of family benefits is not considered), she will receive $1,950 ($1,350 from Social Security and $600 from the long-term disability plan).

Under the *dual-percentage approach*, two percentages are used. The first is applicable to benefits that are provided under the long-term plan when there are no other benefits subject to coordination. A second and higher percentage is applicable to total benefits payable from the long-term plan and other sources subject to coordination.

Example

Assume Theresa's disability income plan provides benefits equal to 60 percent of earnings in the absence of other benefits subject to coordination. If there are benefits subject to coordination, benefits under the insured plan are reduced to the extent that the sum of the benefits under the long-term disability plan and the benefits subject to coordination exceed 70 percent. Using these percentages and the previous example, 70 percent of earnings is $1,750. Because the long-term disability benefit and all the Social Security benefits total $2,850, the long-term disability benefit is reduced by $1,100 if the plan provides for coordination with total family benefits. Therefore, she will receive a total benefit of $1,750 ($1,350 from Social Security and $400 from the long-term plan).

Coordination with other benefits has the potential to totally eliminate a long-term disability benefit. To prevent this from happening, many plans provide (and some states require) that a minimum benefit, such as $50 or $100 per month, be paid. Most plans also contain a provision freezing the amount of any reduction because of Social Security at the initial level that was established when the claim began. Without such a provision, the intended effect of increases in Social Security benefits would be erased by equivalent reductions in other disability income benefits provided to the employee. This is seen by some regulators as contrary to public policy and thus a reason for requiring insured plans to contain a freeze on the amount of the reduction.

Example

Herb is entitled to receive $2,000 per month in disability income benefits under a long-term plan that contains a provision for full coordination with Social Security. If he initially receives $800 from the long-term plan and $1,200 from Social Security, the $800 continues to be paid under a provision that freezes this amount even if Social Security benefits are increased. If a 5 percent increase is later granted in Social Security benefits, he will receive a total benefit of $2,060.

As a general rule, both the insured and the insurer are better off if the insured is able to collect Social Security benefits for a disability. The insured has an increased overall benefit, and the insurer has a substantially lower claim to pay. Consequently, insurers are often willing to assist claimants by helping them with the filing of Social Security claims and the appealing of decisions denying claims.

Supplemental Benefits

buy-up plan

It is becoming increasingly common to find group long-term disability income plans that provide employees with a base of employer-paid benefits and that allow each covered employee to purchase additional coverage at his or her own expense. For example, a plan may provide basic benefits of 50 percent of earnings and an option for an employee to increase this amount to 60, 66 2/3, or 70 percent of earnings. Such a supplemental or **buy-up plan** is becoming more popular because employers feel the need to control the costs of benefits by shifting a greater burden of the cost to employees.

Some plans are also designed to "carve out" benefits for certain employees, frequently key executives. For example, an employer might design one plan to cover most of its employees, but it might cover top executives with another group plan that provides enhanced benefits in the form of a larger percentage of earnings and a more liberal definition of disability. Another variation of a carve-out plan would provide the executives with a lower benefit percentage than other employees receive, but it could provide supplemental benefits in the form of individual disability income policies. In addition to more favorable policy provisions, a carve-out plan might offer better rate guarantees and an overall higher benefit than a group plan could offer. Furthermore, the portability of the individual policy might be attractive to executives, although it might not necessarily appeal to the employer. In addition, individual policies might be available on a guaranteed-issue basis if the group of executives is large enough.

Catastrophic Benefits Rider

catastrophic benefits rider

A few disability insurers that also sell long-term care insurance have recently started to make available additional benefits in the form of a **catastrophic benefits rider** if the insured suffers a severe disability that includes cognitive impairment or the inability to perform two or more of six activities of daily living. These are the same criteria that trigger benefits in long-term care policies.

The employer can typically purchase benefits that range from an additional 10 to 40 percent of earnings as long as total disability benefits do not exceed a specified limit that may be as high as 100 percent of earnings. The length of time the catastrophic benefits are paid is also selected by the employer and can vary from one year to the duration of the regular disability benefits provided by the policy. In addition, an employer may have the option of adding a flat monthly benefit that is payable if an employee's spouse suffers a cognitive impairment or is unable to perform two or more of activities of daily living.

Other Contract Provisions

Many provisions in group disability income contracts are similar to those in group life insurance contracts. The provisions that are discussed either are unique to group disability income benefit contracts or differ in certain respects from similar provisions found in group life insurance contracts.

Claims

The provisions concerning claims under both short-term and long-term disability income contracts are essentially the same. The insurance company must be notified within a relatively short period—20 or 30 days (or as soon as is reasonably possible)—after the disability for which benefits are being claimed begins. A claim form must then be filed with the insurance company, usually within 90 days after the commencement of the disability or after the end of the week, month, or other time period for which benefits are payable. The claim form normally consists of three statements; one by the employee concerning the disability, another by the attending physician, and a third by the employer indicating the date and reason that active employment ceased. Provisions also require periodic reports from the attending physician or permit the insurance company to request such reports at reasonable intervals. The insurance company also has the right to have the employee examined by a physician of its own choice (and at its own expense) at reasonable intervals during the duration of the claim.

Payment of Benefits

The insurance company is not obligated to make benefit payments until a proof of loss has been filed. Although benefits are usually payable to the employee, a facility-of-payment provision is included to allow payments to a guardian if the employee is physically, mentally, or otherwise incapable of giving a valid release for any payment received. Benefits may be assigned to another party if such an assignment is permissible under state law and the insurance contract.

Rehabilitation

rehabilitation provision

As an incentive to encourage disabled employees to return to active employment as soon as possible, but perhaps at a lower-paying job, most insurance companies include a **rehabilitation provision** in their long-term disability income contracts. This provision permits the employee to enter a trial work period (sometimes referred to as a return-to-work program) of 1 or 2 years in rehabilitative employment. During this time, disability benefits continue but are reduced by some percentage (varying from 50 to 80 percent) of the earnings from rehabilitative employment. For example, with a 50 percent reduction, an employee who is otherwise entitled to a disability benefit of $1,500 per month will have this benefit reduced by only $600 if he or she can earn $1,200 in the new job. If the trial work period indicates that the employee is unable to perform the rehabilitative employment, the original long-term benefits continue and the employee is not required to satisfy a new waiting period.

Often, there are no other provisions in long-term disability income contracts that require the insurance company to aid in the rehabilitation of disabled employees. Insurance companies, however, sometimes provide benefits for rehabilitation when it is felt that the cost of these benefits is offset by shortening an employee's disability period. These benefits may be in the form of physical therapy, job training, adaptive aids to enable a disabled person to perform job functions, or even the financing of a business venture.

In the past, the decision to seek rehabilitation was left to the disabled person. A number of insurers now require the person to undertake rehabilitation or have benefits reduced or stopped.

The rehabilitation of disabled workers is continuing to grow in importance among insurance companies. In fact, the rehabilitative services provided are often used as a selling feature for a company's product. More and more companies are taking a proactive role in managing disability claims by employing more skilled professionals and by intervening earlier in the claims process. In addition to providing rehabilitation benefits, insurance companies are monitoring claims data more closely so that they can better advise employers of areas where action can be taken to reduce the number of future claims.

integrated disability management

Integrated Disability Management. Because early intervention is a key to getting disabled employees back to work sooner, more and more employers are turning to **integrated disability management.** These employers use the same organization to manage the rehabilitation of disabled employees under all their disability programs—short-term, long-term, and workers' compensation. The organization may be the insurance company that provides insurance coverage to the employer or a firm that specializes in disability management. This approach is commonly referred to as integrated disability management, and it applies to both insured and self-funded benefits.

Integrated disability management has several advantages to both the employer and the employees. There is a single centralized claims-reporting system that is easier to understand and less expensive than duplicate programs for each type of coverage. There are consistent treatment protocols for all disabilities, no matter where or when they occurred, and it is easier to measure and track outcomes of return-to-work programs. In addition, there is a lower incidence of fraudulent claims from employees trying to collect under disability plans and workers' compensation at the same time.

Termination

For the most part, the provisions in disability income contracts concerning either the termination of the master contract or an employee's coverage are the same as those found in group life insurance. However, there is one notable exception: A conversion privilege is rarely included, based on the theory that the termination of employment also terminates an employee's income and thus the need for disability income protection. If a conversion privilege is available, an extra charge is made for the coverage.

One other situation should be mentioned. When an employee meets the definition of total disability under a disability income contract, the employee is considered to have terminated employment by reason of ceasing to be an active, full-time employee. Without some provision to the contrary, an employee who resumes work is then required to resatisfy any eligibility requirements, including a new probationary period. However, most group disability income contracts allow the employer to consider disabled employees as not having terminated employment for insurance purposes. The employer may continue coverage as long as it is done on a nondiscriminatory basis and as long as the required premiums are paid. In short-term contracts, coverage is generally continued by the payment of premiums on the same basis as for active employees. However, it is common for long-term contracts to contain a waiver-of-premium provision. This waiver normally begins at the time benefit payments start, not at the beginning of the waiting period.

The only practical effect of continuing coverage on a disabled employee is to guarantee that the employee will again be eligible for disability income benefits after he or she has returned to active employment. The continuation of coverage (or termination of coverage) has no effect on the future disability income benefits to an employee who is currently disabled and therefore entitled to receive benefits.

Additional Benefits

Long-term disability income contracts occasionally provided several types of additional benefits. The most common are a cost-of-living adjustment, a pension supplement, and a survivor's benefit.

cost-of-living adjustment (COLA)

Some disability income plans have a **cost-of-living adjustment (COLA)** so that inflation does not erode the purchasing power of disability income benefits being received. Under the typical COLA formula, benefits increase annually along with changes in the consumer price index.

pension supplement

Many firms make provisions in their pension plan for treating disabled employees as if they were still working and accruing pension benefits. Such a **pension supplement** requires the employer to make contributions to the pension plan on behalf of disabled employees, usually from the employer's current revenues. However, some disability income contracts stipulate that the contributions to fund a disabled employee's accruing pension benefits will be paid from the disability income contract.

Some retirement plans also provide disability income benefits by allowing disabled employees to begin receiving retirement benefits when they are totally and permanently disabled. It is common, however, to limit these early retirement benefits to employees who have satisfied some minimum period of service or who have reached some minimum age. However, the feeling among employee benefit consultants seems to be that it is preferable to have separate retirement and disability income plans.

Some long-term contracts provide a benefit to survivors in the form of continued payments after the death of a disabled employee. In effect, the disability income payments continue, possibly at a reduced amount, for periods ranging up to 24 months, with 3 to 6 months being most common. Payments are generally made only to eligible survivors, who commonly are the spouse and unmarried children under age 21.

Other less common types of additional benefits may also be found. Examples include child-care payments for disabled employees who can work on a part-time basis, spousal disability benefits payable to the employee, benefits to pay premiums for medical expense coverage, and benefits for worksite modification.

FEDERAL TAX TREATMENT

As with group life insurance, employer contributions for an employee's disability income insurance are fully deductible to the employer as an ordinary and necessary business expense if the employee's overall compensation is reasonable. Sick-leave payments are similarly tax deductible. Contributions by an individual employee are considered payments for personal disability income insurance and are not tax deductible.

Income Tax Liability of Employees

In contrast to group life insurance, for which employer contributions may result in some taxable income to an employee, employer contributions for disability income insurance generally result in no taxable income to an employee. However, the payment of benefits under an insured plan or sick-leave plan may or may not result in the receipt of taxable income. To make this determination, it is necessary to look at whether the plan is fully contributory, noncontributory, or partially contributory.

Fully Contributory Plan

Under a fully contributory plan, the entire cost is paid by employee contributions and benefits are received free of income taxation.

Noncontributory Plan

The tax situation for an employee will vary with a noncontributory plan, depending on how an employer designs a disability income plan. Almost all plans follow the usual design described below. However, a few plans are now designed so that an employee can receive benefits on a tax-free basis.

The Usual Design. Under a typical noncontributory plan, the employer pays the entire cost and benefits are included in an employee's gross income. However, the Internal Revenue Code provides a tax credit to persons who are permanently and totally disabled. A tax credit is better than a tax deduction in that it is subtracted from an individual's federal income tax liability rather than deducted from gross income to determine taxable income. For purposes of this tax credit, the IRS uses the Social Security definition of disability; that is, an employee must be unable to engage in any kind of gainful work because of a medically determinable physical condition that has lasted or is expected to last at least 12 months or to result in death.

The Tax-Free Design. A 2004 IRS Revenue Ruling allows an employer to design a disability income plan so that an employee can receive tax-free benefits from a noncontributory plan. In order to receive these benefits, however, the employee must elect to have the employer-paid premium for his or her coverage reported as taxable income. Such an election, which applies separately to each employee covered under a plan, must be made prior to the beginning of a plan year and is irrevocable during that period. The election must also apply to the full cost of the employer-provided coverage.

Few plans have incorporated such an election. It creates administrative burdens for the employer, and most employees prefer to minimize their income tax burden on a current basis. If this option is available, an employee should discuss its implications with a tax advisor before making such an election.

Partially Contributory Plan

Under a partially contributory plan, benefits attributable to employee contributions are received free of income taxation. Benefits attributable to employer contributions are includible in gross income, but employees are eligible for the tax credit described previously.

The portion of the benefits attributable to employer contributions (and thus subject to income taxation) is based on the ratio of the employer's contributions to the total employer-employee contributions for an employee who has been under the plan for some period. For example, if the employer paid 75 percent of the cost of the plan, 75 percent of the benefits would be considered attributable to employer contributions and 25 percent to employee contributions. The time period used to calculate this percentage varies, depending upon the type of disability income plan and the length of time that the plan has been in existence. Under group insurance policies, the time period used is the 3 policy years ending prior to the beginning of the calendar year in which the employee is disabled. If coverage has been in effect for a shorter time, IRS regulations specify the appropriate period that should be used. Similar provisions pertain to contributory sick-leave plans. There is one major exception, however, that stipulates when the period should be based on calendar years rather than policy years. If benefits are provided under individual disability income insurance policies, the proportion is determined on the basis of the premiums paid for the current policy year.

Tax Withholding and Social Security Taxes

Benefits paid directly to an employee by an employer under a sick-leave plan are treated like any other wages for purposes of tax withholding. Disability income benefits paid by a third party (for instance, an insurance company or a trust) are subject to the withholding tax rules and regulations only if the employee requests that taxes be withheld. In both cases, benefits that are attributable to employer contributions are subject to Social Security and Medicare taxes. However, taxes are payable only during the last calendar month in which the employee worked and during the 6 months that follow.

STATE TAX TREATMENT

For income tax purposes, some states consider an individual's taxable income to be the figure shown on the individual's federal income tax return, and those states treat disability income and sick-leave benefits as the federal government does. Although considerable variations exist in other states, disability income and sick-leave benefits are generally treated more favorably than under the federal tax laws and are often totally exempt from state income taxation.

CHAPTER REVIEW

Key Terms and Concepts

disability income insurance
short-term disability (STD) income
  plans
long-term disability (LTD) income
  insurance
sick-leave plan
paid time off (PTO) program
partial disability
own-occupation definition of
  disability

dual (split) definition of disability
exclusion
preexisting-conditions provision
waiting (elimination) period
buy-up plan
catastrophic benefits rider
rehabilitation provision
integrated disability management
cost-of-living adjustment (COLA)
pension supplement

Review Questions

Review questions are based on the learning objectives in this chapter. For example, a [3] at the end of a questions means that the question is based on learning objective 3. If there are multiple objectives, they are all listed.

1. Why does long-term disability have a more severe financial impact on a family than does death? [1]

2. Why is it important to coordinate insured group disability income plans with other sources of disability income benefits? [1]

3. Regarding sick leave plans: [2]

    a. What are the most common eligibility requirements found in sick-leave plans?

    b. What variations are sometimes found in these requirements?

4. Describe the approaches used in determining the duration of benefits under sick-leave plans. [3]

5. Why are long-term disability income plans less likely to cover all employees than short-term disability income plans? [3]

6. Compare insured short-term and long-term disability income contracts with respect to each of the following: [3]

    a. length of probationary periods

    b. the definition of disability

    c.   coverage for partial disabilities

    d.   coverage for nonoccupational disabilities

7.   Identify the exclusions commonly found [3]

    a.   in both short-term and long-term disability income contracts

    b.   in long-term disability income contracts only

8.   What is the rationale for providing disability benefits that are less than an employee's earnings prior to disability? [3]

9.   Compare insured short-term and long-term disability income contracts with respect to the following benefit provisions: [3]

    a.   waiting (elimination) period

    b.   duration of benefits

10. Compare insured short-term and long-term disability income contracts with respect to the following benefit provisions: [3]

    a.   the extent to which benefits are usually reduced for older employees

    b.   the extent to which benefits are usually coordinated with other disability income benefits

11. Lindsay Grant, who earns $1,600 per month, is covered under a group long-term disability income plan that provides benefits equal to 60 percent of predisability earnings. If disabled, she will also receive Social Security disability benefits of $780—$520 as her primary insurance amount and an additional $260 as a family benefit. If the group plan contains a provision reducing benefits to the extent that the long-term disability income benefit and the primary insurance amount exceed 75 percent of earnings, how much will Lindsay receive from each source if she is disabled? [3]

12. Regarding disability income plans: [3]

    a.   What is the nature of supplemental or buy-up disability income plans?

    b.   Why might an employer carve out disability income benefits for employees such as key executives?

13. What provisions are contained in disability income contracts that enable the insurer to verify whether a disability continues to exist? [3]

14. Describe the rehabilitation provision often found in long-term disability income contracts. [3]

15. Regarding disability income plans: [3]

    a. What is the rationale for and role of insurance companies in providing rehabilitation benefits to disabled employees?

    b. What are the advantages of an integrated disability management program?

16. Explain how long-term disability income contracts are sometimes modified to provide [3]

    a. inflation protection

    b. a pension supplement

    c. survivor benefits

17. Under the federal income tax laws, to what extent are employer contributions for disability income insurance [4]

    a. deductible to the employer

    b. taxable as income to an employee

18. Sam Jones has been totally and permanently disabled for the past 2 years and receives a monthly disability benefit of $1,600, consisting of $700 from Social Security and $900 from the long-term disability income plan of Sam's former employer. The plan was contributory, and Sam was required to pay one-third of the cost of his coverage. Other than the disability benefits, Sam and his wife expect to have an adjusted gross income of $12,000 this year from Mrs. Jones's part-time work and interest on their savings.

    What is Sam's tax credit this year for his disability income if he and his wife file jointly? [4]

Review Question Answers

1. In the event of long-term disability and death, income from employment ceases. In the case of long-term disability, however, family expenses—instead of decreasing because of one less family member—may actually increase because of the cost of providing care for the disabled person.

2. A lack of coordination can lead to such a generous level of benefits for employees that absences from work because of disability might be either falsified or unnecessarily prolonged. Alternatively, a lack of coordination can lead to an employee having a gap in coverage from the time a short-term plan ends until a long-term plan or Social Security benefits begin.

3. a. Almost all sick-leave plans are limited to regular full-time employees. Most plans also require that an employee satisfy a short probationary period (commonly 1 to 3 months) before being eligible for benefits.

    b. Benefits may be extended to regular part-time employees. Sick-leave plans may also be limited to certain classes of employees, such as top management or non-union employees.

4. Several approaches are used in determining the duration of benefits.

    •   The most traditional approach credits eligible employees with a certain amount of sick leave each year, such as 10 days. The majority of plans using this approach allow employees to accumulate unused sick leave up to some maximum amount, which rarely exceeds 6 months (sometimes specified as 180 days or 26 weeks). A variation of this approach is to credit employees with an amount of sick leave, such as one day, for each month of service.

    •   Another approach bases the duration of benefits on an employee's length of service. An alternative to this approach provides benefits for a uniform length of time to all employees, except possibly those with short periods of service.

    •   In some instances, an employee is not eligible for sick-leave benefits if he or she is eligible for benefits under social insurance plans, such as workers' compensation. However, most sick-leave plans are coordinated with social insurance programs.

5. Employers are more likely to provide short-term benefits to a wider range of employees, but long-term disability plans often limit benefits to salaried employees because the claims experience of such plans has traditionally been less favorable for hourly paid employees. Claims of hourly paid employees tend to be more frequent, particularly in recessionary times when the possibility of temporary layoffs or terminations increases. Such claims also tend to be of longer duration. Some long-term plans also exclude employees below a certain salary level because this category of employees, like hourly paid employees, is considered to have a reasonable level of benefits under Social Security.

6. a. Long-term disability income plans usually have longer probationary periods than short-term disability income plans. Short-term plans only require that an employee be actively at work on the date he or she is otherwise eligible for coverage, but long-term plans sometimes require an extended period (such as 30 days) on the job without illness or injury before coverage becomes effective.

    b. Virtually all short-term disability income insurance contracts define disability as the total and continuous inability of the employee to perform each and every duty of his or her regular occupation. A few long-term disability income contracts use this same liberal definition. However, the term material duties often replaces the term each and every duty. These contracts often are described as containing an own-occupation definition of disability. Some other long-term disability income contracts define disability as the total and continuous inability of the employee to engage in any and every gainful occupation for which he or she is qualified or shall reasonably become qualified by reason of training, education, or experience.

However, most long-term disability contracts use a dual (or split) definition of disability. Under a dual definition, benefits are paid for some period of time (usually 24 or 36 months) as long as an employee is unable to perform his or her regular occupation. After that time, benefits are paid only if the employee is unable to engage in any occupation for which he or she is qualified by reason of training, education, or experience. Another popular definition of disability found in long-term contracts contains an occupation test and an earnings test.

Finally, short-term contracts usually have the same definition of disability for all classes of employees. Some long-term contracts, however, use different definitions for different classes of employees: one for most employees and a more liberal definition for executives or salaried employees.

   c.   Usually, neither short-term nor long-term contracts cover partial disabilities. Nevertheless, a few plans, which are somewhat more than likely to be long-term contracts, do provide such benefits. However, the amount and duration of such benefits may be limited when compared with those for total disabilities, and the receipt of benefits is usually contingent upon a previous period of total disability.

   d.   The majority of short-term contracts limit coverage to nonoccupational disabilities, because employees have workers' compensation benefits for occupational disabilities. Most long-term contracts, however, provide coverage for both occupational and nonoccupational disabilities.

7.   a.   Common exclusions under both short- and long-term disability income contracts specify that no benefits are paid

- for any period during which the employee is not under the care of a physician

- for any disability caused by an intentionally self-inflicted injury

- unless the period of disability commenced while the employee was covered under the contract

- if the employee is engaged in any occupation for remuneration

- if (or to the extent) benefits are payable under workers' compensation or similar laws

b. Additional exclusions are often found in long-term contracts. These commonly deny benefits for disabilities resulting from

- war, whether declared or undeclared

- participation in an assault or felony. This exclusion may include the commission of any crime.

- mental disease, alcoholism, or drug addiction. However, many contracts provide employees with benefits but limit their duration (such as for 24 months per disability); other contracts provide benefits for an employee who is confined in a hospital or institution that specializes in the care and treatment of such disorders

- preexisting conditions

8. A disabled employee does not have the usual expenses associated with working, such as transportation costs. In addition, disability income benefits are not subject to Social Security and Medicare taxation after a period of time and, depending on the source and amount, may be free of income taxation.

9. a. In the typical short-term contract, there is no waiting period for disabilities resulting from accidents, but a waiting period of 1 to 7 consecutive days is used for disabilities resulting from sicknesses. However, some plans have a single waiting period that applies to disabilities from either accidents or sicknesses; a few plans have no waiting periods for either. Waiting periods longer than 7 days are occasionally used, particularly when there is a sick-leave plan to provide benefits during the initial portion of a disability.

   Although waiting periods in long-term disability income plans may be as short as 30 days or as long as a year or more, most plans use periods of 3 to 6 months, with 6 months most common.

   b. Although short-term contracts may provide benefits up to 2 years (with long-term contracts providing benefits for periods over 2 years), benefits rarely continue for more than a year. In fact, the majority of short-term contracts stipulate that benefits are paid for either 13 or 26 weeks, with the latter period being most prevalent.

   Long-term disability income benefits may be paid for as short a period as 2 years or as long as the lifetime of the disabled employee. In a few cases, the length of the benefit period may differ, depending on whether the disability was a result of an accident or a sickness.

Both short-term disability income plans and long-term plans typically provide for successive disabilities. The majority of contracts stipulate that successive periods of disability that are separated by less than some period (usually varying from 3 to 6 months) of continuous, active full-time employment are considered a single disability, unless the subsequent disability (1) arises from an unrelated cause and (2) begins after the employee has returned to work.

10. a. Although reducing short-term disability income benefits for older employees may be justifiable on a cost basis, few plans have done so.

Long-term disability income benefits, however, are commonly reduced for older employees, and several different approaches are acceptable under the Age Discrimination in Employment Act. In a few cases, benefits are paid until age 70 for any disability that occurred before that age. For disabilities occurring at age 70 or later, benefits are paid for a reduced duration. A more common approach is to use a graded benefit period and give benefits to age 65 for employees who are disabled before a specified age. Employees disabled after the specified age get benefits for a limited duration.

A similar approach uses a sliding level of benefit durations after a certain age. For example, a plan may provide that employees disabled prior to age 60 will receive benefits until age 65. A schedule might then be used for employees who are disabled at age 60 or older.

b. In general, the insurance laws or regulations of most states allow reductions in benefits to be made as a result of benefits from social insurance programs and group insurance or retirement plans provided by the employer. Reductions as a result of benefits from individual disability income contracts are not usually allowed unless the policies were purchased by the employer. For various reasons, including the limited duration of benefits and the desire for simplified operating procedures, coordination with other benefits is less common for short-term plans than in long-term plans.

11. Lindsay will receive the full $780 from Social Security because it is paid regardless of the existence of any benefits payable under a long-term disability income plan.

In the absence of any provision to coordinate benefits, the group plan would pay her 60 percent of her predisability earnings of $1,600 per month, or $960. However, this is reduced to the extent that it, together with her primary insurance amount of $520, exceeds 75 percent of her earnings. Since $960 plus $520 is $1,480 and therefore exceeds $1,200 by $280, the long-term benefit is reduced by that amount to $680.

Thus, Lindsay will receive a total of $1,460 from Social Security and the long-term disability income plan.

12. a. A supplemental or buy-up disability plan allows each covered employee to purchase additional coverage at his or her own expense beyond a base of employer-paid benefits. For example, a plan may provide basic benefits of 50 percent of earnings and an option for an employee to increase this amount to 60, 66 2/3, or 70 percent of earnings.

   b. A carve-out plan for key executives typically provides enhanced benefits in the form of a larger percentage of earnings and a more liberal definition of disability. Another variation of a carve-out plan would provide the executives with a lower benefit percentage than other employees receive, but it could provide supplemental benefits in the form of individual disability income policies. In addition to more favorable policy provisions, a carve-out plan might offer better rate guarantees and an overall higher benefit than a group plan could offer. Furthermore, the portability of the individual policy might be attractive to executives. In addition, individual policies might be available on a guaranteed-issue basis if the group of executives is large enough.

13. Contract provisions require periodic reports from the attending physician or permit the insurance company to request such reports at reasonable intervals. The insurance company also has the right to have the employee examined by a physician of its own choice (and at its own expense) at reasonable time periods during the duration of the claim.

14. This provision permits the employee to enter a trial work period (sometimes referred to as a return-to-work program) of 1 or 2 years in rehabilitative employment. During this time, disability benefits continue but are reduced by some percentage (varying from 50 to 80 percent) of the earnings from rehabilitative employment. If the trial work period indicates that the employee is unable to perform the rehabilitative employment, the original long-term benefits continue and the employee is not required to satisfy a new waiting period.

15. a. Insurance companies sometimes provide benefits for rehabilitation when the cost of these benefits is offset by shortening an employee's disability period.

   More and more companies are taking a proactive role in managing disability claims by employing more skilled professionals and by intervening earlier in the claims process. In addition to providing rehabilitation benefits, insurance companies are monitoring claims data more closely so that they can better advise employers of areas where action can be taken to reduce the number of future claims.

b. There is a single centralized claims-reporting system that is easier to understand and less expensive than duplicate programs for each type of coverage. There are consistent treatment protocols for all disabilities, no matter where or when they occurred, and it is easier to measure and track outcomes of return-to-work programs. In addition, there is a lower incidence of fraudulent claims from employees trying to collect under disability plans and workers' compensation at the same time.

16. a. Some disability income plans have a cost-of-living adjustment (COLA) so that inflation does not erode the purchasing power of disability income benefits being received. Under the typical COLA formula, benefits increase annually along with changes in the consumer price index.

b. Many firms make provisions in their pension plan for treating disabled employees as if they were still working and accruing pension benefits. Such a pension supplement requires that contributions on behalf of disabled employees be made to the pension plan, usually from the employer's current revenues. However, some disability income contracts stipulate that the contributions to fund a disabled employee's accruing pension benefits are paid from the disability income contract.

Some retirement plans also provide disability income benefits by allowing disabled employees to begin receiving retirement benefits when they are totally and permanently disabled.

c. Some long-term contracts provide a benefit to survivors in the form of continued payments after the death of a disabled employee. In effect, the disability income payments continue, possibly at a reduced amount, for periods ranging up to 24 months, with 3 to 6 months being most common. Payments are generally made only to eligible survivors, who commonly are the spouse and unmarried children under age 21.

17. a. Employer contributions for an employee's disability income insurance are fully deductible to the employer as an ordinary and necessary business expense if the employee's overall compensation is reasonable.

b. Under a fully contributory plan, the entire cost is paid by employee contributions and benefits are received free of income taxation. However, the tax situation for an employee will vary with a noncontributory plan, depending on how an employer designs a disability income plan.

- Under a typical noncontributory plan, the employer pays the entire cost and benefits are included in an employee's gross income. However, the Internal Revenue Code provides a tax credit to persons who are permanently and totally disabled.

  A 2004 IRS Revenue Ruling allows an employer to design a disability income plan so that an employee can receive tax-free benefits from a noncontributory plan. In order to receive these benefits, however, the employee must elect to have the employer-paid premium for his or her coverage reported as taxable income.

- Under a partially contributory plan, benefits attributable to employee contributions are received free of income taxation. Benefits attributable to employer contributions are includible in gross income, but employees are eligible for the tax credit described previously.

18. Sam receives no tax credit. The maximum tax credit available to Sam is $1,125. However, it is reduced because the adjusted gross of he and his wife exceeds $10,000 (the $7,200 of disability income benefits plus the $12,000 of other income. This reduction is equal to 7.5 percent of $9,200, or $690. In addition, the credit is also reduced by 15 percent of his annual Social Security benefit of $8,400. This further reduction of $1,260 more than eliminates the tax credit.

Chapter 6

Medical Expense Benefits

Learning Objectives

An understanding of the material in this chapter should enable the student to

1. **Describe the purpose and development of medical expense insurance.**

2. **Explain the reasons for the increasing cost of health care, and identify the measures that employers use to contain health care costs.**

3. **Describe the providers of traditional medical expense insurance plans.**

4. **Discuss basic medical expense benefits and exclusions.**

5. **Describe the characteristics of major medical insurance.**

6. **Describe the types of managed care provisions used in traditional medical expense insurance plans.**

7. **Explain how complementary and alternative medicine play a role in medical expense insurance.**

medical expense insurance

The purpose of **medical expense insurance** is to provide protection against financial losses that result from medical bills because of accident and/or illness. Medical expense insurance is the most significant type of group insurance in terms of both the number of persons covered and the dollar outlay. With the exception of employers with a very small number of employees, virtually all employers offer some type of medical expense plan. In almost all cases, coverage identical to that offered for employees is also available for eligible dependents.

Group medical expense contracts are not as standardized as group life insurance and group disability income insurance. Coverage may be marketed through insurance companies, Blue Cross and Blue Shield plans, health maintenance organizations (HMOs), preferred-provider organizations (PPOs), and the health insurance exchanges. In addition, plans that are partially or totally self-funded (self-insured) provide a large and increasing percentage of the benefits. In contrast to other types of group insurance, benefits may be in the form of services rather than cash payments. Finally, the skyrocketing cost of providing medical expense benefits over a long period has led to changes in coverage and plan design aimed at controlling these costs. Many of these changes have resulted in more similarities among the providers of medical expense coverage than existed in the past.

Over the past 25 years, two major issues—affordability and accessibility of medical care—have led to profound changes in the health care industry. Not only has there been a continued shift to managed care plans, but the entire character of the health care industry has also changed. Where once there was a distinction between the providers of care (such as doctors and hospitals) and the organizations that financed the care (such as insurers, the Blues, and HMOs), this distinction is increasingly blurred. Physicians and hospitals have established HMOs, PPOs, and accountable care organizations. Physicians may be employees of managed care plans. There are those who feel that in the not-too-distant future most Americans will receive their medical expense coverage from one of a small number of large organizations that both provide medical care and finance the cost of that care.

The issues surrounding medical care have also become a concern of government. Many states have enacted programs to make coverage available to the uninsured, including those who work for employers with a small number of employees. At the federal level, the Affordable Care Act was passed in March, 2010 to address many of these concerns.

COMMENTS ON TERMINOLOGY

health insurance

Medical expense insurance is often referred to as **health insurance**. However, this book uses health insurance in a broad sense to mean protection against the financial consequences of poor health. These consequences include incurring medical and dental bills.

But poor health can also result in lost income and additional expenses. In this context, health insurance includes medical expense insurance, dental insurance, disability insurance, and long-term care insurance.

DEVELOPMENT OF MEDICAL EXPENSE COVERAGE

To understand the wide array of medical expense plans available today, it is appropriate to review their historic development.

The history of medical expense plan development spans approximately 90 years.

Prior to the 1930s, medical expenses were borne primarily by the ill or injured persons or their families. It was not unusual for hospitals and physicians to provide care on a charity basis if the patient lacked the resources to pay.

Blue Cross plans developed during the Great Depression. Blue Shield plans followed in the late 1930s. The Blues, as they were called, were the predominant providers of medical expense coverage through the 1940s.

The earliest HMO, the Ross-Loos Clinic, was founded in Los Angeles in 1929. Other HMOs, such as the Kaiser Plans, had their beginnings in the 1930s. HMOs played only a small role in the marketplace for medical expense coverage until the past 30 years.

Insurance companies entered the market for hospital insurance in the 1930s and later added coverage for surgical expenses and physicians' expenses. The major medical insurance policy was introduced in 1949. This comprehensive policy was able to successfully compete with the Blues.

In the mid-1960s, the federal government became a major player in providing medical expense coverage by creating Medicare as a national health insurance program for the elderly and Medicaid to provide health benefits for certain classes of low-income individuals and families.

The Health Maintenance Organization Act of 1973 encouraged the growth of HMOs by providing funding for their development costs and mandating that certain employers make these plans available to employees. In 1974, the passage of ERISA freed self-funded plans from state regulation and hastened the growth of this benefit financing option.

The 1970s and 1980s also saw ever increasing costs for medical care in the United States. About 14 percent of the population, including many employed persons and their families, remained uninsured.

In 1996, the Health Insurance and Portability and Accountability Act was implemented. The next year, the Mental Health Parity Act was enacted. The Children's Health Insurance Program, a federally funded/state administered program offering coverage to hundreds of thousands of lower income parents and several million children, was also created in 1997.

The many efforts by employers to contain costs during the 1980s and 1990s included the following:

- growth in the self-funding of benefits. Much of this growth came from small- and medium-sized employers.

- cost-shifting to employees. It became increasingly common for employers to raise deductibles and require employees to pay a larger portion of their medical expense coverage.

- requiring or encouraging managed care plans. Some employers dropped traditional medical expense plans and offered managed care alternatives only. A more prevalent approach was to offer employees a financial incentive to join managed care plans.

- increased use of managed care plans that are alternatives to HMOs, such as PPOs and point-of-service plans. These approaches often overcome the reluctance of some employees to participate in managed care plans.

A significant change in medical expense plans took place in the 1990s. In 1980, approximately 90 percent of all insured workers were covered under "traditional" medical expense plans, and 5 percent were covered under HMOs. Under the traditional plan, the patient had complete freedom in choosing a doctor or a hospital. The plan paid the medical bills with almost no attempt to control costs or the utilization of services. It is estimated that 10- to 15 percent of the employees under these traditional plans were in totally self-funded plans. The remainder of the employees were split fairly evenly between plans written by insurance companies and the Blues.

By 2014, the majority of employees were covered under plans that control costs and the access to medical care. Over 99 percent of employees were enrolled in managed care plans or high deductible health plans. Less than one percent were in traditional plans that had been redesigned to incorporate varying degrees of managed care.[1] Sixty-one percent of covered workers were in a totally or partially self-funded medical expense plan.[2]

COST CONTAINMENT

Between 2004–2014, there has been a 69 percent increase in average annual health insurance premiums.[3] Reasons for these increases include:

---

1.   The Henry J. Kaiser Family Foundation, *2014 Employer Health Benefits Survey,* Sept. 10, 2014, p. 4.

2.   Ibid, p. 174.

3.   Ibid, p. 1.

- technological advances in such techniques as CAT scans, MRIs, fetal monitoring, and organ transplants that can prolong the life of the terminally ill and increase associated medical expenses

- increasing malpractice suits with awards that outpaced the general rate of inflation

- increases in mandates by the Affordable Care Act and the states that require insurance contracts to provide coverage for certain types of medical care and for treatment by certain types of providers

- an aging population. The incidence of illness increases with age. Current demographics indicate that this trend will be a source of cost increases for several years to come.

Increasing health care costs have become the concern of almost everyone—government, labor, employers, and consumers. Measures employers use to contain costs include:

- benefit plan design
- alternative benefit providers
- alternative funding methods
- claims review
- health education and preventive care
- encouragement of external cost-control systems
- managed care
- consumer-directed plans

Benefit Plan Design

Numerous design features of a medical expense plan can control costs. These have traditionally been in the form of contractual provisions that shift costs to employees. Examples are

- deductibles
- coinsurance
- copayments
- exclusions and limitations
- maximum benefits

In recent years, many design features have been aimed at reducing costs rather than shifting them. In fact, benefit plans are often structured to provide a higher level of benefits if less costly alternatives are used. Examples of these cost-containment features are

- preadmission testing
- second surgical opinions
- coordination of benefits
- the use of alternatives to hospitals (such as skilled-nursing facilities, home health care, hospice care, birthing centers, and ambulatory care centers)
- the use of health savings accounts, health reimbursement arrangements, and other consumer-directed medical expense plans. These plans typically involve the use of high-deductible medical expense policies.

Alternative Benefit Providers

The use of HMOs, PPOs, and point-of-service (POS) plans has been popular for some years as a cost-containment method. These methods have now been joined by accountable care organizations (ACOs).

Alternative Funding Methods

Employers are increasingly turning to funding methods that are alternatives to the traditional insurance company plan or Blue Cross and Blue Shield plan.

Claims Review

There is no doubt that claims review can generate substantial cost savings. In general, the provider of medical expense benefits, a third-party administrator, or some independent outside organization performs this function. At a minimum, claims should be reviewed for patient eligibility, eligibility of the services provided, duplicate policies, and charges that are in excess of usual, customary, and reasonable amounts. Many medical expense plans routinely audit hospital bills, particularly those that exceed some stipulated amount, such as $5,000 or $10,000. They check for errors in such items as length of stay, services performed, and billed charges. Many insurance companies have found that each dollar spent on this type of review results in two or three dollars of savings.

Health Education and Preventive Care

Persons who lead healthy lifestyles tend to have fewer medical bills, particularly at younger ages. Healthier employees save an employer money by taking fewer sick days and having fewer disability claims. For these reasons, employers are increasingly establishing wellness programs and employee-assistance plans. With increasing health awareness among the general population, the existence of these programs also has a positive side effect—the improvement of employee morale.

Encouragement of External Cost-Control Systems

Although a certain degree of cost containment is within the control of employers, the proper control of costs is an ongoing process that requires participation by consumers (both employers and individuals), government, and the providers of health care services. Many agencies and committees of the Department of Health and Human Services carry out these activities at the federal level. This government department has the primary responsibility for identifying health care needs, monitoring resources, establishing priorities, recommending courses of action, and overseeing laws that pertain to health care.

At the state and local level, many employers are active in coalitions whose purpose is to control costs and improve the quality of health care. These groups—which may also involve unions, providers of health care, insurance companies, and regulators—are often catalysts for legislation, such as laws authorizing PPOs and establishing hospital budget-review programs. Some coalitions act as purchasing groups to negotiate lower-cost coverage for members.

Managed Care

managed care

For many years, the buzzword with respect to cost containment has been **managed care**. In a general sense, the term includes any medical expense plan that attempts to contain costs by controlling the behavior of participants. However, in practice many persons use the term to mean different things. At one extreme are traditional plans that require second opinions and/or hospital precertification. At the other extreme are HMOs and PPOs that limit a participant's choice of medical providers, negotiate provider fees, and manage utilization of medical services.

Managed care plans have evolved over the last few years. Today, it is generally felt that a true managed care plan should have five basic characteristics:

- *controlled access to providers.* It is difficult to control costs if participants have unrestricted access to physicians and hospitals. Managed care plans tend to use network primary care physicians as gatekeepers to determine the necessity and appropriateness of specialty care by contracted specialists. By limiting the number of providers, managed care plans are better able to control costs by negotiating provider fees.

- *comprehensive utilization management.* Successful managed care plans perform utilization review at all levels. This involves reviewing a case to determine the type of treatment necessary, monitoring ongoing care, and reviewing the appropriateness and success of treatment after patients receive it.

- *preventive care.* Managed care plans encourage preventive care and the attainment of healthier lifestyles.

- *risk sharing.* Managed care plans are most successful if providers share in the financial consequences of medical decisions. Newer managed care plans have contractual guarantees to encourage cost-effective care.

- *high-quality care.* Managed care plans not only select providers carefully but also monitor the quality of care on a continuing basis.

There seems to be a reasonable consensus among employers and benefit specialists that there is a negative correlation between benefit costs and the degree of managed care—that is, the greater the degree of managed care, the lower the cost. For example, studies generally rank benefit plans in the following order (from highest to lowest) with respect to annual benefit costs:

- traditional insurance company and Blue Cross and Blue Shield plans without utilization management

- traditional insurance company and Blue Cross and Blue Shield plans with utilization management

- PPOs

- point-of-service plans

- independent practice association HMOs

- closed-panel HMOs

Consumer-Directed Health Care

There is considerable interest in the concept of consumer-directed health care. With this approach, employees are put in charge of managing the health care dollars their employers provide. It exposes employees to the true cost of care and involves them in keeping health care expenditures under control.

TRADITIONAL MEDICAL EXPENSE PLANS

traditional (indemnity) medical expense plan

fee-for-service plan

Prior to the mid-1970s, most employees were covered by what is commonly referred to as a **traditional (or indemnity) medical expense plan**. Employees incurred medical expenses and had considerable freedom in choosing the providers of medical care. Insurers paid claims based on charges billed by providers with virtually no attempts to control costs. As a result, a traditional plan is also referred to as a **fee-for-service plan**.

A small number of employees are still covered under plans that are largely traditional in nature. However, these plans have evolved. Although they are still far from what might be called managed care plans, these plans contain provisions designed to control costs, influence the behavior of persons needing medical care, and provide preventive care.

A few employers still offer traditional major medical plans. Although participation by employees is small, one major survey indicated that less than one percent of employees still have the option of selecting such plans.[4] However, many employees are unlikely to do so because of higher premiums, deductibles, and copayments than are found in managed care plans.

The discussion of medical expense plans largely follows the historical development of medical expense plans. Much of the terminology and coverage of legislation introduced here also applies to the managed care approaches to medical care.

PPOs—a major sources of employer provided medical expense coverage—are essentially traditional major medical plans that have evolved over time to provide a higher level of benefits if a covered person receives services or products from a preferred-provider.

---

4.   The Henry J. Kaiser Foundation and Health Research and Education Trust, *Employer Health Benefits Survey, 2014*, p. 4.

PROVIDERS OF COVERAGE

Providers of traditional coverage and other types of medical expense coverage include Blue Cross and Blue Shield plans, insurance companies, HMOs, PHOs, ACOs, and employers using self-funded arrangements.

Form of Benefits

service-benefit concept

indemnity concept

Under the **service-benefit concept**, benefits are expressed in terms of the services that are provided by the hospitals or physicians participating in the plan rather than in terms of dollar amounts. For example, a Blue Cross plan might have provided up to 90 days of hospitalization per year in semiprivate accommodations. Under the **indemnity concept**, an insured would be reimbursed for covered medical expenses incurred up to a maximum dollar amount. There is no contractual relationship between the providers of medical services and the insurance company. For example, an insurance company might provide reimbursement for hospital charges subject to both dollar and duration limits, such as $1,000 per day for 90 days. In both cases, however, any charges in excess of the benefits must be borne by the covered person.

BASIC MEDICAL EXPENSE COVERAGES

It should be noted before this discussion of the different types of basic medical expense coverages the Affordable Care Act (ACA) mandated that qualified health plan coverage must offer essential health benefits (example: ambulatory patient services, hospitalization, emergency services, maternity, newborn care, mental health and substance abuse services, behavioral health services, chronic disease management, rehabilitative services, laboratory services, pediatric services including oral and vision services, prescriptions, and preventive and wellness care) without annual or lifetime maximums or preexisting condition exclusions. Grandfathered health plans may be granted waivers to authorize noncompliance with some ACA mandates.

Hospital Expense Benefits

hospital expense coverage

Hospital expense coverage provides benefits for charges incurred in a hospital by a covered person (that is, the employee or his or her dependents) who is an inpatient or, in some circumstances, an outpatient. Every medical expense contract defines what is meant by a hospital. The actual wording may vary among insurance companies and in some states, but the following definition is typical:

> The term hospital means (1) an institution that is accredited as a hospital under the hospital accreditation program of the Joint Commission on Accreditation of Healthcare Organizations or (2) any other institution that is legally operated under the supervision of a staff of physicians and with 24-hour-a-day nursing service. In no event should the term hospital include a convalescent nursing home or include any institution or part thereof that (1) is used principally as a convalescent facility, rest facility, nursing facility, or facility for the aged; or (2) furnishes primarily domiciliary or custodial care, including training in the routines of daily living; or (3) is operated primarily as a school.

Inpatient Benefits

Hospital inpatient benefits fall into two categories: coverage for room-and-board charges and coverage for "other charges."

Coverage for room-and-board charges includes the cost of the hospital room, meals, and services normally provided to all inpatients, including routine nursing care. Policies usually express the daily room-and-board benefit as the full cost of semiprivate accommodations.

Coverage for other charges (often called miscellaneous charges, ancillary charges, or hospital extras) provides benefits for certain services and supplies ordered by a physician during a covered person's hospital confinement, such as drugs, operating room charges, laboratory services, and X rays. With a few exceptions, only the hospital portion of these charges is covered; any associated charges for such professional services as physicians' fees are not covered under this benefit.

Outpatient Benefits

Today it is common to find coverage for outpatient expenses arising from surgery under hospital expense benefit coverage. The purpose of this benefit is to provide comparable coverage and thus lower hospital utilization when surgical procedures can be performed on an outpatient basis. Note that this benefit covers only hospital charges or charges of outpatient surgical centers (such as the use of operating room facilities), not the surgeon's fee.

Hospital expense contracts commonly provide coverage for emergency room treatment of accidental injuries within some specified period (varying from 24 to 72 hours) after an accident. Many contracts treat emergency room charges incurred immediately prior to hospitalization as inpatient expenses.

Surgical Expense Benefits

surgical expense coverage

Surgical expense coverage provides benefits for physicians' charges associated with surgical procedures. Although one tends to think of a surgical procedure as involving cutting, insurance contracts typically define the term broadly to include such procedures as suturing, electrocauterization, removal of a stone or foreign body by endoscopic means, and the treatment of fractures or dislocations.

Surgical expense coverage normally provides benefits for surgery performed not only in the hospital (either as an inpatient or an outpatient), but also as an outpatient in a free-standing (that is, separate from a hospital) ambulatory surgical center and in a physician's office. To discourage unnecessary hospitalization, some surgical expense benefit contracts actually provide larger benefits if a procedure is performed as outpatient surgery.

Outpatient surgery also results in charges for medical supplies, nurses, and the use of facilities. As mentioned, these charges are often covered if surgery is performed on an outpatient basis in a hospital or outpatient surgical facility.

surgical fee schedule

reasonable-and- customary charge

In providing basic surgical expense benefits, some insurance companies and some Blue Shield plans use a **surgical fee schedule** in which charges are paid up to the maximum amounts specified in the schedule of surgical procedures in the master contract. However, the majority of surgical expense plans follow the approach used in major medical contracts and provide benefits to the extent that surgical charges are reasonable and customary. Unfortunately, the precise meaning of these terms in insurance contracts is vague, and each company determines what it considers reasonable and customary. In general, a

reasonable-and-customary charge (sometimes referred to as a usual, customary, and reasonable charge or prevailing charge) is considered to be a charge that falls within the range of fees normally charged for a given procedure by physicians of similar training and experience within a geographic region.

The usual practice of insurance companies is to pay charges in full as long as they do not exceed some percentile (usually ranging from the 85th to the 95th) of the range of charges for a specific surgical procedure within a certain geographic region. For example, if an insurance company uses the 90th percentile and if for a certain procedure 90 percent of the charges are $300 or less, this is the maximum amount that is paid. The covered person is required to absorb any additional charges if he or she uses a more expensive physician. With computers, insurance companies now have statistics that categorize expenses by geographic regions that are as small as the zip codes of medical-care providers. Thus, $300 may be the maximum reasonable-and-customary amount in one part of a metropolitan area, and $350 may be the reasonable and customary in another part of the same metropolitan area.

Today's Coverage

Today's medical expense plans provide comprehensive coverage that focus more on providing benefits for catastrophic medical expenses. Even with deductibles, copayments, and percentage participation, such plans typically pay from 60–90 percent of medical expenses incurred. The medical expense plans are underwritten by qualified health plans and pay for the actuarial equivalent of 60 to 90 percent of covered medical expenses including essential health benefits.

MAJOR MEDICAL COVERAGE

major medical coverage

Many employees have major medical coverage that protects against catastrophic medical expenses, with few exclusions or limitations. However, employees must often pay part of the cost of these medical expenses because of deductibles and coinsurance provisions.

Comprehensive Major Medical Coverage

comprehensive major medical coverage

With **comprehensive major medical coverage**, a single major medical contract covers practically all medical expenses. Once the insured satisfies the deductible, the contracts cover most medical expenses subject to a coinsurance provision. Most comprehensive medical expense contracts contain modifications of deductibles and/or coinsurance provisions for certain expenses, often resulting in payment of 100 percent of reasonable and customary charges.

Characteristics of Major Medical Coverage

The distinguishing features of major medical expense plans include a broad range of covered expenses, exclusions, limitations, deductibles, coinsurance, and unlimited overall maximum benefits.

Covered Expenses

Major medical plans give broad coverage for necessary expenses incurred for medical services and supplies that a physician has ordered or prescribed. The services and supplies, which the contract specifies, generally include essential health benefits as well as other benefits such as:

- hospital room and board. Some plans also provide benefits for room and board in alternative facilities, such as birthing centers.

- other hospital charges

- charges of outpatient surgical centers

- anesthetics and their administration

- services of doctors of medicine or osteopathy

- professional services of a registered nurse. The services of a nurse midwife, nurse practitioner, and nurse anesthetist may also be covered.

- services of certain other types of providers. Most states mandate that the insurance contract cover services of certain types of providers other than physicians and nurses as long as the service is a covered benefit and the provider is operating within the scope of his or her license. The list of providers varies from state to state and may include one or more of the following: acupuncturists, audiologists, chiropractors, dentists, marriage and family therapists, dietitians, optometrists, physical therapists, physicians' assistants, podiatrists, psychologists, social workers, and speech pathologists.

- prescription drugs
- physical and speech therapy
- diagnostic X-ray and laboratory services
- radiation therapy
- blood and blood plasma
- artificial limbs and organs
- pacemakers
- casts, splints, trusses, braces, and crutches
- rental of wheelchairs and hospital beds
- ambulance services

Even though coverage is broad, major medical contracts contain certain exclusions and limitations.

Exclusions

The list of exclusions varies, but exclusions found in most major medical contracts include charges arising from the following:

- occupational injuries or diseases to the extent that workers' compensation laws or similar legislation provide benefits.
- services furnished by or on behalf of government agencies unless there is a requirement for the patient's medical expense plan to pay for the services. Under federal law, medical expense plans must generally pay benefits to the government for care in Veterans Health Administration or military hospitals on the same basis as they pay for care received elsewhere. However, if a plan does not pay charges in full because of deductibles, coinsurance, or plan limitations, the patient is not responsible for the balance. The exceptions to the law—meaning that the plan is not responsible for payment—include treatment in Veterans Health Administration hospitals for service-connected disabilities and treatment of active-duty members of the armed services in military hospitals.
- care provided by family members or when no charge would be made for the care received in the absence of the insurance contract

- cosmetic surgery, except as required by legislation, unless such surgery is to correct a condition resulting from either an accidental injury or a qualifying birth defect

- experimental or investigational drugs and treatment

- convalescent, custodial, or rest care

- dental care except for (1) treatment required because of injury to natural teeth and (2) hospital and surgical charges associated with hospital confinement for dental surgery. This exclusion is not included if dental coverage is provided under the major medical contract.

- eye refraction, or the purchase or fitting of eyeglasses or hearing aids. Like the dental care exclusion, this exclusion is not included if the major medical coverage provides benefits for vision and hearing care. A separate plan, however, most likely provides these benefits.

- expenses either paid or eligible for payment under Medicare or other federal, state, or local medical expense programs

The use of preexisting-conditions provisions for essential health benefits in group medical expense plans was eliminated by the passage of the Affordable Care Act.

Finally, there are certain types of medical expenses that insurers may or may not exclude. Examples include charges arising from the following:

- treatment for weight reduction and morbid obesity

- sexual transformation or sexual dysfunction

- procedures to restore or enhance fertility, reversal of sterilizations, artificial insemination, or in vitro fertilization

- treatment of injuries incurred while committing a felony

Maternity. Until the passage of the Pregnancy Discrimination Act in 1964, it was not unusual for medical expense contracts to exclude coverage for maternity-related expenses. However, the act requires that benefit plans of employers with 15 or more employees treat pregnancy, childbirth, and related conditions the same as any other illness. The Affordable Care Act removed all limitations for essential health benefits and removed pre-existing condition clauses for essential health benefits including maternity.

Newborns' and Mothers' Health Protection Act

Since 1998, group medical expense plans have been subject to the provisions of the **Newborns' and Mothers' Health Protection Act**. The act prohibits a group medical expense plan or insurer from restricting hospital benefits to less than 48 hours for both the mother and the newborn following a normal vaginal delivery and 96 hours following a cesarean section. Although a new mother, in consultation with her physician, might agree to a shorter stay, a plan or insurer cannot offer a monetary or nonmonetary incentive to the mother for this purpose. For example, follow-up visits from a home health nurse cannot be provided to mothers and children who are discharged early unless these visits are also provided to mothers and children who stayed in the hospital for the full period specified in the act. In addition, the plan or insurer cannot limit provider reimbursement because care was provided within the minimum limits or make incentives available to providers to render care inconsistent with the minimum requirements.

If a plan has deductibles or other benefit restrictions, these cannot be greater during the 48- or 96-hour period than those imposed on any preceding portion of the hospital stay prior to the birth.

Women's Health and Cancer Rights Act

Effect of Women's Health and Cancer Rights Act. The **Women's Health and Cancer Rights Act** amended ERISA and applies to group medical expense plans as well as to individual medical expense insurance. Under the provisions of this federal act, any benefit plan or policy that provides medical and surgical benefits for mastectomy must also provide benefits for the following:

- reconstruction of the breast on which the mastectomy has been performed
- surgery and reconstruction of the other breast to produce a symmetrical appearance
- prostheses
- physical complications of all stages of mastectomy, including lymphedemas

Prior to the act taking effect, such coverage was often not available because of exclusions, particularly exclusions that applied to cosmetic surgery. This coverage may be subject to deductibles and coinsurance provisions as long as they are consistent with those provided for other procedures under the plan or policy. A plan must notify participants of the existence of these benefits on an annual basis.

Limitations

limitations

Major medical plans also contain **limitations** or internal limits for certain types of medical expenses. Although the expenses are covered, the amounts that the contract pays are limited. Plans very rarely pay for charges that exceed what is reasonable and customary. In addition, they often place limitations on the following expenses:

- hospital room and board. Benefits are generally limited to the charge for semiprivate accommodations unless other accommodations are medically necessary.
- dental care, vision and hearing care. When major medical contracts provide this coverage, benefits are frequently subject to schedules and annual limitations.
- ambulance service, such as $250 per trip
- rental or purchase of durable equipment, such as $5,000

Deductibles

deductible

A **deductible** is the initial amount of covered medical expenses an individual must pay before he or she receives benefits under a major medical plan.

initial (straight) deductible

The **initial (or straight) deductible** is used in comprehensive major medical plans. Essentially, a covered person must satisfy this deductible before the plan pays any insurance benefits.

Example

Kirk is covered under a major medical plan that has an annual deductible of $500. He is responsible for the first $500 of medical expenses incurred each year. The major medical plan then pays covered expenses in excess of $500, subject to any limitations or coinsurance.

There are variations in (1) the amounts of the deductible, (2) the frequency with which it must be satisfied, and (3) the expenses to which it applies.

Deductible Amounts

Deductibles are fixed-dollar amounts that apply separately to each person. Although deductibles are normally relatively small, large deductibles are often used for coverage written in conjunction with consumer-directed medical expense plans.

all-causes deductible

In most major medical expense plans, the deductible must be satisfied only once during any given time period (usually a calendar year), regardless of the number of causes from which medical expenses arise. This type of deductible is referred to as an **all-causes deductible**.

family deductible

Deductibles apply to each covered individual, including the dependents of an employee. To minimize the family's burden of satisfying several deductibles, most major medical expense plans also contain a **family deductible**. Once the family deductible is satisfied, future covered medical expenses of all family members are paid just as if each member of the family had satisfied his or her individual deductible.

The most common type waives any deductible requirements for other family members once a certain number of family members (generally two or three) have satisfied their individual deductibles. Two important points should be noted. First, major medical benefits are paid for each individual family member once his or her individual deductible is satisfied, even though the family deductible has not been met. Second, the waiver of any deductible requirements that results from the satisfaction of the family deductible does not apply to medical expenses incurred prior to the date the deductible is satisfied.

Example

Assume a family deductible is satisfied when each of three family members incurs $200 in covered medical expenses. If a fourth family member has had $60 in medical expenses up to that point, future medical expenses for that person will be paid under the major medical coverage. The $60, however, is not covered. In effect, the satisfaction of the family deductible freezes the deductible for each family member at the lesser of the individual deductible or the amount of medical expenses incurred up to that time.

Certain high deductible policies used with health savings accounts contain a variation of the family deductible under which a single aggregate deductible applies to the family.

common accident provision

Most major medical expense contracts contain a **common accident provision**, whereby if two or more members of the same family are injured in the same accident, the covered medical expenses for all family members are at most subject to a single deductible, usually equal to the individual deductible amount. This deductible establishes the maximum amount of medical expenses an employee must bear for his or her family before major medical benefits are paid. Sometimes the employee may actually bear a smaller portion of the medical expenses if the amount satisfies the family or individual deductibles.

Example

If each of three family members incurs $300 of medical expenses in an accident under a plan that contains a $200 individual deductible, at least $700 of these expenses is covered under the major medical contract. If due to previous medical expenses only $40 is needed to satisfy the family deductible, then $860 of these expenses is covered under the major medical plan.

Deductible Frequency

calendar-year deductible

An all-causes deductible usually applies to medical expenses incurred within a 12-month period, typically a calendar year (January 1 to December 31). Under such a **calendar-year deductible**, expenses incurred from January 1 apply toward the deductible. Once it has been satisfied, the major medical plan pays the balance of any covered expenses incurred during the year, subject to limitations and coinsurance.

carryover provision

Many plans with a calendar-year deductible also have a **carryover provision** that allows any expenses (1) applied to the deductible and (2) incurred during the last 3 months of the year also to be applied to the deductible for the following year. No carryover is allowed if the deductible for the year is satisfied prior to the last 3 months of the year.

Example

Assume Ed satisfies only $450 of a $500 deductible prior to October 1. If less than $50 of covered expenses is incurred in the last 3 months of the year, the deductible is not totally satisfied for the year, but this amount can be applied to the deductible for the following year. If $50 or more of covered expenses are incurred in this

> 3-month period, not only is the deductible satisfied for the year but this amount
> ($50) can also be applied to the deductible for the following year.

accumulation period

benefit period

Medical expenses used to satisfy the deductible for each illness or accident must be
incurred within a specified **accumulation period**. The accumulation period is normally a
calendar year. Once the deductible for an accumulation period has been met, benefits are
paid for a **benefit period**. In medical expense insurance, this period usually begins when
the deductible is satisfied. Once the benefit period ends, an individual must again satisfy
the deductible before a new benefit period begins.

Coinsurance

coinsurance

Major medical expense plans contain a coinsurance provision, whereby the plan pays only
a specified percentage (in most cases, 80 percent) of the covered expenses that exceed the
deductible. The term **coinsurance** as used in this book refers to the percentage of covered
expenses that a medical expense plan pays. Thus, a plan with 80 percent coinsurance,
sometimes referred to as an 80/20 plan, pays 80 percent of covered expenses and a person
who receives benefits under the plan must pay the remaining 20 percent. It has been
argued that having such provisions is a financial incentive for employees to control their
use of medical care because they must bear a portion of the cost of any expenses incurred.

percentage participation

copayment

In some plans, there is a specified percentage participation, such as 20 percent. As commonly used, **percentage participation** refers to the percentage of covered medical
expenses that a medical expense plan does not pay and that a person receiving benefits
must pay. Note that percentage participation is sometimes referred to as a **copayment**,
but that terminology usually implies a fixed-dollar amount that an insured must pay for a
covered service. To make the matter even more confusing, some insurers refer to the percentage participation, rather than their portion of the benefit payment, as coinsurance.

Example

Karl's comprehensive major medical expense plan has a $500 calendar-year deductible and an 80 percent coinsurance provision that applies to all expenses. If Karl incurs $1,200 of covered medical expenses during the year, he will receive a $560 reimbursement from the insurance company, calculated as follows:

Covered expenses	$1,200
Minus deductible	−500
	$700
Times coinsurance percentage	× .80
	$ 560

Karl will have to pay the remaining $640 from his own pocket (that is, the deductible plus 20 percent of those expenses exceeding the deductible).

Just as deductibles vary, so do coinsurance provisions. Sometimes different coinsurance percentages apply to different categories of medical expenses. For example, outpatient psychiatric charges may be subject to 50 percent coinsurance, and other covered medical expenses may be subject to 80 percent coinsurance. In addition, certain medical expenses are subject to 100 percent coinsurance (such as preventive care), which in effect means that the expenses are paid in full, subject to any limitations.

stop-loss limit

In the case of catastrophic medical expenses, the coinsurance provision could result in an individual having to assume a large dollar amount of his or her own medical expenses. Consequently, many major medical expense plans have a **stop-loss limit** on the amount of out-of-pocket expenses that a covered person must bear during a specified time period. Policies sometimes specified that the coinsurance provision only applies to a limited amount of expenses and that there is full payment of covered expenses over this limit. Such an approach is often referred to as a coinsurance limit.

Example

Eve's medical plan has a $500 deductible, an 80 percent coinsurance provision that applies to the next $5,000 of covered expenses, and full coverage for any remaining covered expenses. Therefore, the most she will pay out of pocket in any year is the $500 deductible and 20 percent of $5,000 (for a total of $1,500).

out-of-pocket limit

Another way of limiting out-of-pocket expenses is to state the maximum dollar amount that any individual (or a family) must bear during a specific period. Once the individual reaches this limit, by paying either deductibles or a percentage of medical expenses, the policy pays additional covered expenses in full. This approach is often referred to as an **out-of-pocket limit**.

Example

Trevor's medical expense plan has a $400 deductible and an 80-percent coinsurance provision. He meets his $2,000 stop-loss limit if total medical expenses reach $8,400. Of this amount, Trevor is responsible for the $400 deductible and 20 percent of the remaining $8,000 (for a total of $2,000). The insurer pays any covered medical expenses in excess of $8,400.

Maximum Benefits

One of two ways is used to determine the maximum benefits that the insurer will pay for any covered person under a major medical contract. The use of a lifetime maximum was most common. The benefit maximum applies separately to each employee and each dependent covered under the contract.

Lifetime Maximum

lifetime maximum

When there was a **lifetime maximum**, the specified overall maximum applied to all medical expenses the insurer paid (after the application of deductibles and coinsurance) during the entire period an individual has coverage under the contract. The Affordable Care Act prohibits the use of lifetime maximums on essential health benefits. Nonessential health benefits may still enforce a lifetime maximum.

internal maximum

In addition to the overall lifetime maximum, some contracts contain an **internal maximum**. For example, a plan may have an unlmited overall lifetime maximum, but a $20,000 lifetime maximum for benefits relating to a specific nonessential health benefit treatment. In other words, the policy will pay only $20,000 for expenses relating to this condition unless the employer is subject to state laws that prevent such an internal maximum.

MANAGED CARE-TYPE PROVISIONS IN TRADITIONAL PLANS

Historically, traditional medical expense plans contained few provisions to manage the care of covered persons, but this situation continues to evolve. Provisions such as preadmission testing, hospital precertification, and second surgical opinions have been around for many years. It is also common for plans to provide benefits for treatment in facilities other than hospitals. The following discussion looks at these types of benefits.

Other managed care provisions and practices that may be found in traditional plans include the following:

- preapproval of visits to specialists
- carve-outs of benefits that the plan can provide cost effectively under arrangements that employ various degrees of managed care. Examples include prescription drugs, mental illness, substance abuse, and maternity management.

Some traditional major medical plans actually make wide use of managed care techniques; the primary factor that prevents them from being called managed care plans is that there are few restrictions on access to providers. Today most traditional plans have evolved into PPOs and use preferred-provider networks.

Preadmission Testing

preadmission testing

The first day or two of hospital confinement, particularly for surgical procedures, were historically devoted to necessary diagnostic tests and X rays. **Preadmission testing** requires the performance of these procedures on an outpatient basis prior to hospitalization and covers the costs as if the person were an inpatient. For benefits to be paid, these procedures must generally be (1) performed before a hospital confinement for surgery has been scheduled, (2) ordered by the same physician who ordered the hospital confinement, (3) performed in the hospital where the confinement will take place, and (4) accepted by the hospital in lieu of the same tests that would normally be performed during confinement. The plan pays benefits even if the preadmission testing leads to a cancellation of the scheduled confinement.

Hospital Precertification

hospital precertification

As a method of controlling costs, most medical expense plans contain utilization review programs. One aspect of these programs is **hospital precertification**. Such a program requires that a covered person or his or her physician obtain prior authorization for any nonemergency hospitalization. Authorization usually must also be obtained within 24 to 48 hours of admissions for emergencies.

The initial reviewer, typically a registered nurse, determines whether hospitalization or some type of alternative care is most appropriate and what the length of stay for the medical condition should be. If the preapproved length of stay is insufficient, the patient's physician must obtain prior approval for any extension.

Most plans reduce benefits if the hospital precertification procedure is not followed. Probably the most common reduction is to pay only 50 percent of the benefit that the plan would otherwise pay. If a patient enters the hospital after a denial of hospital precertification, many plans do not pay for any hospital expenses, while other plans provide a reduced level of benefits.

Second Surgical Opinions

second surgical opinion

In an attempt to control medical costs by eliminating unnecessary surgery, many medical expense plans, both traditional and managed care, provide benefits for a **second surgical opinion**.

Plans often use a voluntary approach for obtaining second surgical opinions. If a physician or surgeon recommends surgery, a covered person can seek a second opinion; the cost is borne by the medical expense plan. Sometimes the benefit is limited to a specific maximum, but usually the plan pays the costs of the second opinion, including X rays and diagnostic tests, in full. Some plans also pay for a third opinion if the first two opinions disagree.

In the last few years, it has become increasingly common for medical expense plans to require mandatory second opinions, which frequently apply only to a specified list of procedures. In most cases, a surgeon selected by the insurance company or other provider of benefits must give the second opinion. If conflicting opinions arise, the plan may require a third opinion.

The plan pays the costs of the second and third opinions in full. In contrast to voluntary provisions, mandatory provisions generally specify that the plan will pay benefits at a reduced level if the insured has surgery either without a second opinion or contrary to the final opinion.

Alternative Facilities for Treatment

Many traditional medical expense plans provide coverage for treatment in facilities that are alternatives to hospitals. The following discussion looks at care received under:

- extended care facility benefits
- home health care benefits
- hospice benefits
- birthing centers

Extended Care Facility Benefits

extended care facility

Many hospital patients recover to a point where they no longer require the full level of medical care provided by a hospital, but they cannot be discharged because they still require a period of convalescence under supervised medical care. An **extended care facility** (often called a convalescent nursing home or skilled-nursing facility) often exists to provide this type of care. To the extent that patients can be moved to such a facility, daily room-and-board charges can be reduced—often substantially.

Extended care facility coverage provides benefits to the person who is an inpatient in an extended care facility, which plans typically define as an institution that furnishes room and board and 24-hour-a-day skilled-nursing care under the supervision of a physician or a registered professional nurse. This definition does not include facilities that are designed as a place for rest or domiciliary care for the aged. In addition, facilities for the treatment of drug abuse and alcoholism are often excluded from the definition.

To receive benefits, the following conditions must usually be satisfied:

- A physician must recommend the confinement.
- Twenty-four-hour-a-day nursing care must be necessary.
- The confinement must commence within (1) 14 days after termination of a specified period of hospital confinement (generally 3 days) for which room-and-board

benefits were payable or (2) 14 days of a previous confinement in an extended care facility for which benefits were payable.

- The confinement must be for the same or a related condition for which the covered person was in the hospital.

Plans provide benefits in much the same manner as under hospital coverage. If they pay hospital expense on a semiprivate accommodation basis, they generally pay extended care facility benefits on the same basis.

Home Health Care Benefits

home health care coverage

Home health care coverage is similar to extended care facility benefits but designed for when the necessary part-time nursing care ordered by a physician following hospitalization can be provided in the patient's home. Coverage is for (1) nursing care (usually limited to a maximum of 2 hours per day) under the supervision of a registered nurse; (2) physical, occupational, and speech therapy; and (3) medical supplies and equipment, such as wheelchairs and hospital beds.

In most cases, the benefits payable are equal to a percentage, frequently 80 percent, of reasonable-and-customary charges. Benefit payments are limited to either a maximum number of visits (such as 60 per calendar year) or to a specified period (such as 90 days after benefits commence). In the latter case, the period may be a function of the unused hospital days, such as 3 days of home visits for each unused hospital day.

Hospice Benefits

hospice care

Hospices for the treatment of terminally ill persons are a relatively recent development in the area of medical care. **Hospice care** does not attempt to cure medical conditions but rather is devoted to easing the physical and psychological pain associated with death. In addition to providing services for the dying patient, a hospice may also offer counseling to family members. Although many people think of a hospice as a separate facility, a dying person can also receive this type of care on an outpatient basis in a home setting. Where hospice care is available, the cost of treating terminally ill patients is usually much less than the cost of traditional hospitalization. Hospice benefits may be subject to a specified maximum benefit, such as $10,000, or a time limit, such as 60 days.

Birthing Centers

birthing center

Another development in medical care is the increasing use of **birthing centers**, separate from hospitals. The cost of using birthing centers is considerably less than using hospitals. Nurse-midwives perform deliveries, and mothers and babies are released shortly after birth. The plan may pay benefits as if the mother had used a hospital and obstetrician, but charges the frequently pay charges in full as an incentive to use these lower-cost facilities.

COVERAGE FOR COMPLEMENTARY AND ALTERNATIVE MEDICINE

complementary and alternative medicine (CAM)

Since the early 1990s, the use of **complementary and alternative medicine (CAM)** increased dramatically, with estimates that over half of the population has used one or more of these types of services as alternatives to conventional treatments covered under medical expense plans. In addition, the majority of physicians have recommended CAM techniques, particularly for treatment of neck and back problems, anxiety, depression, and headaches. Examples of CAM services include the following:

- acupuncture
- biofeedback
- chiropractic treatment
- herbal medicine
- naturopathy
- homeopathy
- hypnosis
- massage therapy
- meditation
- relaxation
- therapeutic touch
- vitamin therapy
- yoga

The attractiveness of these programs has increased over the past several years for a number of reasons. Patients appreciate the rapport they develop with their CAM practitioners, and this is indicated by a higher degree of satisfaction with these practitioners than with their physicians. Patients also like the fact that CAM practitioners are more likely than traditional medical practitioners to actively involve patients in the development of treatment plans. As a result, patients are more likely to follow plans of CAM than they are to follow conventional medical treatment plans. Finally, complications from treatment are less likely than from conventional medical treatment, possibly because of the less-invasive nature of CAM.

Insurers and plan administrators have typically been leery of adding benefits for CAM because they fear increases in claims costs. This will obviously occur if covered persons use CAM in addition to traditional medical treatment. However, they often use it as a replacement for traditional medical treatment. If successful, costs might decrease. There is also concern over the qualifications and training of many of the persons who provide CAM.

Many insurance contracts and managed care plans provide limited benefits for chiropractic treatment and a smaller number cover acupuncture, sometimes due to state mandates. However, benefits are often subject to limitations. Some providers of medical benefits will add other types of CAM to their insurance contracts or managed care plans if the employer is willing to pay an increased premium. Employers may be willing to pay this cost as a response to employee interest or to differentiate their medical expense plan from those of other employers. Results of surveys vary, but it appears that most employers have benefit plans that cover chiropractic services, about 30 percent have plans that cover acupuncture, and about 20 percent have plans that cover some other forms of CAM.

To control costs, coverage of CAM is subject to a variety of controls. These include one or more of the following:

- annual or lifetime dollar limits
- limits on the number of annual visits
- a requirement that treatment is for specified medical conditions
- a requirement for a referral from a primary care physician

CHAPTER REVIEW

Key Terms and Concepts

medical expense insurance
health insurance
Medicaid
Children's Health Insurance Program
  (CHIP)
managed care
traditional (indemnity) medical
  expense plan
fee-for-service plan
service-benefit concept
indemnity concept
first-dollar coverage
hospital expense coverage
surgical expense coverage
surgical fee schedule
reasonable-and-customary charge
major medical coverage
comprehensive major medical
  coverage
Newborns' and Mothers' Health
  Protection Act
Women's Health and Cancer Rights
  Act
limitations
deductible

initial (straight) deductible
all-causes deductible
family deductible
common accident provision
calendar-year deductible
carryover provision
accumulation period
benefit period
coinsurance
percentage participation
copayment
stop-loss limit
out-of-pocket limit
lifetime maximum
internal maximum
preadmission testing
hospital precertification
second surgical opinion
extended care facility
home health care coverage
hospice care
birthing center
complementary and alternative
  medicine (CAM)

Review Questions

Review questions are based on the learning objectives in this chapter. For example, a [3] at the end of a questions means that the question is based on learning objective 3. If there are multiple objectives, they are all listed.

1. What is the purpose of medical expense insurance? [1]

2. Regarding the federal government's role in health care, how did the federal government become a major player in providing medical expense coverage during the 1960s? [1]

3. How was medical expense coverage affected by legislation in the 1970s through the 1990s? [1]

4. Describe the efforts that employers have used in recent years to control the cost of medical expense coverage. [1]

5. What changes have occurred in recent years in the relative market shares of the various methods for providing medical expense coverage? [1]

6. What are some of the reasons for the significant increases in the cost of health care? [2]

7. What are the major components of health care cost containment? [2]

8. How can design features of medical expense plans control costs? [2]

9. How can claims review generate cost savings? [2]

10. What characteristics should be contained in a managed care plan? [2]

11. What is the purpose of consumer-directed health care? [2]

12. Who are the providers of traditional medical expense coverage? [3]

13. Compare Blue Cross and Blue Shield organizations with private insurance companies with respect to each of the following features: [3]

    a. form of benefits provided

    b. types of benefits provided

14. Briefly describe the following basic medical expense coverages: [4]

    a. hospital expense benefits

    b. surgical expense benefits

15. How do insurance contracts typically define a surgical procedure? [4]

16. Explain how most insurance companies determine whether a surgical fee is reasonable and customary? [4]

17. What are the covered expenses for medical coverage? [5]

18. What types of exclusions do major medical contracts commonly contain? [5]

19. How does the Newborns' and Mothers' Health Protection Act affect coverage for maternity under medical expense plans? [5]

20. How does the Women's Health and Cancer Rights Act affect exclusions under medical expense plans? [5]

21. What types of limitations do major medical contracts usually place on the benefits they provide? [5]

22. What is an initial (straight) deductible and how does it apply to major medical plans? [5]

23. What is a family deductible? [5]

24. Explain the carryover provision associated with a calendar-year deductible. [5]

25. Why do different coinsurance percentages sometimes apply to different categories of medical expenses? [5]

26. Describe the methods insurers use to place a limit on the amount of out-of-pocket medical expenses that an individual must bear under the coinsurance provision of a major medical contract. [5]

27. Regarding precertification: [6]

    a.   What is the purpose of hospital precertification?

    b.   What are the possible penalties if the precertification process is not followed?

28. Explain how surgical benefits may be affected by

    (a) voluntary provisions and

    (b) mandatory provisions for second surgical opinions. [6]

29. What conditions must an individual usually satisfy in order to receive benefits for care in an extended care facility? [6]

30. What types of benefits does home health care coverage typically provide? [7]

31. How does hospice care often lower the cost of health care? [6]

32. Explain how medical expense plans might use birthing centers to control medical expenses. [6]

33. Regarding complementary and alternative medicine: [5]

    a.   Why have benefits for complementary and alternative medicine become more attractive in recent years?

b.　How can the cost of coverage for complementary and alternative medicine be controlled?

Review Question Answers

1.　The purpose of medical expense insurance is to provide protection against financial losses that result from medical bills because of accident and/or illness.

2.　The federal government became a major player in providing medical expense coverage by creating national health insurance programs for two segments of the population.

- Medicare provides benefits for persons aged 65 and older and certain disabled persons. The financing of the benefits under this program comes from three sources: government revenue, premiums of Medicare beneficiaries, and the Social Security and Medicare taxes paid by most working persons and their employers.

- The second program—Medicaid—provides health benefits for certain classes of low-income individuals and families.

3.　The passage of ERISA in 1974 thwarted initial state attempts to bring self-funded plans under their insurance regulations. This federal legislation freed self-funded plans from state regulation and hastened the growth of this financing technique.

Another significant piece of legislation was passed—the Health Maintenance Organization Act of 1973. This legislation encouraged the growth of HMOs by providing funding for their development costs and mandating that certain employers make these plans available to employees.

The State Children's Health Insurance Program (SCHIP) provides coverage to uninsured children 18 years old or younger who are from low-income families and who are ineligible for Medicaid.

4.　Employer efforts to contain costs have included the following:

- growth in the self-funding of benefits. Much of this growth came from small- and medium-sized employers.

- cost-shifting to employees. It became increasingly common for employers to raise deductibles and require employees to pay a larger portion of their medical expense coverage.

- requiring or encouraging managed care plans. Some employers dropped traditional medical expense plans and offered managed care alternatives only. A more prevalent approach was to offer employees a financial incentive to join managed care plans.

- increased use of managed care plans that are alternatives to HMOs, such as PPOs and point-of-service plans. These approaches often overcome the reluctance of some employees to participate in managed care plans.

5. In 2014, over 99 percent of employees were enrolled in managed care of high-deductible health plans—either HMOs, PPOs, or point-of-service plans. Less than 1 percent of the employees were in traditional plans. Sixty-one percent of covered employees were in partially or totally self-funded plans.

6. A combination of the following reasons produced significant health care cost increases:

- technological advances which have outpaced inflation
- increasing malpractice suits
- increases in mandates by the Affordable Care Act and the states that require insurance contracts to provide coverage for certain types of medical care and for treatment by certain types of providers. Although in some cases, these mandates simply transfer costs that persons were already paying to insurance companies, they also increase costs by increasing the overall utilization of certain types of care.
- an aging population

7. Major components of health care cost containment may be identified as follows:

- benefit plan design
- alternative benefit providers
- alternative funding methods
- claims review
- health education and preventive care
- encouragement of external cost-control systems
- managed care
- consumer-directed plans

8. Many design features have traditionally been in the form of contractual provisions in a medical expense plan that control plan costs by shifting them to employees. Other

plan design features have been aimed at reducing costs rather than shifting them by providing a higher level of benefits if less costly alternatives are used.

9. Claims review can generate cost savings in several ways. At a minimum, claims should be reviewed for patient eligibility, eligibility of the services provided, duplicate policies, and charges that are in excess of usual, customary, and reasonable amounts. Many medical expense plans routinely audit hospital bills, particularly those that exceed some stipulated amount, such as $5,000 or $10,000. They check for errors in such items as length of stay, services performed, and billed charges. Many insurance companies have found that each dollar spent on this type of review results in two or three dollars of savings.

10. A true managed care plan should have five basic characteristics:

    • controlled access to providers

    • comprehensive utilization management

    • preventive care

    • risk sharing

    • high-quality care

11. The purpose of consumer-directed health care is to put employees in charge of managing the health care dollars their employers provide. It exposes employees to the true cost of care and involves them in keeping health care expenditures under control.

12. Providers of traditional coverage include Blue Cross and Blue Shield plans, insurance companies, and employers using self-funded arrangements.

13. a. Blue Cross and Blue Shield plans involve two separate types of contractual relationships: a plan promises to provide specified services to a member, and it has contracts with providers of services whereby it reimburses the providers for the cost of services rendered to members. In general, plans neither bill members for the cost of covered services nor require them to file claim forms. This type of arrangement generally requires that members receive their services from providers participating in the plan; however, most hospitals and physicians are participants. If members can use nonparticipating providers (such as for emergencies), the plan usually pays benefits on an indemnity basis, as insurance companies do.

    In contrast, an insurance company that writes traditional medical expense coverage agrees only to reimburse a covered person for medical expenses up to the limits specified in the insurance contract. There is no contractual relationship between the providers of medical services and the insurance company. Thus, covered persons must file the appropriate claim forms. The insurance company's obligation (unless the covered person assigns benefits) is only to reimburse the covered person, not to actually pay the providers. However, most hospitals and many other providers require that a patient assign any potential insurance benefits to them before they will render services. In effect, such an assignment requires the insurance company to pay benefits directly to the provider on behalf of the covered person.

Even though a covered person may see little difference in the benefits received from either type of provider, the traditional distinction still exists: The Blues are providing services, whereas insurance companies are providing reimbursement for the cost of services.

b. Competition from insurance companies and increased cooperation between Blue Cross and Blue Shield plans have resulted in the Blues now offering virtually the same coverages as insurance companies. As the Blues expanded their scope of benefits beyond traditional hospital, surgical, and physicians' services, they have frequently included deductible and coinsurance provisions similar to those used by insurance companies.

Today, the Blues and insurance companies are major players in the managed care marketplace. Together they write the majority of PPO coverage and a significant portion of HMO coverage.

Most of the Blues now have their own HMOs, PPOs, and point-of-service plans. Similarly, insurance companies have expanded their offerings. Most insurers that write traditional medical expense coverage also offer PPO products; Some insurers offer only PPOs. A number of large medical expense insurers have entered the HMO market—sometimes through mergers with existing HMOs. Insurance companies also offer a wide array of products and services for use with self-funded plans.

The advantage many insurance companies have had over the Blues has been their ability to offer a wide variety of group benefits, including life insurance coverage and disability income coverage. However, because of changes in state laws and regulations, the Blues can now offer a wider range of group benefits to their members. Nevertheless, the Blues currently write relatively little coverage other than medical expense benefits.

14. a. Hospital expense coverage provides benefits for charges incurred in a hospital by a covered person (that is, the employee or his or her dependents) who is

aninpatient or, in some circumstances, an outpatient. Hospital inpatient benefits fall into two categories: coverage for room-and-board charges and coverage for "other charges." Coverage also extends to outpatient care for expenses arising from surgery. Emergency room treatment of accidental injuries within some specified period (varying from 24 to 72 hours) after an accident is usually covered as well.

    b.   Surgical expense benefits pay physicians' charges associated with surgical procedures performed in a hospital, surgical facility, or a doctor's office.

15. Insurance contracts typically define the term surgery broadly to include such procedures as suturing, electrocauterization, removal of a stone or foreign body by endoscopic means, and the treatment of fractures or dislocations.

16. In general, a reasonable-and-customary charge (sometimes referred to as a usual, customary, and reasonable charge or prevailing charge) is a charge that falls within the range of fees normally charged for a given procedure by physicians of similar training and experience within a geographic region.

17. The services and supplies provided under medical expense coverage generally include essential health benefits as well as other benefits such as:

- hospital room and board. Some plans also provide benefits for room and board in alternative facilities, such as birthing centers.

- other hospital charges

- charges of outpatient surgical centers

- anesthetics and their administration

- services of doctors of medicine or osteopathy

- professional services of a registered nurse. The services of a nurse midwife, nurse practitioner, and nurse anesthetist may also be covered.

- services of certain other types of providers. Most states mandate that the insurance contract cover services of certain types of providers other than physicians and nurses as long as the service is a covered benefit and the provider is operating within the scope of his or her license. The list of providers varies from state to state and may include one or more of the following: acupuncturists, audiologists, chiropractors, dentists, marriage and family therapists, dietitians, optometrists, physical therapists, physicians' assistants, podiatrists, psychologists, social workers, and speech pathologists.

- prescription drugs

- physical and speech therapy

- diagnostic X-ray and laboratory services

- radiation therapy

- blood and blood plasma

- artificial limbs and organs

- pacemakers

- casts, splints, trusses, braces, and crutches

- rental of wheelchairs and hospital beds

- ambulance services

18. Most major medical contracts commonly contain the following exclusions:

- occupational injuries or diseases to the extent that benefits are provided by workers' compensation laws or similar legislation

- services furnished by or on behalf of government agencies unless there is a requirement for either the patient or the patient's medical expense plan to pay for the services

- care provided by family members or when no charge would be made for the care received in the absence of the insurance contract

- cosmetic surgery, except as required by the Women's Health and Cancer Rights Act, unless such surgery is to correct a condition resulting from either an acci-dental injury or a birth defect

- experimental or investigational drugs and treatment

- convalescent, custodial, or rest care

- dental care except for (1) treatment required because of injury to natural teeth and (2) hospital and surgical charges associated with hospital confinement for dental surgery

- eye refraction, or the purchase or fitting of eyeglasses or hearing aids

- expenses either paid or eligible for payment under Medicare or other federal, state, or local medical expense programs

19. The act prohibits a group medical expense plan or insurer from restricting hospital benefits to less than 48 hours for both the mother and the newborn following a normal vaginal delivery and 96 hours following a cesarean section. In addition, a plan cannot require that a provider obtain authorization from the plan or insurer for a stay

within these minimums. Although a new mother, in consultation with her physician, might agree to a shorter stay, a plan or insurer cannot offer a monetary or nonmonetary incentive to the mother for this purpose.

20. Any benefit plan or policy that provides medical and surgical benefits for mastectomy must also provide benefits for the following:

    • reconstruction of the breast on which the mastectomy has been performed

    • surgery and reconstruction of the other breast to produce a symmetrical appearance

    • prostheses

    • physical complications of all stages of mastectomy, including lymphedemas

21. Although the expenses are covered, the amounts that are paid under the contract are limited. Benefits are very rarely paid for charges that exceed what is reasonable and customary. In addition, limitations are often placed on the following expenses:

    • hospital room and board. Benefits are generally limited to the charge for semiprivate accommodations unless other accommodations are medically necessary.

    • dental care, vision and hearing care. When these major medical contracts provide coverage, benefits are frequently subject to schedules and annual limitations.

    • ambulance service, such as $250 per trip

    • rental or purchase of durable equipment, such as $5,000

    • treatment for infertility. Such treatments might be subject to 50 percent coinsurance or a maximum dollar limit.

22. The initial (straight) deductible is used in comprehensive major medical plans. The deductible must be satisfied before the plan pays any insurance benefits.

23. A family deductible is a dollar amount which when satisfied, any future covered medical expenses for all family members will be paid.

24. A carryover provision allows any expenses (1) applied to the deductible and (2) incurred during the last 3 months of the year also to be applied to the deductible for the following year. No carryover is allowed if the deductible for the year is satisfied prior to the last 3 months of the year.

25. Different coinsurance percentages sometimes apply to different categories of medical expenses based on (1) the degree of discretion an insured may have in obtaining

services, (2) the need to limit plan expenses, or (3) a desire to discourage the use of costly services and encourage the use of cost-effective alternatives.

26. • Many major medical expense plans have a stop-loss limit on the amount of out-of-pocket expenses that a covered person must bear during a specified time period. Policies sometimes specified that the coinsurance provision only applies to a limited amount of expenses and that there is full payment of covered expenses over this limit. Such an approach is often referred to as a coinsurance limit.

   • Another way of limiting out-of-pocket expenses is to state the maximum dollar amount that any individual (or a family) must bear during a specific period. Once the individual reaches this limit, by paying either deductibles or a percentage of medical expenses, the policy pays additional covered expenses in full. This approach is often referred to as an out-of-pocket limit.

27. a. Hospital precertification is a program that requires a covered person or his or her physician to obtain prior authorization for any nonemergency hospitalization. Authorization usually must also be obtained within 24 to 48 hours of admissions for emergencies.

   b. Most plans reduce benefits if the hospital precertification procedure is not followed. Probably the most common reduction is to pay only 50 percent of the benefit that the plan would otherwise pay. If a patient enters the hospital after a denial of hospital precertification, many plans do not pay for any hospital expenses, whereas other plans provide a reduced level of benefits.

28. a. Under a voluntary provision, if the first and second opinions diverge, the final choice is up to the patient, and the plan's regular benefits are usually paid for any resulting surgery. As an incentive to encourage second opinions, some plans actually provide larger benefits for a covered person who has obtained a second opinion, even if it does not agree with the first opinion.

   b. In contrast to voluntary provisions, mandatory provisions generally specify that benefits are paid at a reduced level if surgery is performed either without a second opinion or contrary to the final opinion.

29. To receive benefits, an individual must usually satisfy the following conditions :

   • A physician must recommend the confinement.

   • Twenty-four-hour-a-day nursing care must be necessary.

   • The confinement must commence within (1) 14 days after termination of a specified period of hospital confinement (generally 3 days) for which room-and-board benefits were payable or (2) 14 days of a previous confinement in an extended care facility for which benefits were payable.

- The confinement must be for the same or a related condition for which the covered person was in the hospital.

30. Coverage is for (1) nursing care (usually limited to a maximum of 2 hours per day) under the supervision of a registered nurse; (2) physical, occupational, and speech therapy; and (3) medical supplies and equipment, such as wheelchairs and hospital beds.

31. Hospice care can offer lower costs because

- Hospice is devoted to easing the physical and psychological pain associated with death but does not incur the expense of trying to cure medical conditions.

- This type of care can also be provided on an outpatient basis in the dying person's home rather than incur the expense of a separate facility.

- Benefits may be subject to a specified maximum benefit, such as $5,000.

32. In a birthing center, nurse-midwives perform deliveries, and mothers and babies are released shortly after birth. The plan may pay benefits as if the mother had used a hospital and obstetrician, but frequently pay charges in full as an incentive to use these lower-cost facilities.

33. a. Patients develop a good rapport with their complementary and alternative medicine (CAM) practitioners to the extent that they report a higher degree of satisfaction with these practitioners than with their physicians. CAM practitioners are more likely than traditional medical practitioners to actively involve patients in the development of treatment plans. As a result, patients are more likely to follow plans of CAM than they are to follow conventional medical treatment plans. Finally, complications from treatment are less likely than from conventional medical treatment, possibly because of the less-invasive nature of CAM.

   b. Cost control of CAM coverage is achieved through one or more of the following medical expense plan provisions:

   - annual or lifetime dollar limits

   - limits on the number of annual visits

   - a requirement that treatment is for specified medical conditions

   - a requirement for a referral from a primary care physician

Chapter 7

Managed Care Plans

Learning Objectives

An understanding of the material in this chapter should enable the student to

1. **Explain how managed care plans differ from traditional medical expense plans, and describe the reasons for using managed care plans.**

2. **Explain the role of provider networks and utilization management in managed care plans.**

3. **Describe the characteristics of health maintenance organizations (HMOs) and explain the effect of the HMO Act of 1973.**

4. **Describe the characteristics of preferred-provider organizations (PPOs).**

5. **Describe the characteristics of point-of-service (POS) plans.**

6. **Explain the nature of benefit carve-outs, and describe the common types of carve-outs.**

This chapter discusses the concept of managed care, primarily by analyzing the types of managed care plans that are available—health maintenance organizations (HMOs), preferred-provider organizations (PPOs), and point-of-service (POS) plans. A discussion of benefit carve-outs, which often use managed care arrangements, follows. The chapter begins with an introduction to managed care plans and why a person might select managed care in general or a particular managed care plan. There is also a discussion of major features of managed care plans—provider networks and utilization review.

Managed care continues to evolve and is very different today from what it was just a few years ago. Three main types of managed care plans are available: health maintenance organizations (HMOs), preferred-provider organizations (PPOs), and point-of-service (POS) plans. Accountable care organizations (ACOs) are becoming more established due to the Affordable Care Act.

INTRODUCTION TO MANAGED CARE PLANS

Historically, a true managed care plan should have five main characteristics:

- controlled access to providers
- comprehensive utilization management
- preventive care

- risk sharing
- high-quality care

The major characteristic of managed care plans that differentiates them from traditional medical expense plans is probably the limitations on the choice of medical care providers that may be used. The question arises as to whether these choice limitations lead to a different quality of care. Despite these apparent or perceived differences, more than 95 percent of the population is now in some type of managed care plan, and the majority seems reasonably satisfied with the arrangement. In the past few years, much of the growth in managed care has come from employers with fewer than 50 employees. Unlike larger employers, who usually give employees a choice between one or more plans, small employers are more likely to offer a single managed care plan rather than multiple options.

Despite the relatively high level of satisfaction, there has been consumer backlash against managed care that has led to plan changes and legislation, particularly at the state level.

Limited Choice of Medical Providers

Managed care plans attempt to eliminate the unrestricted use of medical care providers by either requiring or encouraging members to use preapproved network providers. The earliest managed care plans, which were HMOs, usually provided no coverage for treatment outside the managed care network. This discouraged enrollment because many Americans valued the choice that had traditionally been available when they needed medical treatment.

The concept of managed care received considerable attention in the late 1960s and early 1970s, culminating in the passage of the Health Maintenance Organization Act of 1973. The act resulted in modest growth of HMO plans, but the real growth that came later for managed care was encouraged by several developments that gave members more choice in selecting providers of medical care, especially primary care physicians.

At the same time, the traditional insurance industry was entering managed care, primarily through the marketing of PPO products, which allowed more flexibility than most HMOs with respect to selection of specialists. In addition, benefits were usually available for treatment received outside a managed care network, although at a reduced payment level.

The popularity of PPO products with both employers and employees forced the HMOs to adopt even more flexibility. They did this through the establishment of point-of-service plans, which covered nonnetwork treatment. The typical POS plan is more flexible than a typical HMO but more restrictive than a typical PPO product.

Survey statistics on the availability of managed care plans to employees vary. One recent survey, however, estimated that 52 percent of employees are enrolled in PPO plans. The percentages for traditional HMOs and POS plans were 14 and 10, respectively. Twenty-four percent of employees are enrolled in a High Deductible Health Plan with an accompanying savings account.[1]

Quality of Care

A difficult question to answer is whether persons covered by managed care plans receive the same quality of care as persons covered under traditional medical expense plans. If the sole objective of a managed care plan is to offer coverage at the lowest possible cost, the quality of care may decline. However, some type of quality assurance program is one aspect of any managed care plan. If properly administered, this type of program can weed out providers who give substandard and unnecessary care. In this regard, managed care plans may be more progressive than the medical field as a whole.

Two developments relate to the quality of care provided by managed care organizations—an increased interest in accreditation and a consumer backlash against some aspects of managed care. This backlash has led to the introduction or passage of laws in many states aimed at solving consumer and provider concerns about access to care, quality of care, and choice.

Accreditation

accreditation

As managed care matured and became more widespread, there was an increasing focus by government, employers, and consumers on quality. This led many employers, particularly large employers, to require that managed care organizations for their employees meet some type of **accreditation** standards. Accreditation does more than just provide consumers with information about health plans. The process, which may cost a managed care organization several thousand dollars, compares it with benchmark standards of quality care. The organization knows where it stands in relation to its competitors and what it must do to become accredited or to achieve a higher level of accreditation.

---

1. The Henry J. Kaiser Foundation and Health Research Education Trust, Employer Health Benefits, 2015 Summary of Findings, 2015, page 3.

National Committee for Quality Assurance (NCQA)

The leading organization for accreditation is the **National Committee for Quality Assurance (NCQA)**, an independent, not-for-profit organization that has been accrediting managed care plans since 1991. It also accredits or certifies a number of other types of programs, including physician organizations and organizations that provide behavioral health care, utilization management, disease management, and credentials verification. Unlike some accrediting organizations, NCQA makes detailed information available to the public. The NCQA rates managed care organizations by evaluating each of the following five areas of performance:

- *Access and service.* Do plan members have access to the care and service they need?

- *Qualified providers.* Does the plan properly credential each physician's qualifications and what do plan members say about their providers?

- *Staying healthy.* Does the plan help people maintain good health and avoid illness?

- *Living with illness.* How well does the plan care for people with chronic conditions?

- *Getting better.* How well does the plan care for people when they become sick?

The possible ratings for each area of performance are best, very good, good, fair, or poor. From this information, the NCQA also gives overall accreditation outcomes to managed care plans. For HMOs and point-of-service plans, these ratings are

- excellent
- commendable
- accredited
- provisional
- denied

For PPOs, they are

- full
- one-year
- provisional
- denied

Health Plan Employer Data and Information Set (HEDIS)

The NCQA also has a set of performance measures that are designed to enable purchasers and consumers to have necessary information to reliably compare the performance of managed care plans. These measures, commonly referred to as the **Health Plan Employer Data and Information Set,** or **HEDIS**, has more than 70 measures that fall into the following categories:

- effectiveness of care

- access/availability of care

- satisfaction with the experience of care

- health plan stability

- use of services

- cost of care

- health plan descriptive information

Examples of a few of the measures that HEDIS reports, which can then be compared with suggested norms, are the following:

- percentage of adolescents receiving immunizations

- percentage of patients receiving beta blocker treatment following a heart attack

- percentage of patients receiving appropriate treatment for asthma

- percentage of women receiving osteoporosis management

Other organizations also play a major role in accrediting various types of health care organizations, including managed care plans, and make their data available to consumers. The Joint Commission on Accreditation of Healthcare Organizations (JCAHO) has accredited hospitals for many years. It can accredit home care organizations, assisted-living facilities, long-term care facilities, behavioral health care organizations, ambulatory care organizations, and laboratory services.

Another major accrediting organization is URAC (formerly the Utilization Review Accreditation Commission). URAC focuses on accrediting specific aspects of managed care, such as health utilization management. Managed care organizations, such as HMOs and PPOs, can have their own utilization management activities accredited if they meet prescribed standards. In addition, URAC accredits the activities of organizations that specialize solely in utilization management and that sell their services to managed care plans which do not have their own utilization management staffs. URAC also accredits organizations with respect to other aspects of managed care, including the following: case management, disease management, call center standards, network credentialing standards, and pharmacy benefit management.

Reactions to Consumer and Provider Concerns

As previously mentioned, the majority of employers and employees are reasonably satisfied with managed care plans but have increasing concerns. However, the satisfaction of physicians and other providers is much more negative, primarily because of decreased control over medical decisions for their patients and a loss of income. As a result, there has been what the media describe as a "backlash against managed care." In some ways, this terminology is inaccurate. First, some of the public's concerns, such as the lack of complete mental health parity and the issue of plans sometimes denying coverage as unnecessary, apply to the entire health care system. Second, although some of the concerns apply to all types of managed care plans, many apply solely to practices of HMOs.

This backlash has had several results:

- States continue to enact legislation that addresses many of the concerns.
- Managed care organizations voluntarily modify their practices in light of legislative activity and competitive forces.
- The federal government continues to grapple with consumer legislation.

State Reform

State legislatures in recent years have passed several types of laws aimed at managed care reform. Many of these laws, which exist in anywhere from 12 to almost all states, are described in the following paragraphs.

antigag-clause legislation

Antigag-Clause Rules. Almost all states have adopted **antigag-clause legislation** that prohibits managed care organizations from having provisions in their contracts that prevent physicians from discussing with patients treatment options that their plan may not cover or from referring very ill patients for specialized care by providers outside the plan.

Grievance, Review, and Appeal Procedures. A concern of many consumers over the years has been that managed care plans did not have adequate procedures to receive complaints or appeals about denials of coverage or to make decisions in a timely fashion. As a result, all states have passed some type of legislation that requires managed care plans to follow specified grievance, review, and appeal procedures. At a minimum, this legislation requires that a plan inform members of the procedures. There is often a specific period in which a plan must respond to a grievance, particularly when a member needs emergency care. Some states have gone further and require an independent external review process if a member is dissatisfied after going through the plan's grievance and appeal process. The decision of the independent review organization is usually binding on the parties.

any-willing-provider law

Any-Willing-Provider Laws. There has been some concern, often by physicians, that managed care organizations unnecessarily limit the access of patients to physicians. As a result, several states have passed an **any-willing-provider law**. These laws require that HMOs and other networks of medical care providers accept any provider who is willing to agree to the plan's basic terms and fees. Managed care plans have opposed this legislation on the basis that it will prevent them from negotiating for the best possible terms with highly qualified and efficient providers.

Mandatory POS Options. Several states have adopted legislation that requires managed care organizations to permit members to seek treatment from nonnetwork providers. The managed care organization must pay a portion, but not all, of the expenses incurred with these providers. In effect, such legislation turns a traditional HMO into a POS plan. In some states, this legislation applies only to HMOs with a minimum number of members, such as 10,000. In other states, HMOs must make a POS option available to employer groups above a certain size, such as 25 employees.

Continuity of Care. One drawback to receiving care through a managed care plan is that continuity of care may be lost if the provider ceases to be a part of the provider network, for whatever reason. Several states have recently addressed this issue through this legislation. For example, one state requires that the managed care plan continue to pay for care for up to 60 days, as long as such a continuation is appropriate. Many of the state laws deal primarily with pregnant patients and may, for example, require coverage to be continued until birth or shortly thereafter for any woman who is in the third trimester of a pregnancy at the time of her obstetrician's departure from the network.

Provider Protection. Most states now require that managed care plans disclose their criteria for selecting medical care providers, give these providers advance notice of contract termination, and provide them with procedures for contesting the termination. One purpose of this legislation is to address the concern that providers who give quality care might lose their provider contract if this care was more expensive or extensive than that the managed care plan deemed necessary.

Emergency Room Coverage. Managed care organizations have been criticized for often refusing to pay for emergency room care, claiming that emergency room treatment was unnecessary. For example, some plans do not pay if a member who goes to an emergency room with chest pains is found to have indigestion rather than a heart attack. The majority of states now require that a plan pay emergency room charges whenever a prudent lay-person considers a situation to be an emergency. In addition, the emergency room cannot delay care to get plan authorization for treatment.

Minimum Stays for Certain Procedures. As a result of concerns that some HMOs were compromising proper health care by forcing new mothers and their babies to leave the hospital too soon, most states adopted laws requiring coverage of minimum stays for mothers and newborns following deliveries. As a rule, these periods coincide with those required by the federal legislation. Most states also mandate that plans provide coverage for minimum stays following surgery for breast cancer. For example, several states mandate coverage for stays of 48 hours for mastectomies and 24 hours for lymph node dissection.

Plastic Surgery Mandates. Because of publicity over several cases in which HMOs denied coverage for reconstructive surgery—for example, to deformed children—several states enacted legislation to require all health insurance contracts or health plans to provide coverage for certain types of reconstructive surgery. This legislation may apply to the repair of birth defects only, or it may apply to a broader list of situations in which reconstruction might be needed because of mastectomies, trauma, infections, tumors, or disease.

Direct Access to Providers. Most states have passed laws to allow women covered under managed care plans to have direct access to obstetricians/gynecologists without obtaining approval or a referral from their health plan. A few states require direct access to other types of providers, such as dermatologists.

Voluntary Reform by Managed Care Organizations

Managed care organizations voluntarily initiate many managed care reforms. Some reforms are probably a result of the natural evolution of any form of financing and pro-viding health care. Other changes have occurred because of competition among managed care organizations for market share. However, most of the reforms probably are reactions to legislation that is proposed or passed by the states. After a few states pass a certain type of managed care legislation, there is often a tendency for managed care organizations nationwide to revise their plans to address the concerns that resulted in the legislation. There then may be little need for other states to adopt similar legislation, and, in fact, legis-latures often do not enact bills if the legislature learns that the managed care industry has already resolved the problem.

REASONS FOR USE OF MANAGED CARE

There are many reasons why employees elect coverage under a managed care plan. First, it may be the only plan the employer provides, although most employers allow a choice of benefit plans. In those situations, the following factors have been identified as reasons why an employee might select a managed care plan, in general, or a particular managed care plan:

- the reputation of the managed care plan. To some extent, this is a function of the managed care plan's experience. In areas where there have been managed care plans for many years, a larger percentage of employees participate. Employees are also concerned with perceived quality of care and are less likely to choose a plan known for frequent coverage denials and difficulty in obtaining referrals to specialists.

- the extent to which employees have established relationships with physicians. Employees are reluctant to elect a managed care option if it requires that they give up a physician with whom they are satisfied. In some cases, of course, this physician may also participate in the managed care plan. In general, new employees are more likely to elect a managed care option if they are new residents of the area or are just entering the labor force.

- costs. Managed care plans are obviously more attractive to employers when they offer a less expensive alternative to coverage under insurance company indemnity plans. As a rule, managed care plans are less expensive, and any employee share of the premium is lower. Even when the premium cost is comparable, there is often broader coverage and no deductibles or percentage participation. If employees view a managed care alternative as being less expensive in the long run, their participation is greater.

In the early days of the growth of managed care, employers were concerned primarily with cost savings when they adopted managed care plans. In a more mature managed care marketplace, employers are concerned with the same factors when they change plans as are employees: reputation, availability of providers, and cost. Throughout most of the late 1990s, the economy was booming, labor markets were tight, and employers faced relatively modest premium increases from year to year. As a result, employers were much more likely than in the past to modify managed care plans or to adopt new plans that were less restrictive, and therefore somewhat more expensive, in their management of care. With greater premium increases and a downturn in the economy, this trend is reversing.

PROVIDER NETWORKS

provider network

Networks of providers of health care services and the contracts that establish them are essential to managed care plans. These plans manage care primarily through the **provider network** that members in the plan are encouraged to use. Members may be required to receive covered medical care services from network providers only, or they must use these providers in order to obtain full plan benefits. To be successful, a managed care plan must create and maintain provider networks that do the following:

- contain qualified providers of health care services
- meet member needs for medical care services
- compensate network providers in a manner that encourages efficient use of resources

Qualified Providers of Health Care Services

credentials

Managed care plans specify the qualifications, known as **credentials**, that providers must have and maintain to be a network participant. Physicians, for example, must document their training, licensure, certification in a specialty, and malpractice insurance coverage.

In addition, they must be free of limitations, suspensions, or impairments that would affect their practice of medicine and hospital admitting privileges. Hospitals and other institutions must be licensed, accredited, and approved for participation in the Medicare program. Generally, a credentialing verification organization hired by the managed care plan obtains the information to determine if a provider has the qualifications that the plan requires. The plan repeats the credentialing process periodically to make sure that network providers continue to meet the required qualifications.

Member Needs for Medical Care Services

A managed care plan's provider network must encompass the broad scope of health services that members may need and be conveniently accessible to those members.

Network providers include physicians, hospitals and other institutions, diagnostic radiology and laboratory services, and therapy services. Among the other institutions in a network are facilities that provide outpatient care, including surgery, rehabilitation, and skilled-nursing care. Although a few managed care plans may hire their health care professionals and own their facilities, most managed care plans establish their networks through contracts with providers. These providers may be solo practitioners or participate in various types of groups under a variety of organizational structures. A provider often participates in several networks and also treats patients who are not members of managed care plans. Plans may also contract with specialty care organizations for specific services. These services may include psychiatric care, substance abuse treatment, rehabilitation, radiology, laboratory and pathology services, transplant surgeries, and prescription drug services.

Networks need to allow members to have reasonably convenient access to the broad range of services that the managed care plan offers. Therefore, managed care plans must develop and maintain sufficient numbers and types of providers to meet member health care needs in a geographic area. In addition, most network physicians must remain open to accepting as patients those members who are new to the plan as well as those who may wish to change providers. As a result, most plans maintain active recruitment and management programs to make sure that their networks keep pace with the needs of their ever-changing member populations in the areas and regions where these members reside. However, competition for members frequently requires managed care plans to expand their networks to offer members a choice of physicians, specialists, and hospitals beyond that required by scope of service and convenience alone.

Provider Compensation

A major objective of managed care plans is cost containment through the efficient use of health care resources. The method of provider compensation is one major component of this objective.

Providers are willing to grant preferred rates to managed care plans because as participants in the plan's network they anticipate an increased number of patients who will utilize their services. Or conversely, they will not lose patients to providers who are network providers. The specific payment method for network providers varies by the type of provider and the negotiating strength of the plan. However, the managed care plan's objective remains the same under any payment arrangement: to control the price of services and the overall increase in the cost of services utilized.

The compensation for services is determined by agreement in advance of the provision of services and a plan cannot change it for a specified period without notification. It also usually requires the agreement of each party. An important part of the contract with a provider outlines the provider's obligation to accept the agreed-upon amount as payment in full, except for copayments and other clearly identified amounts which the provider must collect from plan members.

The payment method also intends, if possible, to have providers participate to some degree in the increased cost of services utilized either through incentive payments for meeting utilization targets or penalties for failure to do so. The payment methods managed care plans use include capitation, modification of the traditional fee-for-service payment system, and per-day and per-case rates.

Capitation

capitation

Although far from dominant, the payment method historically associated with managed care plans is **capitation**. HMOs frequently employ this method for the payment of primary care physicians if each HMO member is required to select or is assigned a primary care physician who is responsible for the member's care. Primary care physicians provide members with basic health care services and coordinate additional care needs through referrals to other network physicians for certain medical specialist services. Under capitation, these physicians receive a fixed payment per month for each member without regard to the services a member may receive in any particular month. These rates reflect likely utilization of services by the plan's members based on age and gender and the cost of care in the area. Capitation provides physicians no financial incentives to overtreat patients.

incentive payment program

withhold arrangement

In conjunction with capitation, a managed care plan commonly establishes an **incentive payment program** that rewards physicians who meet budgeted cost and utilization levels for hospital and ancillary services. This program may include other criteria such as meeting member satisfaction and quality standards. Such an incentive program is called a **withhold arrangement** if it imposes financial penalties or decreases compensation for failure to meet these same criteria.

HMOs may also use capitation in some cases for the payment of specialty physicians and services such as substance abuse care and chronic condition management. Although infrequent, payment arrangements for inpatient hospital services may also use capitation.

Modified Fee-For-Service Payments

modified fee-for-service payment system

Despite the cost containment advantages of capitation, a **modified fee-for-service payment system** is the dominant method for compensating physicians in managed care plans. Many specialty physicians in managed care plans and most physicians in PPO networks receive payment in this manner. Managed care organizations also occasionally used it with hospitals.

With this method of compensation, the plan pays providers on a fee-for-service basis, subject to negotiated maximums per procedure. In most cases, this involves a discount from what the physician would charge a patient who did not participate in the managed care plan.

Modified fee-for-service payment arrangements employed by managed care plans often include some element of physician financial involvement in cost containment through rewards or penalties based on success in achieving the plan's utilization and cost targets. These rewards and penalties are similar to the incentive and withhold arrangements discussed previously under capitation payment.

Per-Day and Per-Case Payments

per-day rate

The dominant arrangement used by managed care plans for payment of inpatient hospital services is a negotiated **per-day rate**. With this approach, a plan pays a hospital a specified amount for each day a plan member is hospitalized, regardless of the actual cost of services on any particular day. The rate usually differs by type or level of care such as intensive care, obstetrics, or rehabilitation. The rate may decrease in relation to the days the member stays in the hospital or the aggregate days of stay for all plan members.

per-case rate

diagnosis-related groups (DRGs)

A managed care plan may be able to control costs more effectively by using a **per-case rate** to pay for hospital stays. With this approach, the plan pays a specified fee for all inpatient costs, regardless of a member's length of stay. This fee is based on such factors as a member's principal diagnosis, secondary diagnosis, surgical procedures, age, gender, and presence of complications. This system of classification of services is often referred to as **diagnosis-related groups (DRGs)**.

Managed care plans also often use a per-case rate to reimburse hospitals and other providers for nonphysician services that members receive on an outpatient basis.

UTILIZATION MANAGEMENT

utilization management

> **Utilization management** is the process by which a managed care plan ensures that members use health services effectively and efficiently. Such programs are essential to a managed care plan's control of medical care resource use and plan costs overall. A plan should design the provider compensation methods previously discussed to reinforce utilization management objectives or at least be compatible with them.

> Utilization management programs may be categorized as demand management, referral management, and management of institutional services. Case management and disease management are also important classes of utilization programs that cut across these categories.

Demand Management

demand management

> **Demand management** is a category of utilization management that guides members with respect to their personal health conditions. This category, which aims to reduce member need and use of medical services, includes wellness programs, health risk assessments, and provision of medical information.

Wellness Programs

wellness program

> A **wellness program** promotes the well-being of plan members. One goal of a wellness program is to discover and treat medical conditions before they become severe. A plan may accomplish this goal by providing such benefits as routine physicals and immunizations as well as screening for breast and prostate cancer, high cholesterol, high blood pressure, and diabetes.

A second goal of a wellness program is to reduce health risks by conforming personal behavior to a healthy lifestyle with healthy habits. Exercise and nutrition programs for weight management and fitness as well as smoking cessation programs are common plan benefits to achieve this goal.

Health Risk Assessments

health risk assessment

A **health risk assessment** is an evaluation of a member's health status using self-reported information. In addition to gathering data on health history and current medical conditions, the evaluation also elicits information on a member's behavior and habits. Members may have the option of using the Internet or an intranet to supply the assessment information. Taken together this information identifies the member's potential health care risks and gives the plan the opportunity to advocate member lifestyle and health habit changes that reinforce prevention and wellness programs. The extent to which a member requires counseling is usually left to the primary care physician who receives the health risk assessment from the managed care plan.

Medical Information Programs

medical information programs

Managed care plans have a variety of **medical information programs** that manage utilization by providing professional medical information that members can use for self-care of common conditions or to decide when to seek professional care. This service also provides members with in-depth information on specific diseases and treatment alternatives via newsletters, pamphlets, and authoritative texts. Plans may offer computer programs and Internet Web sites with interactive features to tailor the information to the member's needs. This technology can assist members in conjunction with their physicians to make informed decisions regarding their course of treatment.

Telephone advice lines also provide members with guidance from qualified professionals, usually nurses, regarding their medical care. Advice lines and the other sources of medical information also reinforce prevention and wellness programs while educating members on self-care.

Referral Management

referral management

gatekeeper (care manager)

referral

Referral management is a major function of many managed care plans, usually HMOs and point of service plans that require members to select a primary care physician. With this approach, a primary care physician acts as a **gatekeeper, or care manager**, in that the physician serves as a member's initial contact for medical care and referral for any additional medical services the member may need. The primary care physician must authorize the use of specialty physicians such as dermatologists, cardiologists, and urologists. The authorization, known as a **referral**, means that the primary care physician believes the member's health condition requires treatment by a specialist who is also a participant in the plan's network. Without a referral, the specialist receives no payment or a reduced payment from the plan. In this way the plan controls the cost of specialists' services and the services they may order. It also avoids unnecessary utilization.

The managed care plan does not intervene in the referral decision, but it must capture the authorization information to process the specialist's claim for full payment as a network service. The plan also uses the same information to report to the primary care physician on referral rates and the costs they generate. This may affect the physician's compensation under incentive or penalty payment arrangements.

Management of Institutional Services

Management of institutional services includes three types of review: prospective, concurrent, and retrospective. If the plan, the member, or the provider disputes a coverage decision, the plan usually has an external review process. In this process, outside specialists who do not work directly for the managed care plan determine whether the plan should pay denied benefits after reviewing the facts of the case. Disputes typically involve disagreements over medically necessary care or experimental treatments. Many states require review programs by an independent external party.

Prospective Management

prospective management

Prospective management of hospital and other institutional services is a standard part of a plan's utilization management program. Both inpatient admissions and outpatient procedures may require an authorization. When the plan's medical management department receives an authorization request, a utilization manager, usually a nurse, compares the proposed course of treatment or procedure with medical criteria for care based on the member's diagnosis. If a plan approves the request for an inpatient admission, the plan usually assigns an expected length of stay that allows benefits for that period and sets the anticipated discharge date.

Although the main purpose of the authorization is to avoid unneeded institutional care, the process serves additional purposes. If the course of treatment promises to be complicated and expensive, the plan may earmark the episode for case management. A plan may divert a member initially assigned to inpatient care to an outpatient care setting or to a specialty care organization where services may cost less and/or be more effective.

The participating network provider, either the institution or physician, is responsible for obtaining the authorization, not the member. Under the terms of the contract with the plan, if the institutional care proceeds without an authorization, the network providers may incur a payment reduction or be denied payment. If the member seeks treatment outside the provider network, which a PPO or a point-of-service plan would cover, the plan may still require an authorization. In this case, the member may be responsible for obtaining the authorization and is subject to a benefit penalty for failure to obtain it. In emergencies , the plan does not impose a penalty as long as the plan receives notification within a reasonable time.

Concurrent Management

concurrent management

Concurrent management, also known as continued stay review, is the management of inpatient utilization during a hospital stay. The plan's utilization manager conducts it by telephone or in person. Initially, the utilization manager confirms the member's status to be sure that discharge is planned within the assigned length of stay for which benefits are approved. If the member is recovering more quickly, the utilization manager may pursue an earlier discharge. However, if the hospital stay is expected to exceed the approved period, the utilization manager must reach a decision using medical criteria to authorize or deny coverage for additional days. Rather than deny coverage, the utilization manager usually tries to expedite the discharge. For example, the member's physician and the hospital's own utilization review and discharge-planning departments may agree that home care services and outpatient treatments will allow an earlier discharge. Nevertheless, resolution of disagreements may require a plan's medical director or consulting physician to contact the member's physician regarding the appropriateness of the care with referral to the plan's external review process if necessary.

Retrospective Management

retrospective management

The **retrospective management** of utilization is an evaluation of the patterns of medical care services that members received over a prior period to determine their appropriateness and to take corrective action as needed. The evaluation of utilization patterns, which a plan may do on a provider-specific or plan-wide basis, might show that certain tests and procedures are performed more or less frequently than the norm. The length of stay and charges for certain surgeries at some hospitals may be higher than expected. Retrospective evaluation of utilization patterns allows a plan to concentrate its utilization management efforts more effectively on problem areas. For example, retrospective evaluation might lead to a more stringent concurrent management program for a hospital with excessive lengths of stay. Data shared with providers might also cause some of them to modify their practices when they compare their treatment patterns with those of their peers.

Case Management and Disease Management

Case management and disease management are both programs of a health plan's utilization management department that actively coordinate the care of members who incur or are expected to incur unusually high medical care costs from complex courses of treatment resulting from injury or illness. The coordination often applies to a spectrum of the professional and institutional services previously mentioned with the goal of providing cost-effective care.

case management

disease management

Case management frequently involves a single episode of inpatient care that may occur, for example, because of an automobile accident, heart attack or high-risk pregnancy. By contrast, **disease management** focuses on selected medical conditions that are chronic, severe, and expensive to treat. It attempts to control the course of the disease and avoid the need for expensive medical care services.

Education of members to effectively manage their conditions is an integral part of these programs.

HEALTH MAINTENANCE ORGANIZATIONS

health maintenance organization (HMO)

A **health maintenance organization (HMO)** is an organized system of health care that provides a comprehensive array of medical services on a prepaid basis to voluntarily enrolled persons living within a specified region. HMOs act like insurance companies and the Blues in that they finance health care. However, unlike insurance companies and the Blues, they also deliver medical services.

For many years, prepaid group practice plans (as HMOs were once called) operated successfully in many parts of the country. However, growth was relatively slow until the passage of the Health Maintenance Organization Act of 1973. This act resulted from a belief on the part of the federal government that HMOs were a viable alternative method of financing and delivering health care and thus should be encouraged. In fact, the act also resulted in many employers being required to offer their employees the option of coverage by an HMO instead of by a more traditional medical expense plan. There are approximately 550 HMOs in existence, with the 10 largest plans enrolling about 25 percent of all HMO participants.

Characteristics of HMOs

HMOs have several characteristics that distinguish them from traditional medical expense contracts that insurance companies and the Blues offer.

Comprehensive Care

HMOs offer their members a comprehensive package of health care services, generally including benefits for outpatient services as well as for hospitalization. In the past, members usually got many of these services at no cost except the periodically required premium. However, in today's environment, they typically impose a copayment for certain services. For example, the copayment for physician office visits is usually in the range of

$10 to $50. Some HMOs also have an annual deductible that might apply to some services or to hospitalization only.

Delivery of Medical Services

HMOs provide for the delivery of medical services, which in some cases is performed by salaried physicians and other personnel employed by the HMO. Although this approach is in contrast to the usual fee-for-service delivery system of medical care, some HMOs do contract with providers on a fee-for-service basis.

Members must obtain their care from providers of medical services who have affiliation with the HMO. Because HMOs often operate in a geographic region no larger than one state or a single metropolitan area, this requirement may result in limited coverage for members if they receive treatment elsewhere. Most HMOs do have "out-of-area coverage," but usually only in the case of medical emergencies.

direct-access HMO

HMOs emphasize treatment by primary care physicians to the greatest extent possible. These practitioners provide a gatekeeper function and historically have controlled access to specialists. The traditional HMO covers benefits provided by a specialist only if the primary care physician recommends the specialist. This specialist may be a fellow employee in a group-practice plan or a physician who has a contract with the HMO. The member may have little or no say regarding the specialist selected, which has been one of the more controversial aspects of HMOs and one that has discouraged larger enrollment. In response to consumer concerns, many HMOs now make the process of seeing a specialist easier. Referrals can often be made by nurses in physicians' offices or by staff members of the HMO whom members can contact by telephone. Some HMOs, referred to as **direct-access (or self-referral) HMOs**, allow members to see network specialists without going through a gatekeeper. However, the specialist may have to contact the HMO for authorization before proceeding with tests or treatment. A variation of an HMO, called a *POS plan*, may allow even more choice by incorporating out-of-network benefits as well.

Cost Control

A major emphasis of HMOs is the control of medical expenses. HMOs attempt to provide treatment on an outpatient basis whenever possible. Because insurance companies and the Blues have provided more comprehensive coverage for a hospitalized person in the past, less expensive outpatient treatments were often not performed. This emphasis on outpatient treatment has resulted in a lower hospitalization rate for HMO members than for the population as a whole. However, some of this decreased hospitalization rate over the years appears to be a result of younger and healthier employees having been more likely to elect HMO coverage. This increased emphasis on outpatient treatment has resulted in HMOs often providing better coverage than other types of plans for mental health, alcoholism, or drug addiction if a member receives the treatment outside a hospital setting. However, if the member needs hospitalization, HMOs may have more limited benefits than other types of plans.

HMOs practice a greater degree of utilization management and control than do other types of health plans. In addition to the usual types of prospective review, such as hospital preadmission certification or second surgical opinions, other techniques are often used, such as controlled access to specialists by gatekeepers and preauthorization for certain outpatient procedures. Note that the burden for obtaining preadmission certification or preauthorization for medical procedures in general lies with the plan physician, not the plan member. This is in contrast to traditional medical expense plans and nonnetwork PPO coverage, where that responsibility is on the plan member.

HMOs are more likely than other types of health plans to conduct a high degree of concurrent management while patients are hospitalized. In addition, HMOs closely monitor the practice patterns of physicians. If a physician, for example, orders a higher-than-average number of diagnostic tests or admits a disproportionate number of patients to hospitals, the HMO reviews the situation with the physician to determine whether the physician follows proper practice. If the physician does not, the HMO may help the physician adopt better standards.

Physicians sometimes are not aware of all alternatives to hospitalization or that the medical community has changed its standards regarding the effectiveness and frequency of some diagnostic tests. Working with the physician may result in an effective change in practice patterns or, in extreme cases, the termination of the physician from the plan. HMOs that monitor practice patterns closely may also contact physicians who do not seem to be ordering enough diagnostic tests or who provide lower-than-usual amounts of preventive care.

HMOs also tightly control payments to physicians and other providers of medical services. In some cases, these providers are employees of the HMO. In other cases, HMOs control providers' compensation by capitation or by other arrangements under which the providers share some of the risk for costs that exceed certain levels.

Sponsorship of HMOs

physician-hospital organizations (PHOs)

Traditionally, most HMOs operated as nonprofit organizations and had the majority of members until a few years ago. Most new HMOs are profit making, and the majority of members have coverage under this type of organization. Many members are covered by plans that insurance companies or the Blues sponsor. Sponsorship may also come from physicians, hospitals, labor unions, consumer groups, or private investors. Some recently established HMOs have been formed by **physician-hospital organizations (PHOs)**. A PHO is a legal entity that is formed by one or more physicians' groups and hospitals. It negotiates, contracts, and markets the services of the physicians and the hospitals. PHOs may form their own HMOs, or they may contract with existing HMOs or other types of managed care organizations.

In addition to actually sponsoring and owning HMOs, some insurance companies are actively involved with them in a variety of ways. These include

- consulting on such matters as plan design and administration

- administrative services, such as actuarial advice, claims monitoring, accounting, and computer services

- marketing assistance, such as designing sales literature or selling the products through the agents of insurance companies

- providing hospitalization coverage. HMOs that do not control their own hospital facilities may provide this benefit by purchasing coverage for their members.

- providing emergency out-of-area coverage. An insurance company operating on a national basis may be better equipped to administer these claims than an HMO.

- providing financial support in a variety of ways, including reinsurance if an HMO experiences greater-than-expected demand for services and agreements to bail out financially troubled HMOs

Types of HMOs

closed-panel plans

There are several types of HMOs. The earliest plans can best be described as **closed-panel plans**, under which members must use physicians employed by the plan or by an organization with which it contracts. With most closed-panel plans having many general practitioners, members can usually select their physician from among those accepting new patients and make medical appointments just as if the physician were in private practice. However, there is frequently little choice among specialists because a plan may have a contract with only one physician or a limited number of physicians in a given specialty.

The three different types of closed-panel plans—staff-model HMOs, group-model HMOs, and network-model HMOs—are discussed in more detail below.

open-panel plans

Many newer HMOs have been formed as individual practice associations (IPAs), which are **open-panel plans**. This type of plan has more flexibility with respect to members choosing physicians and the ability of physicians to participate in the plan. IPAs are slightly more prevalent than closed-panel plans.

Staff-Model HMO

staff-model HMO

Under a **staff-model HMO**, the HMO owns its own facilities and hires its own physicians. It may own hospitals, laboratories, or pharmacies, or it may contract for these services. The HMO may also have contracts with specialists to treat members if it is not large enough to justify hiring its own specialists in a given medical field.

Staff-model HMOs pay employees a salary and possibly an incentive bonus. A staff-model HMO offers a great degree of control over costs because it controls the salaries of the physicians who might find themselves unemployed if the HMO is unprofitable or if they do not provide care within the cost and utilization parameters of the HMO.

Despite the potential for cost savings in staff-model HMOs, few have actually been established, primarily because of high start-up costs and high fixed costs once they are operating.

Group-Model HMO

group-model HMO

Under a **group-model HMO**, physicians (and other medical personnel) are employees of another legal entity that has a contractual relationship with the HMO to provide medical services for its members. In most cases, this is an exclusive arrangement and the entity's physicians only treat members of the HMO. These physicians also typically operate out of one or more common facilities.

Under a group-model plan, the HMO may contract with a single provider of medical services or with different providers for different types of services (for example, one contract for physicians' services and another for hospital services). The HMO often pays for services on a capitation basis, which means that the provider of services gets a predetermined fee per month for each member and must provide any and all covered services for this capitation fee. The fee is independent of how the provider compensates its own employees. Under this arrangement, the provider shares the risk in that it loses money if utilization is higher than expected or increases its profit if utilization is lower than expected. Therefore, the provider has a very real incentive to control costs.

Accountable Care Organizations

accountable care organizations

An accountable care organization (ACO) is a cohort of medical providers who, as a group, are accountable for the quality, cost, and efficiency of the care patients receive. Their services are delivered primarily for Medicare beneficiaries. The providers may provide services for primary care and specialty care as well as institutional care. Participants in a successful ACO will share in the savings achieved by providing efficient quality care.

Network-Model HMO

network-model HMO

The most common type of closed-panel plan is the **network-model HMO**. It differs from a group-model HMO in that it contracts with two or more independent groups of physicians to provide medical services to its members. Physician groups that enter into this type of arrangement often also treat non-HMO patients on a fee-for-service basis.

Individual Practice Associations

individual practice association (IPA)

In an **individual practice association (IPA)**, participating physicians practice individually or in small groups at their own offices. In most cases, these physicians accept both non-HMO patients and HMO members. IPAs are open-panel plans because members choose from a list of participating physicians. The number of physicians participating in this type of HMO is frequently larger than the number participating in group practice plans and may include several physicians within a given specialty. In some geographic areas, most physicians may participate; in other geographic areas, only a relatively small percentage of physicians may participate.

IPAs use several methods to compensate participating physicians. The most common is a fee schedule based on the services provided to members. To encourage physicians to be cost effective, it is common for plans to have a provision for reducing payments to physicians if the experience of the plan is worse than expected. On the other hand, the physicians may receive a bonus if the experience of the plan is better than expected. Particularly with respect to general practitioners, some IPA plans pay each physician a flat annual amount for each member who has elected to use him or her. For this annual payment, the physician must see these members as often as necessary during the year.

Mixed-Model HMOs

mixed-model HMO

Some HMOs operate as **mixed-model HMOs**, which means that the organization of the plan is a combination of two or more of the approaches previously described. Such a combination generally occurs as a plan continues to grow. For example, a plan might have been established as a staff-model HMO, and later the HMO decided to expand its capacity or geographic region by adding additional physicians under an IPA arrangement. Some mixed models have also resulted from the merger of two plans that each used a different organizational form.

Extent of HMO Use

There are approximately 86 million employees and dependents covered under HMOs, with the enrollment varying considerably by geographic region. For example, California has approximately 20 million members or 23 percent of the national HMO population enrolled in HMOs.[2] Other states have significantly less HMO enrollment. There are also significant variations by metropolitan area, with most members living in large metropolitan areas.

Some employers offer HMO options only. However, in most cases, employees covered by HMO plans have elected this form of coverage as an alternative to other types of coverage. The administrative details of options that allows choice among different types of plans may be burdensome and expensive for small employers, but they seem to pose few problems for large employers with specialized employee benefit staffs. In many cases, the financial

---

2.   The Henry J. Kaiser Foundation, *statehealthfacts.org,* kff.org/other/state-indicator/total-hmo-enrollment/, Jan, 2015.

consequences to the employer of such an option are insignificant because the employer makes the same contribution on an employee's behalf regardless of which plan an employee selects. The general attitude of employers toward HMOs seems to be somewhat ambivalent: Some employers had been in favor of them, others against, and the majority indifferent. However, according to several recent studies, most employers feel that HMOs have been a very effective technique for controlling benefit costs.

When there is a choice of medical expense plans, most employees do not elect an HMO option unless there is a financial incentive to do so. However, studies have revealed that employees who have elected HMOs are for the most part satisfied with their choice and are unlikely to switch back to another plan as long as the HMO option remains available.

Health Maintenance Organization Act of 1973

Health Maintenance Organization Act

federally qualified HMO

The **Health Maintenance Organization Act of 1973** has had a significant influence on both the interest in and the growth of HMOs. The act introduced the concept of the **federally qualified HMO**. For several years after the act's passage, most HMOs were formed to take advantage of this federal qualification, which entitled them to federal grants for feasibility studies and development (including grants to solicit members) and federal loans (or loan guarantees) to assist them in covering initial operating deficits. In addition, many employers were required to make federally qualified HMOs available to their employees until late 1995.

Requirements for Federal Qualification

To become federally qualified, an HMO must meet certain requirements (set forth in the act) to the satisfaction of the Secretary of Health and Human Services. In return for a periodic prepaid fee, an HMO must provide the specific basic benefits to its members at no cost or with nominal copayments. These include the following:

- physicians' services, including consultant and referral services, up to 10 percent of which may be provided by physicians who are not affiliated with the HMO
- inpatient and outpatient hospital services
- medically necessary emergency health services
- short-term (up to 20 visits) outpatient mental health services

- medical treatment and referral services for alcohol or drug abuse or addiction
- diagnostic laboratory services and diagnostic and therapeutic radiological services
- home health services
- preventive health services, such as immunizations, well-baby care, periodic physical examinations, and family-planning services
- medical social services, including education in methods of personal health maintenance and in the use of health services

The HMO may also provide optional supplemental benefits either as part of its standard benefit package or as optional benefits for which it may charge an additional premium. Some of these include the following:

- vision care
- hearing care
- dental care
- additional mental health services
- rehabilitative services
- prescription drugs

State Regulation

The states heavily regulate HMOs. All states have numerous laws that are enforced by various state officials, often including both the insurance and public health commissioners. In many cases, the state legislation largely duplicates the federal HMO act.

Almost all states have adopted the NAIC Health Maintenance Organization Model Act, which focuses substantially on issues relating to licensing of HMOs and the maintenance of their financial solvency. However, it also addresses numerous other issues, such as the types of activities in which HMOs can engage, the requirement of a quality assurance program, standards for materials given to members, grievance procedures, enrollment periods, and coordination-of-benefits provisions.

PREFERRED-PROVIDER ORGANIZATIONS

A concept that continues to receive considerable attention from employers and insurance companies is the preferred-provider organization. A few PPOs existed on a small scale for many years, but since the early 1980s PPOs have grown steadily in number and in membership. Today, PPOs provide coverage for medical expenses to more Americans than do HMOs, primarily because of the flexibility of covered persons to choose their own medical providers.

What Is a PPO?

preferred-provider organization (PPO)

The term **preferred-provider organization (PPO)** tends to be used in two ways. One way is to apply it to health care providers that contract with employers, insurance companies, union trust funds, third-party administrators, or others to provide medical care services at a reduced fee. Using this definition, a PPO may be organized by the providers themselves or by other organizations, such as insurance companies, the Blues, HMOs, or employers. Like HMOs, they may take the form of group practices or separate individual practices. They may provide a broad array of medical services, including physicians' services, hospital care, laboratory costs, and home health care, or they may be limited only to hospitalization or physicians' services. Some of these organizations are very specialized and provide specific services, such as dental care, mental health benefits, substance abuse services, maternity care, or prescription drugs. This book refers to these providers not as *PPOs* but as *preferred providers or network providers.*

The second use of the term *PPO*, and the one generally assumed when the term is used throughout this book, is to apply it to benefit plans that contract with preferred providers to obtain lower-cost care for plan members. PPOs typically differ from HMOs in several respects. First, the PPO generally pays the preferred providers on a fee-for-service basis as their services are used. However, fees are usually subject to a schedule that is the same for all similar providers within the provider network, and providers may have an incentive to control utilization through bonus arrangements. Second, employees and their dependents are not required to use the practitioners or facilities that contract with the PPO; rather, they can make a choice each time medical care is needed, and the PPO also pays benefits for care provided that nonnetwork providers furnish. However, employees have incentives to use network providers; they include lower or reduced deductibles and copayments as well as increased benefits, such as preventive health care. Third, most PPOs do not use a primary care physician as a gatekeeper; employees do not need referrals to see specialists.

Successful PPOs today emphasize quality care and utilization review. In selecting physicians and hospitals, PPOs look both at the type of care provided and the provider's cost effectiveness. In this era of fierce competition among medical care providers, these physicians and hospitals are often willing to accept discounts in hopes of increasing patient volume. It is also important for a PPO to monitor and control utilization on an ongoing basis and to deal with groups of preferred providers that monitor their own costs and utilization. Generally, however, PPOs do not monitor their preferred providers as closely as HMOs do.

Variations

Over time, PPOs have continued to evolve. A few PPOs compensate providers on a capitation basis, and a few others perform a gatekeeper function. If a member's primary care physician does not recommend a specialist, PPO benefits may be reduced. With these changes, it is sometimes difficult to determine the exact form of a managed care organization. However, those that operate as traditional HMOs generally provide medical expense coverage at a slightly lower cost than do those that operate as traditional PPOs, but there are wide variations among HMOs as well as among PPOs. Therefore, a careful analysis of quality of care, cost, and financial stability is necessary before the selection of a particular HMO or PPO.

exclusive-provider organization (EPO)

Another variation of the PPO is the **exclusive-provider organization, or EPO**. The primary difference is that an EPO does not provide coverage outside the preferred-provider network, except in emergencies and those infrequent cases when the network does not contain an appropriate specialist. This aspect of an EPO makes it very similar to an HMO. The number of EPOs is small.

Sponsorship

The majority of PPOs are owned by insurance companies and the Blues. Some are owned by HMOs to give them another product in their health plan portfolios to offer employers. Others have a variety of ownership forms, including third-party administrators, private investors, and groups of physicians and/or hospitals.

Benefit Structure

centers of excellence

The basic benefit structure of a PPO is very similar to that of the traditional comprehensive major medical contract. The most significant difference is that there is a higher level of benefits for care received from network providers than there is for care received from nonnetwork providers. Many PPOs have extensive networks of preferred providers, particularly in the geographic areas in which they operate, and there is little reason to seek care outside the network. Some of these PPOs also have reciprocity agreements elsewhere with networks of other PPOs and hospitals (called **centers of excellence**) that have excellent outcomes and reputations for certain types of medical procedures, such as cancer treatment, organ transplants, or burn treatment. Under these agreements, the PPO pays benefits as if a member receives care from network providers. Other PPOs have more limited networks, and the need and desire for treatment from nonnetwork providers is greater.

The level of benefits under PPOs may vary because of differences in deductibles, coinsurance, and precertification rules. There may also be a few additional benefits that are available only if a member receives care from a network provider. Finally, the procedures for filing claims also differ. The major purpose of these differences is to encourage an employee or dependent to receive care from preferred providers who agree to charge the plan a discounted fee.

Deductibles

A PPO may have annual deductibles that apply separately to network and nonnetwork charges. For example, these might be $500 and $1,000, respectively. However, some PPOs have no deductible for network charges. A PPO may waive deductibles for some medical services, such as emergency services.

Coinsurance

PPOs often use coinsurance percentages that are 20 percent (and occasionally 30 percent) lower when a member receives care from nonnetwork providers. A frequently found provision applies 90 percent coinsurance to network charges and 70 percent coinsurance to nonnetwork charges. Coinsurance provisions of 100/80, 90/80, 100/70, and 80/60 are also commonly used. As with deductibles, a PPO may waive the percentage participation for certain medical services. In addition, different stop-loss limits or coinsurance caps, such as $1,000 and $3,000, may apply to network and nonnetwork charges.

Although PPOs typically have higher coinsurance percentages for network charges than do traditional major medical plans, a covered person may be responsible for copayments in some circumstances. For example, there might be a copayment, typically ranging from $10 to $25, for each a visit to a primary care physician.

allowable charge

In evaluating PPOs, it is important to determine the basis the PPO uses to apply the coinsurance percentage. For example, assume a plan uses 80 percent coinsurance for nonnetwork charges and that a charge of $100 is incurred for a medical procedure from a nonnetwork provider. Most PPOs first determine whether this charge is usual, customary, and reasonable. If it is, the plan pays $80. If the plan determines that the usual, customary, and reasonable charge is $90, it will be 80 percent of that amount, or $72. However, some plans apply the coinsurance percentage to what they often refer to as an **allowable charge**. In most cases, this is the amount that the PPO pays to network providers for the same procedure.

Precertification Rules

PPOs often have precertification requirements for many types of hospitalizations, out-patient procedures, and medical supplies. For network benefits, the person responsible for obtaining the needed certification is the network provider, and the PPO does not penalize a member if the network provider fails to obtain the proper precertification. (This becomes an issue between the PPO and the provider.) However, this responsibility shifts to the employee or family member for nonnetwork services. If he or she does not obtain a required precertification , there usually is a reduction in benefits. For example, what was once 80 percent coinsurance might shrink to 60 percent.

Additional Network Benefits

For the most part, PPOs pay benefits for the same medical procedures, whether a network or a nonnetwork provider performs them. However, some PPOs cover a few procedures only if a member receives them from network providers.

Claims

No claim forms are required for network services. The covered person merely pays any required copayment, and the provider of medical services does the paperwork needed to receive the additional amounts payable by the plan. Just as in traditional major medical plans, it is the ultimate responsibility of the covered person to file the claims forms necessary to receive benefits for nonnetwork care. Of course, the provider may do much of the paperwork and accept an assignment of benefits.

Regulation

PPOs initially were subject to much less stringent regulation than HMOs with respect to their managed care activities. In fact, they were largely unregulated. As a result, the NAIC created the Preferred Provider Arrangements Model Act, which the majority of states adopted. The act is relatively brief and establishes only a minimal regulatory framework. The act requires that PPOs incorporate cost-containment mechanisms, such as utilization review, to determine whether a service is medically necessary. Covered persons must have reasonable access to medical services. The act also allows PPOs to provide incentives for persons to use the preferred-provider network and to place limitations on the number and types of providers with whom they contract.

Note that most PPO contracts also meet the definition of insurance and are subject to the same regulation by state insurance departments as traditional insurance contracts with respect to contract provisions and benefit mandates.

POINT-OF-SERVICE PLANS

point-of-service (POS) plan

A type of managed care arrangement is the **point-of-service (POS) plan**. A POS plan is a hybrid arrangement that combines aspects of a traditional HMO and a PPO. With a POS plan, participants in the plan elect, at the time they need medical care, whether to receive treatment within the plan's tightly managed network, usually an HMO, or outside the network. POS plans reimburse members for care they receive outside the network in the same manner as described earlier for nonnetwork services under PPO plans.

open-ended HMO

There are two basic types of POS plans: the open-ended HMO and the gatekeeper PPO. An **open-ended HMO** is by far the most common form and is the HMO industry's response to the demand for more consumer flexibility in the choice of providers, even though it increases costs somewhat. It essentially consists of traditional HMO coverage with an endorsement for nonnetwork coverage. It can take the basic form of any of the HMOs previously described. However, at any time, a member can elect to go outside the HMO network of medical care providers.

gatekeeper PPO

It can be argued that any PPO is actually a POS plan. However, the normal usage of the term POS implies a higher degree of managed care than is found in most PPOs. A **gatekeeper PPO** requires that the PPO participant elect a primary care physician in the manner of an HMO participant. This physician acts as a gatekeeper to control utilization and refer members to specialists within the PPO network. However, any time that a member needs care, he or she can elect to go outside the network. A traditional PPO or insurance company that does not own an HMO generally forms this type of PPO.

Under some POS plans, a covered person can go outside the plan's network without informing the plan of this fact. In other POS plans, the person must notify the gatekeeper that he or she will seek such treatment. Even though the gatekeeper has no power to prevent the nonnetwork treatment, the gatekeeper may be able to convince the person that proper treatment is available within the network. Furthermore, the gatekeeper can better manage future medical care by being aware of all medical treatment that a person is receiving.

MULTIPLE-OPTION PLANS

multiple-option plan

At one time, an employer who wanted to make an HMO or POS option available to employees had to enter into a separate contractual arrangement with an HMO. Several insurance companies and Blue Cross and Blue Shield plans now provide all these options under a single medical expense contract, referred to as a **multiple-option plan**. For example, one insurer markets a so-called quadruple-option plan that gives employees the choice of a high-deductible health plan, a PPO, an HMO, or a POS plan.

These plans offer certain advantages to the employer. First, administration is easier because all elements of the plan are purchased from a single provider. Second, costs may be lower because the entire plan, including the HMO, may be subject to experience rating.

COMPARISON OF TYPICAL MEDICAL EXPENSE PLANS

The various types of medical expense plans, and how they differ, have been previously discussed. Although variations within each type of plan exist, some generalizations can be made. The table below summarizes these. The degree of managed care increases as one moves from left to right in the table. However, the cost of the plans, on the average, decreases as the degree of managed care increases. In addition, a higher degree of managed care is generally associated with lower annual premium increases by a plan.

Table 7-1 Sample Comparison of Health Insurance Plans				
	Traditional Major Medical Contracts	PPOs	POS Plans	HMOs
Provider Choice	Unlimited	Unlimited in network, but benefits are greater if network provider is used	Unlimited in network, but benefits are greater if network provider is used	Network providers must be used; care from non-network providers covered only in emergencies
Use of Gatekeeper	None	None	Used for care by network specialists	Used for access to specialists
Out-of-pocket Costs	Deductibles and percentage participation	Deductibles and percentage participation, which are lower if network providers are used; may have small copayment for network services	Small copayments for network services; deductibles and percentage participation for nonnetwork services	Small copayments for some services
Utilization Review	Traditionally little, but a few techniques are likely to be used now	More than traditional plans, but less than HMOs; network provider may be subject to some controls	Like HMOs for network services; like PPOs for non-network services	Highest degree of review, including financial incentives and disincentives for providers
Preventive Care	Covered with no cost-sharing	Covered with no cost-sharing	Covered with no cost-sharing	Covered with no cost-sharing
Responsibility for Claims Filings	Covered person	Plan provider for network services; the covered person for non-network services	Plan provider for network services; the covered person for non-network services	Plan providers

BENEFIT CARVE-OUTS

The use of benefit carve-outs by medical expense plans has grown in recent years, often as a method of cost containment that uses managed care techniques. In addition, many medical expense plans have come to realize that they cannot always provide as high a quality of care as can a well-managed specialty provider. Carve-outs for prescription drugs, vision care, dental care, and behavioral health have been common for a number of years.

The Nature of Carve-Outs

A benefit carve-out is coverage under a medical expense plan for a health care service that has been singled out for individual management by a party other than the employer's health plan (or the employer if a plan is self-funded). Some types of carve-outs predate managed care as it is now known. For example, many employees have long had coverage under separate prescription drug plans. However, the early emphasis under these plans was on discounts with preferred providers of prescription drugs. Today, prescription drug plans and other types of carve-outs use a wider variety of managed care techniques.

An employer can purchase a medical expense plan to provide benefits to its employees for most types of medical care and then enter into a separate contract with another provider for the carved-out benefit. However, in most cases, it is the insurance company, Blue Cross and Blue Shield plan, HMO, or PPO that enters into the carve-out arrangement with a "subcontractor" that manages the benefits. From the standpoint of employers and employees, the benefit is part of the provider's plan.

Vendors who provide carve-outs often act as managed care plans for a single medical expense benefit and take on the characteristics of HMOs or PPOs. They also have learned over time that a unique benefit structure should accompany their type of specialty care. This is one reason why mental health and prescription drug benefits are often subject to different deductibles, copayments, or benefit limitations than those used for most types of medical expenses.

Reasons to Use Carve-Outs

There are several reasons for using benefit carve-outs. These include the following:

- The carve-out can save money. A good carve-out vendor should be able to provide products and services in a cost-effective manner and pass along savings from these efficiencies.

- The carve-out may result in a shifting of financial risk and a better ability to budget. One way of controlling costs is to select a carve-out vendor that the plan pays on a capitated basis. This shifts much of the financial risk of higher-than-average claims to the carve-out vendor.

- The carve-out vendor may be better able to build a network of specialists. For some diseases or medical conditions, even very large HMOs or PPOs have too few claims to justify the establishment of their own in-plan network. The carve-out vendor may also be able to provide better outcomes data because of the vendor's size and expertise.

- The carve-out vendor may increase employer and employee satisfaction by lowering plan costs, providing high-quality care with the use of well-regarded specialists, and providing easier access to medical products and services.

Possible Concerns about Carve-Outs

A benefit plan must enter into carve-out arrangement with care. Today, many vendors claim they can properly perform the required tasks, but benefit plan administrators some-times find themselves dissatisfied. Therefore, proper evaluation of vendors is vital. Questions that need to be answered include the following:

- How does the carve-out vendor credential providers?
- Is the carve-out vendor financially able to deliver what it promises?
- Does the carve-out vendor have the management expertise to deliver what it promises?
- Why is the carve-out vendor in business? Providers of medical products and services often market carve-out arrangements, and this may result in their having the expertise to run a high-quality operation. On the other hand, it is important to distinguish these arrangements from those whose primary goal is to increase sales of the provider's products and services.
- Will the carve-out vendor keep a patient's primary-care physician informed about the patient's treatment? This information is essential if the primary-care physician is to properly coordinate patient care.

Types of Carve-Outs

There are numerous types of benefit carve-outs, including

- prescription drugs
- vision benefits
- behavioral health
- disease management

Prescription Drugs

The cost of prescription drugs is over 10 percent of all medical expense claims, and the percentage continues to grow. This increase results from several factors. One is the availability and prescribing of high-priced new pharmaceutical products. Another factor is increased use arising from several sources that include (1) the aging population, which uses more prescription drugs, (2) increased advertising to consumers, and (3) the shift from inpatient to outpatient treatment, resulting in more intensive pharmaceutical treatments. Finally, there are new drugs for many previously untreatable conditions. As a result, benefit plans often carve out prescription drugs in an attempt to control costs.

pharmacy benefit manager

Pharmacy Benefit Managers. A **pharmacy benefit manager** administers prescription drug plans on behalf of self-funded employers, HMOs, PPOs, insurance companies, Blue Cross and Blue Shield plans, and third-party administrators. PBMs may be affiliated with pharmaceutical companies, large retail chains, or benefit providers, such as insurance companies. They may also be independently owned.

The online capabilities of PBMs enable them to offer considerable flexibility in designing a prescription drug program for a specific employer or benefit plan provider.

In addition to developing networks for the dispensing of prescription drugs, PBMs typically also do the following:

- drug utilization review. This practice compares information gathered from a patient's medical and prescription drug records to determine such factors as overutilization, underutilization, drug-to-drug interactions, improper drugs for pregnant patients, early refills, and therapeutic duplication.

- physician profiling and education. A PBM can identify and counsel physicians whose prescribing patterns lie outside acceptable variations from established benchmarks.

- pharmacy profiling and education. PBMs might contact pharmacies about making more use of generic substitutions if they fill or recommend large amounts of brand-name drugs.

- patient profiling and education. Patients treated for hypertension can be identified and sent educational materials on their condition. This material focuses on the risks associated with the condition, safety issues associated with drug treatment, and the importance of complying with prescribed drug regimens. PBMs can also identify and contact patients who fail to refill needed medication.

PBMs are also increasingly developing disease management programs that focus on diagnostic aids identification, treatment guidelines, education, and outcomes measurement for specific diseases. PBMs may also be involved in the overall case management of a patient.

formulary

therapeutic substitution

PBMs have been leaders in the integration of formularies into prescription drug plans. A **formulary** is a list of preferred medications for a specific medical condition developed by a committee of pharmacists and physicians. PBMs provide this list to physicians with the hopes that it will positively affect their prescribing behavior. A formulary informs physicians of approved uses of new drugs on the market, appropriate uses for existing drugs, and appropriate times for generic and therapeutic substitutions. A **therapeutic substitution** is a drug with a similar therapeutic effect as the prescribed drug. Unlike generic substitution, which patients or pharmacists can often make, a physician must make a therapeutic substitution.

Some prescription drug plans do not have a price differential for a patient if a physician prescribes a nonformulary drug. However, PBMs offer plans that either cover formulary drugs only (referred to as closed formularies) or provide a financial incentive for patients to use them.

prescription drug plan

The typical **prescription drug plan** covers the cost of drugs (except those dispensed in a hospital or in an extended care facility) for which either state or federal law requires a prescription. Drugs for which prescriptions are not required by law (often referred to as over-the-counter drugs) are usually not covered even if a physician orders them on a prescription form. One frequent exception to this general rule is injectable insulin, which most plans cover despite the fact that in many states it is a nonprescription drug. There is no coverage for charges to administer drugs or the cost of the therapeutic devices or appliances, such as bandages or hypodermic needles. It is also common to limit benefits to a specific quantity of drugs. In some plans, this quantity is expressed as the amount normally prescribed by physicians; in other plans, it is expressed as a supply for a certain time period, often 30 or 34 days.

step therapy

Drug plans increasingly require precertification for the use of certain expensive drugs. Some plans also use **step therapy** under which approval for higher-cost medications is contingent upon a member first trying lower-cost, often well-established drugs to see if they are effective.

tiered structure

Most prescription drug plans have a copayment that a covered person pays for any prescriptions filled; in some cases, it is a flat amount that usually varies from $5 to $20 per prescription. Most plans, however, use a **tiered structure** under which different copayments (or percentage participation) apply to different types of prescription drugs. Some plans have one copayment amount for generic drugs and a higher one for brand-name drugs. A three-tier structure, such as a $10 copayment for generic drugs, $25 for brand-name formulary drugs, and $45 for brand-name nonformulary drugs, has rapidly become the most widely used option. A few plans have a four-tier structure under which a higher copayment or a significant percentage participation applies to a list of lifestyle and/or expensive specialty drugs. For these drugs, the copayment may be $50 to $100.

Some plans provide financial incentives for prescriptions filled by mail-order pharmacies or on the Internet, typically a 90-day supply for two 30-day copayments.

Prescription drug plans use two basic methods to provide coverage: a reimbursement approach and a service approach. Under plans using a reimbursement approach, a covered individual personally pays the cost of prescription drugs. The person may be able to use any pharmacy he or she chooses or may be required to use a participating pharmacy. A claim for reimbursement is then filed with the provider of benefits, either by the employee or electronically by the pharmacy. The plan makes reimbursement (subject to any copayments) to the covered person on the basis of either billed charges or reasonable-and-customary charges.

Although coverage for prescription drugs under major medical plans is often on a reimbursement basis, the majority of prescription drug plans use a service approach. Under this approach, drugs are provided to covered persons by participating pharmacies upon receipt of prescriptions, proper identification (usually a card issued by the plan), and any required copayments. The pharmacy then bills the provider of coverage (usually electronically) for the remaining cost of any prescription filled. This provider may be a PBM, a Blue Cross and Blue Shield plan, an HMO, an insurance company, or a third-party administrator acting on behalf of either an insurance company or an employer with a self-insured plan. Because of the specialization that can be used in handling many small claims and the need to establish a system of participating pharmacies, most insurance companies, except for a few large ones, use PBMs for their prescription drug plans.

Vision Benefits

Carve-out vision benefits may be provided by any organization that provides medical coverage, plans of state optometric associations patterned after Blue Shield, closed-panel HMO-type plans established by local providers of vision services, vision care PPOs, or third-party administrators.

vision plan

More than half of the persons covered under employer-provided medical expense plans have some type of **vision plan**, and the majority of this coverage is under some type of carve-out arrangement. Despite concerns with rising benefit costs in recent years, vision care is one type of benefit that employers continue to add. Routine eye exams can result in better overall health care because certain other types of health problems—such as high blood pressure, diabetes, and kidney problems—are first discovered during the course of such routine exams. Proper vision correction can also result in fewer accidents and greater productivity by minimizing eyestrain and headaches.

Vision plans occasionally provide benefits on a reasonable-and-customary basis or subjects them to a flat yearly benefit that applies to any covered expenses. Normally, however, plans use a benefit schedule that specifies the type and amounts of certain benefits and the frequency with which the plan will provide them. Below is an example of one such schedule. If a provider of vision services writes a plan, it is common for a discount, such as 20 percent, to be available for costs incurred with the provider that are not covered by the schedule of benefits. Some plans provide most benefits on a service basis rather than having a maximum benefit. However, these plans usually cover only the cost of basic frames, which the covered persons can upgrade at an additional expense.

Exclusions commonly exist for any extra charge for plastic lenses or the cost of safety lenses or prescription sunglasses. Vision plans generally provide benefits for eye examinations by either an optometrist or an ophthalmologist, and they sometimes provide larger benefits if a covered person uses the latter. Vision care plans do not pay benefits for necessary eye surgery or treatment of eye diseases because these are covered under the regular coverage of a medical expense plan. However, many vision plans make benefits available for elective procedures to improve vision, such as LASIK surgery. The benefit is usually in the form of a discounted fee from a provider who has a relationship with the plan.

Table 7-2 Vision Benefits	
Type of Benefit	**Maximum Amount**
Any 12-month Period	
Eye examination	$ 60
Lenses, pair	
single vision	50
bifocal	75
trifocal	100
lenticular (variable lenses)	150
contact (when medically necessary)	300
contact (when not medically necessary)	125
Any 24-month Period	
Frames	75

Behavioral Health

Providing behavioral health benefits has always been an area of difficulty for medical expense plans. With rapidly increasing costs for behavioral health, employers and providers of benefit plans are increasingly carving out this benefit by contracting with vendors that use managed care techniques.

behavioral health program

Characteristics of a successful **behavioral health program**, whether it is a carve-out arrangement or not, should include the following:

- the use of case management to design and coordinate treatment plans and to monitor the need for follow-up care

- a mechanism for referring a patient to the program. In many cases, this is through a primary-care physician gatekeeper. However, behavioral health programs are increasingly coordinated with employee-assistance programs.

- the development of a provider network that specializes in behavioral health. In addition to physicians, the network will include psychologists and therapists. It will also include alternatives to hospital treatment, such as residential centers, halfway houses, and structured outpatient programs. A plan may or may not provide benefits if a covered person obtains nonnetwork treatment. If it is covered, there is usually a lower benefit level than for network treatment.

- patient access to care on a 24-hour basis. Persons who have behavioral health problems often need immediate crisis intervention. Of course, the plan needs to communicate well the availability of such care.

Disease Management

Traditionally, medical expense plans have focused on the treatment of sickness rather than prevention and education. Even though this philosophy changed with managed care, there has often been less-than-complete attention paid to controlling chronic conditions that can lead to frequent and often expensive medical intervention. The list of chronic conditions is lengthy; a few of the conditions on this list are asthma, diabetes, heart disease, high blood pressure, arthritis, allergies, back pain, and multiple sclerosis. Many chronic conditions are high maintenance, and most are not curable. However, proper control can reduce hospitalization for the condition and related complications. In addition, it may increase the patient's longevity and quality of life. As managed care has evolved, the concept of disease management has taken on increasing importance, sometimes through the use of carve-outs for certain chronic conditions. The two most commonly carved-out chronic conditions are probably diabetes and asthma.

Traditional case management begins with an episode of illness, whereas disease management begins prior to it. Disease management programs attempt to identify persons with chronic conditions as early as possible so that proper treatment can minimize future spells of illness. In this regard, it is important to work with primary care physicians so that they can steer patients toward the disease management program.

Disease management programs have a network of providers who deliver the needed care and prevention. These include physicians as well as nurses who provide patient counseling and education and who may even make home visits. Education about a chronic condition is crucial in that a disease management program is much more effective if a patient understands how to manage his or her lifestyle in light of the condition. It is also important for a disease management program to involve pharmacists, because patients with chronic diseases are often on maintenance drugs, the effectiveness of which can be influenced by prescription drugs that the patient might take for other illnesses. A disease management program also has procedures for reacting to emergencies and providing ambulatory care following a hospitalization.

CHAPTER REVIEW

Key Terms and Concepts

accreditation

National Committee for Quality Assurance (NCQA)

Health Plan Employer Data and Information Set (HEDIS)

antigag-clause legislation

any-willing-provider law

provider network

credentials

capitation

incentive payment program

withhold arrangement

modified fee-for-service payment system

per-day rate

per-case rate

diagnosis-related groups (DRGs)

utilization management

demand management

wellness program

health risk assessment

medical information programs

referral management

gatekeeper (care manager)

referral

prospective management

concurrent management

retrospective management

case management

disease management

health maintenance organization (HMO)

direct-access HMO

physician-hospital organizations (PHOs)

closed-panel plans

open-panel plans

accountable care organization (ACO)

staff-model HMO

group-model HMO

network-model HMO

individual practice association (IPA)

mixed-model HMO

Health Maintenance Organization Act

federally qualified HMO

preferred-provider organization (PPO)

exclusive-provider organization (EPO)

centers of excellence

allowable charge

point-of-service (POS) plan

open-ended HMO

gatekeeper PPO

multiple-option plan

pharmacy benefit manager

formulary

therapeutic substitution

prescription drug plan

step therapy

tiered structure

vision plan

behavioral health program

Review Questions

Review questions are based on the learning objectives in this chapter. For example, a [3] at the end of a questions means that the question is based on learning objective 3. If there are multiple objectives, they are all listed.

1. How do managed care plans attempt to eliminate the unrestricted use of medical care providers? [1]

2. What are the purposes of accreditation of managed care organizations? [1]

3. What areas of performance does the NCQA evaluate when it evaluates a managed care organization for accreditation? [1]

4. Regarding HEDIS: [1]

    a. What is the purpose of the Health Plan Employer Data and Information Set (HEDIS)?

    b. What type of information about health plans does HEDIS measure?

5. Regarding managed care backlash: [1]

    a. Why may the terminology "backlash against managed care" be somewhat inaccurate?

    b. In a general sense, what have been the results of this backlash?

6. Briefly describe the purpose of each of the following types of state reform aimed at managed care. [1]

    a. antigag-clause rules

    b. grievance, review, and appeal procedures

    c. any-willing-provider laws

    d. mandatory POS options

    e. continuity of care

    f. provider protection

    g. emergency room coverage

    h. minimum stays for certain procedures

    i. plastic surgery mandates

    j. direct access to providers

7. Why have managed care reforms often been initiated voluntarily by managed care organizations? [1]

8. What are the factors that might lead an employee to elect a particular managed care plan? [1]

9. What is the role of provider networks in managed care plans? [2]

10. How does a managed care plan determine whether it has qualified providers of medical care services? [2]

11. How do managed care plans address member needs for medical care services? [2]

12. Regarding provider contracts: [2]

    a. Why are providers willing to grant preferred rates to managed care plans?

    b. What are the important aspects of a contract with a provider?

13. Describe each of the following methods that managed care plans use to compensate providers: [2]

    a. capitation

    b. modified fee-for-service

    c. per-day rate

    d. per-case rate

14. What is the relationship between a managed care plan's utilization management and its provider compensation methods? [2]

15. How do each of the following demand management programs guide members with respect to their personal health conditions? [2]

    a. wellness programs

    b. health risk assessments

    c. medical information programs

16. What is the role of a gatekeeper in a managed care plan? [2]

17. How do managed care plans usually settle disputes about coverage decisions? [2]

18. What is the role of each of the following in the management of institutional services? [2]

   a.   prospective management

   b.   concurrent management

   c.   retrospective management

19. Describe the characteristics of HMOs that distinguish them from insurance companies. [3]

20. In addition to sponsoring HMOs, how are insurance companies actively involved with them? [3]

21. Explain how HMOs may vary with respect to each of the following: [3]

   a.   choice of medical providers

   b.   reimbursement of physicians

22. Why are there a small number of staff-model HMOs, even though they offer a significant potential for cost savings? [3]

23. How does an individual practice association differ from a closed-panel HMO? [3]

24. What factors account for the use of mixed-model HMOs? [3]

25. Regarding HMO federal qualification? [3]

   a.   Why might an HMO seek federal qualification?

   b.   What requirements must be satisfied by an HMO to obtain federal qualification ?

26. What type of state regulation applies to HMOs? [3]

27. What must a successful PPO do in addition to seeking discounts from preferred providers? [4]

28. What are the characteristics of PPOs with respect to each of the following? [4]

   a.   deductibles

   b.   coinsurance

   c.   maximum benefits

29. How may each of the following differ under a PPO depending on whether network or nonnetwork services are used? [4]

   a.   precertification rules

   b.   benefits received

    c.   claims

30. To what extent are PPOs subject to state regulation? [4]

31. How does a POS plan differ from a traditional PPO? [5]

32. What advantages do multiple-option plans have for employers? [5]

33. Regarding benefit carve-outs: [6]

    a.   What are the reasons for using benefit carve-outs?

    b.   What are the concerns about benefit carve-outs?

34. What are the functions performed by pharmacy benefits managers? [6]

35. Explain the differences between a reimbursement approach and a service approach to providing prescription drug benefits. [6]

36. Why do employers continue to add vision plans? [6]

37. Describe the nature of vision care plans. [6]

38. What are the characteristics of a successful behavior health program? [6]

39. Regarding disease management: [6]

    a.   How does disease management differ from traditional case management?

    b.   What are the characteristics of a typical disease management program?

Review Question Answers

1. Managed care plans attempt to eliminate the unrestricted use of medical care providers by either requiring or encouraging members to use preapproved network providers.

2. Accreditation compares a managed care organization with what are considered benchmark standards of quality care. The organization knows where it stands in relation to its competitors and also what must be done to become accredited or to achieve a higher level of accreditation. The results of the process provide consumers with important comparative information about health plans.

3. The NCQA rates the following five areas of performance:

    • access and service

- qualified providers

- staying healthy

- living with illness

- getting better

4. a. HEDIS is a set of performance measures that are designed to enable purchasers and consumers to have necessary information to reliably compare the performance of managed care plans.

    b. HEDIS has more than 50 measures that fall into the following categories:

        - effectiveness of care

        - access/availability of care

        - satisfaction with the experience of care

        - health plan stability

        - use of services

        - cost of care

        - health plan descriptive information

5. a. First, some of the public's concerns, such as the lack of complete mental health parity and the issue of plans sometimes denying coverage as unnecessary, apply to the entire health care system not just to managed care plans. Second, although some of the concerns apply to all types of managed care plans, many apply solely to practices of HMOs.

    b. This backlash has had several results:

        - States continue to enact legislation that addresses many of the concerns.

        - Managed care organizations voluntarily modify their practices in light of legislative activity and competitive forces.

        - The federal government continues to grapple with consumer legislation.

6. a. Antigag clauses prohibit managed care organizations from having provisions in their contracts that prevent physicians from discussing with patients treatment options that their plan may not cover or from referring very ill patients for specialized care by providers outside the plan.

    b. Plans are to inform members, usually in writing, of plan grievance, review, and appeal procedures. In addition, a plan must respond to a grievance, particularly when a member needs emergency care. Some states require an independent external review of a plan's grievance and appeal decisions.

c. Any-willing-provider laws require that HMOs and other network plans accept any provider who is willing to agree to the plan's basic terms and fees.

d. The managed care organization must pay a portion, but not all, of the expenses incurred when a member obtains treatment from nonnetwork providers.

e. In certain cases, managed care plans must assure continuity of patient care with the same provider if that provider ceases to be a part of the provider network. For example, a pregnant patient's care by her obstetrician may continue until birth or shortly thereafter for any woman in the third trimester of a pregnancy at the time of her obstetrician's departure from the network.

f. Managed care plans must disclose their criteria for selecting medical care providers, give these providers advance notice of contract termination, and provide them with procedures for contesting the termination.

g. Managed care plans must pay emergency room charges whenever a prudent layperson considers a situation to be an emergency. In addition, care cannot be delayed to get plan authorization for treatment.

h. Minimum stays, which typically coincide with federal legislation, are required for mothers and newborns following deliveries. Most states also mandate that plans provide coverage for minimum stays following surgery for breast cancer.

i. Health insurance contracts and health plans must provide coverage for certain types of reconstructive surgery. Required coverage may apply to the repair of birth defects only, or it may apply to a broader list of situations in which reconstruction might be needed because of mastectomies, trauma, infections, tumors, or disease.

j. Women must have direct access to obstetricians/gynecologists without obtaining approval or a referral from their health plan. Direct access to other types of providers, such as dermatologists, may also be required.

7. Some voluntary reforms result from the natural evolution of new forms of financing and providing health care. Other changes have occurred because of competition among managed care organizations for market share. However, most voluntary reforms probably are reactions to legislation that is proposed or passed by the states.

8. The reasons why a particular managed care plan might be selected are:

   • the reputation of the managed care plan

   • the extent to which employees have established relationships with physicians

- costs

9. Managed care plans manage care primarily through the provider network that members in the plan are encouraged to use. Members may be required to receive covered medical care services from network providers only, or they must use these providers in order to obtain full plan benefits.

10. Physicians must document their training, licensure, certification in a specialty, and malpractice insurance coverage. In addition, they must be free of limitations, suspensions, or impairments that would affect their practice of medicine and hospital admitting privileges. Hospitals and other institutions must be licensed, accredited, and approved for participation in the Medicare program.

11. Managed care plans must develop and maintain sufficient numbers and types of providers to meet member health care needs in a geographic area. In addition, most network physicians must remain open to accepting as patients those members who are new to the plan as well as those who may wish to change providers. As a result, most plans maintain active recruitment and management programs to make sure that their networks keep pace with the needs of their ever-changing member populations in the areas and regions where these members reside.

12. a. Providers in the plan's network anticipate an increased number of patients who will utilize their services. Or conversely, they will not lose patients to providers who are network providers.

    b. Compensation for services is determined in advance of their provision and cannot be changed for a specified period without notification and agreement. Significantly, providers are obliged to accept the agreed-upon amount as payment in full.

    Providers usually participate to some degree in increased costs due to utilization of services either through incentive payments for meeting utilization targets or penalties for failure to do so.

13. a. Physicians receive a fixed payment per month for each member without regard to the services a member may receive in any particular month. The payment reflects likely utilization of services by the plan's members based on age and gender and the cost of care in the area. Capitation provides physicians no financial incentives to overtreat patients. In conjunction with capitation, a managed care plan commonly establishes an incentive payment program that rewards physicians who meet budgeted cost and utilization levels for hospital and ancillary services, as well as member satisfaction and quality standards.

b.   The plan pays providers on a discounted fee-for-service basis, subject to negotiated maximums per procedure.

This arrangement often includes some element of physician financial involvement in cost containment through rewards or penalties based on success in achieving the plan's utilization and cost targets.

c.   The plan pays a hospital a specified amount for each day a plan member is hospitalized, regardless of the actual cost of services on any particular day. The rate usually differs by type or level of care such as intensive care, obstetrics, or rehabilitation. The rate may decrease in relation to the days the member stays in the hospital or the aggregate days of stay for all plan members.

d.   The plan pays a specified amount for all services a member receives at hospital or facility, whether as an inpatient or outpatient, regardless of the length of the stay or number of services provided. This amount is calculated using such factors as a member's principal diagnosis, secondary diagnosis, surgical procedures, age, gender, and presence of complications.

14.   A plan should design provider compensation methods to reinforce utilization management objectives or at least be compatible with them.

15.   a.   Discovering and treating medical conditions before they become severe may be accomplished through such plan benefits as routine physicals and immunizations as well as screening for breast and prostate cancer, high cholesterol, high blood pressure, and diabetes.

Exercise and nutrition programs for weight management and fitness as well as smoking cessation programs are common plan benefits to reduce health risks by conforming personal behavior to a healthy lifestyle with healthy habits. .

b.   In addition to gathering data on health history and current medical conditions, a health risk assessment also elicits information on a member's behavior and habits. Taken together this information identifies the member's potential health care risks and gives the plan the opportunity to advocate member lifestyle and health habit changes that reinforce prevention and wellness programs.

c.   Improved utilization management occurs when members are provided with medical information they can use for self-care of common conditions or to decide when to seek professional care. Medical information programs can assist members in conjunction with their physicians to make informed decisions regarding their specific diseases, treatment alternatives, and the course of treatment.

16. The gatekeeper, or care manager, serves as a member's initial contact for medical care and referral for any additional medical services the member may need. The primary care physician authorizes the use of specialty physicians and issues the referral for specialty care.

17. If the plan, the member, or the provider disputes a coverage decision, the plan usually has an external review process. In this process outside specialists who do not work directly for the managed care plan determine whether the plan should pay denied benefits after a review of the facts of the case.

18. a. Prospective management is a utilization management program for inpatient admissions and outpatient procedures that may require an authorization. Although the main purpose of the authorization is to avoid unneeded institutional care, the plan may use the program to earmark the episode for case management, especially if treatment promises to be complicated and expensive. A plan may divert a member initially assigned to inpatient care to another setting where services may cost less and/or be more effective.

    b. Concurrent management, also known as continued stay review, is the management of inpatient utilization during a hospital stay.

    c. The retrospective management of utilization is an evaluation of the patterns of medical care services that members received over a prior period to determine their appropriateness and to take corrective action as needed.

19. Distinguishing HMO characteristics may be summarized under the following headings:

    • Comprehensive Care

        – Members receive a comprehensive package of health care benefits that generally include broad outpatient services as well as for hospitalization, typically with modest copayments. HMOs emphasize preventive care and include such services as routine physicals and immunizations.

    • Delivery of Medical Services

        – HMOs provide for the delivery of medical services, which in some cases is performed by salaried physicians and other personnel employed by the HMO. Typically, Members must obtain their care from providers of medical services in a specific geographic area who have an affiliation with the HMO. HMOs are likely to emphasize treatment by primary care physicians who also serve as gatekeepers controlling access to specialists.

    • Cost Control

    – Outpatient treatment and preventive medicine avoid expensive medical treatment and lower hospitalization rates. HMOs emphasize utilization management which includes preadmission authorization and concurrent review and retrospective review. Payments to physicians and other providers are controlled through incentives to contain costs and lower utilization.

20. Insurance company involvement with HMOs can take the following forms:

- consulting on such matters as plan design and administration
- administrative services, such as actuarial advice, claims monitoring, accounting, and computer services
- marketing assistance, such as designing sales literature or in a few cases, the agents of insurance companies have been used to market HMOs
- providing hospitalization coverage for member of HMOs that do not control their own hospital facilities
- providing emergency out-of-area coverage
- providing financial support in a variety of ways, including reinsurance

21. a. With most closed-panel plans having several general practitioners, members can usually select their physician from among those accepting new patients and make medical appointments just as if the physician were in private practice. However, there is frequently little choice among specialists because a plan may have a contract with only one physician or a limited number of physicians in a given specialty. Many newer HMOs have been formed as individual practice associations (IPAs), which are open-panel plans. This type of plan has more flexibility with respect to members choosing physicians and the ability of physicians to participate in the plan. IPAs are slightly more prevalent than closed-panel plans.

    b. Reimbursement of physicians vary based on the type of HMO.

- Staff-model HMOs pay their physicians as employees using salaries, possibly with an incentive bonuses.
- Under a group-model, the HMO often pays for services on a capitation basis for each member and must provide any and all covered services for this capitation fee. The fee is independent of how the provider compensates its own employees.
- Physician groups that enter into a network model arrangement often treat non-HMO patients on a fee-for-service basis.

- The most common method of compensating physicians in an individual practice association is a fee schedule. Such plans typically have a provision for reducing payments if the experience of the plan is worse than expected or providing a bonus if the experience of the plan is better than expected.

22. A staff-model HMO has high start-up costs and high fixed costs once they are operational.

23. Unlike closed-panel plan HMOs, individual practice association (IPA) plans provide a larger list of physicians, including specialists, from which members may choose. IPA physicians are more likely to be paid on a fee-for-service basis. Finally, it is unusual for IPAs to own their own hospitals. Instead, they enter into contracts with local hospitals to provide the necessary services for their members.

24. Mixed-model HMOs generally develop from plans initially established as a staff-model plans that continue to grow. Such a plan can more easily expand its capacity or geographic region by adding additional physicians under an IPA arrangement. Some mixed models have also resulted from the merger of two plans that each used a different organizational form.

25. a. The HMO Act of 1973 entitled HMOs to federal grants for feasibility studies and development and federal loans or loan guarantees to assist them in covering initial operating deficits. It also exempted federally qualified HMOs from restrictive laws in many states that had effectively prevented the establishment of HMOs. HMOs also feel that the federal qualification grants them a "seal of approval" from the federal government. In addition, from a marketing perspective, some employers will only deal with federally qualified HMOs. Federal qualification continues to be one way that HMOs can satisfy certain qualifications necessary to provide coverage for Medicare recipients.

   b. The HMO must provide specific basic benefits to its members at no cost or nominal copayments including:

   - physicians' services with network access requirements
   - inpatient and outpatient hospital services
   - medically necessary emergency health services
   - short-term outpatient mental health services
   - medical treatment and referral services for alcohol or drug abuse or addiction
   - diagnostic laboratory services and diagnostic and therapeutic radiological services

- home health services

- certain preventive health services

- medical social services, including education in personal health maintenance and use of health services

The HMO may also provide supplemental or optional benefits including:

- vision care

- hearing care

- dental care

- additional mental health services

- rehabilitative services

- prescription drugs

HMOs must also meet requirements for fiscally sound operations and an ongoing quality assurance program.

26. Almost all states have adopted the NAIC Health Maintenance Organization Model Act, which focuses substantially on issues relating to licensing of HMOs and the maintenance of their financial solvency. However, it also addresses numerous other issues, such as the types of activities in which HMOs can engage, the requirement of a quality assurance program, standards for plan information materials given to members, grievance procedures, enrollment periods, and coordination-of-benefits provisions.

27. Successful PPOs today emphasize quality care and utilization review. In selecting physicians and hospitals, PPOs look both at the type of care provided and the provider's cost effectiveness. It is also important for a PPO to monitor and control utilization on an ongoing basis and to deal with groups of preferred providers that monitor their own costs and utilization.

28. a. A PPO may have annual deductibles that apply separately to network and non-network charges. A PPO may waive deductibles for some medical services, such as emergency or preventive care.

    b. PPOs often use coinsurance percentages that are 20 percent (and occasionally 30 percent) lower when care is received from nonnetwork providers. A frequently found provision applies 90 percent coinsurance to network charges and 70 percent coinsurance to nonnetwork charges. Although PPOs typically have higher coinsurance percentages for network charges than do traditional major medical plans, a covered person may be responsible for modest copayments in some circumstances.

c. Although there are variations, many PPOs have separate lifetime maximums, with $1 million being common for nonnetwork benefits. The lifetime maximum for network benefits is seldom less that $2 million and may even be unlimited.

29. a. For network benefits, the person responsible for obtaining the needed certification is the network provider, and the PPO does not penalize the covered person if the network provider fails to obtain the proper precertification. However, this responsibility shifts to the employee or family member for nonnetwork services. If he or she does not obtain a precertification when required, there usually is a reduction in benefits.

b. A few procedures may be covered only if they are received from network providers. For example, routine physical exams may be covered only in the network.

c. No claim forms are required for network services. The covered person merely pays any required copayment, and the provider of medical services does the paperwork needed to receive the additional amounts payable by the plan.

30. PPOs initially were subject to much less stringent state regulation than HMOs with respect to their managed care activities. However, the NAIC created the Preferred Provider Arrangements Model Act, which the majority of states adopted. The act requires that PPOs incorporate cost-containment mechanisms, such as utilization review, to determine whether a service is medically necessary. Covered persons must have reasonable access to medical services. The act also allows PPOs to provide incentives for persons to use the preferred-provider network and to place limitations on the number and types of providers with whom they contract.

31. The normal usage of the term POS implies a higher degree of managed care requirements than is found in most PPOs. For example, unlike PPO plans, POS plans may require a member to notify the primary care physician/gatekeeper that treatment outside of the network is being sought.

32. These plans offer certain advantages to the employer. First, administration is easier because all elements of the plan are purchased from a single provider. Second, costs may be lower because the entire plan, including the HMO, may be subject to experience rating.

33. a. The reasons include the following:
    - The carve-out can save money.

- The carve-out may result in a shifting of financial risk to the vendor and a better ability to budget.

- The carve-out vendor may be better able to build a network of specialists.

- The carve-out vendor may increase employer and employee satisfaction by lowering plan costs, providing high-quality care through the use of well-regarded specialists, and providing easier access to medical products and services.

b. Concerns include the following:

- How does the carve-out vendor credential providers?

- Is the carve-out vendor financially able to deliver what it promises?

- Does the carve-out vendor have the management expertise to deliver what it promises?

- Why is the carve-out vendor in business? It is important to distinguish cost-effective, high quality arrangements from those whose primary goal is to increase sales of the provider's products and services.

- Will the carve-out vendor keep a patient's primary-care physician informed about the patient's treatment?

34. In addition to developing networks for the dispensing of prescription drugs, pharmacy benefit managers typically also do the following:

- drug utilization review

- physician profiling and education

- pharmacy profiling and education

- patient profiling and education

35. Under plans using a reimbursement approach, a covered individual personally pays the cost of prescription drugs. A claim for reimbursement is then filed with the provider of benefits, either by the employee or electronically by the pharmacy. Reimbursement is made to the covered person on the basis of either billed charges or reasonable-and-customary charges.

Under the service approach, used by most prescription drug plans, drugs are provided to covered persons by participating pharmacies upon receipt of prescriptions, proper identification, and any required copayments. The pharmacy then bills the provider of coverage for the remaining cost of any prescription filled.

36. Routine eye exams can result in better overall health care because certain other types of health problems—such as high blood pressure, diabetes, and kidney problems—are first discovered during the course of such routine exams. Proper vision correction can also result in fewer accidents and greater productivity by minimizing eyestrain and headaches.

37. Vision care plans provide benefits for routine eye examination and vision correction through prescription eyewear (frames and lenses) or contact lenses. Normally, plans use a benefit schedule that specifies the type and amounts of certain benefits and the frequency with which the plan will provide them. Vision plans generally provide benefits for eye examinations by either an optometrist or an ophthalmologist, and they sometimes provide larger benefits if the latter is used. Non-covered services, such as Lasik surgery, and non-covered items such as upgraded frames are usually available at discount from a vision care provider who has a relationship with the plan.

38. Characteristics of a successful behavioral health program should include the following:

- the use of case management to design and coordinate treatment plans and to monitor the need for follow-up care

- a mechanism for referring a patient to the program. In many cases, this is through a primary-care physician gatekeeper

- the development of a provider network that specializes in behavioral health

- patient access to care on a 24-hour basis

39. The following statements summarize characteristics of a typical disease management program.

    a. Traditional case management begins with an episode of illness, whereas disease management begins prior to it. Disease management programs attempt to identify persons with chronic conditions as early as possible so that proper treatment can minimize future spells of illness.

    b. • Disease management programs have a network of providers, including pharmacists, who deliver the needed care and prevention.

       • Education about a chronic condition is crucial. A disease management program is much more effective if a patient understands how to manage his or her lifestyle in light of the condition.

       • A disease management program involve pharmacists, because patients with chronic diseases are often on maintenance drugs, the effectiveness of which can be influenced by prescription drugs that the patient might take for other illnesses.

- A disease management program also has procedures for reacting to emergencies

Chapter 8

Consumer-Directed Medical Expense Plans

Learning Objectives

An understanding of the material in this chapter should enable the student to

1. **Describe the general approaches to consumer-directed medical expense plans.**

2. **Describe the nature and provisions of health reimbursement arrangements (HRAs).**

3. **Describe the nature and provisions of health savings accounts (HSAs).**

consumer-directed medical expense plan

Recent years have seen considerable interest in the concept of the **consumer-directed medical expense plan**. Such plans, also referred to by such names as consumer-driven health care and consumer-choice plans, give the employee increased choices and responsibilities with the selection of his or her own medical expense coverage. Some consumer-directed models also have a greater accountability for health plans and health care providers, particularly with respect to disclosing information to help consumers make better-informed decisions.

GENERAL APPROACHES

There are two general approaches to consumer-directed medical expense plans—defined-contribution medical expense plans and the use of savings accounts.

Defined-Contribution Medical Expense Plans

defined-contribution medical expense plan

Even though some consumer-directed approaches for medical expense plans are still relatively new, they have existed in the form of the **defined-contribution medical expense plan** for some time. For example, many employers make two or more medical expense plans available to their employees, such as an HMO, a PPO, and an indemnity plan. The employer contribution to the cost of coverage for each plan may be a dollar amount that is pegged to a fixed percentage of the cost of the least expensive plan, usually an HMO. Therefore, an employee who elects a more expensive PPO or indemnity plan must make a greater out-of-pocket contribution for his or her coverage than if the HMO had been selected. Certain forms of cafeteria plans also incorporate a defined-contribution approach for medical expense plans.

Example

The Weir Corporation makes three medical expense plans available to its employees—an HMO, a point-of-service plan, and a PPO. For self-only coverage, the corporation pays an amount equal to 90 percent of the cost of the least expensive plan, which is the HMO. For the three plans, the employee contribution is as follows:

	Total Monthly Premium	Employer Contribution	Employee Contribution
HMO	$344.00	$309.60	$34.40
POS Plan	413.34	309.60	103.74
PPO	523.86	309.60	214.26

The corporation uses a similar approach to determine the cost of dependent coverage for which it contributes an amount equal to 50 percent of the cost of HMO coverage.

There is no question that defined-contribution plans over time have driven large numbers of employees to medical expense plans with higher degrees of managed care. However, managed care plans historically have provided a broad scope of coverage, including prescription drugs, yet limited the member's payment for these services to relatively modest copayments. In doing so, these plans greatly diminish the motivation of their members to contain costs when they seek services. From a member's viewpoint, the broad array of services is available for only the cost of the copayments. Even as many managed care plans have become less restrictive, copayment levels have often changed little. This is changing as more employers adopt or revise their medical expense plans so that employees have higher deductibles and larger copayments. In 2013, the American Association of Preferred Provider Organization estimates that 45 million people were enrolled in CDHPs, up from 39 million in 2012—a 15 percent growth rate.[1]

---

1.   American Association of Preferred Provider Organizations, Survey of Consumer-Directed Health Plans, aappo. interactivemedialab.com/resources/research.aspx, 2015.

Use of Savings Accounts

high-deductible health plan (HDHP)

Newer types of defined-contribution medical expense plans have features other than just fixed employer contributions. At a minimum, these approaches force employees to make financial decisions involving their health care. Typically, an employer might provide employees with a medical expense plan that has a very high deductible, perhaps as much as $5,000 per year. This type of plan is often referred to as a **high-deductible health plan (HDHP)**. The employer also contributes a lower or equal amount, such as $2,500 per year, to some type of savings account from which the employee can make withdrawals to pay medical expenses that the health plan does not cover because of the deductible. These funds are often withdrawn with an electronic payment card (such as a debit card), which has a dollar limit equal to the available savings account balance. The employee can carry forward any unused amount in the account without it affecting the next year's contribution to the account. Such a plan gives the employee an immediate incentive to purchase medical care wisely because, if the amount in the account is exceeded, the employee will have to pay the full cost of medical expenses out of his or her own pocket until the plan's high deductible is satisfied. The plan often incorporates a preferred-provider network of health care professionals. As long as an employee receives medical treatment within the network, any charges that the employee must pay because of the deductible are limited to the amount negotiated with the preferred provider.

The rationale for using a high-deductible medical expense plan along with a savings account is that significant cost savings can occur for two primary reasons. First, the expensive cost of administering and paying small claims is largely eliminated, as demonstrated by the fact that a major medical policy with a $2,500 deductible can often be purchased for about one-half the cost of a policy with a $250 deductible. Second, employees now have a direct financial incentive to avoid unnecessary care and to seek out the most cost-effective form of treatment.

A small number of employers have used this approach for some time with positive results. Costs have been lowered or have risen less rapidly than would otherwise be expected. Reactions of employees have generally been favorable, but until federal legislation in the late 1990s there was one major drawback—employer contributions to a savings account constituted taxable income to employees.

This type of medical expense plan has its critics. They argue that employees will minimize treatment for minor medical expenses and preventive care that would have been covered under a plan without a high deductible. Critics contend that this avoidance of medical care may lead to major expenses that could have been averted or minimized with earlier treatment. Another criticism is that a high-deductible plan tends to favor healthy individuals and those in high tax brackets. A third criticism is that this type of medical expense plan does not focus on the problem of the uninsured. In rebuttal to this criticism, proponents argue that any technique that lowers costs for employers will ultimately benefit everyone and encourage small employers to provide coverage that would have previously been unaffordable. A final criticism is that these plans are just another way of shifting more medical costs to employees.

Most consumer-directed medical expense plans that use the savings-account approach, however, only make a single medical expense plan available to employees.

Two tax-favored approaches use savings accounts:

- health reimbursement arrangements (HRAs)
- health savings accounts (HSAs)

HRAs can only be established by employers for their employees. HSAs can be established by either employers or individuals.

It is common for employers to establish flexible spending accounts (FSAs) so that their employees can elect before-tax salary reductions to pay for unreimbursed medical expenses. There are those who argue that FSAs are a form of consumer-directed health plan. However, they can be viewed primarily as an aspect of a cafeteria plan that provides federal income tax benefits to employees when they are properly used.

HEALTH REIMBURSEMENT ARRANGEMENTS

health reimbursement arrangements (HRAs)

Some employers provide their employees with high-deductible medical expense plans and create a savings account for each covered employee under which he or she can obtain reimbursement for certain medical expenses that are not covered under a high-deductible plan. However, there was uncertainty about the tax treatment of such reimbursements, particularly if employees carry over account balances to subsequent plan years. This uncertainty was settled in 2002 when the IRS issued a ruling that specifically allowed such tax-favored **health reimbursement arrangements (HRAs)** as long as specified criteria were satisfied. HRAs are the dominant form of consumer-directed health plans. By 2013, 10 percent of large employers offered HRAs to their employees.[2]

Requirements for Health Insurance Plans

Although HRAs are almost always used with high-deductible insurance plans, there is no requirement for the size of the deductible. In fact, a plan with any size deductible can be used. The deductible can also be waived for certain services, including prescription drugs and preventive services.

Eligibility

HRAs can be established by any size employer for its employees, but they cannot be established by or for self-employed persons.

Contributions

Contributions to an HRA must be made solely by the employer. However, employees may be required to pay part of the premium for the underlying medical expense coverage. Some employers make a single annual contribution to each employee's HRA account. Other employers make contributions that are spread throughout the year, such as each pay period.

There is no requirement that employers make contributions to a trust or custodial account. In fact, HRAs are typically unfunded, and the employer contributions are merely credits to a savings account. Reimbursements are then paid from the employer's current revenue, at which time the employer receives an income tax deduction.

Contributions in an employee's account can be carried over to subsequent years to the extent they have not been withdrawn to reimburse eligible medical expenses.

Distributions

Under IRS rules, employees can take tax-free distributions from an HRA as reimbursement only for medical expenses that are not paid by any other medical expense plan. The medical expenses may be for the employee, his or her spouse, or any other persons who are dependents for tax purposes.

---

2.   Ibid.

The reimbursements may be for any medical expenses that would be deductible, ignoring the 10 percent of adjusted gross income threshold, if the employee itemized his or her income tax deductions. Tax-free withdrawals therefore are permitted for the purchase of COBRA continuation coverage, Medicare premiums, and Medicare supplement policies. They are also permitted for the purchase of long-term care insurance up to specified deductible limits.

Despite the broadness of the IRS rules, an employer can design an HRA to reimburse only specific types of medical expenses. For example, an HRA might provide reimbursement for copayments, percentage participation, deductibles, and expenses that the employer's medical expense plan does not cover. Reimbursements for required employee premiums for the medical expense coverage are generally not allowed.

HRAs that are unfunded (as is usually the case) are treated as self-funded medical reimbursement plans and are subject to the nondiscrimination rules applicable to such plans. Therefore, if HRAs are set up on a discriminatory basis, highly compensated employees may be taxed on all or a portion of any benefits they receive.

Termination of Employment

At termination of employment, an employee's HRA usually terminates. Unlike HSAs and Archer MSAs, however, HRAs are treated as group health plans and generally subject to COBRA requirements. If any employee elects this option, he or she has access to unused balances in the HRA account during the COBRA continuation period.

An employer can (but is not required to) allow a terminated employee to spend down an HRA balance for unreimbursed medical expenses incurred after termination of employment. Indeed, the employer may set up the HRA so that the funds are dedicated in whole or in part for use in an employee's retirement years.

Example

Ned's employer provides each employee with a high-deductible health insurance plan that has a $2,500 annual deductible for each employee and covered dependent. The deductible does not apply to certain preventive services. There is no cost to Ned for his coverage, but he must pay 50 percent of the cost for his wife.

In addition, Ned's employer contributes $2,000 at the beginning of each year to an HRA for unreimbursed medical expense incurred by either Ned or his wife.

The unused balance in the HRA carries over from year to year. After retirement, the employer allows Ned to use these remaining funds to pay any unreimbursed medical expense, which would include premiums for Medicare or Medicare supplement policies.

HEALTH SAVINGS ACCOUNTS

health savings accounts (HSAs)

In addition to providing prescription drug coverage for older Americans, the Medicare Prescription Drug, Improvement, and Modernization Act established **health savings accounts (HSAs)**. HSAs are designed as successors to Archer MSAs, which are briefly discussed later, and the two have many features in common. However, they also have some notable differences that make HSAs more attractive than Archer MSAs and available to a much larger pool of consumers.

HSAs were allowed as early as 2004. Various surveys indicate that by 2009 there were 6 to 7 million people with high-deductible health plans that met the criteria for them to also have HSAs. About three-quarters of these people have such health plans through employer-provided medical expense arrangements, but only about half of this group have either established HSAs or had their employers establish HSAs for them.

General Nature

An HSA is a personal savings account from which unreimbursed medical expenses, including deductibles, percentage participation, and copayments, can be paid. The HSA must be in the form of a tax-exempt trust or custodial account established in conjunction with a high-deductible health (medical expense) plan. An HSA is established with a qualified trustee or custodian in much the same way that an IRA is established. Any insurance company or bank (as well as certain other financial institutions) can be a trustee or custodian, as can any other person or entity already approved by the IRS as a trustee or custodian for IRAs.

HSAs are individual trusts, which prohibits a husband and wife from having a joint HSA. But as long as both are eligible, each may have a separate HSA. Some insurers that sell high-deductible health plans for use with HSAs also market the HSA accounts; other insurers leave it to the purchasers of a high-deductible health plan to establish their HSAs with other institutions.

Even though employers can sponsor HSAs, these accounts are established for the benefit of individuals and are portable. If an employee changes employers or leaves the workforce, the HSA, including the balance in the account, remains with the individual.

Eligibility

Employees, the self-employed, and anyone else can establish HSAs as long as they meet the following rules for qualification:

- The individual must be covered by a high-deductible health plan. That plan may be insured or self-insured if offered by an employer as long as it meets the criteria for a qualifying high-deductible plan.

- The individual is not eligible to be claimed as a dependent on another person's federal income tax return.

- With some exceptions, a person who is covered under a high-deductible health plan is denied eligibility for an HSA if he or she is covered under another health plan that does not meet the definition of a high-deductible plan but that provides any benefits that are covered under the high-deductible health plan. The exceptions include coverage for accident, disability, dental care, vision care, and long-term care as well as liability insurance, insurance for a specified disease or illness, and insurance paying a fixed amount per period of hospitalization. Participation in a typical FSA would make an individual ineligible to participate in an HSA unless the FSA only provided reimbursement for types of expenses not covered under the high-deductible health plan.

An employer can establish HSAs for its employees, or an individual (whether employed or not) may establish his or her own HSA.

High-Deductible Health Plan

For purposes of HSA participation, a high-deductible health plan is defined as having the following deductibles and annual out-of-pocket limitations for covered services. These figures are for 2016 and subject to annual inflation adjustments:

- In the case of self-only coverage, the deductible must be at least $1,300, and annual out-of-pocket expenses cannot exceed $6,550.

- In the case of family coverage, the deductible must be at least $2,600, and annual out-of-pocket expenses cannot exceed $13,100.

If these high-deductible plans use preferred-provider networks, they can have higher out-of-pocket limits for services provided outside the network, and any deductibles for nonnetwork services are not taken into account when determining the out-of-pocket limits specified above.

One point should be emphasized about the deductible for family coverage. It is not a family deductible as was described in the discussion on major medical insurance. In that situation, there is an individual deductible that applies to each family member as well as a separate deductible for the family. This is sometimes referred to as an embedded deductible, and the policy pays benefits for any family member once his or her deductible is satisfied, even if the family deductible is not yet met.

In the case of a high-deductible policy used with an HSA, there will usually not be an individual deductible if a policy is written for a family. Rather, there will be a single deductible—referred to as a common deductible—that must be satisfied before any benefits are payable, even if all claims are for one family member. It is permissible, however, to use an embedded deductible, but only if the individual deductible is equal to at least the required HSA family deductible of $2,600.

The following incurred expenses do not count toward the plan's required deductible and out-of-pocket limit:

- payments for services not covered by the high-deductible health plan
- payments for services received from nonnetwork health care providers, if the plan uses a preferred-provider network
- amounts above a plan's reasonable allowable specific service maximums
- amounts in excess of reasonable and customary fees
- penalties for failure to obtain a plan-required certification

Nevertheless, copayments and required percentage participation count toward the out-of-pocket limit, even if the plan does not consider them as contributing toward the satisfaction of the deductible. In addition, the deductible amount counts towards the out-of-pocket limit. However, employee contributions paid for the coverage do not count.

Contributions

Contributions to an HSA may be made solely by individuals who have such accounts. They may also be made by employers that provide their employees with a high-deductible health plan.

Individual Contributions

Individuals often fund HSAs without employer contributions because they are not employees or because their employer makes no contribution to HSAs. Contributions must be in the form of cash, and they are deductible for federal income tax purposes even if the individual does not itemize deductions.

The maximum annual contribution to an HSA in 2016 is $3,350 if the account holder has self-only coverage and $6,750 if the account holder has family coverage. These amounts are subject to annual indexing for inflation. As a result of the Tax Relief and Health Care Act of 2006, the full maximum contribution is allowed even if it exceeds the policy deductible amount under the high-deductible health plan.

If both a husband and wife establish an HSA and have family coverage (that is, a single policy covering both of them), they can allocate the maximum contribution in any way they determine. If they have separate policies, each is subject to the limits that apply to self-only coverage.

Individuals aged 55 or older are also permitted an additional annual catch-up contribution of up to $1,000. If both a husband and wife are aged 55 or older, the catch-up contribution is available to each of them only if they have separate HSAs.

Annual contributions can be made in a lump sum or spread out over time. However, the contributions for a specific tax year cannot be made before the tax year begins or after the taxpayer's original filing date (without extensions) for that tax year. For most individuals, this is the earlier of April 15 of the following year or the date a return is filed. This is similar to the rules for IRA contributions.

If an individual stops participating in an HSA during a tax year, the actual HSA contribution that can be deducted for the tax year is limited to 1/12 of the annual amount, as described previously, times the number of months that an individual is eligible for HSA participation. Until 2007, the same rule applied if an individual began participating in an HSA after January of the tax-year—only a proportionate contribution could be made. The Tax Relief and Health Care Act changed the rule as long as an individual is still eligible to participate in an HSA during the last month of a tax-year. In such a situation, the individual is allowed to make the full annual tax-deductible contribution for the year. However, if he or she fails to remain eligible for an HSA for at least 12 months thereafter (other than because of death or disability), the contribution for the prior year that is attributable to months when the account holder did not have an HSA is includible in gross income and subject to a 20 percent penalty tax.

An excess contribution occurs to the extent that contributions to an HSA exceed the tax-deductible limits or are made for an ineligible person. The account holder is subject to a 6 percent excise tax on excess contributions (including those made by an employer) for each year these contributions are in an account. This excise tax can be avoided if the excess amount and any net income attributable to the excess amount are removed from the HSA prior to the last day prescribed by law, (including extensions) for filing the account holder's income tax return. The net income attributable to the excess contributions is included in the account holder's gross income for the tax year in which the distribution is made.

Employer Contributions

Many persons with HDHPs have their coverage under an employer-provided plan, and their employer may make contributions to the HSAs of employees. Employer contributions belong to the employee and are nonforfeitable. The employer might make the maximum annual contribution as previously described. However, it is also possible that the employer contribution will contribute a lower amount. In this case, an employee can make any remaining allowable contribution.

An employer that contributes to HSAs is subject to a nondiscrimination rule that requires the employer to make comparable contributions for all employees who have HSAs. Failure to comply with this rule subjects the employer to an excise tax. However, full-time employees and part-time employees (those working fewer than 30 hours per week) are treated separately. The comparability rule generally requires that the employer contribute either the same dollar amount for each employee or the same percentage of each employee's deductible under the health plan. However, it is permissible for an employer to make larger contributions for nonhighly-compensated employees than for highly compensated employees.

HSA Account Growth

Unused amounts in an HSA accumulate on a tax-free basis and carry over to subsequent years without limit. The size of an HSA balance carried over from prior years has no effect on a current year's contribution.

Distributions from an HSA

An individual can usually take distributions from an HSA at any time, but the trust or custodial document may put reasonable restrictions on both the frequency and minimum amount of distributions. Generally, accounts are set up so that they can be accessed with debit cards or checks written by the account holder as an alternative to actually filing for reimbursement. The amount of the distribution can be any part or all of the account balance. Subject to some exceptions, distributions of both contributions and earnings are excludible from an account holder's gross income if used to pay medical expenses of the account holder and the account holder's legal spouse and tax dependents as long as these expenses are not paid by other sources of insurance. There is no requirement that these family members be covered by a high-deductible health insurance plan. If both a husband and wife have HSAs, the reimbursement for any family can come from either or both HSAs but together cannot exceed the amount of the unreimbursed expense.

For the most part, the eligible medical expenses are the same ones that would be deductible, ignoring the 10 percent of adjusted gross income limitation, if the account holder itemized his or her income tax deductions. Tax-free withdrawals are permitted for the purchase of COBRA continuation coverage or for the purchase of health coverage while an individual receives unemployment compensation. They are also permitted for the purchase of long-term care insurance up to certain deductible limits. However, tax-free withdrawals are not otherwise permitted for the purchase of health insurance by persons under age 65.

Even though contributions cannot be made after an individual reaches age 65 and becomes a Medicare beneficiary, tax-free distributions can still be used for any future qualified medical expenses, which include premiums for original Medicare, Medicare prescription drug coverage, Medicare Advantage plans, and medical expense coverage under employer-sponsored plans. However, an account holder cannot use tax-free distributions to pay premiums for a Medicare supplement policy.

From a financial planning standpoint, account holders may want to wait until after retirement or age 65 to take HSA distributions as long as they have the resources to pay for unreimbursed medical expenses prior to that time. This will allow their HSA balances to grow on a tax-favored basis for use in their older years when unreimbursed medical expenses may be higher and/or income may be lower.

Distributions are permitted for other reasons, but they are subject to income taxation and possibly to a 20 percent penalty tax. However, the penalty tax does not apply in the case of distributions after an individual's death, disability, or the attainment of age 65.

Example

Kirby has a balance of $7,000 in his HSA. At age 67, he rediscovered his childhood sweetheart and fell madly in love. She agreed to marry him and he wants to give her a big diamond ring. Because she told Kirby that she would take care of him for life, he decided to cash in his HSA and apply the proceeds to purchase the ring.

His tax accountant informed Kirby that this arrangement would not be a qualified medical expense. He can withdraw the funds without penalty because he is at least age 65, but the $7,000 must be included in his gross income for federal income tax purposes.

Termination of Employment

Former employees, including retirees, may continue HSAs that were established prior to termination of employment, and the rules for contributions and distributions are as previously described.

Retirees who did not have an HSA prior to retirement can establish one at that time as long as all the proper rules are satisfied. Such an HSA may present an opportunity for a retiree to reduce income taxes. However, the requirement of having a high-deductible plan will probably negate this advantage if an individual has substantial medical expenses.

Example

Kathleen, a widow, retired at age 60 from her job as an attorney. She likes the concept of consumer-directed health plans and has decided to establish an HSA. In order to be eligible for the HSA, she purchased a major medical policy with an annual deductible of $2,500. She plans to make the maximum allowable contribution to the HSA until she is eligible for Medicare. She will then use her HSA balance to pay her Medicare premiums.

There are fees involved in establishing an HSA. These fees may affect any potential tax advantages if an HSA is established near the time of Medicare enrollment.

Estate Tax Treatment of HSAs

Upon death, the remaining balance in an HSA is includible in the account holder's gross estate for estate tax purposes. If the beneficiary of the account is a surviving spouse, the HSA belongs to the spouse and he or she can deduct the account balance in determining the account holder's taxable estate. The surviving spouse can then use the HSA for his or her medical expenses. If the beneficiary is someone other than the spouse, the HSA ceases to exist, and the beneficiary must include the fair market value of the account in his or her gross income for tax purposes. If no beneficiary is named, the tax is payable by the estate or the beneficiary of the estate.

Establishing and Maintaining HSAs

There are a number of issues that need to be evaluated by an individual who has the option to establish an HSA. Perhaps the most important question is whether such an account is appropriate. After a person decides to establish an HSA, issues such as account fees, investment options for funds, and record keeping must be addressed.

Appropriateness of HSAs

For some persons, an HSA is very appropriate and offers significant tax benefits and financial planning opportunities. For other persons, an HSA may not be an attractive financial commitment. An HSA's viability depends on individual circumstances such as income, tax rates, the funds available to fund such an account, when account balance will be withdrawn, earnings on account funds, and account fees. Some of these issues are addressed in the following example.

Example

John and his wife, both aged 50, no longer have any dependent children. They are self-employed and have a joint income of $150,000. For the last few years, they have had an HSA-compatible policy with a $5,000 deductible, but have not established HSAs. They are in good health and have paid all unreimbursed medical expenses from current income. Their financial advisor has suggested that one or both of them should establish an HSA. They have decided to do so, and make an annual contribution of $5,000, which is an affordable financial commitment. This will result in an annual income tax savings of $1,300 (based on IRS estimates). They have also decided to continue paying any unreimbursed medical expenses from current income and to let the HSA funds accumulate until they retire at age 65. They plan on investing the funds and expect them to grow at about 5 percent per year. If this return is achieved, they will have a fund of about $100,000 when they retire. They will then withdraw amounts as needed on a tax-free basis to pay their Medicare premiums.

Account Fees

One factor that varies widely among financial institutions that offer HSAs is the fees that they charge. If an individual uses an HSA that has been established by his or her employer, the employer may pay some of these fees. But no matter how an account is established, a potential account holder should look at the fees and their impact on the account balance. Unfortunately, this is not always easy to do. Although financial institutions often have information about their HSAs on Web sites or in print, the fee structure is often conspicu-ously absent or hard to locate. Unlike other types of financial products, such as IRAs, there are no requirements to provide potential account holders with a prospectus that details the fees. Therefore, it is often necessary to ask specific questions. As the next example demonstrates, these fees may have an effect on the decision to establish an HSA. Even if an HSA is an obvious choice, the account balance will be affected by the fee structure.

HSA fees fall into several categories that might include one or more of the following:

- *account setup fee.* This is a one-time fee to establish the HSA. Such fees typically range from $0 to $50, with $15 or $20 being common.

- *annual fee.* An HSA may have an annual fee that ranges up to $200, but amounts of $10 to $20 are most common.

- *monthly maintenance fee.* An HSA may have a monthly maintenance fee that ranges up to $10, but amounts like $2 to $3 seem most common. Although there may be both a monthly maintenance fee and an annual fee, this is very uncommon; there is usually one or the other. In either case, the amount of the fee may be lower for higher account balances.

- *transaction fee.* An HSA may have a fee that is levied on each transaction. The fee may apply to contributions, but is most likely to be levied on withdrawals only. Fees may be as high as $5, but $.25 to $.50 are quite common. Sometimes a few transactions are allowed without a fee, but fees are levied on transactions in excess of this number.

- *account closing fee.* It is not unusual for an HSA to have an account closing fee that can range up to $25 or $30, although $10 is a more common amount.

Investment Options for HSA Funds

Financial institutions often offer several types of investment options for HSA funds. Account holders can invest HSA funds in essentially the same manner as IRA funds. Allow-able investments include bank accounts, annuities, certificates of deposit, stocks, mutual funds, and bonds. Investments in life insurance policies or most types of collectibles are prohibited. In addition, an HSA trust or custodial agreement may limit the investment options available.

Although mutual funds and stocks may result in the best return over a number of years, they are probably unsuitable if an account holder has modest amounts in an HSA that will be used for medical expenses in the near future. Like many types of investments, they will fluctuate in value over time. Such investments may also be unavailable unless an account holder has an account balance of several thousand dollars.

In most cases, an individual will be using some type of bank account that allows easy access to the available funds. In this case, it is important to evaluate the return that these funds will earn, which is set by each bank. In some cases, nothing is paid unless the account exceeds a minimum balance, such as $1,000. Interest rates may also vary by the size of the account's average daily balance. In still other cases, a specified interest rate, which can change, is paid on any size balance. Even with these variations, there are significant differences among banks.

Record Keeping

Custodians and trustees for HSAs report the amount of annual contributions to and distributions from each HSA to the IRS. Under IRS rules, it is the account holder's responsibility to determine whether distributions from HSAs are for eligible medical expenses. Therefore, individuals who establish such accounts should maintain records in case they are audited. They should also become familiar with the types of expenses that are deductible.

ARCHER MEDICAL SAVINGS ACCOUNTS

Archer MSAs Archer medical savings accounts, commonly referred to as Archer MSAs, were the predecessors to HSAs. Fewer than 100,000 were ever established. Many account holders have terminated Archer MSAs or rolled them over to HSAs. Although new Archer MSAs can no longer be established, the few persons who have them can still make contributions if they continue to meet the eligibility requirements.

Archer MSAs are similar to HSAs with respect to account growth and estate tax treatment. However, they have a number of notable differences that include the following:

- Eligibility to make contributions is limited to the self-employed and employees of small employers with 50 or fewer employees.
- The required high-deductible policy has somewhat different deductible amounts and out-of-pocket limits. The deductible must apply to all covered expenses, including preventive care.
- Contributions are limited to 65 percent of the policy deductible for the high-deductible health plan.
- The account holder or the employer, but not both, can make contributions.

- Distributions for medical expenses of a family member is not allowed in any year that contributions are made unless the family member is covered under a high-deductible health plan.

A COMPARISON CHART

The following table compares HRAs, HSAs, and Archer MSAs.

Table 8-1 Savings Accounts Comparison			
	HRAs	**HSAs**	**Archer MSAs**
Persons eligible	Employees only	Anyone	Employees of employer with 50 or fewer employees and self-employed
Use of high-deductible health plan with account	Not required but usually used	Required	Required
Waiver of deductible requirement for preventive care	Permitted	Permitted	Not allowed
Contribution	By employer	By employer, employee, or both	By employer or employee but not both
Qualified medical expenses	Any unreimbursed medical expenses allowed by the employer and Internal Revenue Code, including insurance premiums	Most but not all unreimbursed medical expenses allowed by the Internal Revenue Code; some restrictions on insurance premiums	Most but not all unreimbursed medical expenses allowed by the Internal Revenue Code; some restrictions on insurance premiums
Taxation of distribution to participants	Tax free if for qualified medical expenses only	Tax free if for qualified medical expenses; other distributions subject to taxation and possibly penalty tax	Tax free if for qualified medical expenses; other distributions subject to taxation and possibly penalty tax
Portability	No—account usually terminates with employment	Yes—account owned by employee	Yes—account owned by employee
COBRA	Applies	Does not apply	Does not apply
Funding	Account usually unfunded and paid from employer's current revenue	Account must be funded	Account must be funded

CHAPTER REVIEW

Key Terms and Concepts

consumer-directed medical expense
  plan
defined-contribution medical
  expense plan
high-deductible health plan (HDHP)

health reimbursement arrangements
  (HRAs)
health savings accounts (HSAs)
Archer MSAs

Review Questions

Review questions are based on the learning objectives in this chapter. For example, a [3] at the end of a questions means that the question is based on learning objective 3. If there are multiple objectives, they are all listed.

1. Why have defined-contribution medical expense plans failed to contain medical care expenses? [1]

2. One technique for containing medical expenses is to use a savings account with a high-deductible medical expense policy. [1]

    a. What is the nature of this savings account?

    b. What is the rationale for this technique?

    c. What are the criticisms of this technique?

3. Regarding HRAs: [2]

    a. Who is eligible for an HRA?

    b. Who can make contributions to an HRA?

    c. How are HRAs funded?

4. Regarding HRAs: [2]

    a. When can employees take tax-free distributions from an HRA?

    b. When are tax-free withdrawals permitted?

5. What happens to an employee's HRA at termination of employment? [2]

6. Regarding HSAs: [3]

    a. Describe the general nature of health savings accounts (HSAs).

    b.   Who are eligible to establish and maintain them?

7.   Regarding HSAs: [3]

    a.   For purposes of HSAs, what is a high-deductible health plan?

    b.   What expenses do not count toward the plan's required deductible and out-of-pocket limits?

8.   Regarding HSAs: [3]

    a.   Who can make contributions to HSAs?

    b.   What is the federal income tax treatment of HSA contributions?

    c.   What contributions can be made to HSAs?

    d.   What is the nature of a catch-up contribution?

    e.   When can contributions be made?

    f.   What are excess contributions, and what is their implication?

9.   Regarding HSAs: [3]

    a.   When can an account holders take distributions from an HSA?

    b.   How are distributions taxed?

    c.   To what extent an account holder take tax-free distributions to pay long-term care insurance premiums?

10. Regarding HSAs: [3]

    a.   What effect does termination of employment have on HSAs?

    b.   How are HSAs treated for estate tax purposes?

11. What factors should be considered in determining the appropriateness of HSAs? [3]

12. What types of fees might be charged to HSA account holders? [3]

13. What types of investment options are available to HSA account holders? [3]

14. Why is record keeping particularly important with respect to HSA distributions? [3]

15. Regarding Archer MSAs: [3]

    a.   How are Archer MSAs similar to HSAs?

    b.   How do Archer MSAs differ from HSAs?

Review Question Answers

1. Historically, defined-contribution plans encouraged managed care plans as least expensive alternatives that provide a broad scope of coverage, yet limited a member's payment for services to modest copayments. From a member's viewpoint, the broad array of services is available for only the cost of the copayment. As a result, these plans greatly diminish the motivation of their members to contain costs when they seek services.

2. a. Contributions to the account may be made by the employer up to a specified amount equal the health plan's deductible, for example, such as $2,500. From this account the employee can make withdrawals to pay medical expenses that the health plan does not cover because of the deductible. The employee can carry forward any unused amount in the account and add it to the next year's employer contribution. If the amount in the account is exceeded, the employee will have to pay the full cost of medical expenses out of his or her own pocket until the health plan's deductible is satisfied.

   b. First, the expensive cost of administering and paying small claims is largely eliminated. Second, employees now have a direct financial incentive to avoid unnecessary care and to seek out the most cost-effective form of treatment.

   c. Critics contend that avoidance of minor medical and preventive care because of the high deductible may lead to major expenses that could have been averted or minimized with earlier treatment. Another criticism is that this type of medical expense plan does not focus on the problem of the uninsured. A final criticism is that these plans are just another way of shifting more medical costs to employees.

3. a. HRAs can be established by any size employer for its employees, but they cannot be established by or for self-employed persons.

   b. Contributions to an HRA must be made solely by the employer.

   c. HRAs are typically unfunded, and the employer contributions are merely credits to a savings account.

4. a. Under IRS rules, employees can take tax-free distributions from an HRA as reimbursement only for medical expenses that are not paid by any other medical expense plan.

   b. Tax-free withdrawals are permitted for the purchase of COBRA continuation coverage, Medicare premiums, and Medicare supplement policies. They are also permitted for the purchase of long-term care Insurance up to the tax-deductible limits on premiums.

5.   At termination of employment, an employee's HRA usually terminates. Unlike HSAs and Archer MSAs, however, HRAs are treated as group health plans and generally subject to COBRA requirements. If any employee elects this option, he or she has access to unused balances in the HRA account during the COBRA continuation period.

6.   a.   An HSA is a personal savings account from which unreimbursed medical expenses, including deductibles, percentage participation, and copayments, can be paid. The HSA must be in the form of a tax-exempt trust or custodial account established in conjunction with a high-deductible health (medical expense) plan. Any insurance company or bank (as well as certain other financial institutions) can be a trustee or custodian.

HSAs are individual trusts, which prohibits a husband and wife from having a joint HSA. But as long as both are eligible, each may have a separate HSA.

HSAs (and their balances) are portable even when established by an employer and remain with the individual when an employee changes employers or leaves the workforce.

b.   Employees, the self-employed, and anyone else can establish HSAs as long as they meet the following rules for qualification:

•   The individual must be covered by a qualified high-deductible health plan.

•   The individual is not eligible to be claimed as a dependent on another person's federal income tax return.

•   With some exceptions, a person who is covered under an high-deductible health plan is denied eligibility for an HSA if he or she is covered under another health plan that does not meet the definition of a high-deductible plan but that provides any benefits that are covered under the high-deductible health plan.

7.   a.   A high-deductible health plan (HDHP) is defined as having the following deductibles and annual out-of-pocket limitations for covered services. These figures are for 2016 and subject to annual inflation adjustments:

•   In the case of individual coverage (often referred to as self-only coverage), the deductible must be at least $1,300, and annual out-of-pocket expenses cannot exceed $6,550.

- In the case of family coverage, the deductible must be at least $2,600, and annual out-of-pocket expenses cannot exceed $13,100.

In the case of an HDHP used with an HSA, there will usually not be an individual deductible if a policy is written for a family. Rather, there will be a single deductible—referred to as a common deductible—that must be satisfied before any benefits are payable, even if all claims are for one family member. It is permissible, however, to use an individual deductible, but only if it is at least equal to the required HSA family deductible ($2,600 in 2016).

b. Expenses that do not count toward the plan's required deductible and out-of-pocket limits include:

- payments for services not covered by the high-deductible health plan

- payments for services received from nonnetwork health care providers, if the plan uses a preferred-provider network

- amounts above a plan's reasonable specific service or lifetime maximums

- amounts in excess of reasonable and customary fees

- penalties for failure to obtain a plan-required certification

8. a. Contributions to an HSA may be made solely by individuals who have such accounts. They may also be made by employers that provide their employees with a high-deductible health plan. It is possible that both the employer and employee may contribute to the account as long as the combined contributions do not exceed the annual maximum.

b. Contributions by an individual are deductible for federal income tax purposes even if the individual does not itemize deductions. Contributions by an employer are tax deductible to the employer and are not included in an employee's gross income or subject to Social Security, Medicare, and other employment taxes.

c. The maximum annual contribution to an HSA in 2016 is $3,350 if the account holder has self-only coverage and $6,750 if the account holder has family coverage. These amounts are subject to annual indexing for inflation. If both a husband and wife establish an HSA and have family coverage (that is a single policy covering both of them), they can allocate the maximum contribution as they wish. If they have separate policies, each is subject to the limits that apply to self-only coverage.

An account balance from an Archer MSA can be rolled over to an HSA on a tax-free basis. Similarly, an account balance from an existing HSA can be rolled over to a new HSA. Recent legislation also allows certain other types of tax-free rollovers from HRAs, health FSAs, and IRAs in specific circumstances.

d. Individuals aged 55 or older are also permitted an additional annual catch-up contribution of up to $1,000. If both a husband and wife are aged 55 or older, the catch-up contribution is available to each of them only if they have separate HSAs.

e. Annual contributions can be made in a lump sum or spread out over time. However, the contributions for a specific tax year cannot be made before the tax year begins or after the taxpayer's original filing date (without extensions) for that tax year. For most individuals, this is the earlier of April 15 of the following year or the date a return is filed. This is similar to the rules for IRA contributions.

f. An excess contribution occurs to the extent that contributions to an HSA exceed the tax-deductible limits or are made for an ineligible person. The account holder is subject to a 6 percent excise tax on excess contributions for each year these contributions are in an account unless they and any income attributable to them are removed from the HSA prior to the last day prescribed by law. The net income attributable to the excess contributions is included in the account holder's gross income for the tax year in which the distribution is made.

9. a. An individual can usually take distributions from an HSA at any time, but the trust or custodial document may put reasonable restriction on both the frequency and minimum amount of distributions.

b. Subject to some exceptions, distributions of both contributions and earnings are excludible from an account holder's gross income if used to pay medical expenses of the account holder and the account holder's legal spouse and tax dependents as long as these expenses are not paid by other sources of insurance.

c. Distributions for the purchase of long-term care insurance are permitted up to specified tax-deductible limits on premiums based on an individual's age which are subject to cost-of-living adjustments.

10. a. Retirees can continue HSAs that were established prior to retirement, and the rules for contributions and distributions are as previously described. As long as they are not yet Medicare eligible, retirees who did not have an HSA when they were actively employed can establish one at that time as long as all the proper rules are satisfied.

b. Upon death, the remaining balance in an HSA is includible in the account holder's gross estate for estate tax purposes. If the beneficiary of the account is a surviving spouse, the HSA belongs to the spouse and he or she can deduct the account balance in determining the account holder's taxable estate. The surviving spouse can then use the HSA for his or her medical expenses. If the beneficiary is someone other than the spouse, the HSA ceases to exist, and the beneficiary must include the fair market value of the account in his or her gross income for tax purposes. If no beneficiary is named, the tax is payable by the estate or the beneficiary of the estate.

11. The appropriateness of an HSA depends on individual circumstances such as income, tax rates, the funds available to fund such an account, when account balances will be withdrawn, earnings on account funds, and account fees.

12. The fees that an HSA might have include one or more of the following:

    - account set up fee

    - monthly maintenance fee

    - transactions fee

    - account closing fee

13. Account holders can invest HSA funds in essentially the same manner as IRA funds. Allowable investments include bank accounts, annuities, certificates of deposit, stocks, mutual funds, and bonds.

14. Under IRS rules, the account holder is responsible for determining whether distribution from HSAs are for eligible medical expenses. Therefore, individuals who establish such accounts should be familiar with the types of expenses that are deductible and maintain records in case they are audited.

15. a. Archer MSAs are essentially identical to HSAs with respect to account growth and estate tax treatment.

    b. Archer MSAs differ from HSAs in the following ways:

        - Eligibility to make contributions is limited to the self-employed and employees of small employers with 50 or fewer employees.

        - The required high-deductible policy has somewhat different deductible amounts and out-of-pocket limits. The deductible must apply to all covered expenses, including preventive care.

        - Contributions are limited to 65 percent of the policy deductible for the high-deductible health plan.

        - The account holder or the employer, but not both, can make contributions.

- Distributions for medical expenses of a family member is not allowed in any year that contributions are made unless the family member is covered under a high-deductible health plan.

Chapter 9

Provisions and Tax Treatment of Medical Expense Plans

Learning Objectives

An understanding of the material in this chapter should enable the student to

1. **Describe the eligibility provisions found in medical expense plans.**

2. **Explain the coordination-of-benefits process.**

3. **Explain the relationship between employer-provided medical expense coverage and Medicare.**

4. **Identify the circumstances under which employer-provided coverage may terminate, and explain how coverage can be continued.**

5. **Describe the procedures for processing medical expense claims and the HIPAA administrative standards.**

6. **Explain the tax implications of group medical expense premiums and benefits for employers and employees and the tax changes implemented by the Affordable Care Act.**

This chapter is devoted primarily to a discussion of many of the major provisions in medical expense plans, whether an employer self-funds the plan benefits or provides them through a traditional insurance contract, HMO, or PPO. Although the provisions in medical expense plans may stand alone as part of the employer's plan, most of them are incorporated into the contracts that fund the plan's benefits. Certain provisions are either unique to medical expense plans or different from those found in other types of group benefits. These provisions pertain to eligibility, coordination of benefits, the effect of Medicare, termination (including postretirement benefits), and claims.

ELIGIBILITY FOR MEDICAL EXPENSE COVERAGE

The eligibility requirements for medical expense coverage are essentially the same as those for group term insurance—an employee must usually be in a covered classification, must satisfy any probationary period, and generally must be full time.

Group health plans may condition eligibility on commencement of employment. Therefore, an employee who fails to start work on what would otherwise have been his or her initial day of employment, even because of health reasons, can be denied coverage until he or she begins work. If there is a probationary period, such as 90 days of continuous employment, a plan cannot treat an absence from work for a health reason as a break in this period.

Eligibility requirements may vary somewhat if an employer changes carriers for a plan's benefits. Note that the following discussion refers to the employer's plan with benefits paid by the previous carrier as the old plan and the employer's plan with benefits paid by the new carrier as the new plan. In actuality, the employer still has the same medical expense plan. It has only been modified with the use of a new insurance carrier or other financing mechanism and, possibly, a different level of benefits. This is a material modification to a group health plan, and ERISA requires that the plan administrator notify participants of this change by a summary of material modification.

Even though only a few states have adopted them, most insurers follow the procedures established by the National Association of Insurance Commissioners (NAIC) Group Coverage Discontinuance and Replacement Model Regulation for medical expense coverage (and possibly other group coverages). This regulation stipulates that a new plan provide coverage to anyone who (1) was covered under the old plan at the date it was discontinued and (2) is in an eligible classification of the new plan.

There are two final points about the transfer of coverage. First, the new plan will not pay benefits for expenses that the old plan covered under an extension-of-benefits provision (discussed later). Second, when applying any deductibles or probationary periods under the new plan, credit is often given for the satisfaction (or partial satisfaction) of the same or similar provisions during the last 3 months of the old plan. For example, assume that the employer transfers coverage in the middle of a calendar year and the new plan contains the same $500-a-year calendar deductible as the old plan. If an employee has already satisfied the deductible under the old plan, no new deductible is required for the remainder of the calendar year provided that (1) the expenses used to satisfy the deductible under the old plan satisfy the deductible under the new plan, and (2) the expenses were incurred during the last 3 months of the old plan. If only $340 of the $500 was incurred during those last 3 months, the employee is subject to an additional $160 deductible under the new plan for the remainder of the calendar year.

Dependent Eligibility for Medical Expense Benefits

Typically, the same medical expense benefits that a plan provides for an eligible employee are also available for that employee's dependents. Conversely, dependent coverage is rarely available unless the employee also has coverage. As long as an employee authorizes any necessary payroll deductions, dependent coverage is typically effective on the same date as the employee's coverage. If the employee does not elect coverage under a contributory plan within 31 days after dependents are eligible, future coverage is generally available only during an open enrollment period or when a qualifying event occurs. Newly acquired dependents (by birth, marriage, or adoption) are eligible for coverage as of the date they gain dependent status. As a rule, the employee must take a positive action to enroll such new dependents in order for their coverage to become effective. However, a newborn child has automatic coverage for the first 31 days following birth.

dependent

The term **dependent** most commonly refers to an employee's spouse who is not legally separated from the employee and any eligible dependent children (including stepchildren and adopted children) under the age of 26. Under the ACA mandates, student status, tax dependency, employment status, marital status, and other requirements are no longer relevant to continue a dependent child's coverage to age 26.

In addition, coverage may also continue for children who are incapable of earning their own living because of a physical or mental infirmity. Such children are considered dependents as long as this condition exists, but periodic proof of the condition is normally required. If an employee has dependent coverage, all newly acquired dependents (by birth, marriage, or adoption) have automatic coverage.

A few plans define "dependent" more widely to include grandchildren, parents, and siblings who live with the employee.

Federal Rules for Children's Medical Coverage

Federal legislation in the early 1990s brought the federal government into the picture with a series of rules designed to better guarantee that benefits are available to children. Some of these rules pertain to eligibility.

Medical Coverage for Adopted Children

If a work-related group medical expense plan provides coverage for dependent children of participants or beneficiaries, it must provide benefits for adopted children or children placed for adoption under the same terms and conditions that apply to natural children. For purposes of this change, a child is defined as a person under the age of 18 at the time of adoption or placement for adoption. Placement for adoption occurs at the time in the adoption process when the plan participant or beneficiary assumes and retains the legal duty for the total or partial support of a child to be adopted.

Medical Child Support Orders

Employer-sponsored medical expense plans must recognize qualified medical child support orders by providing benefits for a participant's children in accordance with the requirements of such an order.

medical child support order

A **medical child support order** is a court judgment, decree, or order that (1) provides for child support with respect to the child of a group plan participant or provides benefit coverage to such a child, is ordered under state domestic relations law, and relates to benefits under the plan or (2) enforces a state medical support law enacted under the new Medicaid rules discussed below. The support order then becomes *qualified* if it meets two additional requirements. First, the order must create or recognize the right of the child to receive benefits to which the plan participant or other beneficiary is entitled under a group plan. Second, the order must include such information as the name and last known mailing address of the plan participant and the child, a reasonable description of the coverage to be provided, the period for which coverage must be provided, and each plan to which the order applies.

Because of a lack of uniformity among medical child support orders and difficulty for employers in determining whether they are qualified, the Department of Labor and the Department of Health and Human Services have jointly developed a National Medical Support Notice (NMSN) that state courts and agencies must use. When properly completed, the NMSN meets the requirements of a qualified medical child support order. The NMSN has two parts, both of which are sent to the employer. Within 20 days, the employer must respond to the agency that sent the order if coverage is not available for any reason. If coverage is available, part B of the form must be sent to the plan administrator if it is not the employer. Within 40 days after receiving the NMSN, the employer's plan must provide coverage for the dependent child. If the plan administrator is not the employer, the administrator must notify the employer of the amount to withhold from the worker's pay.

Medicaid Rules

The legislation encouraged the states (under threat of losing some Medicaid reimbursement) to adopt a series of laws relating to medical child support. One of these laws prohibits plan administrators from denying enrollment of a child under a parent's insurance plan on any of the following grounds:

- The child was born out of wedlock.

- The child is not claimed as a dependent on the parent's federal income tax return.
- The child does not reside with the parent or in the insurer's service area.

In addition, a second law provides that if a court orders a parent to provide medical support, the parent's plan must enroll the child without regard to any enrollment restrictions. If the parent fails to enroll the child, enrollment can be made by the child's other parent or by the state Medicaid agency. The employer is required to withhold from the parent's compensation any payments that the parent must make toward the cost of coverage.

Benefits for Domestic Partners

domestic partners

In the mid-1980s, the plans of a few employers began to make coverage available for unmarried **domestic partners**. For example, one plan covers unmarried couples as long as they live together, show financial interdependence and joint responsibility for each other's common welfare, and consider themselves life partners. This type of requirement is typical, as is the additional requirement that the employee's relationship must have lasted some specified minimum period, such as 6 or 12 months. The employee must usually give the employer an affidavit that these requirements have been satisfied. A domestic partner with benefits is often able to enroll his or her dependent children under the plan.

Over 50 percent of large employers now provide medical expense benefits to domestic partners, as do many smaller employers. Most plans provide benefits to domestic partners engaged in either opposite sex or same sex relationships. Some plans provide benefits only to persons of the opposite gender of the employee, and a small number of plans limit benefits only to persons of the same gender.

The number of employees obtaining coverage for domestic partners has been relatively small, with many employers experiencing enrollment of less than one percent when only partners of the same gender are covered. Some employers have experienced enrollment of up to 5 percent if partners of either gender are covered. (Enrollments of partners of the opposite gender have historically been more than double the enrollments of partners of the same gender.) This low enrollment is due primarily to two factors. First, the domestic partner is probably also working and has medical expense coverage from his or her employer. Second, some employees are unwilling to make their living arrangement or sexual orientation known in the workplace.

COORDINATION OF BENEFITS

Estimates are that the percentage of individuals having duplicate group medical expense coverage is about 10 percent. One such situation occurs if a husband and wife both work and have coverage under their respective employers' plans. If the employer of either spouse also provides dependent coverage on a noncontributory basis, the other spouse (and other dependents if both employers provide such coverage) may be covered under both plans. If dependent coverage is contributory, it is necessary for a couple with children to elect such coverage under one of their plans. However, because a spouse is considered a dependent, he or she may have duplicate coverage when the election is made. Note that this duplicate coverage is avoided if an employee can elect dependent coverage for children only. This option exists under many but not all plans. Duplicate coverage may also arise when

- an employee has coverage at a current job and under a prior employer's plan for retirees
- children are covered under both a parent's and a stepparent's plans
- an employee elects coverage under a contributory plan even though the employee is covered as a dependent under another plan. This could result from ignorance or from an attempt to collect double the amount if a claim should occur. In many cases, the employee elects this coverage because it is broader, even though it still results in an element of duplicate coverage.

Duplicate coverage can also occur if the individual has coverage under a group plan that an employer does not provide, as with children whose parents have purchased accident coverage for them through their schools.

coordination-of-benefits (COB) provision

In the absence of any provisions to the contrary, group medical expense plans are obligated to provide benefits in cases of duplicate coverage as if no other coverage exists. However, to prevent individuals from receiving benefits that exceed their actual expenses, group medical expense plans contain a **coordination-of-benefits (COB) provision**, which establishes priorities for the payment of benefits by each plan covering an individual.

While a COB provision is not required, if one is used it must comply with the appropriate state rules. Most COB provisions are based on the Group Coordination of Benefits Model Regulation promulgated by the NAIC.

Almost all COB provisions apply when other coverage exists through the group insurance plans or other group benefit arrangements of another employer. They may also apply to no-fault automobile insurance benefits and to student coverage that an educational institution either sponsors or provides. However, these provisions virtually never apply (and cannot in most states) to any other insurance contracts that an individual purchases outside the employment relationship.

Determination of Primary Coverage

The usual COB provision stipulates that any other plan without the COB provision is primary. If more than one plan has a COB provision, the following priorities are established:

- Coverage as an employee is usually primary to coverage as a dependent. The exception occurs if a retired person has coverage (1) under Medicare, (2) under a retiree plan of a former employer, and (3) as a dependent of a spouse who is an active employee. In this case, coverage as a dependent is primary, Medicare is secondary, and the retiree plan pays last.

- Coverage as an active employee (or that person's dependent) is primary to coverage as a retired or laid-off employee (or that person's dependent). This rule is ignored unless both plans contain it.

- Coverage as an active employee (or that person's dependent) is primary to a plan that provides COBRA continuation benefits. This rule is also ignored unless both plans contain the rule.

- If the specific rules of a court decree state that one parent must assume responsibility for his or her child's health care expenses, and the plan of that parent has actual knowledge of the terms of the court decree, then that plan is primary.

- If the parents of dependent children are married or are not separated (regardless of whether they have ever been married) or if a court awards joint custody without specifying that one parent has the responsibility to provide health care coverage, the plan of the parent whose birthday falls earlier in the calendar year is primary and the plan of the parent with the later birthday is secondary.

- If the parents of dependent children are not married, are separated (regardless of whether they have ever been married), or are divorced and if there is no court decree allocating responsibility for the child's health care expenses, the following priorities apply:

  - The plan of the parent with custody is primary.

- The plan of the stepparent who is the spouse of the parent with custody is secondary.

- The plan of the parent without custody is tertiary.

- The plan of the stepparent who is the spouse of the parent without custody pays last.

• If none of the previous rules establishes a priority, the plan covering the person for the longest period is primary. If this rule also fails to determine the primary plan, then the plans share the allowable expenses equally.

Determination of Benefits Payable: Some Examples

The following examples demonstrate the mechanics of the previously described COB provision.

Example

Mary has coverage under two medical expense plans, neither of which contains a COB provision.

Plan A provides PPO coverage that pays allowable expenses in full as long as network preferred providers are used. If nonnetwork providers are used, there is (1) a $500 annual deductible, (2) 80 percent coinsurance subject to a $3,000 out-of-pocket limit, and (3) an unlimited lifetime maximum.

Plan B provides traditional comprehensive major medical expense coverage with (1) a $200 calendar-year deductible, (2) 80 percent coinsurance subject to a $1,000 out-of-pocket limit, and (3) a $2 million lifetime maximum.

Assume that Mary incurs the following expenses for a surgical procedure:

Semiprivate room for 4 days at $1,000 per day	$4,000
Other hospital charges	3,500
Surgeon's fees	3,000
Total expenses	$10,500

Assume also that (1) plan A is primary and (2) Mary uses network providers. In this case, plan A would pay the full $10,500, and plan B would pay $9,300 after deductions for the $200 deductible and the $1,000 out-of-pocket limit that applies to the coinsurance provision. Consequently, Mary would collect a total of $19,800, or $9,300 in excess of her actual expenses.

If the example changes so that plan B is primary and Mary uses nonnetwork providers for plan A, plan B will still pay $9,300. However, plan A will only pay $8,000, which is 80 percent of the expenses above the nonnetwork deductible. In this case, Mary would collect $17,300, still significantly more than her actual expenses.

allowable expenses

If a plan uses a COB provision, the plan must first determine whether the provision applies to a given claim. It applies only if the sum of the benefits under the plans involved (assuming there is no provision) exceeds an individual's allowable expenses. **Allowable expenses** are defined as any necessary, reasonable, and customary items of expense, all or a portion of which are covered under at least one of the plans that provides benefits to the person for whom the claim is made. However, under a primary plan, the amount of any benefit reductions resulting from a covered person's failure to comply with the plan's provisions (such as second opinions or precertification) is not an allowable expense. In addition, the difference between the cost of a private hospital room and the cost of a semiprivate hospital room is not an allowable expense unless the patient's stay in a private room is medically necessary. When the allowable expenses are determined, any deductibles, percentage participation resulting from coinsurance provisions, and plan maximum are ignored.

When the COB provision applies, a person can receive benefits equal to 100 percent of his or her allowable expenses and no more.

Example

Assume the same facts as in the previous example, except that each plan contains a COB provision. The entire $10,500 of expenses incurred by Mary are allowable expenses. Because the sum of the benefits otherwise payable under the two plans (either $19,800 or $17,300, depending on which plan is primary) exceeds this amount, the COB provision applies. The primary plan pays its benefits as if no other coverage exists, and the secondary plan (or plans) pays the remaining benefits. If plan A in this example is primary, it will pay $10,500, and plan B will pay nothing because 100 percent of Mary's allowable expenses have been paid. If plan B is primary, it will pay $9,300, and plan A will pay the remaining $1,200 of Mary's allowable expenses.

Determination of Benefits: Some Complexities

In actual practice, the determination of benefits payable may be much more complex than the previous simple example. Although many of these complexities are beyond the scope of this book, a few issues are addressed. These include the following:

- determination of benefits payable by each plan

- coordination of benefits with self-funded plans

Before proceeding further, however, there is one important point: Coordination of benefits is between two (or more) specific plans, each of which has its own rules. Although generalizations can be made, the ultimate benefits a plan pays depends on the specific rules of the plan.

Determination of Benefits Payable by Each Plan

The earlier example lumped expenses together into three broad categories and assumed each plan covered them, except for any deductibles and percentage participation by the insured. An actual benefit calculation looks at every charge billed by the hospital and surgeon and determines to what extent that charge is covered. It is possible that some charges will not be paid in full because they exceed reasonable and customary charges or because of exclusions. In addition, some managed care plans limit benefits for nonnetwork services to what they pay network providers. It is common for this to be significantly below billed charges.

Coordination of Benefits with Self-Funded Plans

Self-funded plans are not bound by the state COB rules that apply to insurance contracts and HMO plans, but as a rule they use provisions that are identical or very similar. However, they are free to use any type of COB provision.

Some self-funded plans use a provision so that their payment as a secondary payer is limited to the amount that would reach the limits of their own plan. For example, assume that two self-funded plans each cover only 80 percent of an insured's medical expenses after a $250 deductible. The secondary payer would pay nothing because the limits of its own plan had already been reached by the primary plan. If the secondary plan had a lower deductible, such as $200, the secondary plan would pay $50. This type of provision, which in effect preserves deductible and coinsurance in the COB process, is not allowed under the NAIC model regulation previously discussed for insured plans.

A few self-funded plans coordinate benefits with plans under which an individual is eligible for coverage, even if that plan does not cover the individual. For example, the self-funded plan might provide coverage for an employee's dependents. If a dependent spouse works outside the home and is eligible for his or her own employer-provided coverage, the self-funded plan would pay on a secondary basis, whether or not the spouse signed up for his or her employer's plan.

Finally, some self-funded plans have been designed so that they are excess or "always secondary" to any other medical expense plan. The extreme situation occurs if a person has coverage under two self-funded plans, each of which takes an always-secondary approach. Each plan pays as if it were secondary. In the earlier example where the insured has $10,500 of covered expenses, this means that plan A pays $2,200 and plan B pays nothing. This total of $2,200 is less than either plan would pay if it were primary. This issue has been the subject of several court cases, and some (but not all) courts have stated that the always-secondary position cannot prevail. Although these courts have ordered an equitable payment of benefits to the covered person, that person has been forced to take the matter to court.

RELATIONSHIP WITH MEDICARE

Because most employees and their dependents are eligible for Medicare upon reaching age 65 (and possibly under other circumstances), a provision that eliminates any possible duplication of coverage is necessary. The simplest solution is to exclude any person eligible for Medicare from eligibility under the group contract. However, in most cases this approach conflicts with the Age Discrimination in Employment Act, which prohibits discrimination in welfare benefit plans for active employees.

Medicare Secondary Rules

Medicare secondary rules

Medicare is often the secondary payer to employer-provided medical expense coverage. Under the **Medicare secondary rules**, employers with 20 or more employees must make coverage available under their medical expense plans to active employees aged 65 or older and to active employees' spouses who are eligible for Medicare. Unless an employee elects otherwise (by not enrolling in the employer's plan), the employer's plan is primary and Medicare is secondary. Except in plans that require large employee contributions, it is doubtful that employees will elect Medicare because federal law prohibits employers from offering active employees or their spouses a Medicare carve-out, a Medicare supplement, or some other incentive not to enroll in the employer's plan.

Medicare is the secondary payer of benefits in certain other situations. One situation involves persons who are eligible for Medicare benefits to treat end-stage renal disease with dialysis or kidney transplants. Medicare provides these benefits to any insured workers (either active or retired workers and regardless of age) and their spouses and dependent children, but the employer's plan is primary only during the first 30 months of treatment. After that, Medicare is primary and the employer's plan is secondary. This rule for renal disease applies to medical expense plans of all employers, not just those with 20 or more employees.

Medicare is also the secondary payer of benefits to disabled employees (or the disabled dependents of employees) under age 65 who are eligible for Medicare and who have coverage under the medical expense plan of large employers (defined as plans with 100 or more employees). Medicare, however, does not pay anything until a person has been eligible for Social Security disability income benefits for 2 years. The rule applies only if an employer continues medical expense coverage for disabled persons; such continuation is not required.

When an employer's plan is primary, Medicare makes payments for any expenses that are covered by Medicare but not by the employer's plan. For purposes of these payments, Medicare deductibles, copayments, and percentage participation generally do not apply. However, Medicare benefits are limited to what would have been paid in the absence of the employer's plan.

Medicare Carve-Outs and Supplements

An employer's plan may cover certain persons aged 65 or older who are not subject to the provisions of the Age Discrimination in Employment Act—specifically, retirees and active employees of firms with fewer than 20 employees. Although there is nothing to prevent an employer from terminating coverage for these persons, many employers provide them with either a Medicare carve-out or Medicare supplement.

Medicare carve-out

With a **Medicare carve-out**, plan benefits are reduced to the extent that benefits are payable under Medicare for the same expenses. (Medicare may also pay for some expenses not covered by the group plan.)

Example

If Karen incurs $1,000 of covered expenses and is not eligible for Medicare, $720 in benefits is paid under her medical expense plan that has a $100 deductible and an 80 percent coinsurance provision. However, if she is eligible for Medicare, and the Medicare allowable amount for the same service is $650, that amount becomes the basis of benefit determination. Medicare typically pays 80 percent of the allowable amount for medical (nonhospital) services, or $520 in this example. The employer's plan would then pay the remaining $130, for a total benefit of $650, thereby relieving Karen of ant out-of-pocket expenses.

Some medical expense plans use a less liberal carve-out approach and reduce covered expenses (rather than benefits payable) by any amounts received under Medicare.

Example

In the previous example, the $130 left unpaid by Medicare would be subject to the employer plan's $100 deductible, unless Karen had already satisfied this amount. If she had not, the plan would pay 80 percent of the remaining $30.

Medicare supplement

As an alternative to using a carve-out approach, some employers use a **Medicare supplement** that provides benefits for certain expenses not covered under Medicare. These include (1) the portion of expenses not paid by Medicare because of deductibles, coinsurance, or copayments, and (2) specified expenses excluded by Medicare, such as vision and dental care. Such a supplement may or may not provide benefits similar to those available under a carve-out plan.

TERMINATION OF COVERAGE

In the absence of any provisions for continuation or conversion, the group medical expense coverage of an employee generally ceases upon the earliest of

- the date on which employment terminates. In some plans, coverage ceases on the last day of the month in which employment terminates.
- the date on which the employee ceases to be eligible
- the date on which the master contract terminates
- the date on which the overall maximum benefit of major medical coverage is received
- the end of the last period for which the employee makes any required contribution

Coverage on any dependent usually ceases on the earliest of the following:

- the date on which he or she ceases to meet the definition of dependent
- the date on which the coverage of the employee ceases for any reason except the employee's receipt of the overall maximum benefit
- the date on which the dependent receives the overall maximum benefit of major medical coverage

- the end of the last period for which the employee makes any required contribution for dependent coverage

However, coverage often continues past these dates because of federal legislation or employer practices.

Continuation of Coverage under COBRA

COBRA

The Consolidated Omnibus Budget Reconciliation Act of 1985 (**COBRA**) requires that group health plans allow employees and certain beneficiaries to elect to have their current health insurance coverage extended at group rates for up to 36 months following a "qualifying event" that results in the loss of coverage for a "qualified beneficiary." The term *group health plan* as used in the act is broad enough to include medical expense plans, dental plans, vision care plans, and prescription drug plans, regardless of whether benefits are self-insured or provided through other entities, such as insurance companies, HMOs, or PPOs. Long-term care and disability income coverages are not included in the definition of group health plan and are not subject to COBRA.

COBRA also applies to voluntary group health plans even if the employee pays the entire premium as long as an employee would not be able to receive the coverage at the same cost if the employment relationship ended. If the voluntary plan has a portability provision whereby an employee can continue the coverage on an individual basis at no increase in cost, then COBRA does not apply.

Certain church-related plans and plans of the federal government are exempt from COBRA, but the act applies to all other employers who had the equivalent of 20 or more full-time employees on at least 50 percent of its typical business days during the preceding calendar year. For example, an employer who has 10 full-time and 16 half-time employees throughout the year has the equivalent of 18 full-time employees and is not subject to COBRA.

Failure to comply with the act results in an excise tax of up to $100 per day for each person denied coverage. The IRS can levy the tax on the employer as well as on the entity (such as an insurer or HMO) that provides or administers the benefits. In addition, employers face a significant liability risk if they fail to notify qualified beneficiaries about the availability of COBRA coverage. There have been legal judgments under which employers have been required to pay uninsured claims that would have been covered if a qualified beneficiary had known about COBRA and elected coverage.

qualified beneficiary

COBRA defines a **qualified beneficiary** as any employee, or the spouse or dependent child of the employee, who on the day before a qualifying event had coverage under the employee's group health plan. HIPAA expanded the definition to include any child who is born to or placed for adoption with the employee during the period of COBRA coverage. This change gives automatic eligibility for COBRA coverage to the child as well as the right to have his or her own election rights if a second qualifying event occurs.

qualifying event

Under the act, each of the following is a qualifying event if it results in the loss of coverage by a qualified beneficiary or an increase in the amount the qualified beneficiary must pay for the coverage:

- the death of the covered employee

- the termination of the employee for any reason except gross misconduct. This includes quitting, retiring, or being fired for anything other than gross misconduct.

- a reduction of the employee's hours so that the employee or dependent is ineligible for coverage

- the divorce or legal separation of the employee and his or her spouse

- for spouses and children, the employee's eligibility for Medicare

- a child's ceasing to be an eligible dependent under the plan

The act specifies that a qualified beneficiary is entitled to elect continued coverage without providing evidence of insurability. The plan must allow the beneficiary to continue coverage identical to that available to employees and dependents to whom a qualifying event has not occurred. Persons electing COBRA continuation can change their coverage when changes are made to the plan covering similarly situated active employees and their dependents. In addition, a qualified beneficiary who moves out of an area served by a region-specific plan must have the right to change coverage if the employer is able to provide coverage under another of its existing plans.

The plan must allow each qualified beneficiary to continue coverage from the qualifying event until the earliest of the following:

- 18 months for employees and dependents when the employee's employment ceases or coverage terminates because of a reduction in hours. This period extends to 29 months for a qualified beneficiary if the Social Security

Administration determines that the beneficiary was or became totally disabled at any time during the first 60 days of COBRA coverage.

- 36 months for other qualifying events
- the date the plan terminates for all employees
- the date the coverage ceases because of a failure to make a timely payment of premium for the qualified beneficiary's coverage. COBRA regulations prohibit a plan from discontinuing coverage because a payment is short by an insignificant amount, which the regulations define as the lesser of $50 or 10 percent of the amount due. The plan must either (1) accept the amount received as satisfying the plan's payment requirement or (2) notify the beneficiary of the amount of the deficiency and grant a reasonable time for it to be paid.
- the date the qualified beneficiary subsequently becomes entitled to Medicare or becomes covered (as either an employee or dependent) under another group health plan, provided the group health plan does not contain an exclusion or limitation with respect to any preexisting condition. If the new plan does not cover a preexisting condition, a qualified beneficiary can continue the COBRA coverage until the earlier of (1) the remainder of the 18- or 36-month period or (2) the time when the preexisting-conditions provision no longer applies. Note that COBRA coverage is not affected by entitlement to benefits under Medicare or coverage under another group plan if this entitlement or coverage existed at the time of the qualifying event.

If a second qualifying event (such as the death or divorce of a terminated employee) occurs during the period of continued coverage, the maximum period of continuation is 36 months. For example, if an employee terminates employment, the employee and family are eligible for 18 months of COBRA coverage. If the employee dies after 15 months, a second qualifying event has occurred for the employee's spouse and dependent children. The normal period of COBRA continuation resulting from the death of an employee is 36 months. However, because the spouse and children have already had COBRA coverage for 15 months, the second qualifying event extends coverage for an additional 21 months.

At the termination of the COBRA period, a plan must offer a qualified beneficiary the right to convert to an individual insurance policy if a conversion privilege is generally available to employees under the plan.

The plan administrator must provide notification of the right to continue coverage at two times. First, when a plan becomes subject to COBRA or when a person becomes covered under a plan subject to COBRA, the administrator must give notification to an employee as well as to his or her spouse, generally within 90 days. A single letter to the employee and spouse satisfies this requirement as long as they reside at the same location. Second, when a qualifying event occurs, the employer must notify the plan administrator, who then must notify all qualified beneficiaries within 14 days. In general, the employer has 30 days to notify the plan administrator. However, an employer may not know of a qualifying event if it involves divorce, legal separation, or a child ceasing to be eligible for coverage. In these circumstances, the employee or family member must notify the employer within 60 days of the event, or the right to elect COBRA coverage is lost. The period for the employer to notify the plan administrator begins when the employer is informed of the qualifying event, as long as this occurs within the 60-day period.

COBRA rules also require plan administrators to provide notification to qualified beneficiaries in two other circumstances. First, if a plan beneficiary receives a notice of a qualifying event and the qualified beneficiary is ineligible for COBRA coverage, the plan administrators must explain why the qualified beneficiary is not entitled to coverage. Second, if the plan terminates COBRA coverage before the end of the maximum duration, the plan administrator must explain when and why the coverage is being terminated and inform the qualified beneficiary of any available rights to other coverage.

Continuation of coverage is not automatic; a qualified beneficiary must elect it. The election period starts on the date of the qualifying event and may end not earlier than 60 days after actual notice of the event to the qualified beneficiary by the plan administrator. Once a beneficiary elects coverage, he or she has 45 days to pay the premium for the period of coverage prior to the election.

Under COBRA, the plan may pass the cost of the continued coverage to the qualified beneficiary, but the cost cannot exceed 102 percent of the cost to the plan for the period of coverage for a similarly situated active employee to whom a qualifying event has not occurred. The extra 2 percent is supposed to cover the employer's extra administrative costs. The one exception to this rule occurs for months 19 through 29 if an employee is disabled, in which case the premium can then be as high as 150 percent. Qualified beneficiaries must have the option of paying the premium in monthly installments. In addition, there must be a grace period of at least 30 days for each installment.

COBRA has resulted in significant extra costs for employers. Precise statistics are difficult to obtain, but one insurer indicates that approximately 20 percent of those persons who are entitled to a COBRA continuation elect coverage. The length of coverage averages almost one year for persons eligible for an 18-month extension and almost 2 years for persons eligible for a 36-month extension. Although significant variations exist among employers, claim costs of persons with COBRA coverage generally run about 150 percent of claim costs for active employees and dependents. Moreover, administrative costs are estimated to be about $20 per month for each person with COBRA coverage.

Continuation of Coverage in Addition to COBRA

Retired Employees

Although not required to do so by the Age Discrimination in Employment Act, some employers continue coverage on retired employees. Some employers continue coverage for the life of an employee, but some employers provide coverage only until the employee is eligible for Medicare. Although a plan may continue coverage for retirees' dependents, it is often limited only to spouses. Retired employees under age 65 usually have the same coverage as active employees have. However, coverage for employees aged 65 or older (if included under the same plan) may be provided under a Medicare carve-out or a Medicare supplement. If there is a lifetime maximum for persons eligible for Medicare, it is often lower than the limit for active employees.

The subject of retiree benefits became a major concern to employers since the Financial Accounting Standards Board (FASB) phased in new rules between 1993 and 1997 for the accounting of postretirement benefits other than pensions. These rules require that employers do the following:

- recognize the present value of future retiree medical expense benefits on the firm's balance sheet with other liabilities
- record the cost for postretirement medical benefits in the period when an employee performs services. This is comparable to the accounting for pension costs.
- amortize the present value of the future cost of benefits accrued prior to the new rules

These rules are in contrast to the long-used previous practice of paying retiree medical benefits or premiums out of current revenue and recognizing these costs as expenses when paid. Although the rules are logical from a financial accounting standpoint, the effect on employers has been significant. Employers who elected to immediately recognize the liability had to show reduced earnings and net worth. Firms that elected to amortize the liability (often because immediate recognition would wipe out net worth) will be affected for years to come.

The FASB rules, along with the increasing cost of medical expense coverage, have resulted in two major changes by employers. First, many employers have reduced or eliminated retiree benefits or are considering such a change. One survey[1] indicates that the number of employers (with over 200 employees) that provide coverage to retirees has dropped from 66 percent in 1988 to 23 percent in 2015. Most of the employers provide coverage prior to Medicare eligibility and about 73 percent of them also provide benefits after Medicare eligibility. Some employers are not altering plans for current retirees or active employees who are eligible to retire. Instead, the changes apply to future retirees only. These changes, which seem to run the gamut, include the following:

- eliminating benefits for future retirees

- shifting more of the cost burden to future retirees by reducing benefits. A plan may accomplish such a reduction by providing lower benefit maximums, covering fewer types of expenses, or increasing copayments.

- adding or increasing retiree sharing of premium costs after retirement

- shifting to a defined-contribution approach to funding retiree benefits. For example, an employer might agree to pay $5 per month toward the cost of coverage after retirement for each year of service by an employee. Thus, an employer would make a monthly contribution of $150 for an employee who retired with 30 years of service, but the employer would make a contribution of only $75 for an employee with 15 years of service. Some plans of this nature are designed so that the employer's contribution increases with changes in the consumer price index, subject to maximum increases (such as 5 percent per year).

- encouraging retirees to elect benefits from managed care plans. With this approach, retirees are required to pay a significant portion of the cost if they continue coverage through a traditional indemnity plan.

A second change is that some employers have explored methods to prefund the benefits. However, there are no alternatives for prefunding that are as favorable as the alternatives for funding pension benefits. One alternative is the use of a 501(c)(9) trust (or VEBA). There are limitations on the deductibility of contributions to a 501(c)(9) trust. Furthermore, an employer can use a 501(c)(9) trust to fund retiree benefits only if it also uses the trust to fund benefits for active employees.

Another alternative is to prefund medical benefits within a pension plan. Contributions are tax deductible, and earnings accumulate tax free. The IRS rules for qualified retirement plans permit the payment of benefits for medical expenses from a pension plan if the following requirements are satisfied:

---

1.   The Henry J. Kaiser Family Foundation and Health Research Education Trust, *Employer Health Benefits, 2015 Summary of Findings, 2015,* page 6.

- The medical benefits must be subordinate to the retirement benefits. A pension plan meets this rule if the cost of the medical benefits provided does not exceed 25 percent of the employer's aggregate contribution to the plan. For many employers, this figure is too low to allow the entire future liability to be prefunded.

- There must be a separate account for the monies allocated to medical benefits. Nonkey employees can have an aggregate account, but separate individual accounts must be maintained for key employees, and medical benefits attributable to a key employee (and his or her family members) can be made only from the key employee's account.

- The employer's contributions for medical benefits must be ascertainable and reasonable.

Although the rules for funding retiree medical benefits in a pension plan are restricted and administratively complex, they offer an employer the opportunity to deduct at least a portion of the cost of prefunded benefits.

Surviving Dependents

A plan can also continue coverage for the survivors of deceased active employees and/or deceased retired employees. However, plans do not commonly continue coverage for the survivors of active employees beyond the period required by COBRA, and coverage for the survivors of retired employees may be limited to surviving spouses. In both instances, the continued coverage is usually identical to what the survivor had prior to the employee's death. It is also common for the employer to continue the same premium contribution level.

Laid-off Employees

An employer may continue medical expense coverage for laid-off workers, and large employers frequently provide such coverage for a limited period. Few employers provide coverage beyond the period required by COBRA, but some employers continue to make the same premium contribution, at least for a limited period.

Disabled Employees

Medical expense coverage can be continued for an employee (and dependents) when he or she has a temporary interruption of employment, including one arising from illness or injury. Many employers also cover employees who have long-term disabilities or who have retired because of a disability. In most cases, this continuation of coverage is contingent on satisfaction of some definition of total (and possibly permanent) disability. When continuing coverage for disabled employees, an employer must determine the extent of employer contributions. For example, the employer may continue the same premium contribution as for active employees, although there is nothing to prevent a different contribution rate—either lower or higher.

Domestic Partners

In general, domestic partners do not meet the definition of qualified beneficiary for purposes of COBRA. However, some employers provide domestic partners who have coverage under the employer's plan with continuation coverage that is similar or identical to what is available under COBRA.

Extension of Benefits

extension of benefits

When coverage terminates rather than continues, most medical expense plans have an **extension of benefits** for any covered employee or dependent who is totally disabled at the time of termination. However, the disability must have resulted from an illness or injury that occurred while the person was covered under the plan's insurance contract. Generally, the same level of benefits is available as before termination. Although some contracts cover only expenses associated with the same cause of disability, other contracts cover any expenses that would have been paid under the terminated coverage, regardless of cause.

As a rule, the extension of benefits generally ceases after 12 months, or when the individual is no longer totally or continuously disabled, whichever comes first.

Conversion

Except when termination results from the failure to pay any required premiums, medical expense contracts usually contain a conversion provision. With such a provision, a plan allows covered persons whose group coverage terminates to purchase individual medical expense coverage without evidence of insurability and without any limitation of benefits for preexisting conditions. Covered persons commonly have 31 days from the date of termination of the group coverage to exercise this conversion privilege, and coverage is then effective retroactively to the date of termination.

This conversion privilege is typically given to any employee who has been insured under the group contract (or under any group contract it replaced) for at least 3 months, and it permits the employee to convert his or her own coverage as well as any dependent coverage. In addition, a spouse or child whose dependent coverage ceases for any other reason may also be eligible for conversion.

State laws and insurance company practices vary with respect to the conversion provision and COBRA. In some cases, conversion is contingent upon an individual electing COBRA coverage and maintaining it for the maximum election period. At that time, a conversion policy is available. In other cases, a person who is eligible for both the conversion privilege and the right to continue the group insurance coverage under COBRA has two choices when eligibility for coverage terminates. He or she can either elect to convert under the provisions of the policy or elect to continue the group coverage under COBRA. If the person makes the latter choice, the COBRA rules specify that the person must again be eligible to convert to an individual policy within the usual conversion period (31 days) after the maximum continuation-of-coverage period ceases. In either situation, policy provisions may also make the conversion privilege available to persons whose coverage terminates prior to the end of the maximum continuation period. If a covered person elects the conversion option, there are no COBRA rights if the conversion policy terminates.

The provider of the medical expense coverage has the right to refuse the issue of a "conversion" policy to anyone (1) who has Medicare coverage or (2) whose benefits under the converted policy, together with similar benefits from other sources, would result in overinsurance according to the insurance company's standards.

Some plans offer a conversion policy that another entity issues. For example, an HMO might enter into a contractual arrangement with an insurance company. In some cases, the HMO and insurance company are commonly owned or have a parent-subsidiary relationship.

Self-funded plans, which are exempt from state laws mandating a conversion policy, may still provide such a benefit. Rather than providing coverage directly to the terminated employee, the plan usually enters into an agreement with an insurance company to make a policy available. This agreement is typically part of a broader contract with the insurer to also provide administrative services and/or stop-loss protection. Because the availability of a conversion policy results in a charge (such as $0.65 per employee per month), most self-funded plans do not provide any continuation of coverage beyond what COBRA requires.

CLAIMS

The handling of medical expense claims is different, depending on whether a plan provides benefits on an indemnity basis or on a service basis. Subrogation provisions may also apply.

Indemnity Benefits

Medical expense contracts that provide benefits on an indemnity basis typically require that the insurance company (or other provider) receive a written proof of loss (a claim form) concerning the occurrence, character, and extent of the loss for which a covered person makes a claim. This form usually contains portions that must be completed and signed by the employee, a representative of the employer, and the provider of medical services.

The period during which an employee must file a claim depends on the provider of coverage and any applicable state requirements. An employee generally has at least 90 days (or as soon as is reasonably possible) after medical expenses are incurred to file. Some insurance companies require notification within a shorter time (such as 20 days) about any illness or injury on which a claim may be based, even though they give a longer time for the actual filing of the form itself.

Individuals have the right to assign their benefits to the providers of medical services. A covered person generally makes such an assignment, which authorizes the insurance company to make the benefit payment directly to the provider by completing the appropriate portion of the claim form. In addition, the insurance company has the right (as it does in disability income insurance) to examine any person for whom a claim is filed at its own expense and with the physician of its own choice.

Service Benefits

Medical expense contracts that provide benefits on a service basis (such as HMOs and the Blues) generally do not require that covered persons file claim forms. Rather, the providers of health care services perform any necessary paperwork and receive reimbursement directly.

For example, when a physician presents a claim, the plan must determine one or more of the following: the physician's status as a network participant; the primary or specialty care nature of the service if rendered by a network participant; and the applicability of an authorization requirement. Depending upon the plan's stringency, the provider's reimbursement may be denied altogether or be far less than the amount charged if the member receives services from a nonnetwork provider or sees a specialist without a required referral. In turn, the payment made to the provider determines whether the enrollee must pay a modest copayment, a more substantial amount under an indemnity benefit as described above, or the total amount if there is a claim denial.

Network providers with capitation payment arrangements file patient encounter forms that in effect are claims that produce no payment for a specific service.

Subrogation

Most plans contain subrogation provisions. If state law allows, they are commonly contained in the group medical expense contracts of HMOs, PPOs, the Blues, and insurance companies. A subrogation provision gives the plan (or the organization providing plan benefits) the right to recover from a third party who is responsible through negligence or other wrongdoing for a covered person's injuries that result in a claim payment. If a covered person receives a settlement from the third party (or their liability insurance company) for medical expenses that the plan has already paid, the covered person must reimburse the plan. The plan also has the right to seek a recovery from the party at fault for benefits paid if the person who receives benefits does not take legal action.

HIPAA ADMINISTRATIVE STANDARDS

protected health information (PHI)

An important result of HIPAA is the various administrative standards that it imposes on medical expense plans. The act authorizes the Secretary of the Department of Health and Human Services (HHS) to set administrative standards for the privacy, security, and electronic exchange of personal health information, which the act refers to as **protected health information (PHI)**. PHI is individually identifiable health information that is transmitted or maintained in electronic or other media, including both written and oral communications. It specifically includes genetic information.

Entities subject to these standards include health plans, health information data processors (known as *clearinghouses*) and health care providers. For purposes of the standards, HIPAA broadly defines *health plan*s to include essentially all individual policies and group plans that provide or pay the cost of medical care, both public and private. However, self-administered plans with fewer than 50 participants are not included in the definition. The definition extends to most insurance companies that provide medical, dental, vision, prescription drug, and long-term care insurance. Employers and plan sponsors are also subject to the rules to the extent they handle PHI.

The administrative standards impose significant penalties for noncompliance. Civil penalties, increased under recent legislation, now encompass five tiers that range from a low of $100 per violation, not to exceed $25,000 per calendar year, to as high as $50,000 per violation, not to exceed $1.5 million per calendar year. The Secretary of Health and Human Services determines the penalty based on the nature and extent of the harm resulting from the violations. However, the Secretary may use a corrective action plan in place of a penalty.

Violations relating to PHI under the standards may also result in criminal penalties. These penalties can be as high as (1) $50,000 and one year in prison for obtaining or disclosing PHI; (2) $100,000 and 5 years in prison for obtaining PHI under false pretenses; and (3) $250,000 and 10 years in prison for obtaining or disclosing PHI information with the intent to sell, transfer, or use it for commercial advantage, personal gain, or malicious harm.

In addition, if there is a breach of PHI, the covered entity is required to notify the affected person within 60 days after discovery. If the breach affects more than 500 individuals, the covered entity must notify the Secretary of HHS and media outlets. Personal health record vendors must also notify individuals of a breach of PHI. A breach is the unauthorized acquisition, access, use, or disclosure of patient health information. Although the law allows certain exceptions to this definition when the disclosure occurs in good faith, an inadvertent disclosure is considered a breach if it results in information being disclosed outside of the confines of a covered entity.

The Secretary of HHS has the responsibility not only for the creation of the standards for PHI, but also for their enforcement. Subject to the Secretary's jurisdiction, the recent legislation also grants limited authority to the state attorneys general who can bring law suits in federal court on behalf of state residents for the enforcement of these HIPAA provisions.

The HIPAA provisions that authorize the creation of these standards are known collectively as *administrative simplification* because of the consistency and efficiency they seek to achieve. These provisions generate extensive regulations that the following headings summarize:

- privacy standards
- security standards
- identifier standards
- transaction and code set standards

Privacy Standards

privacy standards

Privacy standards provide the first comprehensive federal protection for the privacy of personal health information. At the same time, many states have their own privacy rules and federal standards do not override those rules if they contain stricter provisions. The federal privacy standards extend protection to all PHI relating to physical or mental health condition, the provision of health care, or the payment for the provision of health care.

Covered entities generally have to adopt written procedures regarding certain privacy issues. These include who has access to protected information, how the entity will use PHI, and when the entity may disclose information. Covered entities must also train their employees in privacy procedures and designate a privacy officer who is responsible for ensuring that the employees follow the procedures.

Under the privacy standards, individuals have significant rights to control and understand how their health information is used. These rights include the following:

- Providers and health plans must give patients and members a clear written explanation of how the covered entity may use and disclose health information.

- Patients must be able to see and obtain copies of their health records and to make amendments. In addition, a history of nonroutine disclosures of personal health information must be available to patients.

- Individuals must give a separate authorization for nonroutine and most non-healthcare-related disclosures of their personal health information. The sale of patient health information for marketing purposes is an example of a disclosure requiring such an authorization. Individuals also have the right to request restrictions on the uses and disclosures of their information.

- Individuals have the right to file a formal complaint with a covered provider or health plan, or with HHS, about violations of the privacy regulations or the policies and procedures of the covered entity.

The standards do allow use and disclosure of PHI without authorization for specified purposes. All other purposes require an individual's authorization. A covered entity must also establish an agreement with any business associate to which it discloses personal health information in the conduct of the covered entity's business.

Use and Disclosure without Specific Authorization

A covered entity may use or disclose PHI without written authorization for treatment, payment, or health care operations, or in other situations permitted by the privacy standards.

Treatment, Payment, or Health Care Operations. *Treatment* includes the provision, coordination, and management of health care and related services by health care providers. *Payment* consists of a health plan's activities to obtain premium, determine or fulfill responsibilities for coverage and provision of benefits, and provide reimbursement for health care services to an individual. Payment also extends to the activities of a health care provider to obtain payment for services. However, recent legislation allows patients to pay for their services out-of-pocket and request nondisclosure of services for claim payment or other operational purposes. *Health care operations* covers a broad spectrum of administrative services that support or otherwise relate to the delivery of health care services including such insurance functions as underwriting, rating, and reinsurance. Covered entities are required to provide, upon the patient's request, an accounting of health information made through an electronic health record system for any of these purposes.

Other Situations. The privacy standards allow disclosure of personal health information without an individual's authorization for several other purposes or situations that include the following:

- informal situations in which the individual may be asked directly or has the opportunity to agree or object, such as in the case of a pharmacist dispensing a prescription to a person acting on the patient's behalf
- incidental uses and disclosures such as when a health plan employee discusses a patient's health claim on the phone and may be overheard by another employee who is not authorized to handle personal health information
- public interest and benefit activities such as research, public health and safety, and law enforcement

Authorized Use and Disclosure

For purposes other than those previously identified, a covered entity must request an individual's written authorization. *Authorization* is defined as a specific written permission from individuals to use and disclose their personal health information. Examples of situations that would require an individual's authorization are disclosures to an insurer for coverage purposes, to an employer of results of a preemployment physical, or to a pharmaceutical firm for its own marketing purposes. Although the standards do not dictate the specific form, an authorization must be in plain language and contain specific items among which are the information to be disclosed, persons disclosing and receiving the information, expiration date, and right to revoke the authorization.

In limited circumstances, a covered entity may condition treatment, payment, enrollment, or benefits on an individual's granting an authorization. For instance, a health plan may condition enrollment on an authorization to obtain personal health information to establish eligibility for enrollment or for underwriting or premium determination.

Business Associate Agreements

business associate

The privacy standards not only require that a covered entity ensure compliance by its workforce, but they also contain requirements for agreements between a covered entity and its business associates. A **business associate** is a person or organization, other than a member of the covered entity's workforce, that performs services for a covered entity that involve PHI. These services may be legal, actuarial, accounting, consulting, data aggregation, management, administrative, accreditation, or financial functions.

The recent legislation requires noncovered entities such as health information exchanges, regional health information organizations, e-prescribing gateways, and personal health record vendors to have business associate agreements with covered entities for the electronic exchange of PHI. Perhaps, more significantly, HIPAA violations can now be enforced directly against business associates as well as covered entities.

A covered entity's agreement with a business associate must do the following:

- ensure that the business associate establishes safeguards to protect the confidentiality of, integrity of, and appropriate access to PHI

- assure that the agents and subcontractors to whom the business associate provides PHI meet the same standards and report to the covered entity any security incident of which they become aware

- authorize termination of the contract if the business associate commits a material violation of the privacy provisions

The privacy standards do not specifically mention agents and brokers, and the HHS has issued no guidance on their role under the standards. There seems to be a general (but not unanimous) consensus, however, that agents or brokers are business associates if they have access to PHI. As a result, covered entities may ask agents or brokers with whom they deal to sign a business associate contract.

Security Standards

security standards

The **security standards** require covered entities to implement measures to maintain reasonable and appropriate administrative, physical, and technical safeguards for electronic PHI. These safeguards aim to protect the integrity, confidentiality, and availability of the PHI that a covered entity creates, receives, stores, or transmits. They must also protect against reasonably anticipated threats or hazards to the security or integrity of the data and unauthorized use or disclosure of the information. Policies and procedures must effectively control physical access to the data and establish technical security measures to protect networks, computers, and other electronic devices. Business associate agreements as required by the privacy standards must also contain these safeguards.

Although the scope of the security standards is limited to PHI in electronic form, the privacy standards, previously discussed, provide a security requirement for all PHI, regardless of form or medium.

Identifier Standards

identifier standards

Historically, providers, employers, and health plans have used nonstandard identification formats when conducting business with each other. Each physician, for example, has a different provider number with each insurer or health plan to which he or she submits claims. The **identifier standards** will ensure the use of uniform identifiers among these health care organizations in order to reduce errors, uncertainty, and duplication. The employer identification standard adopted for electronic transactions is an employer's tax identification number or employer identification number assigned by the Internal Revenue Service. Health care providers and health plans now have unique identifiers.

Transaction and Code Set Standards

transaction and code set standards

Standard data elements and electronic processes are expected to promote cost effective, efficient, accurate, and prompt health care transactions. The **transaction and code set standards apply to code systems** for diagnosis and treatment as well as data fields and electronic formats for transmitting data. Transactions subject to the national electronic standards include health claims or claims status, patient encounters, benefit eligibility inquiries, enrollments and disenrollments, provider and premium payments, referral certifications and other authorizations, and related communications. Providers that use nonelectronic transactions with private health plans are not required to adopt and use the standards.

FEDERAL TAX TREATMENT

In many respects, the federal tax treatment of group medical (including group dental) expense premiums and benefits parallels that of other group coverage if they are provided through an insurance company, a Blue Cross and Blue Shield plan, an HMO, or a PPO, etc. Contributions by the employer for an employee's coverage or the coverage of the employee's dependents are tax deductible to the employer as long as the employee's overall compensation is reasonable. As a rule, employer contributions do not create any income tax liability for an employee. Moreover, benefits are usually not taxable to an employee.

There are, however, some aspects of the tax treatment of medical expense coverage that are unique to this type of employee benefit or need a little further explanation. These include tax liability from employer contributions, taxation of benefits, deductible employee contributions, special rules for self-funded medical expense plans, and a credit for certain individuals.

Tax Liability from Employer Contributions

Under IRS rules, there is no tax liability from employer contributions to the cost of medical expense coverage for an employee, the employee's spouse, or the employee's dependents. For purposes of these rules, a dependent includes two categories of persons—a qualifying child and a qualifying relative.

It is important to make two points. First, the definition of dependent for purposes of medical expense coverage is different from the definition that applies for most income tax purposes. Second, the definition is worded in such a way that an employee's domestic partner would not likely qualify as a dependent. Therefore, the value of any employer-provided coverage for the employee's domestic partner, minus any employee contributions, represents taxable income to the employee.

Taxation of Benefits

Except in very rare situations, medical expense plans are designed so that benefits received do not create any income tax liability for an employee. There are two situations in which taxable income could occur, however. The first is if benefits exceed actual medical expenses. Should this occur, the excess is taxable to the extent it is attributable to employer contributions.

Second, tax-free benefits must be for "medical expenses" as determined by the IRS. For example, such procedures as routine cosmetic surgery and teeth whitening do not meet the IRS definition of medical expenses and create taxable income if a taxpayer receives benefits for them.

Limitations and exclusions in medical expense plans typically prevent either of these two situations from occurring.

Deductible Employee Contributions

One major difference between group medical expense coverage and other forms of group insurance is that a portion of an employee's contribution for coverage may be tax deductible as a medical expense if that individual itemizes his or her income tax deductions. The Internal Revenue Code allows individuals to deduct certain medical care expenses including dental expenses for which they received no reimbursement. This deduction is limited to expenses (including amounts paid for insurance) that exceed 10 percent of the person's adjusted gross income.

As mentioned earlier in this book, the IRS considers a sole proprietor, partner, member of a limited liability company (LLC), or more-than-2-percent shareholder of an S corporation to be a self-employed person. If an organization pays the cost of medical expense coverage for a self-employed person (including dependent coverage), this amount constitutes taxable income to the self-employed person. However, the self-employed person is entitled to an income tax deduction for this amount. The deduction, however, cannot exceed the individual's earned income from the organization that provides the medical expense plan. In addition, the deduction is available only if the self-employed person is not eligible to participate in any subsidized medical expense plan of another employer of the self-employed person or the person's spouse. It is important to recognize that this is not an itemized deduction, but rather it is a deduction in arriving at adjusted gross income.

There is one circumstance under which a self-employed person, other than a more-than-2-percent owner-employee of an S corporation, can receive a 100 percent deduction for his or her medical expense coverage. This occurs only if the spouse is a bona fide employee of the self-employed person. The medical coverage is then provided to the spouse, who elects dependent coverage for the self-employed person. The self-employed person then pays the entire premium and takes a business deduction for the medical expense coverage provided to an employee. However, the IRS indicates that it will challenge such an arrangement if the spouse's involvement in the business consists of nominal or insignificant services that have no economic substance or independent significance. Note that if there is a significant investment of the spouse's separate assets in the business, the spouse is a joint owner and treated as a self-employed person rather than an employee for purposes of the medical expense insurance.

Self-Funded Plans

self-insured medical reimbursement plan

highly compensated individual

The tax situation may be different if an employer provides medical expense benefits through a self-funded plan (referred to in the Internal Revenue Code as a **self-insured medical reimbursement plan**), under which employers either (1) pay the providers of medical care directly or (2) reimburse employees for their medical expenses. If a self-funded plan meets certain nondiscrimination requirements for highly compensated employees, the employer can deduct benefit payments when it makes them, and the employee has no taxable income. If a plan is discriminatory, the employer still receives an income tax deduction. However, all or a portion of the benefits received by "highly compensated individuals," but not by other employees, is treated as taxable income. The IRS defines a **highly compensated individual** as (1) one of the five highest-paid officers of the firm, (2) a shareholder who owns more than 10 percent of the firm's stock, or (3) one of the highest-paid 25 percent of all the firm's employees. There are no nondiscrimination rules if a plan is not self-funded and provides benefits through an insurance contract, a Blue Cross and Blue Shield plan, an HMO, or a PPO.

To be considered nondiscriminatory, a self-funded plan must meet certain requirements regarding eligibility and benefits. The plan must provide benefits (1) for 70 percent or more of "all employees," or (2) for 80 percent or more of all eligible employees if 70 percent or more of all employees are eligible. The employer can then exclude the following from the all-employees category without affecting the plan's nondiscriminatory status:

- employees who have not completed 3 years of service
- employees who have not attained age 25
- part-time employees. Anyone who works fewer than 25 hours per week is automatically considered a part-time employee. The employer may also count persons who work 25 or more but fewer than 35 hours per week as part-time as long as

other employees doing similar work for the employer have substantially more hours.

- seasonal employees. Anyone who works fewer than 7 months of the year is automatically considered a seasonal employee. Persons who work between 7 and 9 months of the year may also be considered seasonal as long as other employees have substantially more months of employment.

- employees who are covered by a collective-bargaining agreement if accident-and-health benefits were a subject of collective bargaining

Even if a plan fails to meet the percentage requirements regarding eligibility, it can still qualify as nondiscriminatory as long as the IRS is satisfied that the plan benefits a classification of employees in a manner that does not discriminate in favor of highly compensated employees. The IRS makes this determination on a case-by-case basis.

To satisfy the nondiscrimination requirements for benefits, the employer must provide the same type and amount of benefits to all employees covered under the plan, regardless of their compensation. In addition, the employer cannot treat the dependents of other employees less favorably than the dependents of highly compensated employees. However, because the IRS considers diagnostic procedures part of a self-funded plan for purposes of the nondiscrimination rule, a higher level of this type of benefit is permissible for highly compensated employees.

If a plan is discriminatory in either benefits or eligibility, highly compensated employees must include the amount of any "excess reimbursement" in their gross income for income tax purposes. If highly compensated employees receive any benefits that are not available to all employees covered under the plan, the IRS considers these benefits an excess reimbursement. For example, if a plan pays 80 percent of covered expenses for employees in general, but 100 percent for highly compensated employees, the extra 20 percent of benefits constitutes taxable income.

If a self-funded plan discriminates in the way it determines eligibility, highly compensated employees have excess reimbursements for any amounts they receive. The amount of this excess reimbursement is determined by a percentage that is calculated by dividing the total amount of benefits highly compensated employees receive (exclusive of any other excess reimbursements) by the total amount of benefits paid to all employees (exclusive of any other excess reimbursements).

If a plan provides benefits only for highly compensated employees, all benefits received are considered an excess reimbursement, because the percentage is 100 percent.

SOME TAX CHANGES INTRODUCED BY THE AFFORDABLE CARE ACT

Small Group Tax Credit

Small businesses receive a tax credit of up to 50 percent of the employer's cost to provide eligible health coverage for its employees. For tax-exempt small businesses, the tax credit is up to 35 percent.

Play-or-Pay Tax

Employers with 200 or more employees may be required to offer affordable health care coverage to their employees. If they do not offer health care coverage, they will have to pay a tax of up to $2,000 per year per employee. If the coverage being offered is deemed not to be affordable and the employee obtains coverage through a state health benefit exchange, the employer will be subject to a similar tax. Coverage is deemed to be unaffordable if the employer's contribution to the premium is less than 60 percent of the cost or the contribution requirement for the employee is above 9.5 percent of the employee's household income. If none of these circumstances occur and the employee still goes to the state health benefit exchange for coverage, the employer will not be subject to the tax.

Other Changes Affecting Taxation

The Affordable Care Act created other mandates that directly or indirectly affect tax revenue. A partial list of these changes includes:

- Over-the-counter drugs are excluded from reimbursement for qualified health care accounts such as HRAs and FSAs unless ordered with a prescription.

- The tax penalty for reimbursement of ineligible medical expenses from a qualified health care account was increased from 10 and 15 percent to 20 percent.

- The maximum family contribution to a flexible spending account is capped at $2,500.

- The deduction threshold for unreimbursed medical expenses for federal income tax purposes is 10 percent of adjusted gross income.

- The tax rate on wages for Medicare Part A increased by 0.9 percent from 1.45 percent to 2.35 percent on earnings over designated levels.

CHAPTER REVIEW

Key Terms and Concepts

dependent
medical child support order
domestic partners
coordination-of-benefits (COB)
  provision
allowable expenses
Medicare secondary rules
Medicare carve-out
Medicare supplement
COBRA
qualified beneficiary

qualifying event
extension of benefits
protected health information (PHI)
privacy standards
business associate
security standards
identifier standards
transaction and code set standards
self-insured medical reimbursement
  plan
highly compensated individual

Review Questions

Review questions are based on the learning objectives in this chapter. For example, a [3] at the end of a questions means that the question is based on learning objective 3. If there are multiple objectives, they are all listed.

1. What is the effect of the NAIC Model Regulation on Group Coverage Discontinuance and Replacement when an employer transfers group insurance coverage? [1]

2. What dependents are typically eligible for coverage under a medical expense plan? [1]

3. How does federal legislation mandate benefits for adopted children? [1]

4. Regarding medical child support orders: [1]

   a. What is a medical child support order?

   b. What makes such an order qualified?

   c. What are the obligations of a plan administrator who receives a medical child support order?

5. How does federal legislation modify Medicaid rules with respect to benefits for children? [1]

6. Regarding domestic partner coverage: [1]

   a. What requirements must often be satisfied in order for a medical expense plan to provide coverage to a domestic partner?

    b.   How do plans differ with respect to the groups of persons who might be eligible for domestic partner benefits?

7.   A child in the custody of her mother is covered as a dependent under the major medical coverage of both her father and her stepfather. Explain which coverage is primary if both coverages are subject to a coordination-of-benefits provision that conforms to the NAIC model provisions. [2]

8.   Holly incurred $5,000 of medical expenses that, except for deductibles and coinsurance, are fully covered under the medical expense plan provided by her employer. She is also covered as a dependent under her husband's plan. Holly's plan has a $100 deductible and an 80 percent coinsurance provision; her husband's plan has a $200 deductible and a 90 percent coinsurance provision. How much will Holly collect from each plan if the traditional coordination-of-benefits approach is used? [2]

9.   How might coordination of benefits differ from the usual rules if self-funded plans are involved? [2]

10. Regarding Medicare coverage: [3]

    a.   Under what circumstances is Medicare the secondary payer of medical expense benefits?

    b.   What does Medicare pay if it is secondary?

11. Regarding continuation of coverage: [4]

    a.   In the absence of any provision for continuation or conversion, what circumstances may cause an employee's coverage to cease under a medical expense plan?

    b.   What circumstances may cause a dependent's coverage to cease?

12. Regarding COBRA: [4]

    a.   What employers are subject to the health insurance continuation provisions of COBRA?

    b.   What are the penalties for noncompliance?

13. With respect to the health insurance continuation provisions of COBRA, answer each of the following questions: [4]

    a.   Who are eligible qualified beneficiaries?

    b.   What is a qualifying event?

c. For what length of time must coverage be continued?

14. Regarding COBRA: [4]

    a. When must a plan administrator notify a covered person of his or her rights to continue health insurance coverage under COBRA?

    b. What is the maximum a plan can charge for continuation of health insurance coverage under COBRA?

15. Briefly describe how medical expense coverage provided to retired employees may differ from that provided to active employees. [4]

16. Regarding postretirement coverage: [4]

    a. How do FASB rules affect how employers must account for postretirement medical expense coverage?

    b. How have employers modified medical expense plans as a result of the FASB rules and increasing plan costs?

    c. What options are available to an employer to prefund postretirement medical expense coverage?

17. Regarding termination of coverage: [4]

    a. Under what circumstances is an employee or dependent eligible to convert medical expense coverage that terminates?

    b. What type of coverage can the employee obtain under the conversion provision?

18. How does the claims process differ with respect to medical expense plans providing benefits on a service basis and medical expense plans providing benefits on an indemnity basis? [5]

19. What is the purpose of a subrogation provision in a medical expense plan? [5]

20. How do the HIPAA privacy standards give patients the right to control and understand how their personal health information is used? [5]

21. Regarding HIPAA privacy regulations: [5]

    a. How do the HIPAA privacy regulations affect employers?

    b. Under what circumstances may employers use or disclose protected health information without an employee's written authorization?

22. What must be contained in an employer's agreement with a business associate? [5]

23. What is required by employers under each of the following HIPAA administrative standards? [5]

    a. security

    b. identifier

    c. transaction and code sets

24. To what extent and under what circumstances are contributions for group medical expense coverage deductible for federal income tax purposes if paid by [6]

    a. the employer?

    b. the employees?

25. Under what circumstances do benefits under insured group medical expense plans result in taxable income to an employee? [6]

26. What are the income tax implications if a self-insured medical reimbursement plan is discriminatory? [6]

27. Describe the affect of the following Affordable Care Act mandates on taxation: [6]

    a. the small group tax credit

    b. the play-or-pay tax

    c. the exclusion of over-the-counter drugs from qualified health care accounts

    d. the 20 percent tax penalty for ineligible medical expense reimbursement

    e. capping the family contribution to a flexible spending account

    f. the increase in the deduction threshold for tax deductibility

    g. the increase in Medicare Part A tax rate

Review Question Answers

1. The model regulation stipulates that a new plan provide coverage to anyone who (1) was covered under the old plan at the date it was discontinued and (2) is in an eligible classification of the new plan. If the new plan contains a preexisting-conditions provision, benefits applicable to an individual's preexisting conditions are limited to the lesser of (1) the maximum benefits of the new plan (ignoring the preexisting conditions) or (2) the maximum benefits of the old plan.

2. Person's typically eligible for coverage as dependents are an employee's spouse who is not legally separated from the employee and any unmarried dependent children (including stepchildren and adopted children) under the age of 26.

3. A work-related group medical expense plan that provides coverage for dependent children of participants or beneficiaries must provide benefits for adopted children or children placed for adoption under the same terms and conditions that apply to natural children. A child is defined as a person under the age of 18 at the time of adoption or placement for adoption.

4. a. A medical child support order is a court judgment, decree, or order that (1) provides for child support with respect to the child of a group plan participant or provides benefit coverage to such a child, is ordered under state domestic relations law, and relates to benefits under the plan or (2) enforces a state medical support law enacted under Medicaid rules.

   b. The support order becomes qualified if two additional requirements are met. First, the order must create or recognize the right of the child to receive benefits to which the plan participant or other beneficiary is entitled under a group plan. Second, the order must include such information as the name and last known mailing address of the plan participant and the child, a reasonable description of the coverage to be provided, the period for which coverage must be provided, and each plan to which the order applies.

   c. Within 40 days after receiving the order, the employer's plan must provide coverage for the dependent child. If the plan administrator is not the employer, the administrator must notify the employer of the amount to withhold from the worker's pay.

5. A federal law prohibits plan administrators from denying enrollment of a child under a parent's insurance plan on any of the following grounds:

   • The child was born out of wedlock.

   • The child is not claimed as a dependent on the parent's federal income tax return.

   • The child does not reside with the parent or in the insurer's service area.

   A second law provides that if a court orders a parent to provide medical support, the parent's plan must enroll the child without regard to any enrollment restrictions.

6. a. Unmarried couples may be considered domestic partners as long as they live together, show financial interdependence and joint responsibility for each other's common welfare, and consider themselves life partners. This type of requirement is typical, as is the additional requirement that the employee's relationship must have lasted some specified minimum period, such as 6 or 12 months.

    b. Most plans provide benefits to domestic partners engaged in either heterosexual or homosexual relationships. Some plans provide benefits only to persons of the opposite gender of the employee, and a small number of plans limit benefits only to persons of the same gender.

7. If the father is required by a court decree to provide financial responsibility for the child's medical expenses, her father's coverage is primary. If there is no such court decree, her stepfather's coverage is primary.

8. Holly's total allowable expenses are $5,000. In the absence of a coordination-of-benefits (COB) provision, her plan would pay 80 percent of $4,900, or $3,920. Her husband's plan would pay 90 percent of $4,800, or $4,320. Since the total coverage under the two plans exceeds her allowable expenses, they are paid in full. Her plan, covering an employee, is primary and will pay $3,920. The remaining allowable expenses of $1,080 are paid under her husband's plan.

9. Some self-funded plans use a provision so that their payment as a secondary payer is limited to the amount that would reach the limits of their own plan.

    A few self-funded plans coordinate benefits with plans under which an individual is eligible for coverage, even if that plan does not cover the individual.

    Finally, some self-funded plans have been designed so that they are excess or "always secondary" to any other medical expense plan.

10. a. Under the Medicare secondary rules, employers with 20 or more employees must make coverage available under their medical expense plans to active employees aged 65 or older and to active employees' spouses who are eligible for Medicare. Unless an employee elects otherwise (by not enrolling in the employer's plan), the employer's plan is primary and Medicare is secondary.

Another Medicare-secondary situation involves persons who are eligible for Medicare benefits to treat end-stage renal disease with dialysis or kidney transplants. The employer's plan is primary only during the first 30 months of treatment; after that, Medicare is primary and the employer's plan is secondary. This rule for renal disease applies to medical expense plans of all employers, not just those with 20 or more employees.

Medicare is also the secondary payer of benefits to disabled employees (or the disabled dependents of employees) under age 65 who are eligible for Medicare and who have coverage under the medical expense plan of large employers (defined as plans with 100 or more employees). Medicare, however, does not pay anything until a person has been eligible for Social Security disability income benefits for 2 years.

b. When an employer's plan is primary, Medicare makes payments for any expenses that are covered by Medicare but not by the employer's plan. For purposes of these payments, Medicare deductibles, copayments, and percentage participation generally do not apply. However, Medicare benefits are limited to what would have been paid in the absence of the employer's plan.

11. a. The group medical expense coverage of an employee generally ceases upon the earliest of

- the date on which employment terminates

- the date on which the employee ceases to be eligible

- the date on which the master contract terminates

- the date on which the overall maximum benefit of major medical coverage is received

- the end of the last period for which the employee makes any required contribution

b. Coverage on any dependent usually ceases on the earliest of the following:

- the date on which he or she ceases to meet the definition of dependent

- the date on which the coverage of the employee ceases for any reason except the employee's receipt of the overall maximum benefit

- the date on which the dependent receives the overall maximum benefit of major medical coverage

- the end of the last period for which the employee makes any required contribution for dependent coverage

12. a. Although certain church-related plans and plans of the federal government are exempt from COBRA, the act applies to all other employers who had the equivalent of 20 or more full-time employees on at least 50 percent of its typical business days during the preceding calendar year.

 b. Failure to comply with the act results in an excise tax of up to $100 per day for each person denied coverage. The IRS can levy the tax on the employer as well as on the entity (such as an insurer or HMO) that provides or administers the benefits.

13. a. COBRA defines a qualified beneficiary as any employee, or the spouse or dependent child of the employee, who on the day before a qualifying event had coverage under the employee's group health plan. HIPAA expanded the definition to include any child who is born to or placed for adoption with the employee during the period of COBRA coverage.

 b. Each of the following is a qualifying event if it results in the loss of coverage by a qualified beneficiary or an increase in the amount the qualified beneficiary must pay for the coverage:

   - the death of the covered employee
   - the termination of the employee for any reason except gross misconduct. This includes quitting, retiring, or being fired for anything other than gross misconduct.
   - a reduction of the employee's hours so that the employee or dependent is ineligible for coverage
   - the divorce or legal separation of the employee and his or her spouse
   - for spouses and children, the employee's eligibility for Medicare
   - a child's ceasing to be an eligible dependent under the plan

 c. The plan must allow each qualified beneficiary to continue coverage from the qualifying event until the earliest of the following:

   - 18 months for employees and dependents when the employee's employment ceases or coverage terminates because of a reduction in hours. This period is extends to 29 months for a qualified beneficiary if the Social Security Administration determines that the beneficiary was or became totally disabled at any time during the first 60 days of COBRA coverage.
   - 36 months for other qualifying events
   - the date the plan terminates for all employees

- the date the coverage ceases because of a failure to make a timely payment of premium for the qualified beneficiary's coverage

- the date the qualified beneficiary subsequently becomes entitled to Medicare or becomes covered (as either an employee or dependent) under another group health plan, provided the group health plan does not contain an exclusion or limitation with respect to any preexisting condition

If a second qualifying event (such as the death or divorce of a terminated employee) occurs during the period of continued coverage, the maximum period of continuation is 36 months.

14. a. First, when a plan becomes subject to COBRA or when a person becomes covered under a plan subject to COBRA, the administrator must give notification to an employee as well as to his or her spouse, generally within 90 days. Second, when a qualifying event occurs, the employer must notify the plan administrator, who then must notify all qualified beneficiaries within 14 days. In general, the employer has 30 days to notify the plan administrator.

Recent changes to COBRA rules also require plan administrators to provide notification to qualified beneficiaries in two other circumstances. First, if a plan beneficiary receives a notice of a qualifying event and the qualified beneficiary is ineligible for COBRA coverage, the plan administrators must explain why the qualified beneficiary is not entitled to coverage. Second, if COBRA coverage is terminated before the end of the maximum duration, the plan administrator must explain when and why the coverage is being terminated and inform the qualified beneficiary of any available rights to other coverage.

b. The cost cannot exceed 102 percent of the cost to the plan for the period of coverage for a similarly situated active employee to whom a qualifying event has not occurred. The one exception to this rule occurs for months 19 through 29 if an employee is disabled, in which case the premium can then be as high as 150 percent.

15. Although a plan may continue coverage for retirees' dependents, it is often limited only to spouses. Retired employees under age 65 usually have the same coverage as active employees have. However, coverage for employees aged 65 or older (if included under the same plan) may be provided under a Medicare carve-out or a Medicare supplement. If there is a lifetime maximum for persons eligible for Medicare, it is often lower than the limit for active employees.

16. a. These rules require that employers do the following:

- recognize the present value of future retiree medical expense benefits on the firm's balance sheet with other liabilities

- record the cost for postretirement medical benefits in the period when an employee performs services. This is comparable to the accounting for pension costs.

- amortize the present value of the future cost of benefits accrued prior to the new rules

b. Modifications to retiree medical expense plans include the following:

- eliminating benefits for future retirees

- shifting more of the cost burden to future retirees by reducing benefits. A plan may accomplish such a reduction by providing lower benefit maximums, covering fewer types of expenses, or increasing copayments.

- adding or increasing retiree sharing of premium costs after retirement

- shifting to a defined-contribution approach to funding retiree benefits

- encouraging retirees to elect benefits from managed care plans

c. One alternative is the use of a 501(c)(9) trust (or VEBA). However, there are limitations on the deductibility of contributions to a 501(c)(9) trust. Furthermore, an employer can use such a trust to fund retiree benefits only if it also uses the trust to fund benefits for active employees.

Another alternative is to prefund medical benefits within a pension plan. Contributions are tax deductible, and earnings accumulate tax free if certain requirements are met.

17. a. Typically, medical expense contracts usually contain a conversion provision at termination of employment which has lasted at least 3 months. Covered persons commonly have 31 days from the date of termination of the group coverage to exercise this conversion privilege, and coverage is then effective retroactively to the date of termination.

In some cases, depending on state law, conversion is contingent upon an individual electing COBRA coverage and maintaining it for the maximum election period. At that time, a conversion policy is available. In other cases, a person who is eligible for both the conversion privilege and the right to continue the group insurance coverage under COBRA has two choices when eligibility for coverage terminates. He or she can either elect to convert under the provisions of the policy or elect to continue the group coverage under COBRA. If the person makes the latter choice, the COBRA rules specify that the person must again be eligible to convert to an individual policy within the usual conversion period after the maximum continuation-of-coverage period ceases. In either situation, policy provisions may also make the conversion privilege available to persons whose coverage terminates prior to the end of the maximum continuation period.

b.   A person whose coverage terminates only has the right to purchase a contract on an individual basis at individual rates. Most Blue Cross and Blue Shield plans and some HMO plans offer a conversion policy that is similar or identical to the terminated group coverage. However, most insurance companies offer a conversion policy (or a choice of policies) that contains a lower level of benefits than existed under the group coverage.

18. Benefits paid on an indemnity basis typically require that the insurance company (or other benefit provider) receive a written proof of loss (that is, a claim form) concerning the occurrence, character, and extent of the loss for which a covered person makes a claim. This form usually contains portions that must be completed and signed by the employee, a representative of the employer, and the provider of medical services and returned to the insurance company for the benefit payment to be made to the insured. By completing an assignment of benefits on the appropriate portion of the claim form, the insured authorizes the insurance company to make the benefit payment directly to the provider.

Medical expense contracts that provide benefits on a service basis (such as HMOs and the Blues) generally do not require that covered persons file claim forms. Rather, the providers of health care services perform any necessary paperwork and are then receive reimbursement directly. A person covered under an indemnity contract generally makes an assignment, which authorizes the insurance company to make the benefit payment directly to the provider.

19. A subrogation provision gives the plan (or the organization providing plan benefits) the right to recover from a third party who is responsible through negligence or other wrongdoing for a covered person's injuries that result in a claim payment.

20. •   Providers and health plans must give patients and members a clear written explanation of how the covered entity may use and disclose health information.

     •   Patients must be able to see and obtain copies of their health records and to make amendments. In addition, a history of nonroutine disclosures of personal health information must be available to patients.

- Individuals must give a separate authorization for nonroutine and most non-health-care-related disclosures of their personal health information, such as for marketing purposes. Individuals also have the right to request restrictions on the uses and disclosures of their information.

- Individuals have the right to file a formal complaint with a covered provider or health plan, or with HHS, about violations of the privacy regulations or the policies and procedures of the covered entity.

21. a. The standards do allow use and disclosure of protected health information (PHI) without authorization for specified purposes. All other purposes require an individual's authorization. A covered entity must also establish an agreement with any business associate to which it discloses personal health information in the conduct of the covered entity's business.

    b. A covered entity may use or disclose PHI without written authorization for treatment, payment, or health care operations, or in other situations permitted by the privacy standards.

22. An employer, as a covered entity, must establish agreements with business associates that contain provisions to do the following:

    - ensure that the business associate establishes safeguards to protect the confidentiality of, integrity of, and appropriate access to PHI

    - assure that the agents and subcontractors to whom the business associate provides PHI meet the same standards and report to the covered entity any security incident of which they become aware

    - authorize termination of the contract if the business associate commits a material violation of the privacy provisions

23. a. The security standards require covered entities to implement measures to maintain reasonable and appropriate administrative, physical, and technical safeguards for electronic PHI.

    b. The identifier standards require an employer to use its tax identification number or employer identification number assigned by the Internal Revenue Service for business transactions with health providers and health plans.

    c. Employers must use the transaction and code set standards applicable to code systems for diagnosis and treatment as well as data fields and formats for transmitting data electronically relating to: health claims or claims status; patient encounters; benefit eligibility inquiries; enrollments and disenrollments; provider and premium payments; referral certifications and other authorizations; and related communications.

24. a. Contributions by an employer for an employee's coverage or the coverage of the employee's dependents are tax deductible to the employer as long as the employee's overall compensation is reasonable. As a general rule, there is no tax liability for an employee from employer contributions to the cost of medical expense coverage for an employee, the employee's spouse, or the employee's dependents. Moreover, benefits are usually not taxable to an employee.

    However, a sole proprietor, partner, member of a limited liability company (LLC), or more-than-2-percent shareholder of an S corporation is considered a self-employed person. If an organization pays the cost of medical expense coverage for a self-employed person (including dependent coverage), this amount constitutes taxable income to the self-employed person. However, the self-employed person is entitled to an income tax deduction for this amount. Nevertheless, an exception occurs if the spouse is a bona fide employee of the self-employed person. The medical coverage is then provided to the spouse, who elects dependent coverage for the self-employed person. The self-employed person then pays the entire premium and takes a business deduction for the medical expense coverage provided to an employee.

    b. An employee's contribution for coverage may be tax deductible as a medical expense if that individual itemizes his or her income tax deductions. This deduction is limited to expenses (including amounts paid for insurance) that exceed 10 percent of the person's adjusted gross income.

25. The first circumstance is if benefits exceed actual medical expenses. Should this occur, the excess is taxable to the extent it is attributable to employer contributions.

    The second circumstance occurs if the benefits fail to meet the definition of "medical expenses" as determined by the IRS. For example, benefits for procedures such as routine cosmetic surgery and teeth whitening do not meet the IRS definition of medical expenses and create taxable income if a taxpayer receives benefits for them.

26. If a plan is discriminatory in either benefits or eligibility, highly compensated employees must include the amount of any "excess reimbursement" in their gross income for income tax purposes. For example, if a plan pays 80 percent of covered expenses for employees in general, but 100 percent for highly compensated employees, the extra 20 percent of benefits constitutes taxable income. If a plan

provides benefits only for highly compensated employees, all benefits received are considered an excess reimbursement, because the percentage is 100 percent.

27. a. The small group tax credit gives small employers savings on their net cost for health coverage for their employees by reducing their tax liability.

   b. The play-or-pay tax will generate tax revenue as the tax penalty is collected from large employers.

   c. By excluding standard over-the-counter medications from qualified health care accounts with the Affordable Care Act, the tax rules slowed down the tax advantage of those qualified health care accounts by converting the dollars used to purchase these medications to after-tax dollars.

   d. The increase in the tax penalty for ineligible medical expense reimbursements from 10 or 15 percent to 20 percent will generate additional tax revenue.

   e. By capping the family contribution to a health flexible spending account at $2,500, the total FSA tax sheltered dollars are decreased, thus increasing a family's potential tax liability.

   f. By increasing the federal income tax deduction threshold for deductibility of medical expenses, a person's tax liability is increased.

   g. The increase in Medicare Part A tax rate will generate more dollars to support the Medicare program.

Chapter 10

Cafeteria Plans

Learning Objectives

An understanding of the material in this chapter should enable the student to

1. **Explain the rationale for and the nature of cafeteria plans.**

2. **Describe the types of cafeteria plans.**

3. **Identify the obstacles to cafeteria plans, and explain how they might be overcome.**

4. **Explain the issues that employers face in designing a cafeteria plan.**

cafeteria plan

Many organizations have benefit programs in which all (or almost all) of the employees can design their own benefit packages by purchasing benefits with a prespecified amount of employer dollars from a number of available options. Generally, such a **cafeteria plan** (often referred to as a *flexible benefit plan, cafeteria compensation plan,* or *Sec. 125 plan*) also allows employees to purchase additional benefits on a payroll-deduction basis.

RATIONALE FOR CAFETERIA PLANS

The growth in employee benefits has caused two problems. First, some employers feel that many employees do not recognize and appreciate the magnitude of their employee benefits because, as benefits increase, employee appreciation often seems to decrease. Advocates of cafeteria plans argue that by giving employees a stated dollar amount with which they must select their own benefits (from a list of options), employees become more aware of the actual cost of these benefits and are more likely to appreciate the benefits they choose.

A second problem is that the inflexible benefit structure of conventional employee benefit plans does not adequately meet the various benefit needs of all employees, often leading to employee dissatisfaction. For example, single employees may resent the medical coverage that married employees receive for their families because the single employees receive no benefit of corresponding value. Similarly, employees who have no dependents often see little value in life insurance and would prefer other benefits. Those who favor the concept of cafeteria plans feel that such dissatisfaction can be minimized if employees have the option to select their own benefits. Advocates of cafeteria plans argue that this increased employee satisfaction will result in a better employee-retention record and in greater ability to attract new employees.

Some employers see the cafeteria approach to benefit planning as an opportunity to control escalating benefit costs. Because a cafeteria plan is essentially a defined-contribution plan rather than a defined-benefit plan, it provides a number of opportunities for controlling increases in costs. For example, it may encourage employees to choose medical expense options that have larger deductibles or a greater degree of managed care so they can more efficiently use the fixed number of dollars allotted to them under the plan. A cafeteria plan may also enable the employer to pass on to the employees any increased benefit costs that result from having to comply with legislation that mandates additional benefits. In addition, because increases in employer contributions for optional benefits are not directly related to increases in benefit costs, the employer can grant percentage increases in the amounts available for benefits that are less than the actual overall increase in employee benefit costs.

Early cafeteria plans were designed primarily to meet the varying needs of employees. In contrast, employers are much more likely to institute newer plans as a cost-saving technique.

NATURE OF CAFETERIA PLANS

In its purest sense, a cafeteria plan is an employee benefit plan that allows an employee to have some choice in designing his or her own benefit package by selecting different types or levels of benefits that are funded with employer dollars. At this extreme, a benefit plan that allows an employee to select an HMO as an option to an insured medical expense plan can be classified as a cafeteria plan. However, the more common use of the term cafeteria plan denotes something much broader—a plan in which employees can make choices among several different types of benefits and possibly cash.

constructive receipt

Prior to the addition of Sec. 125 to the Internal Revenue Code, the use of cafeteria plans had potentially adverse tax consequences for an employee. If an employee had a choice among benefits that were normally nontaxable (such as medical expense insurance) and benefits that were normally taxable (such as life insurance in excess of $50,000 or cash), then the doctrine of **constructive receipt** would apply. Constructive receipt is the doctrine whereby a deduction (especially a pre-tax deduction) must be elected prior to earning the dollars that are affected. This would result in an employee's being taxed as if he or she had elected the maximum taxable benefits that could have been obtained under the plan. Therefore, if an employee could elect cash in lieu of being covered under the employer's medical expense plan, an employee who elected to remain in the medical expense plan would have taxable income merely because cash could have been elected. Obviously, this tax environment was not conducive to the use of cafeteria plans unless the only benefits they offered were normally of a nontaxable nature.

Permissible Benefits

qualified benefit

Sec. 125 of the Code defines a cafeteria plan as a written plan under which all participants are employees and under which all participants may choose between two or more benefits consisting of (1) qualified benefits and (2) cash. A **qualified benefit** essentially includes any welfare benefits excluded from taxation under the Internal Revenue Code except scholarships and fellowships, transportation benefits, educational assistance, no-additional-cost services, employee discounts, and de minimis fringe benefits. The latter include dependent life insurance coverage in amounts of $2,000 or less. The Health Insurance Portability and Accountability Act (HIPAA) expanded this list of exceptions to include medical savings accounts (MSAs) and any product that insurers advertise, market, or offer as long-term care insurance. Thus, medical expense benefits (other than MSAs and long-term care insurance), disability benefits, accidental death and dismemberment benefits, vacations, and dependent-care assistance (such as day-care centers) can be included in a cafeteria plan as a tax-favored benefit. Recent legislation allows employers to include HSAs in cafeteria plans. The Code also permits group term life insurance to be included, even in amounts exceeding $50,000. In general, a cafeteria plan cannot include benefits that defer compensation except for a qualified Sec. 401(k) or similar plan.

The term *cash* is actually broader than it would otherwise appear. In addition to the actual receipt of dollars, a benefit is treated as cash as long as (1) it is not a benefit specifically prohibited by Sec. 125 as cash and (2) it is provided on a taxable basis. This latter provision means that either (1) the employee pays the cost of the benefit with after-tax dollars on a payroll-deduction basis or (2) the employee uses employer dollars to obtain the benefit, but the employer reports the cost of the benefit as taxable income for the employee. This rule allows the inclusion of group automobile insurance or long-term care insurance in a cafeteria plan but not on a tax-favored basis. It also allows long-term disability coverage to be provided on an after-tax basis so that disability income benefits can be received tax free.

The list of benefits that Sec. 125 specifically prohibits from being treated as cash includes any benefits provided under Sec. 117 (scholarships and tuition expenses) and Sec. 132 (various fringe benefits, such as discounts and transportation benefits) of the Internal Revenue Code.

As long as a benefit plan offering choice meets the definition of a cafeteria plan, the issue of constructive receipt does not apply. Employees have taxable income only to the extent they elect normally taxable benefits—group term life insurance in excess of $50,000 and cash. An employer can have a benefit plan that offers choice but does not meet the statutory definition of a cafeteria plan. In such a case, the issue of constructive receipt comes into play if the plan contains any benefits that normally result in taxable income.

Choice of Medical Expense Plans

Employers often allow employees a choice of medical expense plans for themselves and their dependents. However, there is often confusion over whether this choice constitutes a cafeteria plan. If it does, the employer needs to comply with the rules of Sec. 125 and ERISA or be subject to the statutory penalties for noncompliance.

Assume an employer has a noncontributory medical expense plan that allows employees to elect among two or more managed care plans. If this is the only choice offered to employees, it is not a cafeteria plan because there is no cash option. It is only a choice among qualified benefits.

Now assume that an employer gives employees the option of electing either a noncontributory managed care plan or an indemnity plan for which the employee must make a monetary contribution on an after-tax basis. Again, by itself this is not a cafeteria plan because there is no option of electing cash. However, if employees can pay their share of the premiums for the indemnity plan on a before-tax basis through a premium-conversion plan, the employer has created a cafeteria plan under Sec. 125. Because salary reductions technically become employer dollars, the IRS treats the employees who elect salary reductions as having chosen between cash and a qualified benefit.

Some employers allow an employee to elect out of medical expense coverage and receive cash. For example, some employees may feel that they do not need coverage under the employer's plan because they are adequately covered under their spouse's plans. If the cost to provide coverage to employees is $2,000 per year, the employer might feel financially justified in offering these employees $1,000 to waive coverage. Because these employees have a choice between the medical expense coverage and cash, the employer has created a cafeteria plan.

Benefit Election

Sec. 125 requires that employees make benefit elections under a cafeteria plan prior to the beginning of a plan year. They generally cannot change these elections for that plan year except under certain specified circumstances and if the plan or IRS regulations allow such changes. Although there is no requirement that a cafeteria plan allow any changes other than those required by regulations, most plans permit changes under some or all of the other specified circumstances. Note, however, that new benefit elections can always be made for subsequent plan years during specified election periods prior to each plan year.

IRS regulations regarding election changes during a plan year allow new cafeteria plan elections for specified changes in status. The acceptable changes in status include the following:

- a change in legal marital status. This includes marriage, death of a spouse, divorce, legal separation, or annulment.

- a change in the number of dependents. This can result from birth, adoption, commencement or termination of an adoption proceeding, or death.

- a change in the employment status of the employee, the employee's spouse, or the employee's dependents. This includes the termination or commencement of employment, a change in worksite, or a change in employment (such as number of hours worked) that affects the eligibility of an employee, spouse, or dependent under a cafeteria plan or other qualified benefit plan.

- a change in dependent status. This includes the satisfaction of or ceasing to satisfy dependent status because of age, student status, or any similar circumstance.

- the commencement or termination of an adoption agreement if adoption assistance is provided through a cafeteria plan

The regulations specify that any new cafeteria plan election because of a change in status is permissible only if any employee, spouse, or dependent gains or loses eligibility for coverage, and the cafeteria plan election change must correspond with that gain or loss in coverage. For example, if a spouse dies, an employee could delete medical expense coverage for the spouse but could not change coverage for other dependents. As a rule, the loss of eligibility for coverage for a cafeteria plan benefit would only allow an employee to decrease the amount of an election. However, there is one exception to this rule. If an election results from the loss of medical expense coverage, an increase in the amount of an election to pay for the COBRA coverage for the individual who lost coverage is permissible.

The regulations also allow affected participants in cafeteria plans to make election changes because of specified changes in the cost or coverage of benefits under the cafeteria plan. However, the IRS does not allow election changes for these reasons for health benefits under flexible spending accounts (FSAs). Note that the need for election changes during the plan year of a cafeteria plan is minimized if an employer's plan years for its benefit plans correspond to the plan year for its cafeteria plan.

Employees can make election changes if the cost of a benefit plan increases or decreases and, under the terms of the plan, they are required to make a corresponding change in their payments. In addition, it is permissible for employees to make election changes because of significant cost increases or decreases of a benefit plan. In the case of significant cost increases, an employee can do one of the following: increase payments, change to another benefit package providing similar coverage, or revoke the benefit election and drop coverage if no similar coverage is available. In the case of significant cost decreases, employees currently with coverage and those who elected a different benefit option can revoke their current elections and elect the cost-reduced coverage. Employees who previously elected not to participate in the plan may also elect coverage. There is one exception to the rules that apply to cost changes: A new benefit election is not allowed because of a change in the cost of dependent care expenses if the dependent care provider is a relative of the employee.

Similarly, election changes by employees are permissible if there are certain changes in coverage. If there is a significant curtailment, but no loss, of coverage (such as significantly increased deductibles and copayments), a cafeteria plan may permit the employee to revoke an election change and make a new election for coverage under another benefit package option providing similar coverage. If the curtailment involves a loss of coverage (such as an HMO ceasing to be available), an employee can make a new election for a similar option or revoke the benefit election if no similar coverage is available. If a plan adds or improves a benefit, the plan may allow an employee to revoke an existing option and elect an option with the new or improved benefits. In addition, a plan may permit benefit changes if there is a loss of coverage for an employee, spouse, or dependent under a group health plan sponsored by a government or educational institution. Lastly, a benefit election is permitted if it corresponds with changes in another employer plan (such as that of a spouse or dependent) (1) if the change in the other plan is permitted by any of the rules mentioned previously or (2) if the cafeteria plan allows participants to make an election for a period of coverage different from that under the other employer plan.

Even if none of the above rules are met, employees may make election changes in cafeteria plans as a result of changes in coverage or premiums because of any of the following:

- special enrollment rights under HIPAA
- COBRA
- entitlement to Medicare or Medicaid

- Family and Medical Leave Act requirements
- legal judgments, decrees, or orders that result from divorce, legal separation, annulment, or change in legal custody

Finally, a recent change to cafeteria plan regulations allows an employee to make changes in pre-tax HSA salary reductions on a monthly basis or upon loss of eligibility for an HSA.

Payroll Deductions and Salary Reductions

Under some cafeteria plans, employees can only allocate a predetermined employer contribution for benefits. Other cafeteria plans allow employees to obtain additional benefits with optional payroll deductions or salary reductions.

Many cafeteria plans that provide a wide array of benefits allow an employee to elect an after-tax payroll deduction to obtain additional benefits. For example, under a cafeteria plan an employee might have a $300 per month employer contribution with which to select varying types and levels of benefits. If the benefits the employee chooses cost $340, the employee has two options—either to decrease the benefits selected or to authorize a $40 payroll deduction. Even though the payroll deduction may be on an after-tax basis, the employee gains to the extent that the additional benefits are available at a lower cost through a group arrangement than in the individual marketplace.

Sec. 125 also allows employees to purchase certain benefits on a before-tax basis with a premium-conversion plan or an FSA. Premium-conversion plans or FSAs, both of which are technically cafeteria plans, can be used by themselves or incorporated into a more comprehensive cafeteria plan. They are most commonly used alone by small employers who are unwilling to establish a broader plan, primarily for cost reasons. The cafeteria plans of most large employers contain one or both of these arrangements as an integral part of the plan.

Before-tax salary reductions reduce taxable income for federal income tax purposes. In most (but not all) states, they also reduce income subject to state tax.

Premium-Conversion Plans

premium-conversion plan

A **premium-conversion plan** (also called a *premium-only plan,* or *POP*) allows an employee to elect a before-tax salary reduction to pay his or her premium contribution to any employer-sponsored health or other welfare benefit plan. For example, an employer might provide medical expense coverage to employees at no cost but make a monthly charge for dependent coverage. Under a premium-conversion plan, the employee can pay for the dependent coverage with a before-tax salary reduction.

As a rule, employers establish premium-conversion plans for medical and dental expenses only. If such plans are used for group term life insurance, the cost of coverage in excess of $50,000 must be reported as income, defeating the purpose of the salary reduction. If these plans are used for disability income coverage, benefits are taxable as noncontributory employer-provided coverage because the amount of any salary reduction is considered to be the employer's money.

Flexible Spending Accounts

flexible spending account (FSA)

A **flexible spending account (FSA)** allows an employee to elect a before-tax salary reduction to fund three types of benefits. FSAs can be used to fund health care expenses not covered by the employer's plan (referred to as a health FSA) and for dependent-care expenses (referred to as a dependent-care FSA). A health FSA includes benefits for both medical and dental expenses. Employers can limit eligibility for health FSAs to employees who are enrolled in one of the employer's medical expense plans.

Reimbursements for eligible expenses are typically made monthly or quarterly. An employee must determine the amount of the salary reduction prior to the beginning of the plan year. Once the amount is set, an employee may make changes only under the specified circumstances previously mentioned for benefit elections. An employee must make a separate election for a each type of FSA, and the employer must account for the funds separately. Monies from a salary reduction for one type of expense (such as medical and dental bills) cannot be used as reimbursement for another type of expense (such as dependent care).

If the monies in an FSA are not fully used during a plan year for incurred expenses, the employee historically forfeited the remaining account balance. The Treasury Department now allows up to $500 of health FSA funds to be carried over into the next plan year—thus modifying the "use it or lose it" standard.

Under ERISA rules, employers may use forfeitures to

- defray the administrative costs of the plan
- protect the underwriting integrity of the plan. This includes the use of these funds to reimburse the plan for benefits paid that exceed a terminated employee's contributions. For example, an employee who contributed $100 per month

for medical expenses might be eligible to collect a full annual reimbursement of $1,200 in the first month of participation. If the employee terminated employment at that time, the plan would have paid out $1,100 more than it had taken in.

- reallocate contribution to the following plan year. Such reallocations must be on a per capita basis for all participants and cannot be based on amounts each employee originally contributed.

The ERISA rules specifically prohibit the donating of forfeitures to charity or the reversion of such amounts to the employer for general business expenses.

Effective January 1, 2013, the maximum contribution to a medical flexible spending account is $2,500 per family.

An election to participate in an FSA program not only reduces salary for federal income tax purposes but also lowers the wages on which an employee pays Social Security and Medicare taxes. As a result, those employees who are below the wage-base limit after the reduction pay less in Social Security taxes, and their future income benefits under Social Security may also be smaller. However, the reduction in benefits is small in most cases unless the salary reduction is large. Note that the employer's share of Social Security and Medicare tax payments also decreases. In some cases, the employer's savings are actually large enough to fully offset the cost of administering the FSA program.

Most health FSAs limit benefits to unreimbursed medical and dental expenses that would be deductible under Sec. 213 of the Internal Revenue Code if an employee was eligible to itemize these expense for income tax purposes. An employer, however, can have a more restricted list of eligible expenses for purposes of FSA reimbursement.

Employers are permitted to make payments from an FSA only after an employee provided substantiation of the expense from a third-party. This substantiation must include information about the service or product received, the date of the service or sale, and the amount of the expense. In addition, in the case of a health FSA, the employee must certify that he or she has not been reimbursed from another health plan and will not seek such reimbursement.

The IRS specifically allows the use of electronic payment cards to make health FSA reimbursements as long as certain criteria are satisfied. Such cards, which can be in the form of debit or credit cards, allow an employee to get immediate reimbursement rather than having to submit FSA claims. They also reduce paper administration for the employer. The required criteria for the use of these cards include annual employee certification that the card will be used only for eligible expenses and that it will be used at vendors that have health-related merchant codes.

An FSA is subject to COBRA rules as long as the FSA provides any of the benefits of a group health plan. However, it is not necessary for the FSA to make coverage available beyond the current plan year as long as the maximum amount paid by an employee for a full plan year of coverage equals or exceeds the maximum benefit available under the FSA for the plan year. For almost all FSAs, this will be the case. For the remainder of the current plan year, the employer needs to offer COBRA coverage only if the maximum benefit available for the remainder of the plan year exceeds the amount that the employer can charge for COBRA coverage during the remainder of the plan year.

IRS regulations state that any employee is allowed to be reimbursed for full annual health FSA funds at any time during the year regardless of the total year to date contributions. Health FSAs must allow an amount equal to the full annual contribution to be taken as benefits any time during the year. However, the IRS regulations do allow a choice in reimbursement policies for other types of benefits, such as dependent-care expenses. For these benefits, most plans limit aggregate benefits to the total contributions made until the time benefits are received.

Effect of Salary Reductions

The use of salary reductions under a cafeteria plan can have a significant effect on an employee's spendable income by lowering taxes paid.

Example

Charlie is a single employee with an annual income of $75,000. He pays $1,000 per year toward the cost of his employer-provided medical expense coverage. He expects to have $2,000 in unreimbursed medical and dental expenses for the year. Charlie's marginal federal income tax bracket is 27 percent. This percentage is increased to 30 because of state income taxes. Charlie's standard deduction and exemptions for income tax purposes are $15,000.

Without a cafeteria plan, Charlie's federal and state taxes are calculated as follows:

Annual income	$75,000
Minus standard deduction and exemptions	−15,000
Taxable income	$60,000
Income taxes (.30 × $60,000)	$18,000
Social Security and Medicare taxes (.0765 × $75,000)	5,738
Total taxes	$23,738

If Charlie participates in his employer's premium-conversion plan and FSA, Charlie's taxes are calculated as follows:

Annual income	$75,000
Minus contribution for premium-conversion plan	−1,000
Minus FSA contribution	−2,000
Minus standard deduction and exemptions	−15,000
Taxable income	$57,000
Income taxes (.30 × $57,000)	$17,100
Social Security and Medicare taxes [.0765 × ($75,000 − $3,000)]	5,508
Total taxes	$22,608

Health FSAs and Consumer-Directed Health Plans

Health FSAs are generally used by employees to obtain tax-favored benefits for otherwise nonreimbursable medical and dental expenses. There is no requirement that an employee be covered under any specific type of medical insurance plan.

It is possible for an employee to have coverage under an HRA and to elect a salary reduction for a health FSA. However, reimbursements from the health FSA can be made only (1) after amounts available under the HRA are exhausted or (2) for expenses that are not reimbursable under the HRA. For example, the latter situation might occur if the HRA did not cover dental expenses. In no case can reimbursements be received for the same expenses from both an HRA and an FSA.

The rules for health savings accounts (HSAs) effectively eliminate their use with traditional health FSAs, because FSAs are considered to be health insurance plans that provide benefits for the types of expenses covered under a high-deductible health plan. However, there are some exceptions. It is permissible for an HSA participant to have a limited-purpose health FSA that provides benefits only for expenses (such as dental bills or the cost of eyeglasses) that are not covered by the high-deductible health plan. In addition, an FSA is acceptable if it makes no reimbursements for expenses incurred before the minimum annual deductible for an HSA is satisfied.

TYPES OF PLANS

Core-Plus Plans

core-plus plan

Probably the most common type of full-fledged cafeteria plan is a **core-plus plan**, which offers a basic core of benefits to all employees, plus a second layer of optional benefits that permits an employee to choose which benefits he or she will add to the basic benefits. These optional benefits can be "purchased" with dollars, or credits, that are given to the employee as part of the benefit package. If these credits are inadequate to purchase the desired benefits, an employee can make additional purchases with after-tax contributions or with before-tax salary reductions under a premium-conversion plan and/or an FSA.

Perhaps the best way to demonstrate how cafeteria plans operate is to include a brief description of some existing plans.

> ### Example
>
> The first example is the core-plus plan of an educational organization with 3,000 employees. Although this type of plan is common, the list of optional benefits in this example is more extensive than what is found in most cafeteria plans.
>
> All employees receive a minimum level of benefits, called basic benefits, as follows:
>
> - term life insurance equal to one-half of salary
> - travel accident insurance (when on the employer's business)
> - disability income insurance
> - 2 to 4 weeks' vacation
>
> Employees are also given flexible credits, equal to between 3 and 6 percent of salary (depending on length of service, with the maximum reached after 10 years), which can be used to purchase additional or "optional" benefits. There is a new election of benefits each year, and no carryover of any unused credits is allowed. The optional benefits are the following:
>
> - an array of medical expense options. Although there is no charge for HMO coverage, a charge is made for coverage under an indemnity plan, and additional flexible credits are given if a person elects no medical expense coverage.
> - additional life insurance, up to 4½ times salary

- accidental death insurance when the basic travel accident insurance does not apply
- dental insurance for the employee and dependents
- up to 2 weeks' additional vacation time
- cash

If an employee does not have enough flexible credits to purchase the desired optional benefits, additional amounts may be contributed on a payroll-deduction basis for all but more vacation time. In addition, a salary reduction may be elected for contributions to an FSA that provides dependent-care-assistance benefits.

A variation of the core-plus approach is to have the core plan be an "average" plan for which the employee makes no contribution. If certain benefits are reduced, the employee may then receive credits that can be used either to increase other benefits or, if the plan allows, to increase cash compensation. Additional benefits can typically be obtained through employee payroll deductions.

Example

This plan covers 15,000 nonunion employees in one division of a major industrial conglomerate. Employees may elect to reduce certain benefits and receive credits that can be used to purchase additional benefits, taken in cash, or contributed to the company's 401(k) plan. Additional benefits may be purchased on a payroll-deduction basis.

The plan applies to four types of benefits:

- medical expense insurance
- employee life insurance
- accidental death and dismemberment insurance
- dependent life insurance

Several medical expense insurance options are available. The standard coverage, for which there is neither a charge nor a credit, is a point-of-service plan. Employees may elect a traditional indemnity plan, but this option results in a charge. Several HMO options are also available, all of which result in credits.

There are several employee life insurance options that range from one-half to 5 times salary. The standard coverage, for which there is no credit or charge, is 1½ times salary.

Modular Plans

modular plan

Another type of cafeteria plan is a **modular plan** in which an employee has a choice among several predesigned benefit packages. Typically, at least one of the packages can be selected without any employee cost. If an employee selects a more expensive package, he or she is required to contribute to the cost of the package. Some employers may also include a bare-bones benefit package, which results in cash being paid to an employee who selects it.

Under some cafeteria plans using this approach, the predesigned packages may have significant differences. A comparison of two packages may show one to be better than others in certain cases but inferior in other cases. Other employers using this approach have virtually identical packages, with the major difference being in the option selected for the medical expense coverage. For example, the plan of one large bank offers a traditional insured plan, two HMOs, and a PPO.

Modular plans are popular with employers for two reasons. First, adverse selection can be more easily controlled under modular plans than under core-plus plans. Second, modular plans are easier to administer and communicate. For both these reasons, small employers who have full-fledged cafeteria plans are most likely to take a modular approach.

Example

A large financial institution's cafeteria plan covers almost 20,000 employees. There are seven predesigned benefit packages that can be chosen, with each package designed for a specific segment of the employee population. Each package has one of three medical expense plans and varying amounts of group term life insurance. The packages contain differing combinations of dental insurance, vision coverage, and dependent care benefits. All offer the same level of disability income coverage.

A "cost" is associated with each package. Some packages cost an employee nothing, others require an employee contribution, and at least one option has a negative cost, meaning that an employee who selects it gets additional cash compensation. The cost of each package can vary for two reasons. First, an employee can elect whether to have medical expense coverage for dependents. Second, HMO and PPO choices differ in many of the employee locations.

Salary-Reduction-Only Plans

salary-reduction-only plan

The final example is a **salary-reduction-only plan**, which consists solely of the three types of salary reductions that can be used in a cafeteria plan: a premium-conversion option, a health FSA, and a dependent-care FSA.

Example

In a small nonprofit organization's plan, employees are allowed to elect salary reductions for each of the following:

- the employee's share of the cost of medical and dental insurance premiums for dependents under a premium-conversion plan. (Under this plan, the employer pays the full cost of the employee's coverage.)

- qualifying medical care expenses under a health FSA. These are any medical and dental expenses normally deductible on an employee's federal income tax return (without regard to any gross income limitations). Note that these deductible expenses must not have been reimbursed by insurance.

- eligible dependent-care expenses under a dependent-care FSA. These are expenses for the types of benefits that could be provided in a qualified dependent-care-assistance program. The maximum annual salary reduction for this category of benefits is limited to $5,000 to prevent the plan from being discriminatory because too large a portion of the benefits would be provided to highly compensated employees.

Employees can request reimbursements for medical care and dependent-care expenses at the end of each month and must file an appropriate form with supporting documentation (bills and receipts).

The maximum reimbursement at any time for dependent-care expenses is the accumulated amount in an employee's account.

OBSTACLES TO CAFETERIA PLANS

Certain obstacles must be overcome before a cafeteria plan can be successfully implemented. Proper plan design would seem sufficient to overcome many of these obstacles. However, it must be realized that any organization that adopts a cafeteria plan other than a simple FSA or premium-conversion plan faces a complex, potentially costly, and time-consuming project.

Legislative Environment

Undoubtedly, the largest obstacle to cafeteria plans for many years was the unsettled federal income tax picture. The passage of the Tax Reform Act in 1984 and the IRS issuance of regulations governing cafeteria plans finally clarified this issue significantly. Since then the number of cafeteria plans has grown significantly, particularly among large firms. However, almost every year, a federal tax bill alters Sec. 125 in some way, new IRS regulations are issued, or proposals for change are made by elected officials. The benefits that can be included in a cafeteria plan are changed, the nondiscrimination rules are altered, or the rules for FSAs are "clarified."

Meeting Nondiscrimination Rules

Sec. 125 imposes complex nondiscrimination tests on cafeteria plans, causing many employees to view cafeteria plans unfavorably. If these tests are not met, adverse tax consequences for key employees and/or highly compensated employees may actually result in higher taxable income for these employees than if no cafeteria plan existed. From a practical standpoint, the test is usually met if an employer has a full-fledged cafeteria plan that applies to all employees. However, care must be exercised in designing a plan that either covers only a segment of the employees or has only a small percentage of employees participating. The latter situation often occurs with FSAs.

Concentration Test

Under the concentration test, no more than 25 percent of the tax-favored benefits provided under the plan can go to key employees (as defined for the Sec. 79 nondiscrimination rules). This test is a particular problem if an employer has a large percentage of key employees and if key employees, being higher paid, contribute large amounts to an FSA.

If a plan fails the concentration test, key employees must include in gross income the maximum taxable benefits that could have been elected under the plan. In effect, these employees are subject to the doctrine of constructive receipt.

Eligibility Test

Cafeteria plans are subject to eligibility tests. No employee can be required to complete more than 3 years of employment as a condition for participation and the employment requirement for each employee must be the same. In addition, any employee who satisfies the employment requirement and is otherwise entitled to participate must do so no later than the first day of the plan year following completion of the employment requirement unless the employee has separated from service in the interim. The plan must also offer benefit structures and eligibility guidelines that do not discriminate in favor of the highly compensated individuals.

highly compensated employees

The third part of the test requires that eligibility for participation must not be discriminatory in favor of **highly compensated employees**, who are defined as any of the following:

- officers whose compensation is more than $170,000 in 2015

- shareholders who own more than 5 percent of the voting power or value of all classes of the firm's stock

- employees who are more than one percent owners with compensation over $150,000 per year

If a plan fails its eligibility discrimination test, highly compensated employees must include in gross income the maximum taxable benefits they could have elected under the plan.

Nondiscriminatory Contributions and Benefits

Cafeteria plans cannot discriminate in favor of highly compensated participants with respect to contributions or benefits. Sec. 125 states that a cafeteria plan is not discriminatory if the plan's nontaxable benefits and total benefits (or the employer contributions allocable to each) do not discriminate in favor of highly compensated employees. In addition, a cafeteria plan providing health benefits is not discriminatory if contributions under the plan for each participant include an amount equal to one of the following:

- 100 percent of the health benefit cost for the majority of similarly situated (that is, family or single coverage) highly compensated employees

- at least 75 percent of the health benefit cost for the similarly situated participant with the best health benefit coverage

Contributions exceeding either of these amounts are nondiscriminatory if they bear a uniform relationship to an employee's compensation.

Simple Cafeteria Plans

simple cafeteria plan

It has been historically more challenging for smaller employers to meet the discrimination testing rules for cafeteria plans. The Affordable Care Act amended the Internal Revenue Code effective January 1, 2011, in a way that created additional safe harbor protection for discrimination testing for plans that qualify as **simple cafeteria plans**. Employers who have employed less than 100 employees during either of the 2 preceding years are eligible to establish a simple cafeteria plan. Once established, an employer may continue the simple cafeteria plan until it employs on average 200 or more employees on the business days during the year. Once the employer employs 200 or more employees, the employer may offer the cafeteria plan through the end of the plan year. There are additional employee eligibility and employer contribution rules for simple cafeteria plans.

Employer's Obligation

Under the most liberal cafeteria plan, each employee has an unrestricted choice of the benefits his or her employer provides. Some critics of this concept argue that both the motivational and the security aspects of a cafeteria plan may be damaged by unwise employee selection because many employees may not have the expertise to select the proper benefits. In addition, there is concern about the organization's moral and perhaps legal obligation to prevent employees from financial injury through faulty decisions. These concerns have been incorporated into the design of most plans presently in existence. Employees are given both certain basic benefits that provide a minimum level of security and a series of optional benefits on top of the basic ones.

Negative Attitudes

Employees, insurers, and unions have expressed some negative attitudes toward cafeteria plans. No cafeteria plan can be truly successful without the support of the employees involved. To win the employees' initial support and to overcome any potential negative attitudes, companies that contemplate the development of such programs must spend a considerable amount of time and resources in making sure that employees are adequately informed about (1) the reasons for the proposed program, (2) its advantages and disadvantages, and (3) its future implications. For best results, the opinions of employees should be solicited and weighed, and employees should be involved in various aspects of the decision-making process.

Some insurers have been reluctant to participate in cafeteria plans because of concern about the problem of adverse selection as a result of employee choice. However, as explained below, the problem of adverse selection can be minimized.

Unions have also had a negative attitude. Union management often feels that bargaining for a cafeteria plan is contrary to the practice of bargaining for the best benefit program for all employees. There is also a concern that the employer will use a cafeteria plan primarily as a cost-containment technique to pass on the cost of future benefit increases to union members. Consequently, except for premium-conversion plans and FSAs, the existing programs often apply only to nonunion employees.

Adverse Selection

When employees have a choice in selecting benefits, the problem of adverse selection arises. This means that employees who are likely to have claims tend to pick the benefits that minimize their out-of-pocket costs. For example, an employee who previously selected a medical expense option with a high deductible might switch to a plan with a lower deductible if medical expenses are ongoing. An employee who previously rejected dental insurance is likely to elect this benefit if dental care is anticipated in the near future.

Adverse selection is a problem whether a plan is insured or self-funded. The problem even exists outside of cafeteria plans if employees have choices. However, the degree of choice within a cafeteria plan tends to increase the potential costs unless actions are taken to combat the problem.

Several techniques are used to control adverse selection in cafeteria plans. Benefit limitations and restrictions on coverage can be included if a person wishes to add or change coverage at a date later than initial eligibility. This technique has been common in contributory benefit plans for many years. Another technique is to price the options accordingly. If an option is likely to encourage adverse selection, the cost to the employee for that option should be higher than what would have been charged if the option had been the only one available. Such pricing has been difficult in the past, but it is becoming easier and more accurate as more experience with cafeteria plans develops. The control of adverse selection is also one reason for the use of predesigned package plans. If, for example, the medical expense plan in one option is likely to encourage adverse selection, the option may not include other benefits for which adverse selection is also a concern (such as dental benefits). To further counter increased costs from the medical expense plan, the option may also offer minimal coverage for other types of benefits.

Cost

An organization that adopts a cafeteria plan will incur initial development and administrative costs that are over and above those of a more traditional benefit program. Some of this extra cost is the value of the employee hours that must be spent in preparing the program for implementation and complying with complex IRS regulations. Another sizable portion must be paid for the reprogramming of the organization's computer system to include necessary information and to accept the employees' benefit elections. ERISA also requires the annual filing of Form 5500.

At one time, although the cost of a cafeteria plan was beyond the means of all but large employers, package plans developed by many insurers now make it a viable option for smaller employers.

Continuing costs depend on such factors as the benefits included in the plan, the number of options available with each benefit, the frequency with which employees may change benefit elections, and the number of employees covered by the plan. The firms with cafeteria plans have incurred increased costs because of the need for additional employees to administer the program and additional computer time to process employee choices. However, the costs have been regarded as small in relation to the total cost of providing employee benefits. In addition, as cafeteria plans have grown in popularity, many vendors have developed software packages that can be used by employees to enroll and make benefit changes and to provide other administrative functions more cost effectively.

Selection among benefits, particularly a wide variety of benefits, is often daunting for many employees. As a result, an employer may also need to incur additional costs to provide employee counseling, either with their own employees or from outside financial planning specialists.

ISSUES IN PLAN DESIGN

Before establishing a cafeteria program, an employer must be sure a valid reason exists for converting the company's traditional benefit program to a cafeteria approach. For example, if there is strong employee dissatisfaction with the current benefit program, the solution may lie in clearly identifying the sources of dissatisfaction and making appropriate adjustments in the existing benefit program, rather than making a shift to a cafeteria plan. However, if employee dissatisfaction arises from widely differing benefit needs, conversion to a cafeteria plan may be quite appropriate. Beyond having a clearly defined purpose for converting from a traditional benefit program to a cafeteria program and being willing to bear the additional administrative costs associated with a cafeteria approach, the employer must face a number of considerations in designing the plan.

Type and Amount of Benefits to Include

Probably the most fundamental decision an employer must make in designing a cafeteria plan is determining what benefits to include. An employer that wants employees to view the plan as meeting their differing needs must receive employee input concerning the types of benefits they perceive as most desirable. An open dialogue with employees will undoubtedly lead to suggestions that every possible employee benefit be made available. It is important that the employer establish certain ground rules regarding the benefits that are acceptable.

The employer must decide whether the plan should be limited to the types of benefits provided through traditional group insurance arrangements or be expanded to include other benefits. At a minimum, it is important to ensure that an overall employee benefit program provides employees with protection against all major areas of personal risk. This suggests a benefit program with at least some provision for life insurance, disability income protection, medical expense protection, and retirement benefits, but it is not necessary that all these benefits be included in a cafeteria plan. For example, most employers have a retirement plan separate from their cafeteria plan because of Sec. 125 requirements. Other employers make a 401(k) plan one of the available cafeteria options.

In some respects, a cafeteria plan may be an ideal vehicle for providing less traditional types of benefits. Two examples are extra vacation time and child care. Some plans allow an employee to use flexible credits to purchase additional days of vacation. When available, this option has proven a popular benefit, particularly among single employees. In recent years, employers have been under increasing pressure to provide care for employees' children, which represents an additional cost if added to a traditional benefit program. Employees who include child-care benefits in a cafeteria plan can pay for the cost of such benefits, possibly with dollars from an FSA. However, lower-paid employees may be better off financially by paying for child care with out-of-pocket dollars and electing the income tax credit available for dependent-care expenses.

The greater the number of benefits, particularly optional benefits, the greater the administrative costs. A wide array of options may also be confusing to many employees and require extra personnel to counsel employees or to answer their questions.

Level of Employer Contributions

An employer has considerable latitude in determining the amount of dollars that are available to employees to purchase benefits under a cafeteria plan. These dollars may be a function of one or more of the following factors: salary, age, family status, and length of service.

The major difficulty arises in situations in which the installation of a cafeteria plan is not accompanied by an overall increase in the amount of the employer's contributions to the employee benefit plan. Each employee should be provided with enough dollars so that he or she can purchase optional benefits that, together with basic benefits, are at least equivalent to the benefits provided by the older plan.

Offering Premium-Conversion and FSA Options

Premium-conversion and FSA options, either by themselves or as part of a broader cafeteria plan, enable employees to lower taxes and therefore increase spendable income. Ignoring administrative costs, there is probably no reason not to offer employees these options for such benefits as dependent care or for health insurance premiums. However, salary reductions for unreimbursed medical expenses pose a dilemma. Although such deductions save taxes for an employee, they may also result in nearly 100 percent reimbursement for medical expenses, which may negate many cost-containment features in the employer's medical expense plan.

Offering an FSA for unreimbursed medical expenses also means that employees will need to submit medical information for reimbursement. They may be reluctant to do this if they fear that the employer will know about their medical conditions. For this reason, and because of HIPAA privacy provisions, many employers use an external administrator to process FSA claims.

Change of Benefits

Because employees' needs change over time, a provision regarding their ability to change their benefit options must be incorporated in a cafeteria plan. As a rule, changes are allowed prior to the beginning of the plan year. Additional changes may be allowed as long as they are permissible under Sec. 125 regulations.

Two situations may complicate the issue of the frequency with which benefits may be changed. First, the charges to employees for optional benefits must be adjusted periodically to reflect experience under the plan. If the charges for benefits rise between dates on which employees may change benefit selections, the employer must either absorb these charges or pass them on to the employees, probably through increased payroll deductions. Consequently, most cafeteria plans allow benefit changes on annual dates that are the same as the dates when charges for benefits are recalculated as well as the date on which any insurance contracts providing benefits under the plan are renewed.

The second situation arises when the amount of the employer's contribution is based on compensation. If an employee receives a pay increase between selection periods, should he or she be granted more dollars to purchase additional benefits at that time? Under most cafeteria plans, the dollars available to all employees are calculated only once a year, usually before the date by which any annual benefit changes must be made. Any changes in the employee's status during the year have no effect on the employer's contribution until the date on which a recalculation is made in the following year.

CHAPTER REVIEW

Key Terms and Concepts

cafeteria plan
constructive receipt
qualified benefit
premium-conversion plan
flexible spending account (FSA)

core-plus plan
modular plan
salary-reduction-only plan
highly compensated employees
simple cafeteria plan

Review Questions

Review questions are based on the learning objectives in this chapter. For example, a [3] at the end of a questions means that the question is based on learning objective 3. If there are multiple objectives, they are all listed.

1. What are the advantages of cafeteria plans? [1]

2. Regarding benefits offered under a cafeteria plan: [1]

    a. What types of welfare benefits can an employer provide under a cafeteria plan?

    b. What types of retirement benefits can an employer provide?

    c. What is meant by a cash benefit?

3. Is a choice among medical expense plans a cafeteria plan? Explain. [1]

4. Regarding cafeteria plan elections: [1]

    a. When must an employee make a benefit election under a cafeteria plan?

    b. Explain the circumstances under which an employee can change these elections.

5. Why may it be advantageous for an employee to purchase benefits through a cafeteria plan on an after-tax basis? [1]

6. Why are premium-conversion plans usually limited only to premiums for medical and dental coverage? [1]

7. What types of benefits are usually funded by salary reductions under a flexible spending account (FSA)? [1]

8. Why is it necessary for an employee to plan FSA deductions wisely? [1]

9. What is the maximum contribution to an FSA? [1]

10. Jane contributes $200 per month to an FSA to fund medical expenses not covered by her employer's health insurance plan. In March, Jane incurred her first unreimbursed expenses for the year in the amount of $1,850. What is the maximum reimbursement Jane can receive from the FSA for these expenses at that time? [1]

11. What types of FSAs can be used with health savings accounts (HSAs)? [1]

12. What is the most popular type of cafeteria plan? [2]

13. Why might modular cafeteria plans be popular among employers? [2]

14. What types of cafeteria plans are most likely to have problems in meeting nondiscrimination rules? [3]

15. Regarding discrimination testing in cafeteria plans: [3]

    a. Describe the concentration test that applies to cafeteria plans.

    b. What are the tax consequences if a plan fails this test?

16. Regarding eligibility tests in cafeteria plans: [3]

    a. Describe the eligibility test that applies to cafeteria plans.

    b. What are the tax consequences if a plan fails this test?

17. What circumstances make a cafeteria plan nondiscriminatory with respect to contributions and benefits? [3]

18. How can employers overcome employee objections about cafeteria plans? [3]

19. Why do cafeteria plans often apply only to nonunion employees? [3]

20. What techniques can be used to control adverse selection in a cafeteria plan? [3]

21. What extra costs are likely to be incurred because of the adoption of a cafeteria plan? [3]

22. Briefly discuss the following issues that must be addressed when designing a cafeteria plan: [4]

    a. the type and amount of benefits to include

    b. the level of employer contributions

    c. the use of a premium-conversion plan or FSA

    d. the ability of employees to change benefits

Review Question Answers

1. Cafeteria plans provides an opportunity to control benefit costs because they are defined contribution plan rather than defined-benefit plans. A cafeteria plan can pass on to the employees any increased benefit costs that result from benefit mandates. In addition, the employer can grant percentage increases in the amounts available for benefits that are less than the actual overall increase in employee benefit costs.

2. a. Medical expense benefits (other than MSAs and long-term care insurance), disability benefits, accidental death and dismemberment benefits, vacations, and dependent-care assistance (such as day-care centers) can be included in a cafeteria plan as a tax-favored benefit. Recent legislation allows HSAs to be offered under cafeteria plans. The Code also permits group term life insurance to be included, even in amounts exceeding $50,000.

    b. In general, a cafeteria plan cannot include benefits that defer compensation except for a qualified Sec. 401(k) or similar plan.

    c. In addition to the actual receipt of dollars, a benefit is treated as cash as long as (1) it is not a benefit specifically prohibited by Sec. 125 as cash and (2) it is provided on a taxable basis. This latter provision means that either (1) the cost of the benefit is paid by the employee with after-tax dollars on a payroll-deduction basis or (2) employer dollars are used to obtain the benefit, but the employer reports the cost of the benefit as taxable income for the employee.

3. A choice among medical expense plans is a cafeteria plan only if the employee has the option to elect cash as an alternative to the medical expense plan.

4. a. Sec. 125 requires that benefit elections under a cafeteria plan be made prior to the beginning of a plan year.

    b. IRS regulations allow new cafeteria plan elections for specified changes in status that include the following:

    - a change in legal marital status
    - a change in the number of dependents
    - a change in the employment status of the employee, the employee's spouse, or the employee's dependents
    - a change in dependent status
    - the commencement or termination of an adoption agreement if adoption assistance is provided through a cafeteria plan

Except for health benefits under flexible spending accounts (FSAs), the regulations also allow affected participants in cafeteria plans to make election changes because of specified changes in the cost of coverage or benefits under the cafeteria plan.

In addition, election changes are permitted in cafeteria plans because of any of the following:

- special enrollment rights under HIPAA

- COBRA

- entitlement to Medicare or Medicaid

- Family and Medical Leave Act requirements

- legal judgments, decrees, or orders that result from divorce, legal separation, annulment, or change in legal custody

Finally, a recent change to cafeteria plan regulations allows an employee to make changes in pre-tax HSA salary reductions on a monthly basis or upon loss of eligibility for an HSA.

5. Even though the payroll deduction is on an after-tax basis, the employee gains to the extent that the additional benefits are available at a lower cost through a group arrangement than in the individual marketplace.

6. If such plans are used for group term life insurance, the cost of coverage in excess of $50,000 must be reported as income, thereby defeating the purpose of the salary reduction. If they are used for disability income coverage, benefits are taxable as non-contributory employer-provided coverage.

7. FSAs can be used to fund health care expenses not covered by the employer's plan and for dependent-care expenses.

8. If the monies in an FSA are not fully used during a plan year (or up to 2½ months after the plan year if allowed by the employer), the employee forfeits the remaining account balance over $500.

9. The maximum annual contribution per family effective January 1, 2013 is $2,500.

10. IRS regulations allow Jane to take reimbursements equal to her full annual contribution for health benefits any time during the year. Because these will total $2,400, she can take a reimbursement in March for the entire $1,850 of expenses incurred. Note that this rule does not apply to other types of benefits (such as dependent care)

provided by the FSA, and the plan could limit total reimbursements to the amounts actually contributed up to the time these benefits are received.

11. An HSA participant may have a limited health FSA that provides benefits only for expenses (such as dental bills or the cost of eyeglasses) that are not covered by the high-deductible health plan. In addition, an FSA is acceptable if it makes no reimbursements for expenses incurred before the minimum annual deductible for an HSA is satisfied.

12. The most common type of full-fledged cafeteria plan is a core-plus plan, which offers a basic core of benefits to all employees, plus a second layer of optional benefits that permits an employee to choose which benefits he or she will add to the basic benefits.

13. First, adverse selection can be more easily controlled under modular plans than under core-plus plans. Second, modular plans are easier to administer and communicate.

14. Care must be exercised in designing a plan that either covers only a segment of the employees or has only a small percentage of employees participating.

15. a. Under the concentration test, no more than 25 percent of the tax-favored benefits provided under the plan can go to key employees (as defined for the Sec. 79 nondiscrimination rules).

    b. Key employees must include in gross income the maximum taxable benefits that could have been elected under the plan.

16. a. Cafeteria plans must satisfy all parts of a three-part eligibility test. The first part of the test stipulates that no employee be required to complete more than 3 years of employment as a condition for participation and that the employment requirement for each employee be the same. Under the second part, any employee who satisfies the employment requirement and is otherwise entitled to participate must do so no later than the first day of the plan year following completion of the employment requirement unless the employee has separated from service in the interim. The third part of the test requires that eligibility for participation must not be discriminatory in favor of highly compensated employees.

    b. If a plan fails this test, highly compensated employees must include in gross income the maximum taxable benefits they could have elected under the plan.

17. A cafeteria plan providing health benefits is not discriminatory if contributions under the plan for each participant include an amount equal to one of the following:

- 100 percent of the health benefit cost for the majority of similarly situated (that is, family or single coverage) highly compensated employees

- at least 75 percent of the health benefit cost for the similarly situated participant with the best health benefit coverage

18. Companies that contemplate the development of such programs must spend a considerable amount of time and resources in making sure that employees are adequately informed about (1) the reasons for the proposed program, (2) its advantages and disadvantages, and (3) its future implications. For best results, the opinions of employees should be solicited and weighed, and employees should be involved in various aspects of the decision-making process.

19. Union management often feels that bargaining for a cafeteria plan is contrary to the practice of bargaining for the best benefit program for all employees. There is also a concern that the employer will use a cafeteria plan primarily as a cost-containment technique to pass on the cost of future benefit increases to union members.

20. • Benefit limitations and restrictions on coverage can be included if a person wishes to add or change coverage at a date later than initial eligibility.

   • The cost to the employee for an option that is likely to cause adverse selection should be higher than what would have been charged if the option had been the only one available.

   • Predesigned package plans may separate a specific plan that is prone to adverse selection, such as medical expense plan, from other plan benefits for which adverse selection is also a concern (such as dental benefits) or offer minimal coverage for such other benefits.

21. • Extra development and administrative costs include the value of the employee hours that must be spent in preparing the program for implementation and complying with complex IRS regulations. Another sizable portion must be paid for the reprogramming of the organization's computer system to include necessary information and to accept the employees' benefit elections. ERISA also requires the annual filing of Form 5500.

   • Continuing costs may be incurred because of the need for additional employees to administer the program and additional computer time to process employee choices which may be frequent due to the number of available options and the number of employees covered.

- An employer may also need to incur additional costs to provide employee counseling regarding selection among benefits.

22. a. Employee input on their differing needs must be obtained without creating unreasonable expectations by establishing certain ground rules regarding the benefits that are acceptable to the employer. Because employees should have some protection against traditional areas of major personal risk, the program should have at least some provision for life insurance, disability income protection, medical expense protection, and retirement benefits, although all these benefits need not be included in a cafeteria plan.

   At the same time, a cafeteria plan may be an ideal vehicle for providing less traditional benefits, such as extra vacation time and child care. The value and tax implications for various classes of employees should be considered as well. Finally, the management of an employer's administrative costs associated with numerous benefits and options must also be considered.

   b. Each employee should be provided with enough dollars so that he or she can purchase optional benefits that, together with basic benefits, are at least equivalent to the benefits provided by the older plan.

   c. When used for unreimbursed medical expenses, a premium-conversion plan may negate many cost-containment features in the employer's medical expense plan. Employees may be reluctant to submit medical information for reimbursement under an FSA if they fear that the employer will know about their medical conditions. As a result, many employers use an external administrator to process FSA claims.

   d. As a rule, changes are allowed prior to the beginning of the plan year. Additional changes may be allowed as long as they are permissible under Sec. 125 regulations. To avoid the complications of having employees change benefits during a plan year due to cost experience under the plan or compensation increases, the employer usually makes sure all such changes due to these factors occur or become effective with new plan year for which employees may make their elections.

Chapter 11

Other Group Benefits

Learning Objectives

An understanding of the material in this chapter should enable the student to

1. **Explain why an employer may provide an array of benefits for employees.**

2. **Identify the sources of group dental insurance benefits and understand the provisions contained in dental insurance contracts.**

3. **Explain why long-term care insurance is needed, and understand the provisions found in group long-term care products.**

4. **Describe the types of uninsured benefits offered by employers.**

Employee benefits are divided into five categories:

- legally required social insurance payments
- payments for private insurance and retirement plans
- payments or other benefits for time not worked
- extra payments to employees
- services to employees

There are variations among employers, but typically about one-quarter of the sum spent on employee benefits is devoted to payments for legally required social insurance programs. Almost one-half is spent on employee benefits devoted to payments for retirement plans and group insurance which would include coverages such as dental and long-term care. Often overlooked is the significance of all the remaining types of benefits that employers may provide to employees, which as a group account for between one-quarter and one-third of the employee benefit dollars employers spend. Because the list is extensive, it is not possible to describe every benefit, but more common benefits will be discussed in this chapter.

Discussion begins with group dental insurance.

GROUP DENTAL INSURANCE

dental insurance

Dental insurance is a specialized form of health insurance to pay for normal dental care as well as care needed because of accidents. Dental coverage is one of the more popular ancillary benefits offered by employers.

Group dental insurance contracts have been largely patterned after group medical expense contracts, and they contain many similar, if not identical, provisions. Like group medical expense insurance, group dental insurance has many variations. Dental plans may be limited to specific types of services, or they may be broad enough to cover virtually all dental services. In addition, coverage is available from various types of providers, and benefits can be in the form of either services or cash payments.

Managed care has significantly affected the evolution of group dental insurance plans. However, this evolution has been somewhat different from that of medical expense plans. Group dental plans are more likely to provide benefits on a traditional fee-for-service basis. However, these traditional plans are also more likely to take a managed care approach to providing benefits. The most common example of this is the emphasis on providing a higher level of benefits for preventive care. As group dental plans have become more prevalent, the percentage of persons receiving preventive care has continued to increase. As a result, the percentage of persons needing care for more serious dental problems has continued to decrease.

One other difference between group medical expense plans and group dental plans is that providers of managed dental care arrangements have been more likely to offer coverage to very small groups.

The federal tax treatment of dental insurance premiums and benefits is the same as the tax treatment for medical expense premiums and benefits.

Providers of Dental Coverage

There are several providers of dental coverage which provide benefits in different ways:

- Insurance companies—offer coverage through an indemnity or PPO basis based on reasonable and customary fees

Delta Dental Plans

- Dental service plans such as **Delta Dental Plans**—dentists provide service benefits on a contractual basis but could also provide benefits through a PPO basis

dental health maintenance organization (DHMO)

- Managed care plans—often sponsored by insurance companies or other entity. These plans contain a strong emphasis on preventive care to hold down future costs. The **dental health maintenance organization (DHMO)** which operates like an HMO or point-of-service plans may be used.

direct reimbursement

- Self-funded plans (also called **direct reimbursement** plans)—can be administered by the employer or a TPA. The employee visits a dental provider and submits a paid bill to the employer for reimbursement based on a plan design.

discount plans

- **Discount plans**—noninsured plans that offer discounts on dental services when a participating provider is used by the employee or dependent. Discounts may be in the 20–30 percent range.

Contractual Provisions

Although group dental insurance contracts have been patterned after group medical expense contracts, some of their provisions are different, and others are unique to dental coverage. These provisions pertain to eligibility, benefits, exclusions, benefit limitations, predetermination of benefits, and termination.

Eligibility

In contributory plans, most employers use the same eligibility requirements for dental coverage as they use for medical expense coverage. However, some employers have different probationary periods for the two coverages. Probationary periods are used because members of a group who previously had no dental insurance usually have a large number of untreated dental problems. In addition, because many dental care expenditures are postponable, an employee who anticipates coverage under a dental plan in the future will be inclined to postpone treatment that is not crucial. Therefore, the adverse selection potential for dental plans is higher than for other benefits.

Dental insurance contracts contain several provisions that try to minimize this problem, including one or a combination of the following:

- reducing benefits (usually by 50 percent) for a period of time (such as one year) following the late enrollment

- reducing the maximum benefit to a low amount (such as $100 or $200) for the year following the late enrollment

- excluding some benefits for a certain period (such as one or 2 years) following the late enrollment period. This exclusion may apply to all dental expenses except those that result from an accident, or it may apply only to a limited array of benefits (such as orthodontics and prosthetics).

Benefits

One common characteristic of dental insurance is the inclusion of benefits for both routine diagnostic procedures (including oral examinations and X rays) and preventive dental treatment (including teeth cleaning and fluoride treatment). There is clear evidence that the cost of providing these benefits is more than offset by the avoidance of the expensive dental procedures that a person may require when a condition is not discovered early or when a preventive treatment has not been received.

In addition to benefits for diagnostic and preventive treatment, benefits for dental expenses may be available for these types of dental treatment:

- restoration (including fillings, crowns, and other procedures used to restore the functional use of natural teeth)

- oral surgery (including the extraction of teeth as well as other surgical treatment of diseases, injuries, and defects of the jaw)

- endodontics (treatment for diseases of the dental pulp within teeth, such as root canals)

- periodontics (treatment of diseases of the surrounding and supporting tissues of the teeth)

- prosthodontics (the replacement of missing teeth and structures by artificial devices, such as bridgework and dentures)

- orthodontics (the prevention and correction of dental and oral anomalies through the use of corrective devices, such as braces and retainers)

For plan design purposes, these treatments are usually divided into categories of dental services. Although there are variations, the following is a common list of such categories:

- service level I—preventive and diagnostic services

- service level II—minor restorative procedures, including fillings, inlays, onlays, and veneers

- service level III—major restorations, including crowns, bridges, and implants, as well as other major services involving endodontics, periodontics prosthodontics and oral surgeries

- service level IV—orthodontic services

Most dental plans provide benefits for the first three service levels. Coverage for service level IV is generally optional.

Benefit Payment Methods

Dental plans use several types of benefit payment methods. Plans that pay benefits on an indemnity basis usually make payments on the basis of reasonable-and-customary charges. Most plans have annual deductibles in the neighborhood of $50 to $100. However, the deductible typically does not apply to level I services. Coinsurance is also common. It is typically 80 percent or higher for level I services, with 100 percent being the most common. Level II services are usually subject to coinsurance in the range of 70 to 85 percent. Level III and level IV services typically have coinsurance of between 50 and 60 percent.

Dental plans with a PPO structure usually have deductibles and coinsurance similar to indemnity plans except that they use higher coinsurance percentages when a covered person receives services from network providers. They also pay network benefits on the basis of negotiated charges with providers.

DHMO plans do not usually use deductibles and coinsurance for most service levels as long as a covered person uses network providers. However, the member may be responsible for varying copayments for level II and level III services. Level IV services are usually subject to coinsurance, often 50 or 60 percent.

Exclusions

All dental plans have exclusions, but their number and type vary. Some of the more common exclusions are charges for the following:

- services that are purely cosmetic, unless necessitated by an accidental bodily injury sustained while a person is covered under the plan. (Orthodontics, although often used for cosmetic reasons, can usually also be justified as necessary to correct abnormal dental conditions.)

- replacement of lost, missing, or stolen dentures, or other prosthetic devices

- duplicate dentures or other prosthetic devices

- services that do not have uniform professional endorsement

- occupational injuries to the extent that workers' compensation laws or similar legislation provides benefits

- services furnished by or on behalf of government agencies, unless there is a requirement to pay

- certain services that began prior to the date that coverage for an individual was effective (for example, a crown for which a tooth was prepared prior to coverage)

Limitations

Dental insurance plans also contain numerous limitations to control claim costs and to eliminate unnecessary dental care. In addition to deductibles and coinsurance, virtually all dental plans have overall benefit maximums. Except for DHMOs, which usually do not have a calendar-year limit, most plans contain a calendar-year maximum (varying from $500 to $2,500) but no lifetime maximum. Benefits for orthodontics are subject to a separate lifetime maximum, typically between $500 and $2,000.

Most dental plans limit the frequency with which some benefits are paid. Routine oral examinations and teeth cleaning are usually limited to once every 6 months, and full mouth X rays to once every 24 or 36 months.

The typical dental plan also limits benefits to the least expensive type of accepted dental treatment for a given dental condition. For example, if either a gold or amalgam (silver) filling can be used, benefit payments are limited to the cost of an amalgam filling, even if a gold filling is inserted.

Predetermination of Benefits

About half of dental contracts provide for a pretreatment review of certain dental services by the insurance company. Although this procedure is usually not mandatory, it does allow both the dentist and the patient to know, prior to treatment, just how much the plan will pay. In addition, it enables the insurance company (or other provider of benefits) to have some control over the performance of unnecessary or more-costly-than-necessary procedures, by giving patients an opportunity to seek less costly care (possibly from another dentist) if they learn that benefits are limited.

predetermination-of- benefits provision

In general, the **predetermination-of-benefits provision** (which goes by several names, such as precertification or prior authorization) applies only in nonemergency situations and when a dentist's charge for a course of treatment exceeds a specified amount (varying from $200 to $300). The dentist in effect files a claim form (and X rays if applicable) with the insurance company just as if the treatment had already been performed. The insurance company reviews the form and returns it to the dentist. The form specifies the services that are covered and the amount of reimbursement. If the services are actually performed, the insurance company makes payment to the dentist after the claim form has been returned with the appropriate signatures and the date of completion.

When the predetermination-of-benefits provision is not followed, the plan still pays benefits. However, neither the dentist nor the covered person will know in advance what services the insurance company covers or how much the insurance company will pay for these services.

Termination

Coverage under dental insurance plans typically terminates for the same reasons it terminates under medical expense coverage.

A plan may still provide benefits for a dental service after termination as long as (1) the charge for the service was incurred prior to the termination date, and (2) treatment is completed within 60 or 90 days after termination. For example, the charge for a crown or bridgework is incurred once the preparation of the tooth (or teeth) has begun, even though the actual installation of the crown or bridgework (and the billing) does not take place until after the coverage terminates.

Rarely is there any type of conversion privilege for dental benefits. However, dental coverage is subject to the continuation rules of COBRA.

Examples of Major Plan Types

Dental benefit plans are classified as indemnity plans or managed care plans. As with medical expense insurance, different plan types may be available.

The following tables are examples of an indemnity plan, a PPO plan and a DHMO plan with a point-of-service option. All three plans are typical of their plan types, but variations do exist.

Table 11-1 Sample Dental Indemnity Plan Benefits Summary	
Service Level	**Benefits**
Level I—Preventive	100% of R & C*
Level II—Minor Restorative	80% of R & C*
Level III—Major Restorative	50% of R & C*
Level IV—Orthodontia	50% of R & C*
Deductible†	$75 (individual) $150 (family)
Orthodontia Lifetime Maximum	$2,000
Annual Maximum for Other Benefits	$2,000
*Reasonable and customary—charge determined by the plan based on prevailing fees charged by dentists in the area †Not applicable to service level I	

Table 11-2 Sample Dental PPO Plan Benefits Summary		
Service Level	**In-Network Benefits**	**Out-of-Network Benefits**
Level I—Preventive	100% of negotiated charge*	100% of R & C†
Level II—Minor Restorative	85% of negotiated charge*	75% of R & C†
Level III—Major Restorative	50% of negotiated charge*	50% of R & C†
Level IV—Orthodontia	50% of negotiated charge*	50% of R & C†
Deductible‡	$50 (individual) $100 (family)	$75 (individual) $100 (family)
Orthodontia Lifetime Maximum	$2,000	$2,000
Annual Maximum for Other Benefits	$2,000	$2,000
*Negotiated charge—fee that the dentist participating in the network accepts as payment in full †Reasonable and customary—charge determined by the plan based on prevailing fees charged by dentists in the area ‡Not applicable to service level I		

Service Level	DHMO Benefits	POS Benefits
Level I—Preventive	Fully paid	100% of R & C*
Level II—Minor Restorative	$10 copay	80% of R & C*
Level III—Major Restorative	$50 to $250 copay†	50% of R & C*
Level IV—Orthodontia	50% of negotiated charge‡	50% of R & C*
Deductible	Not applicable	$75 (individual)‡‡
		$150 (family)‡‡
Orthodontia Lifetime Maximum	Not applicable	$2,000
Annual Maximum for Other Benefits	Not applicable	$2,000

Table 11-3
Sample DHMO with Point-of-Service (POS) Option Plan Benefits Summary

*Reasonable and customary—charge determined by the plan based on prevailing fees charged by dentists in the area

†Amount varies depending on treatment or service

‡Negotiated charge—fee that the DHMO-participating dentist accepts as payment in full

‡‡Not applicable to service level I

GROUP LONG-TERM CARE INSURANCE

long-term care insurance

In the 1980s, insurance companies started to market long-term care insurance policies to individuals. **Long-term care insurance** provides coverage for at least 12 months to persons who need nonacute care for their health needs, often in the form of personal care services. Many of the earlier policies had limited benefits and expensive premiums. As the products evolved, benefits improved while premiums remained stable or decreased. As is often the case, the availability of coverage in the individual marketplace led to interest in long-term care insurance as an employee benefit. Today about 24 percent of employers offer long-term care coverage for at least some of their employees.[1]

Employers have been slow and cautious in adopting long-term care insurance plans for several reasons:

1. The individual long-term care insurance market is still in an evolving state after many years, due partially to the lack of adequate actuarial data to design and price coverage.

1. Society of Human Resource Management, *2014 Benefits Survey,* p. 9.

2. The tax treatment for employees is less favorable than that for many other types of employee benefits. As a result, most group long-term care plans have been financed solely by employee contributions. However, the Health Insurance Portability and Accountability Act (HIPAA) now provides favorable tax treatment for long-term care insurance, but within limits.

3. Long-term care insurance cannot be included in a cafeteria plan on a tax-favored basis.

4. Participation in group plans has been modest because older employees often do not see the need for coverage, or it is too expensive.

Before a description of the existing plans is undertaken, it is important to discuss the need for long-term care protection, the sources already available to meet this need, NAIC model legislation, and the effect of HIPAA.

Need for Long-Term Care

An Aging Population

Long-term care has traditionally been thought of as a problem primarily for older Americans. The population aged 65 or over (over 46 million people) is the fastest-growing age group; today it represents about 14.5 percent of the population, a figure that is expected to increase to about 81 million people by 2050.

A great percentage of the elderly have age-related conditions that require varying degrees of assistance to enable them to perform normal daily activities. In some cases, they receive this assistance in other types of supportive-living arrangements, such as assisted living facilities and adult foster homes. In many cases, however, the elderly remain in their own homes or the homes of relatives and receive their care from relatives, home health agencies, and community-based programs. The latter programs include meals on wheels and adult day care centers.

The elderly are not the only group of persons who need long-term care. Many younger persons are unable to care for themselves because of handicaps resulting from birth defects, mental conditions, illnesses, or accidents.

Increasing Costs

As of 2011, almost $134 billion was spent on institutional care (such as nursing home-type care), $58 billion on community-based care (such as churches, support groups, community sponsored centers, etc.), and $234 billion on informal care (such as home health care).[2]

The out-of-pocket payments for long-term care by individuals who must use personal resources can be astronomical. Although the average nursing home stay is 2½ years, some stays exceed the average by many years. In 2012, a semi-private nursing home room average cost was approximately $81,030 per year. A private room averaged almost $90,520 per year. Assisted living center rooms were almost $42,600 per year. Home health care averaged $21 per hour.[3] By 2045, the annual cost of nursing home care is expected to approximate $319,000 with comparable increases in home care charges.[4]

Inability of Families to Provide Full Care

Traditionally, family members have provided long-term care, often at considerable personal sacrifice and stress. However, it is becoming more difficult for families to provide long-term care for these reasons:

- geographic dispersion of family members
- increased participation in the paid workforce by women and children
- fewer children in the family
- more childless families
- higher divorce rates
- inability of family members to provide care because they, too, are growing old

Inadequacy of Insurance Protection

Private medical expense insurance policies (both group and individual) almost always have an exclusion for convalescent, custodial, or rest care. Some policies do provide coverage for extended-care facilities and for home health care. In both cases, the purpose is to provide care in a manner that is less expensive than care in a hospital. However, these policies provide benefits only if a person also needs medical care; they do not provide benefits if a person is merely "old" and needs someone to care for him or her.

---

2.   Congressional Budget Office, *Rising Demand for Long-Term Services and Support for Elderly People,* page 9.

3.   The MetLife Mature Market Institute, *Market Survey of Long-Term Care Costs,* October 2012.

4.   American Council of Life Insurance, *Long-Term Care Insurance: Protection for the Future,* from its Web site at acli.org.

Medicare is also inadequate because it does not cover custodial care unless a person needs this care along with the medical or rehabilitative treatment provided in skilled-nursing facilities or under home health care benefits.

Sources of Long-Term Care Financing

There are several sources other than insurance that are available for financing long-term care; however, there are drawbacks associated with each.

1. Personal financial resources—Few individuals have sufficient retirement income and assets to fully meet their potential long-term care expenses.

2. Relatives or friends—In some cases, family members may act as caregivers themselves; in other cases, they may give financial support to provide care or pay for long-term care insurance premiums. The support of relatives, however, may not last forever. Aging children may not have the financial resources to continue the same level of support because of their own long-term care needs.

3. Medicaid—The Medicaid program in most states provides benefits, which usually include nursing home care and home health care, to the "medically needy." A person, however, is not eligible unless he or she is either poor or has a low income and has exhausted most other assets (including those of a spouse). There is often a social stigma associated with accepting public assistance.

    One strategy that people sometimes use to qualify for Medicaid is to give assets away at the time they need nursing home care and ultimately rely on Medicaid. However, Medicaid reduces benefits (or postpones their onset) if assets were disposed of at less than their fair market value within a specific period (called the look-back period) prior to Medicaid eligibility. The Deficit Reduction Act of 2005 lengthened this period from 3 to 5 years for most transfers. One approach is to purchase long-term care insurance in an amount sufficient to provide protection for the length of the look-back period.

partnership program

4. Partnership program—Several states attempt to encourage better coverage for long-term care by waiving or modifying certain Medicaid requirements if a person carries a state-approved long-term care insurance policy. Such a policy is part of a state **partnership program** under which insurers issue policies that meet requirements established by the state. A person who purchases such coverage is able to retain a higher-than-usual amount of assets if he or she exhausts the insurance benefits and is then otherwise able to qualify for Medicaid.

continuing-care retirement community (CCRC)

5. Continuing-care retirement communities—The concept of the **continuing-care retirement community (CCRC)**, also referred to as a life care facility, is growing in popularity as a source of meeting long-term care needs. Residents in a CCRC pay an "entrance fee" that allows them to occupy a dwelling unit. Residents pay a monthly fee that includes meals, some housecleaning services, and varying degrees of health care. If a person needs long-term care, he or she must give up the independent living unit and move to the assisted-living or nursing home portion of the CCRC, but the monthly fee normally remains the same.

    The disadvantages of this option are that the cost of a CCRC is beyond the reach of many persons, and a resident must be in reasonably good health and able to live independently at the time he or she enters the facility.

6. Cash Value Life Insurance—A few insurers now include long-term care benefits in some cash value life insurance policies. Essentially an insured can begin to use these accelerated benefits while he or she is still living. Any benefits received reduce the future death benefit payable to heirs.

NAIC Model Legislation

NAIC model legislation focuses on two major areas—policy provisions and marketing. Highlights of the criteria for policy provisions include the following:

*   Insurance companies cannot use certain words or terms in a policy unless they specifically define them in accordance with the model legislation.

*   Policies must be guaranteed renewable or noncancelable.

*   There is a prohibition against limitations and exclusions except in the following cases:

    –   preexisting conditions

    –   mental or nervous disorders (but this does not permit the exclusion of Alzheimer's disease)

    –   alcoholism and drug addiction

    –   illness, treatment, or medical condition arising out of war, participation in a felony, service in the armed forces, suicide, and aviation if a person is a non-fare-paying passenger

    –   treatment in a government facility and services available under Medicare and other social insurance programs

- No policy can provide coverage for skilled-nursing care only or provide significantly more coverage for skilled care in a facility than for lower levels of care.

- The definition of preexisting condition cannot be more than 6 months prior to the effective date of coverage.

- Insurance companies cannot base eligibility for benefits on a prior hospital confinement or higher level of care.

- Insurance companies must offer the applicant the right to purchase coverage that increases in the amount of benefits based on reasonable anticipated increases in the cost of services covered by the policy.

- Insurance companies must offer the applicant a nonforfeiture benefit option.

- A policy must contain a provision that makes the policy incontestable after 2 years on the grounds of misrepresentation alone.

The following provisions of the model legislation pertain to marketing:

- All prospective applicants must receive an outline of coverage at the time of initial solicitation. Among the information this outline must contain is (1) a description of the coverage, (2) a statement of the principal exclusions, reductions, and limitations in the policy, (3) a statement of the terms under which the policy can be continued in force or terminated, (4) a description of the terms under which the policy may be returned and the premium refunded, (5) a brief description of the relationship of cost of care and benefits, and (6) a statement whether the policy is intended to be tax qualified.

- All prospective applicants must receive a shopper's guide.

- The policy must allow covered persons to have a free 30-day look at their policy or certificate of insurance during which they may terminate the policy or enrollment in the group plan as of the initial date of coverage.

- An insurance company must establish procedures to ensure that any comparisons of policies by its agents or other producers are fair and accurate and to prohibit the sale or issuance of excessive insurance.

- Applications for insurance must be clear and unambiguous so that an applicant's health condition can be properly ascertained. The application must also contain a conspicuous statement near the place for the applicant's signature that says the following: "If your answers to this application are incorrect or untrue, the company has the right to deny benefits or rescind your policy."

Effect of Health Insurance Portability and Accountability Act (HIPAA)

The Health Insurance Portability and Accountability Act (HIPAA) made the tax treatment of long-term care insurance more favorable. However, this favorable tax treatment is available only if long-term care insurance policies meet prescribed standards. It is important to emphasize that the long-term care changes in the act are primarily changes in the income tax code. States still have the authority to regulate long-term care insurance contracts.

Eligibility for Favorable Tax Treatment

qualified long-term care insurance contract

The act provides favorable tax treatment to a **qualified long-term care insurance contract**. Most, if not all, policies insurers use in the employer marketplace are this type of contract, which is defined as any insurance contract that meets all the following requirements:

- The only insurance protection provided under the contract is for qualified long-term care services.

- The contract cannot pay for expenses that are reimbursable under Medicare. However, this requirement does not apply to expenses that are reimbursable if (1) Medicare is a secondary payer of benefits or (2) benefits are payable on a per diem basis.

- The contract is guaranteed renewable.

- The contract does not provide for a cash surrender value or other money that can be borrowed or paid, assigned, or pledged as collateral for a loan.

- The insurance company uses all refunds of premiums and policyowner dividends as future premium reductions or future benefit increases.

- The policy must comply with various consumer protection provisions. For the most part, these are the same provisions contained in the NAIC model legislation and already adopted by most states.

qualified long-term care services

The act defines **qualified long-term care services** as necessary diagnostic, preventive, therapeutic, curing, treating, and rehabilitative services, and maintenance or personal care services that (1) a chronically ill person requires and (2) a licensed health care practitioner prescribes in a plan of care.

chronically ill individual

> A **chronically ill individual** is one who has been certified as meeting one of the following requirements, often referred to as benefit triggers:

activities of daily living (ADLs)

- The person is expected to be unable to perform, without substantial assistance from another person, at least two **activities of daily living (ADLs)** for a period of at least 90 days due to a loss of functional capacity. The act allows six ADLs: eating, bathing, dressing, transferring from bed to chair, using the toilet, and maintaining continence. A qualified long-term care insurance contract must contain at least five of the six.

- Substantial supervision is required to protect the individual from threats to health and safety because of severe cognitive impairment.

Federal Income Tax Provisions

The IRS treats a qualified long-term care insurance contract as accident and health insurance. With some exceptions, the IRS treats expenses for long-term care services, including insurance premiums, like other medical expenses. However, there is a cap on the amount of personally paid long-term care insurance premiums that a taxpayer can claim as medical expenses. The following table shows these limits, which are based upon a covered individual's age and subject to cost-of-living adjustments, for 2015.

Table 11-4 Sample Long-Term Care Deductible Limits (2015)	
Age	**Annual Deductible Limit per Covered Individual**
40 or younger	$ 380
41–50	710
51–60	1,430
61–70	3,800
Older than 70	4,750

Any employer contributions for group contracts are deductible to the employer and do not result in any taxable income to an employee. An employer cannot offer coverage through a cafeteria plan on a tax-favored basis. In addition, if an employee has a health flexible spending account for unreimbursed medical expenses, any reimbursements for long-term care services must be included in the employee's income. However, a person may pay long-term care premiums from a health savings account without tax consequences, up to the limits listed above.

Benefits a covered person receives under a qualified long-term care insurance contract are tax-free with one possible exception. Under contracts written on a per diem basis, proceeds are excludible from income up to $330 per day in 2015.

Policy Characteristics

Eligibility for Coverage

The typical eligibility rules apply to long-term care products. At a minimum, coverage is available for an active employee and/or spouse. Many products also provide coverage to retirees and to other family members, such as children, parents, parents-in-law, and possibly adult children. There is a maximum age for eligibility, but it is frequently as high as 85 and may be higher.

Cost

As previously mentioned, the cost of long-term care coverage is almost always borne by the employee. Initial premiums are usually in 5-year age brackets and increase significantly with age. Once an employee elects coverage, premiums remain level and do not increase when a person enters another age bracket. Coverage is guaranteed renewable, so premiums can only increase by class.

Under most plans, premiums are payable for life. Virtually all plans contain a waiver-of-premium provision that becomes effective when a covered person starts to receive benefits.

Types of Care Covered

There are many types of care for which a long-term care policy may provide benefits including nursing home care, assisted-living care, hospice care, Alzheimer's facility care, home health care, care coordination, and alternative sources of care. A long-term care policy may provide benefits for one, several, or all of these types of care.

nursing home care

skilled care

intermediate care

custodial care

> Nursing Home Care. **Nursing home care** encompasses skilled care, intermediate care, and custodial care in a licensed facility. **Skilled care** (also called skilled-nursing care) consists of daily nursing and rehabilitative care that can be performed only by, or under the supervision of, skilled medical personnel and must be based on a doctor's orders. **Intermediate care** involves occasional nursing and rehabilitative care that must be based on a doctor's orders and can be performed only by, or under the supervision of, skilled medical personnel. **Custodial care** is primarily to handle personal needs, such as walking, bathing, dressing, eating, or taking medicine, and someone without professional medical skills or training can usually provide them.

bed reservation benefit

> The **bed reservation benefit**, which continues payments to a long-term care facility for a limited time (such as 20 days) if a patient temporarily leaves because of hospitalization or any other reason. Without a continuation of payments, the bed may be assigned to someone else and unavailable upon the patient's release from the hospital.

assisted-living care

> Assisted-Living Facility Care. **Assisted-living care** is provided in facilities that care for the frail elderly who are no longer able to care for themselves but do not need as high a level of care as a nursing home provides.

> Hospice Care. Hospice care is devoted to easing the physical and psychological pain associated with death. A hospice may also offer counseling to family members. A hospice may be a separate facility, in the dying person's home, or the home of a relative or friend. Most long-term care insurance policies that provide benefits for hospice care make no distinction in the setting.

> Alzheimer's Facility Care. Most states require long-term care insurance policies to cover Alzheimer's disease and related forms of degenerative diseases and dementia under the same terms as they cover other conditions that qualify an individual as chronically ill.

Home Health Care. Home health care is much broader than just part-time skilled care, therapy, part-time services from home health aides, and help from homemakers. It may also include benefits for one or more of the following:

- the purchase or rental of needed medical equipment and emergency alert systems
- modifications to the home such as a ramp for a wheelchair or bathroom modifications

adult day care

- **adult day care**, which is received at centers specifically designed for the elderly who live at home but whose spouses or families cannot be available during the day

respite care

- **respite care** allows occasional full-time care for a person who is receiving home health care to give family caregivers a needed break
- caregiver training, which is the training of a family member or friend to provide care so that a person can remain at home
- a homemaker companion, who is an employee of a state-licensed home health care agency. The companion may assist with such tasks as cooking, shopping, cleaning, bill paying, or other household chores.
- prescription drugs and laboratory services typically provided in hospitals and nursing homes

care coordination

Care Coordination. Many policies provide **care coordination**, which is the services of a care coordinator who works with an insured, his or her family, and licensed health care practitioners to assess a person's condition, evaluate care options, and develop an individualized plan of care that provides the most appropriate services.

Benefit Variations

There are almost as many variations among long-term care policies as there are insurance companies writing the product. These benefit variations fall into three broad categories:

facility-only policy

1. **Facility-Only Policies.** Many early long-term care policies (nursing home policies) were designed to provide benefits only if the insured was in a nursing home. The term **facility-only policy** is often used to describe a broader type of policy, and the term, in its most generic sense, includes nursing home as well as other facility coverages.

home health care only policy

2. **Home Health Care Only Policies.** Home health care only policies were originally developed for use either as an alternative to nursing home policies or to complement such policies if more comprehensive coverage was desired. A **home health care only policy** provides benefits for care outside an institutional setting.

   Many insurers only write home health care coverage as part of a broader comprehensive policy.

comprehensive long-term care insurance policy

3. **Comprehensive Policies.** Most group long-term care policies that insurers write today are **comprehensive policies** which combine benefits for facility care and home health care into a single contract.

Benefit Amounts

When purchasing long-term care coverage, the employee selects the level of benefit he or she desires from the available options. Most plans offer at least three daily benefits such as $100, $150, or $200.

Most policies provide the same level of benefits for all types of institutional care. However, many allow applicants to select home health care limits that may vary from 50 percent to 100 percent of the benefit for institutional care.

Policies pay benefits in one of two basic ways: reimbursement or per diem.

reimbursement basis

Reimbursement Policies. The majority of group policies pay benefits on a **reimbursement basis**. These contracts reimburse the insured for actual expenses up to the specified policy limit. Tax-qualified policies that provide benefits on a reimbursement basis must be coordinated with Medicare except when Medicare is the secondary payer of benefits.

per diem basis

Per Diem Policies. Some policies provide benefits on a **per diem basis** once the insured is actually receiving care. This means that a policy pays benefits regardless of the actual cost of care. In this case, a policy with a daily benefit of $200 will pay $200 even if actual long-term care charges for the day are only $150. Insurers seldom coordinate per diem benefits with any benefits that are payable under Medicare.

Period of Benefits

To determine the period of benefits under a long-term care insurance policy, it is necessary to look at the waiting period and the maximum duration of benefits.

Waiting Period. The applicant is required to select a period of time that must pass after long-term care commences but before benefit payments begin. Many long-term care insurers refer to this period as a waiting period. Most insurers allow an applicant to select from among three to five optional waiting periods from 30 to 180 days.

There are several ways that policies count home health care services for purposes of the waiting period. Some policies count only those days when an insured receives services for which there is a charge and that the policy covers after the insured satisfies the waiting period. Some policies count each week as 7 days toward the satisfaction of the waiting period if the insured received services on any number of days in the week, even one day.

One final comment about the waiting period concerns its relationship to the requirement that tax-qualified policies cannot pay benefits for the inability to perform ADLs unless this inability is expected to last at least 90 days. If an insured is certified as being unable to perform the requisite number of ADLs for at least 90 days, benefit payments will start after the satisfaction of the waiting period, be it 0, 20, 60, or any other specified number of days. If the insured makes a recovery after the waiting period is satisfied but before the end of the 90-day period, the insured is fully entitled to any benefits received because the period was expected to be at least 90 days.

Maximum Duration of Benefits. The applicant has a choice as to the maximum period for which the policy will pay benefits, often referred to as the benefit period. This period begins from the time benefit payments start after satisfaction of the waiting period. The benefit period is a period that applies to the aggregate time the insurer pays policy benefits. When the insurer pays the maximum benefits, the policy will terminate.

Most insurers require the applicant to select the benefit period from several available options such as 2, 3, 4, 5, and 6 years as well as lifetime benefits.

shared benefit

A few policies use the concept of a **shared benefit** when a husband and wife have coverage under the same policy or with the same insurer. Under this concept, each spouse can access the other spouse's benefits. For example, if each spouse has a 4-year benefit period and one spouse has exhausted his or her benefits, benefit payments can continue by drawing on any unused benefits under the other spouse's policy. In effect, one spouse could have a benefit period of up to 8 years as long as the other spouse receives no benefit payments.

Restoration

Many policies written with less than a lifetime benefit period provide for restoration of full benefits if the insured previously received less-than-full policy benefits and has not required long-term care for a certain time period, often 180 days. If a policy does not have this provision, the policy reduces maximum benefits for a subsequent claim by the benefits previously paid.

Inflation Protection

Most states require that a long-term care policy offer some type of automatic inflation protection. Under some group contracts, the employer has the choice to decide which option is available. However, in other products, each employee makes the selection from what the insurer offers. The applicant is given the choice to select a standard option, decline the option, or possibly select an alternative option. The cost of an automatic-increase option is built into the initial premium, and the insurer levies no additional premium at the time of an annual increase. As a result of the NAIC model act and HIPAA, the standard provision found in almost all policies is a 5 percent benefit increase that compounds annually over the life of the policy. Under such a provision, the amount of a policy's benefits increases by 5 percent each year over the amount of benefits available in the prior year.

If an insured does not select an automatic-increase option, some insurers allow a policyowner to increase benefits without evidence of insurability on a pay-as-you-go basis at specified intervals such as every one, 2, or 3 years. Each benefit increase results in a premium increase based on attained-age rates for the additional coverage.

Increases in benefits are often inadequate to offset actual inflation in the annual cost of long-term care, which has been in the double digits over the last decade.

Eligibility for Benefits

Almost all tax-qualified contracts use the same two criteria for determining benefit eligibility, with the insured being required to meet only one of the two. The first criterion is that the insured is expected to be unable, without substantial assistance from another person, to perform two of the six ADLs that are acceptable under HIPAA for a period of at least 90 days due to loss of functional capacity. The second criterion is that substantial supervision is required to protect the individual from threats to health and safety because of severe cognitive impairment.

Underwriting

Several levels of underwriting may apply to employer-sponsored groups for long-term care insurance. These levels include guaranteed issue, modified guaranteed issue, simplified issue, and full underwriting.

- Guaranteed issue underwriting—for employees but only if the group meets certain criteria that minimize adverse selection. They seldom use guaranteed-issue underwriting for applicants other than employees.

- Modified guaranteed-issue underwriting—the insurer accepts most applicants. However, they ask some medical questions on the application, and the answers to these questions may result in the declination of the application. As long as there are no unsatisfactory answers to these questions, the insurer requests no further medical information and issues coverage.

- Simplified-issue underwriting—the insurer tends to ask more medically related questions than it uses with modified guaranteed-issue underwriting. Only if the answers to these questions are unsatisfactory does the insurer request further medical information—such as an attending physician's statement—or further medical assessments.

- Full underwriting—underwriting as in the individual marketplace. Insurers are most likely to use this type of underwriting in the group marketplace for very small groups and for persons other than employees.

Renewability

Long-term care policies currently being sold are guaranteed renewable, which means that the insurer cannot cancel an individual's coverage except for nonpayment of premiums. Although the insurer cannot raise premiums based on a particular applicant's claim, they can (and often do) raise premiums by class.

Nonforfeiture Options

nonforfeiture benefit

Most companies give an applicant for long-term care insurance the right to elect a **nonforfeiture benefit**. With a nonforfeiture benefit, the insured will receive some value such as a shortened benefit period for a policy if the policy lapses because the required premium is not paid in the future. There may be an in-force time requirement before the nonforfeiture benefit is valid.

Portability

If an insured is no longer eligible for employer-sponsored coverage, he or she can elect to continue coverage. For an individual policy paid through payroll deductions, the insured needs only to make arrangements with the insurer to pay the premium on a direct-bill basis.

For a group policy, the NAIC model regulations require that the insurer provide the insured with a basis for continuation or conversion of coverage. Under a continuation of coverage, the insured retains coverage under the group contract but pays premiums directly to the insurer. Under a conversion of coverage, the insured is issued an individual policy that must be identical or equivalent to the group coverage. The premium for the converted policy is based on the rates for the individual policy at the insured's attained age when the original group coverage was obtained.

GROUP LEGAL EXPENSE PLANS

legal expense plans

Legal expense plans, which cover the legal expenses of employees, have been a common benefit in several European countries for many years. However, until the mid-1970s, the concept was not widely used in the United States. The plans that did exist were almost always established by unions and were financed from general union funds. Usually, attorneys who were employed by the unions provided the legal services, and the only services covered were those limited to job-related difficulties, such as suspensions or workers' compensation disputes.

Over time, the number of employees with legal expense benefits continued to grow. This growth, however, was modest, primarily due to the fact that employers cannot offer legal expense benefits to employees on a tax-favored basis. Despite this fact, estimates are that 23 percent of employers make some type of plan available to at least some of their employees.[5] However, this percentage has changed little for several years.

Types of Plans

The types of group legal expense plans vary significantly in the ways they provide legal services. Benefits can be self-funded or purchased from another organization.

Existing plans fall into one of three types of arrangements:

- referral and discount plans
- telephone access plans
- comprehensive plans

Referral and Discount Plans

referral and discount plan

The most basic form of legal expense plan is a **referral and discount plan**. The plan refers members to an attorney who provides services based on a fee schedule or at a discount from his or her usual fees, but the plan member pays the attorney's charges. In some cases, the plan may refer members to attorneys who provide free services, such as a clinic for low-income persons or an attorney hot line of a local bar association.

Access Plans

telephone access plan

This form of legal expense plan, sometimes also called a **telephone access plan**, provides plan members with unlimited legal consultation over the telephone for most legal matters. The plan may also provide simple legal services, such as the preparation of wills or powers of attorney or the review of legal documents. The plan refers members to an attorney for more complex legal matters.

Access plans are often available for $5 to $10 per month per member.

5.　Society for Human Resource Management, *2013 Benefits Survey*, Table H-2, p. 44.

Comprehensive Plans

legal HMO

Most legal expense plans are comprehensive plans, and premiums usually fall in the range of $10 to $25 per month per member, depending on the level of services the plan provides. This type of plan is sometimes referred to as a **legal HMO**.

A comprehensive plan covers telephone consultation and in-office visits and trial work of attorneys. Most plans cover 80–90 percent of a member's potential legal services.

Comprehensive plans usually contain a list of covered services. Although there are significant variations among plans, most cover at least the following:

- unlimited legal advice by telephone
- document review and preparation
- name changes
- adoptions
- purchase or sale of primary residences
- eviction defense
- civil actions
- driver's license suspension
- juvenile court proceedings
- consumer protection
- bankruptcy
- IRS audits
- debt collection
- child custody and support
- divorce, but possibly only for the covered employee and not dependents

If a particular legal service that is required is not on the list of covered services, there may be some limited coverage as long as the plan does not otherwise exclude the service. This limited service, for example, may be in the form of telephone consultation or a limited amount of work by the attorney, such as 2 to 4 hours per family per year. Additional services may be available at discounted rates.

Legal expense plans have exclusions, and common exclusions include the following:

- business activities or transactions
- preparation of tax returns
- class-action suits
- actions involving the legal expense plan
- actions involving the employer
- actions involving the union that bargained for the coverage
- cases that have contingent fees

Members of comprehensive plans can choose an attorney through:

1. a closed panel where there is a network of attorneys providing services at a small out-of-pocket fee for the member
2. an open panel where the member can use any attorney normally with a deductible and coinsurance
3. a modified panel which operates much like a medical PPO plan

Current Tax Treatment

The cost of a legal expense plan is deductible for the employer. Employees, however, have taxable income to the extent of employer payments. If the employer prefunds the plan with an insurance contract or other arrangement, the employee has taxable income based on his or her share of the employer-paid premium and receives benefits tax free. If an employer self-funds a plan, the employee's taxable income is the value of the benefits the plan pays.

PAYMENTS OR OTHER BENEFITS FOR TIME NOT WORKED

Vacations

In terms of employer cost, the most significant benefit is paid vacations. Unlike many other countries, the United States has no laws that mandate vacation benefits.

Most plans are based on the employee's length of service, and the number of vacation days given to any particular employee normally increases over time. There is usually a short waiting period (3 to 6 months) during which employees are ineligible for vacations, but for competitive reasons there is often no waiting period for management employees. The following is one employer's benefit schedule for its vacation plan:

Table 11-5 Sample Benefit Schedule for Vacation Plan	
Length of Service	**Vacation Days**
First 6 months	0
After 6 months	1 for each month in the remaining calendar year (max. of 10)
1–5 years	10
6–15 years	15
16 years or more	20

Some firms have different schedules for different classes of employees, with higher-paid employees tending to have more vacation time. In contrast to many types of benefits, employers often give vacation benefits to part-time employees.

An employer must also address several major issues in properly designing a vacation plan. One is the treatment of unused vacation days. Some employers can require employees to forfeit any unused vacation days or allow employees to carry over unused days to the next year, subject to certain limitations. Another issue is the question of vacation timing. In general, vacations may not be allowed during busy work times. Other issues employers must address are those of how to treat unused vacation days upon termination of employment if a state does not require payment for these days and whether to treat sicknesses and holidays occurring during vacation periods as vacation days.

The compensation employees receive during periods of vacation is treated the same as compensation for time worked and is taxed accordingly.

Holidays

Employers normally pay employees for certain holidays. At a minimum, employees in the United States usually receive pay for

- New Year's Day
- Memorial Day
- the Fourth of July
- Labor Day
- Thanksgiving

- Christmas

Most employees receive at least 6 and often as many as 11 or 12 additional holidays, which may include

- Martin Luther King's Birthday
- Washington's Birthday
- Lincoln's Birthday
- Presidents' Day
- Cesar Chavez Day
- Good Friday
- Columbus Day
- the Friday after Thanksgiving
- Veterans Day
- Christmas Eve
- New Year's Eve
- the employee's birthday
- other religious holidays
- various state holidays

For most companies, management decides which holidays to give, subject to collective bargaining if applicable.

floating holidays

Some companies, realizing that not all employees want to take the same holidays, try to satisfy these needs by adopting holiday plans that include a minimum number of scheduled holidays coupled with a specific number (often two or three) of **floating holidays** to be taken at an employee's option. Usually, there is no requirement that the days taken actually be holidays, so in effect they become additional vacation days in lieu of holidays. Floating holidays are usually granted on an annual basis and cannot be carried over to the next year.

Like vacation pay, holiday pay is taxed as regular income.

Personal Time Off with Pay

Because personal situations that require an employee to be away from work occasionally arise, many employers allow employees to take time off with pay for certain reasons, the more common of which are the following:

sabbatical leave

funeral leave

- reserve/National Guard duty. Laws sometimes require that employees get time off for reserve or National Guard duty, but there is no stipulation that pay continue during this period. However, many employers pay their employees the difference between their regular pay and any compensation received for reserve or National Guard duty of short duration.

- jury duty. Most employers grant (and may be required to grant) time off for jury duty. Because the courts usually provide compensation to jurors for their duty, some employers pay only the difference between this amount and an employee's regular pay. Many employers continue regular compensation with no deduction.

- **funeral (bereavement) leave**. Employers often allow up to 5 days funeral (bereavement) leave with pay for the death of an immediate family member. At a minimum, this usually includes the death of a parent, child, spouse, or other relative residing in the household.

- **sabbatical leave**. Sabbatical leaves are well established as employee benefits at educational institutions. Typically, faculty members are permitted an extended leave of a semester or a year after a specified period of service, such as 7 years. During the sabbatical leave, the faculty member receives full or partial pay while performing no services for the employer. Noneducational employers sometimes provide similar benefits to professional employees to give them an opportunity to engage in research or study that is not directly job related.

- observation of religious holidays. Although most businesses in the United States treat Christmas and Easter as holidays, not all employees are Christians. Therefore, employees of other faiths may be allowed time off to observe certain major religious days associated with their faith.

Employers may combine most or all days off with pay into a single program of personal time off (PTO).

Personal Time Off without Pay (Family Leave)

family leave

Over the last two decades, an increasing number of American employers have voluntarily begun to allow employees to take time off without pay. Reasons for such leave may include active military duty, extended vacations, honeymoons, education, the birth or adoption of a child, and the illness of a family member. Usually, such time off has been subject to the approval of the employer. **Family leave** is becoming more and more common as many states and the federal government adopt family-leave legislation.

Federal Family and Medical Leave Act

Family and Medical Leave Act

In 1993, the first federal family-leave legislation—the **Family and Medical Leave Act**—became effective. Unlike some federal legislation, it applies not only to private employers but also to nonprofit organizations and government entities, including Congress. The provisions of this legislation cover only a small percentage of the nation's employers but approximately two-thirds of all employees.

The legislation applies only to employers who have more than 50 employees within a 75-mile radius. To comply with the 50-employee requirement, an employer needs only to have that many employees during each workday of 20 or more calendar weeks during the current or preceding calendar year. Part-time employees and employees on unpaid leaves of absence are included in the calculation.

With some exceptions, an employer must provide a full-time or part-time employee up to 12 weeks of unpaid leave in any 12-month period under the following circumstances:

- because of the birth of the employee's child
- because of the placement of a child in the employee's home for adoption or foster care
- to care for the employee's child, spouse, or parent with a serious health condition
- for the employee's own serious health condition that makes it impossible to work
- because of a qualifying exigency arising if an employee's spouse, child, or parent is on (or has been called to) active duty in the armed forces in support of a contingency operation. Examples of a qualifying exigency include providing child care or getting financial affairs in order.

In 2008, legislation amended the act to require up to 26 weeks of leave within a 12-month period for an employee to care for a service member with a serious injury or illness incurred in the line of active duty. The service member can be a spouse, child, parent, or next of kin.

The act defines a *serious health condition* as one that requires continuing treatment from a health care provider. The regulations implementing the act generally define this as meaning that the condition will require absence from work, school, or regular daily activities for more than 3 calendar days. However, the regulations also include treatment for pregnancy and certain chronic conditions, such as diabetes and asthma, as being serious health conditions even though treatment at any time may last less than 3 days. In addition, the definition includes health problems that are not ordinarily incapacitating on a day-to-day basis, but for which a person is undergoing a series of multiple treatments such as chemotherapy. The regulations specifically exclude the following from the definition of a serious health condition: common colds, upset stomach, and routine dental problems. Stress is also excluded, but mental illness arising from stress can qualify.

In most cases, the rules allow employees to take leave intermittently or by working a reduced week, but only with the employer's approval. The exception is that leave because of a person's or family member's serious health condition may be taken whenever medically necessary.

An employer is allowed to substitute an employee's accrued paid leave for any part of the 12-week period of family leave. In addition, an employer can deny leave to a salaried employee within the highest-paid 10 percent of its workforce if the leave would create a substantial and grievous injury to the organization's operations.

During the period of leave, an employer has no obligation to continue an employee's pay or most benefits except medical and dental benefits, and the employee is ineligible for unemployment compensation. The employee must continue to pay any required plan contributions and must be given a 30-day grace period for such payments.

Upon returning from leave, an employer must generally give an employee his or her former job or one that is equivalent. The employee regains any benefits that he or she enjoyed prior to the leave without having to meet any requalification requirements. With respect to retirement plans, an employer must treat any period of leave as continued service for purposes of vesting and eligibility to participate. There is an exception to this requirement for restoration of employment that applies to employees who are among the highest paid 10 percent of the employees employed by the employer within a 75-mile radius of the facility at which the employee works. Employers can deny restoration of employment (1) if it is necessary to prevent substantial and grievous economic injury to the operations of the employer and (2) if the employer notifies the employee of the fact at the time the employer determines that such injury would occur.

An employer should have a clear, written family-leave policy that is consistently enforced. In establishing this policy, the employer should address such issues as

- eligibility requirements
- employee certification of need for leave
- employee rights upon returning from leave
- employer rights if employee terminates at end of leave

The federal law requires an employer to post a notice explaining the Family and Medical Leave Act, a sample of which is available in material from the U.S. Department of Labor, the administrator of the law. In addition, if an employer does not provide employees with guidance about their rights and obligations under the act in employee manuals or handbooks, it must provide this information to an employee at the time he or she requests leave.

EXTRA PAYMENTS TO EMPLOYEES

Educational Assistance

For 2015, the Internal Revenue Code provides favorable tax treatment to employees for the first $5,250 of annual education assistance received from their employers. In order for benefits to be tax free, the employer's plan cannot discriminate with respect to eligibility in favor of officers, shareholders, highly compensated employees, or their dependents. In addition, no more than 5 percent of the benefits may be paid to shareholders or owners (or their dependents) who are more-than-5-percent owners of the firm.

Eligible benefits include tuition, fees, and books for courses, including graduate education. The costs of supplies and equipment are also included as long as employees do not retain them after completion of the course. Reimbursements for meals, lodging, and transportation associated with educational expenses cannot be received tax free. In addition, courses involving sports, games, or hobbies are ineligible for favorable tax treatment. Although an employer's plan can pay for any of these types of courses, an employee is taxed on the value of the employer's contribution to his or her cost.

Moving-Expense Reimbursement

To attract new employees and to encourage current employees to move to suit the employer's needs, many businesses provide reimbursement for moving expenses. Such reimbursement is includible in an employee's income, but the employee has certain offsetting income tax deductions if specified rules are satisfied. To receive the deductions, the employee must have moved because of a change in job location. In addition, the employee must satisfy both a distance test and a time test. The distance test requires that the employee's new workplace be at least 50 miles farther from the employee's old residence than the employee's old workplace (or old residence if the employee was previously unemployed). The time test requires that the employee work full time in the general location of the new residence for at least 39 weeks during the 12 months following the move. An employee may take the applicable deductions in anticipation of satisfying the time test, but additional taxes are payable if the time test is not ultimately met.

If all the preceding rules are satisfied, an employee may deduct the following expenses:

- transportation expenses in moving household goods and personal effects
- travel and lodging expenses (but not meal expenses) in moving to the new residence

An employer may pay for other expenses, such as expenses to sell an old residence, premove travel to find a new residence, or temporary living costs at the new location. Because these reimbursements are taxable income without a corresponding deduction, the employer may give the employee a bonus to offset the increased tax.

Service Awards

Many employers provide awards to employees for length of service. These awards are often nominal for short periods of service (5 or 10 years) and may consist of such items as key chains, flowers, or pens. Awards typically increase in value for longer periods of service, and employees may have some choice in the award received.

If the value of a service award is $400 or less, it is not included in an employee's income. Service awards of higher value may also be excludible from an employee's income if they are *qualified plan awards*. However, the total amount excludible from an employee's income for qualified plan awards (which also include awards for safety) cannot exceed $1,600 per year. Employers must provide qualified plan awards under a permanent written program that does not discriminate in favor of highly compensated employees. In addition, the average annual cost of all awards under the plan cannot exceed $400.

Holiday Bonuses and Gifts

Many employers, particularly at Christmas time, give gifts or bonuses to employees. Because the value of such gifts is typically small, some employees tend to resent gifts of money. Therefore, such gifts as liquor or a ham are often given.

As with service awards, a holiday gift does not result in taxation for an employee as long as the market value of the gift is small.

SERVICES TO EMPLOYEES

No-Additional-Cost Services

no-additional-cost services

Employers in many service industries provide their employees with free or discounted services, often referred to as **no-additional-cost services**. An example is airline tickets to employees of airlines. As long as the following rules are satisfied, the cost of these services is not includible in an employee's gross income for tax purposes:

- The services cannot be provided on a basis that discriminates in favor of highly compensated employees.

- The employer must not incur any significant additional cost or lost revenue in providing the services. For example, giving a standby ticket to an airline employee if there are unsold seats on a flight satisfies this requirement, but giving an airline ticket to an employee when potential paying customers are denied seats does not.

- The services must be those that are provided in the employer's line of business in which the employee actually works. Therefore, if a business owns both an airline and a chain of hotels, an employee of the hotels can be given a room as a tax-free benefit but not an airline ticket. However, unrelated employers in the same line of business, such as airlines, may enter into reciprocal arrangements under which employees of any party to the arrangement may obtain services from the other parties.

Employee Discounts

Just as no-additional-cost services are an important employee benefit in certain service industries, discounts on the merchandise sold by manufacturers and retailers are an important benefit to employees in these industries. Discounts may also be provided on services sold by other types of businesses, such as the commission charged by a brokerage house or insurance company.

Rules similar to those discussed for no-additional-cost services apply to discounts. Employees have no taxable income as long as the discounts are made available on a nondiscriminatory basis and are provided on goods or services ordinarily sold to nonemployees in the employer's line of business in which the employee works. However, there are some additional rules. Discounts received on real estate or on personal property normally held as an investment (for example, gold coins or securities) are not received tax free. Furthermore, there is a limit on the size of a discount that can be received tax free. The discount for merchandise cannot exceed the gross profit percentage of the price at which the merchandise is offered for sale to customers. For example, if an employer has a gross profit margin of 40 percent on a particular product and an employee purchases the merchandise at a 50 percent discount, the extra 10 percent is taxable income to the employee. In the case of services, including insurance policies, the tax-free discount cannot exceed 20 percent of the price at which the employer offers the service is to nonemployee customers in the normal course of business. The type of service that employees cannot receive tax free involves loans that financial institutions give to employees at a discounted rate of interest.

Dependent-Care Assistance

Changes in society and the workforce often create changing needs for both employers and employees. When the workforce was largely male and most families had two parents, caring for children and older parents frequently was the female spouse's responsibility. As the number of families headed by two wage earners or by single parents has increased, so has the need for dependent care. This change in demographics has also created problems for employers. Caring for family members can lead to increased absenteeism, tardiness, turnover, and time taken as family leave.

dependent-care assistance plan (DCAP)

The nature of employee benefit plans has changed as employers have increasingly responded to the need for dependent care and many employers have established a **dependent-care assistance plan (DCAP)**. Child-care benefits are increasingly common, and a small but growing number of firms also make elder-care benefits available. Firms that have dependent-care assistance plans generally feel that such plans alleviate the problems cited in the previous paragraph. Furthermore, the availability of the benefit often makes it easier to hire new employees.

In addition to a formal dependent-care assistance plan, there are other ways in which employers can respond to employee needs to care for family members. These include flexible work schedules, part-time employment, job sharing, salary reduction options under cafeteria plans, and family-leave policies that are more liberal than those required by federal and state laws.

Child-Care Plans

child-care plan

Employers can provide several alternative types of benefits under a **child-care plan**. A few employers maintain on-site day-care centers, and the number is growing. On the other hand, some employers have closed on-site centers and provide alternative forms of assistance because of problems encountered with on-site centers such as hiring qualified child-care providers, potential liability, licenses, and underutilization.

Probably the most common approach is to provide reimbursements to employees who make their own arrangements for child care, either at child-care centers or in their own home or the home of a caregiver. Employers sometimes tie reimbursement to pay levels, with lower-paid workers receiving higher reimbursements.

Elder-Care Benefits

Benefits to care for elderly dependents are much less prevalent than benefits for child care, but the need for them continues to grow as parents live longer. In addition, as many couples have delayed having children until later in life, they have become part of what is often referred to as the sandwich generation. They must care for elderly parents at the same time they are raising their own children.

elder-care benefit

Although an **elder-care benefit** may take a variety of forms, frequently it is much like the benefit provided under a child-care plan. Within limits, the employer may pay for costs associated with home care for elderly dependents or care at day-care facilities for the elderly. One interesting development in this area is the establishment of centers that care for both children and the elderly, with the elderly assisting in such activities as the feeding and teaching of the children. Studies have shown that the two groups are very compatible.

Tax Treatment of Benefits

Under the Internal Revenue Code, dependent care is a tax-free benefit to employees up to statutory limits as long as a plan meets certain requirements. The amount of benefits that an employee can receive tax free is limited to $5,000 for single persons and married persons who file jointly and to $2,500 for married persons who file separately. The benefits must be for care to a qualifying individual—a child under age 13 for whom the employee is allowed a dependency deduction on his or her income tax return or a taxpayer's spouse or other dependent who is mentally or physically incapable of caring for himself or herself. Although benefits must generally be for custodial care only, the plan can pay educational expenses at the kindergarten or preschool level.

Dependent-care benefits are subject to rules around eligibility, nondiscrimination, communication, and reporting. If a plan does not meet the rules, highly compensated employees are taxed on the amount of benefits received. However, the benefits for other employees still retain their tax-free status.

Even if an employer does not provide assistance for dependent care, other tax-saving options may be available to employees. Under the Code, a tax credit (subject to limits) is available for child-care expenses. In addition, the employer may have the opportunity to make before-tax contributions to a cafeteria plan that includes dependent care as an option.

Adoption Assistance

adoption assistance plan

Although many types of benefits have long been available to natural parents because of the birth of a child, comparable benefits historically have not been available to adoptive parents. Over the last few years, some employers have instituted an **adoption assistance plan**. Even before the passage of family-leave legislation, many employers had established comparable leave policies for natural parents and adoptive parents. For example, if an employer allowed maternity leave (either paid or unpaid) for a new mother, no distinction was made between natural mothers and adoptive mothers. Leave may also be available for time involved in qualifying for the adoption and taking possession of the child.

A smaller number of employers provide reimbursement for some or all of the following expenses associated with adoption:

- legal fees
- adoption agencies' fees

- the birth mother's medical expenses
- the adoptive parents' medical expenses for physical examinations required by the adoption source
- the child's uninsured medical expenses
- foster care charges for the child prior to placement with the adoptive family
- transportation expenses associated with taking custody of the child
- extra expenses associated with foreign adoptions

Reimbursements are generally available only to employees who have satisfied some minimum service requirement, most commonly one year. Amounts typically range from $1,000 to $3,000 per adoption, but the plan may pay higher amounts for adoptions involving handicapped children or children from a foreign country. There may also be a lifetime cap, such as $6,000.

Employer payments for qualified adoption expenses are excludible from an employee's gross income if an employer has an adoption-assistance program that satisfies IRS requirements in 2015.

Qualified adoption expenses include reasonable and necessary adoption fees, court costs, attorney's fees, travel expenses, and other expenses directly related to the legal adoption of an eligible child, defined as a child who is under age 18 or who is incapable of caring for himself or herself. Expenses incurred in adopting a spouse's child or carrying out a surrogate parenting arrangement are not qualified adoption expenses, nor are expenses that are reimbursed from other sources. In addition, expenses to adopt a child with special needs are not qualified adoption expenses unless the adoption becomes final.

There is a tax credit available to all taxpayers for adoption expenses, but the credit is not available for expenses that are paid by employer-provided adoption assistance regardless of whether the employer paid the expenses through an adoption-assistance program. However, a taxpayer can use the credit for expenses not reimbursed by an employer's plan.

Wellness Programs

Traditional benefit programs have been designed to provide benefits (1) to employees and their dependents for their medical expenses and disabilities or (2) to their dependents if the employee should die prematurely. In the last few years, it has become more common for an employer, particularly a large corporation, to initiate a wellness program that is designed to promote the well-being of employees (and possibly their dependents). Some wellness programs focus on the discovery and treatment of medical conditions before they become severe and result in large medical expenses, disabilities, or death. Other programs focus on changing employees' lifestyles in order to eliminate the possible causes of future medical problems. Many firms also feel these programs increase productivity by improving the employees' sense of well-being, their work attitudes, and their family relationships.

Medical Screening Programs

medical screening program

The use of a **medical screening program** to discover existing medical conditions is not new, but it has often covered the costs (frequently up to some dollar limit) of routine physical examinations only for selected groups of management employees.

In recent years, there has been a significant increase in the number of employers that sponsor periodic medical screening programs that detect specific medical problems, such as hypertension (high blood pressure), high cholesterol levels, diabetes, breast cancer, prostate cancer, and colorectal cancer. In many cases, such screenings are conducted at the employment site during regular working hours. Screenings are sometimes available at little or no cost through such organizations as the American Red Cross, the American Heart Association, or the American Cancer Association.

Lifestyle-Management Programs

lifestyle-management program

A **lifestyle-management program** is primarily designed to encourage employees and often their dependents to modify their behavior so that they lead healthier lives. Most of these programs strive to discover and eliminate conditions that increase the likelihood of cardiovascular problems. Some of these conditions (such as obesity and smoking) are obvious, but medical screening can also detect less obvious conditions like hypertension, high cholesterol levels, and the degree of an employee's physical fitness. The types of programs often instituted to promote cardiovascular health include the following:

- smoking-cessation programs
- fitness programs
- weight-reduction programs
- nutrition programs
- stress-management programs

These programs may be available to any employees who express an interest in them, or they may be limited only to those employees who have been evaluated and found to be in a high-risk category for cardiovascular disease. Generally, these evaluations and meetings to describe the programs and their value are conducted during regular working hours. However, the programs themselves are usually conducted during nonworking hours, possibly at lunchtime or just after work.

Many wellness programs are designed to include employees, their spouses, and sometimes other family members. In many instances, it is not possible to change an employee's lifestyle unless the lifestyle of his or her entire family also changes. For example, it is not very probable that an employee will stop smoking if his or her spouse also smokes and is making no attempt to stop. Similarly, a weight-reduction or nutrition program is probably more effective if all family members alter their eating habits.

Programs designed to eliminate alcohol or drug abuse are another example of lifestyle management. Participation may be voluntary or it can be mandatory for employees who are known to have alcohol or drug problems.

The employer may either conduct these wellness activities on the premises or use the resources of other organizations. For example, overweight employees might be sent to Weight Watchers, employees with alcohol problems might be encouraged to attend Alcoholics Anonymous, etc.

Employers in increasing numbers are subscribing to wellness newsletters and distributing them to employees. To encourage wellness for the entire family, these newsletters are often mailed to employees' homes.

Effect of HIPAA

Provisions of HIPAA affect wellness programs that provide rewards for adherence to health promotion and disease prevention programs. These rewards might be in the form of premium discounts or rebates, or modification of deductibles or copayments. With an exception mentioned later, HIPAA does not permit such rewards unless a wellness program meets the following requirements:

- The rewards for the wellness programs, together with rewards from any other wellness programs, cannot exceed 20 percent of the "cost" of coverage under a medical expense plan. If only an employee is eligible to participate in the program, the cost is that of employee-only coverage, even if the employee has family coverage. If any class of dependents can also participate, then the cost is what the employee and that class of dependents would pay for coverage.

- The program must be reasonably designed to promote good health or prevent disease.
- The program must give eligible participants the opportunity to qualify for the reward at least once a year.
- The reward must be available to all similarly situated individuals.

The program must have a reasonable alternative standard to obtain the reward for persons who cannot satisfy the otherwise applicable standard because meeting the standard is unreasonably difficult or not medically advisable. For example, if a premium discount were allowed for nonsmokers, a person with an addiction to nicotine would need to have an alternative standard to receive the reward. The standard might be to participate in a smoking cessation course. However, the reward could be conditioned on participation only, not whether the course was successful.

The HIPAA regulations provide an exception to the requirements for a bona fide wellness program if a reward is based solely on an individual's participation in a wellness program. HIPAA uses the following as examples of programs that are acceptable:

- reimbursing employees, without regard to health factors, for the cost of health club memberships
- voluntary testing for specific health problems and making recommendations for their treatment
- waiving copayments and deductibles for well-baby visits
- reimbursing employees for the costs of smoking cessation programs without regard to whether a participant quits smoking

Tax Treatment of Benefits

Because medical screening programs are treated as medical expenses for tax purposes, employees have no taxable income as a result of merely participating in these programs. Unless the cost of providing lifestyle-management programs is minimal, participation probably results in taxation to employees. The costs of programs that promote general health, such as smoking cessation or weight control, are not considered medical expenses. Although the cost of providing these programs to employees is deductible by the employer, an employee incurs taxable income unless the purpose of the program is to alleviate a specific medical problem. However, there is one exception to this general rule. Employees incur no taxable income because of being provided with or using athletic facilities that are located on the employer's premises.

As a rule, rewards for participating in wellness programs represent taxable income to employees. For example, a $50 gift card for an employee, who filled out a health questionnaire and shared it with his or her physician, is taxable income. However, with some exceptions, premium discounts or rebates, or modification of deductibles and copayments are not taxable to employees. In addition, gifts of small value, such as a coffee mug, are tax free.

Employee-Assistance Programs

employee-assistance program

As the trend toward fostering wellness in the workplace continues, it is increasingly common for an employer to establish an **employee-assistance program**. These programs help employees with certain personal problems through a plan that provides

- treatment for alcohol or drug abuse

- counseling for mental problems and stress

- counseling for family and marital problems

- financial, legal, and tax advice

- referrals for child care or elder care

- crisis intervention

Numerous studies have shown that proper treatment of these problems is very cost effective and leads to reduced sick days, hospital costs, disability, and absenteeism. It is also argued that employee morale and productivity are increased because of the concern shown for employees' personal problems.

Employees can access employee-assistance programs through a referral from an employer or directly. Dependents can usually use the employee assistance program and can often seek help without the employee's knowledge.

Access to an employee-assistance program is through a counselor who may be a company employee, but most often an employer establishes the plan through a professional organization that specializes in such programs. Information that a counselor provides to the employee is kept confidential. Most plans have 24-hour counseling available through either a telephone hot line or on-duty personnel. If the counselor cannot solve an employee's problem, it is the counselor's responsibility to make a preliminary determination about the type of professional help the employee should receive. In many cases, this treatment is available under existing medical expense or legal expense plans or through community agencies. The employer usually pays the costs of other types of treatment totally or in part. As long as the treatment is for alleviating medical conditions, including mental illness, an employee has no taxable income. If the treatment is for a nonmedical condition, the employee has taxable income as the result of employer payments.

Transportation/Free Parking

qualified transportation fringe benefit

Some employers have long provided transportation benefits in many forms to employees as a fringe benefit. The Internal Revenue Code provides favorable tax treatment to transportation benefits that meet the definition of a **qualified transportation fringe benefit**, which includes the following:

- transportation in a commuter highway vehicle with a capacity of at least six adults other than the driver if such transportation is in connection with travel between the employee's residence and place of employment. Traditional vanpools, in which one employee usually has possession of an employer-provided vehicle to drive other employees to work, come under this definition as long as these criteria are satisfied.

- transit passes. These include any pass, token, fare card, voucher, or similar item entitling a person to transportation as long as it is on a mass transit system or in a commuter highway vehicle as previously described.

- qualified parking. This includes parking provided on or near the business premises of the employer or near a location from which the employee commutes to work by using a mass transit facility or a commuter highway vehicle.

- qualified bicycle commuting reimbursement. This includes reasonable expenses for the purchase of a bicycle as well as bicycle repair and storage. An employee must use the bicycle for a substantial portion of travel between his or her residence and place of employment.

The value of the benefit under a qualified transportation fringe is excluded from gross compensation up to specified amounts, which are subject to cost-of-living adjustments. The 2015 figures are:

- $130 per month in the aggregate for any transit passes and transportation in a commuter highway vehicle

- $250 per month for qualified parking

- $20 per month for qualified bicycle commuting reimbursement.

Personal Use of Company Cars

Employers often provide employees with company cars (or other types of vehicles). In addition to using a vehicle for business purposes, an employer may allow an employee to use the car for commuting to and from work and for other personal purposes. However, an employee who drives a company car for personal use must include the value of this use in his or her taxable income.

The employer determines the method for valuing the use of a car, and several choices are available. The most common method for valuing the car is for the employer to report an annual cost that is a percentage of the car's annual lease value. This value is determined by a table prepared by the IRS and is based on a car's fair market value unless an employer can clearly justify a lower value. For example, under this table, a car with a fair market value of $20,000 to $20,999 has an annual lease value of $5,600. This figure is then multiplied by the ratio of personal-use miles to total miles. If 20 percent of the miles driven are personal miles, the employer must report $1,120 of income for the employee. The employee must also report additional income if the employer pays for gas.

A second method is for the employer to annually report the entire lease value of the car as taxable income. If the employer uses this alternative, the employee can claim an income tax deduction for any business use of the vehicle if the employee itemizes his or her deduction. However, the deduction is subject to the 2 percent floor requirement for miscellaneous deductions. This alternative is less favorable to the employee but administratively less burdensome to the employer.

A third alternative is to report a value that is based solely on the employee's use of the vehicle. Under IRS regulations, a flat mileage rate may be used for each personal mile driven. The mileage rate, which is adjusted annually, is 57.5 cents per mile in 2015. This alternative is available only if a car's fair market value does not exceed a specified value and one of the following criteria is satisfied: (1) more than 50 percent of the car's use is for business, (2) the car is used each day in an employer-sponsored commuting pool, or (3) the car is driven at least 10,000 miles per year and is used primarily by employees.

Subsidized Eating Facilities

Employers often provide fully or partially subsidized eating facilities for employees. Lunch is the most commonly served meal, but breakfast and dinner may also be served. Such facilities offer a place for employees to discuss common issues and may minimize the chance that employees will take prolonged lunch periods at off-site restaurants. The popularity of these facilities tends to vary with the price of meals, the convenience of alternative places to eat, and the quality of the food served.

The subsidized value of meals served to employees is excluded from taxable income as long as the meals are (1) provided on the business premises and (2) furnished for the convenience of the employer. In general, meals are considered to be furnished for the employer's convenience if there are inadequate facilities in the area for employees to obtain meals within a reasonable period. If the requirements regarding the business premises and/or the convenience of the employer are not satisfied, the subsidized value of any meals consumed by employees is included in taxable income.

Employees are not allowed to deduct any portion of the cost they pay for individual meals. However, if an employee is required to have a fixed periodic charge for meals deducted from wages or salary (such as $15 per week), this amount is excluded from taxable income.

CHAPTER REVIEW

Key Terms and Concepts

dental insurance
Delta Dental Plans
dental health maintenance organization (DHMO)
direct reimbursement
discount plans
predetermination-of- benefits provision
long-term care insurance
partnership program
continuing-care retirement community (CCRC)
qualified long-term care insurance contract
qualified long-term care services
chronically ill individual
activities of daily living (ADLs)
nursing home care
skilled care
intermediate care
custodial care
bed reservation benefit

assisted-living care
respite care
adult day care
care coordination
alternative plan of care
facility-only policy
home health care only policy
comprehensive long-term care insurance policy
reimbursement basis
per diem basis
shared benefit
nonforfeiture benefit
legal expense plans
referral and discount plan
telephone access plan
legal HMO
floating holidays
sabbatical leave
funeral leave
family leave
Family and Medical Leave Act

no-additional-cost services
dependent-care assistance plan
   (DCAP)
child-care plan
elder-care benefit
adoption assistance plan

medical screening program
lifestyle-management program
employee-assistance program
qualified transportation fringe benefit

Review Questions

Review questions are based on the learning objectives in this chapter. For example, a [3] at the end of a questions means that the question is based on learning objective 3. If there are multiple objectives, they are all listed.

1. What are some of the reasons why employers may offer specific types of employee benefits? [1]

2. Who are the providers of dental expense coverage? [2]

3. What types of limitations does a plan often impose on benefits for a person enrolling in a dental insurance plan after the end of his or her initial eligibility period? [2]

4. Why are dental insurance plans more likely than medical expense plans to include benefits for routine examinations and preventive medicine? [2]

5. What are the usual categories of dental treatment? [2]

6. What types of payment methods do dental plans use? [2]

7. What types of exclusions do dental plans often contain? [2]

8. Describe the limitations that dental expense plans often use to control claim costs and to eliminate unnecessary dental treatment. [2]

9. To what extent does a dental expense plan pay benefits if the predetermination-of-benefits provision has not been followed? [2]

10. Under what circumstances do dental expense plans still pay benefits after the termination of coverage? [2]

11. What are the reasons why employers have taken a cautious approach in adopting long-term care insurance plans? [3]

12. What factors result in the need for long-term care? [3]

13. What sources other than long-term care insurance coverage are available to meet the need for long-term care? [3]

14. What are the highlights of the NAIC model legislation regarding long-term care? [3]

15. With respect to the Health Insurance Portability and Accountability Act (HIPAA), define each of the following: [3]

    a. qualified long-term care insurance contract

    b. qualified long-term care services

    c. chronically ill person

    d. activities of daily living

16. What are the income tax advantages associated with a qualified long-term care insurance contract? [3]

17. Who might be eligible for coverage under a long-term care insurance policy? [3]

18. Describe the broad categories of care for which a long-term care insurance policy might provide benefits? [3]

19. Compare facility-only policies, home health care only policies, and comprehensive long-term care insurance policies. [3]

20. What are the ways in which a long-term care insurance policy might pay benefits? [3]

21. What types of variations are found in long-term care insurance policies with respect to each of the following? [3]

    a. waiting periods

    b. maximum duration of benefits

22. What are the usual criteria to receive benefits under a tax-qualified long-term care insurance policy? [3]

23. What are the levels of underwriting that might apply to employer-sponsored groups for long-term care insurance? [3]

24. What is the nonforfeiture benefit available in a group long-term care insurance policy? [3]

25. What happens to group long-term care coverage if an employee leaves the group? [3]

26. Regarding legal expense plans: [4]

    a. What types of legal services are covered under most comprehensive legal expense plans?

    b. What are the common exclusions?

    c. What are the approaches by which a plan member may be able to select an attorney?

27. What is the current tax treatment of group legal expense plans? [4]

28. Regarding vacation plans: [4]

    a. Describe the basic characteristics of vacation plans.

    b. What are the major issues that an employer must address in designing a vacation plan?

29. How can an employer design a holiday plan that meets the needs of employees who would prefer to take different holidays? [4]

30. What is the income tax treatment of vacation and holiday benefits? [4]

31. Briefly describe how employers might treat employee absences because of each of the following: [4]

    a. reserve/National Guard duty

    b. jury duty

    c. funeral (bereavement) leave

32. Regarding FMLA: [4]

    a. Under what circumstances is an employer subject to the federal Family and Medical Leave Act?

    b. Under what conditions can an employee request leave under the act?

    c. How are pay and benefits affected by the act if an employee takes a leave?

33. With respect to the favorable tax treatment of educational assistance under the Internal Revenue Code, explain each of the following: [4]

    a. amount of educational assistance that may be received tax free

    b. types of educational assistance that may be received

    c. nondiscrimination rules that apply

34. What conditions must be satisfied in order for an employee to deduct moving expenses? [4]

35. Sam Driscoll incurred the following expenses in moving from Pennsylvania to New Mexico for his employer: [4]

Transportation of personal possessions	$4,500
Travel and lodging while moving	$2,000
Meals while moving	$ 500
Premove travel, lodging, and meals, while looking for a new apartment	$1,600
Penalty for settling an unexpired lease in Pennsylvania	$ 500

Sam's employer paid him $8,600 in reimbursement for these expenses.

a. To what extent is this reimbursement includible in Sam's income?

b. To what extent can Sam deduct these expenses?

36. Under what circumstances can no-additional-cost services be received tax free by employees? [4]

37. To what extent can employers provide the following discounts to employees on a tax-free basis? [4]

a. 5 percent discount on residential lots sold by a developer

b. 30 percent discount on merchandise sold by a retailer

c. 10 percent discount on policies sold by an insurance company

38. Compare and contrast the benefits that may be available under child-care plans and elder care plans. [4]

39. Regarding dependent-care plans: [4]

a. What amount of benefits can employees receive tax free under a dependent-care assistance plan?

b. What requirement must a plan satisfy in order for employees to receive dependent-care assistance as a tax-free employee benefit?

40. Regarding qualified adoption expenses: [4]

a. What are qualified adoption expenses?

b. To what extent can they be received tax free?

41. Regarding wellness programs: [4]

a. What are the advantages that may offset the costs of wellness programs?

b. Why are many wellness programs designed to include family members of employees?

c. How do provisions of HIPAA affect wellness programs?

d. How are wellness benefits taxed?

42. Regarding EAPs: [4]

a. What types of problems are often treated by employee-assistance plans?

b. Briefly describe the way in which an employee-assistance plan operates.

c. How are employee-assistance benefits taxed?

43. Regarding transportation fringe benefits: [4]

a. What is a qualified transportation fringe?

b. To what extent can an employer provide a qualified transportation fringe without an employee having taxable income?

44. Describe the alternatives that an employer can consider to value the use of a personal car that is provided to an employee. [4]

45. Under what circumstances can an employer provide subsidized meals to employees on a tax-free basis? [4]

Review Question Answers

1. There are many reasons why employer provide a certain array of benefits: to satisfy specific needs of its employees, for competitive reasons, or because of traditions within its locality or industry. Collective bargaining, the personal whims of the employer, and federal and state laws may also play a role.

2. Insurance companies, dental service plans, the Blues, and managed care plans offer group dental benefits. Although each of these providers might specialize in a certain type of dental product, many offer several types of products in their portfolios. Like medical expense coverage, a significant portion of dental coverage is also self-funded. An employer may self-administer the plan or use the services of a third-party administrator.

3. Such limitations include one or a combination of the following:

- reducing benefits (usually by 50 percent) for a period of time (such as one year) following the late enrollment

- reducing the maximum benefit to a low amount (such as $100 or $200) for the year following the late enrollment

- excluding some benefits for a certain period (such as one or 2 years) following the late enrollment period

4. There is clear evidence that the cost of providing these benefits is more than offset by the avoidance of the expensive dental procedures that a person may are require when a condition is not discovered early or when a preventive treatment has not been received.

5. The categories of dental treatment are:

- service level I—preventive care and diagnostic services

- service level II—minor restorative procedures, including fillings, inlays, onlays, and veneers

- service level III—major restorations, including crowns, bridges, and implants, as well as other major services involving endodontics, periodontics, prosthodontics, and oral surgeries

- service level IV—orthodontic services

6. Indemnity plans usually make payments on the basis of reasonable-and-customary charges. Most have annual deductibles in the neighborhood of $50 to $100. However, the deductible typically does not apply to level I services. Coinsurance is also common.

Dental plans with a PPO structure usually have deductibles and coinsurance similar to indemnity plans except that they use higher coinsurance percentages when a covered person receives services from network providers. They also pay network benefits on the basis of negotiated charges with providers.

DHMO plans do not usually use deductibles and coinsurance for most service levels as long as a covered person uses network providers. However, the member may be responsible for varying copayments for level II and level III services. Level IV services are usually subject to coinsurance, often 50 or 60 percent.

7. Some of the more common exclusions are charges for the following:

- services that are purely cosmetic, unless necessitated by an accidental bodily injury sustained while a person is covered under the plan

- replacement of lost, missing, or stolen dentures, or other prosthetic devices
- duplicate dentures or other prosthetic devices
- oral hygiene instruction or other training in preventive dental care
- services that do not have uniform professional endorsement
- occupational injuries to the extent that workers' compensation laws or similar legislation provides benefits
- services furnished by or on behalf of government agencies, unless there is a requirement to pay
- certain services that began prior to the date that coverage for an individual was effective

8. Except for DHMOs, most plans contain a calendar-year maximum (varying from $500 to $2,500).

   Most dental plans limit the frequency with which some benefits are paid. Routine oral examinations and teeth cleaning are usually limited to once every 6 months (or twice a year), and full mouth X rays to once every 24 or 36 months.

   The typical dental plan also limits benefits to the least expensive type of accepted dental treatment for a given dental condition.

9. When the predetermination-of-benefits provision is not followed, the plan still pays benefits. However, neither the dentist nor the covered person will know in advance what services the insurance company covers or how much the insurance company will pay for these services.

10. A plan may still provide benefits for a dental service after termination as long as (1) the charge for the service was incurred prior to the termination date, and (2) treatment is completed within 60 or 90 days after termination.

11. First, the individual long-term care insurance market is still in an evolving state after many years, due partially to the lack of adequate actuarial data to design and price coverage.

    Second, the tax treatment for employees is less favorable than that for many other types of employee benefits. As a result, most group long-term care plans have been financed solely by employee contributions. However, the Health Insurance Portability and Accountability Act (HIPAA) now provides favorable tax treatment for long-term care insurance, but within limits.

Third, long-term care insurance cannot be included in a cafeteria plan on a tax-favored basis.

Finally, participation in group plans has been modest because older employees often do not see the need for coverage, or it is too expensive.

12. The following factors support the need for long-term care:

    • an aging population

    • increasing costs

    • inability of families to provide full care

    • inadequacy of insurance protection

13. These other sources include personal financial resources, relatives and friends, Medicaid, continuing care retirement communities, and cash value life insurance policies.

14. Highlights of the criteria for long-term care policy provisions include the following:

    • Insurance companies cannot use certain words or terms in a policy unless they specifically define them in accordance with the model legislation.

    • Policies must be guaranteed renewable or noncancelable.

    • There is a prohibition against limitations and exclusions except in the following cases:

        – preexisting conditions

        – mental or nervous disorders (but this does not permit the exclusion of Alzheimer's disease)

        – alcoholism and drug addiction

        – illness, treatment, or medical condition arising out of war, participation in a felony, service in the armed forces, suicide, and aviation if a person is a non-fare-paying passenger

        – treatment in a government facility and services available under Medicare and other social insurance programs

    • No policy can provide coverage for skilled-nursing care only or provide significantly more coverage for skilled care in a facility than for lower levels of care.

    • The definition of preexisting condition cannot be more than 6 months prior to the effective date of coverage. In addition, insurance companies can exclude coverage for a confinement for this condition only if it begins within 6 months of the effective date of coverage.

- Insurance companies cannot base eligibility for benefits on a prior hospital confinement or higher level of care.

- Insurance companies must offer the applicant the right to purchase coverage that increases in the amount of benefits based on reasonable anticipated increases in the cost of services covered by the policy.

- Insurance companies must offer the applicant a nonforfeiture benefit option.

- A policy must contain a provision that makes a policy incontestable after 2 years on the grounds of misrepresentation alone.

The following provisions of the model legislation pertain to marketing:

- All prospective applicants must receive an outline of coverage at the time of initial solicitation. Among the information this outline must contain is (1) a description of the coverage, (2) a statement of the principal exclusions, reductions, and limitations in the policy, (3) a statement of the terms under which the policy can be continued in force or terminated, (4) a description of the terms under which the policy may be returned and the premium refunded, (5) a brief description of the relationship of cost of care and benefits, and (6) a statement whether the policy is intended to be tax qualified.

- All prospective applicants must receive shopper's guide.

- The policy must allow covered persons to have a free 30-day look at their policy or certificate of insurance during which they may terminate the policy or enrollment in the group plan as of the initial date of coverage.

- An insurance company must establish procedures to ensure that any comparisons of policies by its agents or other producers are fair and accurate and to prohibit the sale or issuance of excessive insurance.

- Applications for insurance must be clear and unambiguous so that an applicant's health condition can be properly ascertained.

15. a. A qualified long-term care insurance contract is defined as any insurance contract that meets all the following requirements:

    - The only insurance protection provided under the contract is for qualified long-term care services.

    - The contract cannot pay for expenses that are reimbursable under Medicare. However, this requirement does not apply to expenses that are reimbursable if (1) Medicare is a secondary payer of benefits or (2) benefits are payable on a per diem basis.

- The contract is guaranteed renewable.

- The contract does not provide for a cash surrender value or other money that can be borrowed or paid, assigned, or pledged as collateral for a loan.

- The insurance company uses all refunds of premiums and policyowner dividends as future premium reductions or future benefits increases.

- The policy must comply with various consumer protection provisions. For the most part, these are the same provisions contained in the NAIC model legislation and already adopted by most states.

    b. The act defines qualified long-term care services as necessary diagnostic, preventive, therapeutic, curing, treating, and rehabilitative services, and maintenance or personal care services that (1) a chronically ill person requires and (2) and a licensed health care practitioner prescribes in a plan of care.

    c. A chronically ill individual is one who has been certified as meeting one of the following requirements, often referred to as benefit triggers:

- The person is expected to be unable to perform, without substantial assistance from another person, at least two activities of daily living (ADLs) for a period of at least 90 days due to a loss of functional capacity.

- Substantial supervision is required to protect the individual from threats to health and safety because of severe cognitive impairment.

    d. The six ADLs are: eating, bathing, dressing, transferring from bed to chair, using the toilet, and maintaining continence. A qualified long-term care insurance contract must contain at least five of the six.

16. • The IRS treats expenses for long-term care services, including insurance premiums, like other medical expenses.

- Any employer contributions for group contracts are deductible to the employer and do not result in any taxable income to an employee.

- Benefits a covered person receives under a qualified long-term care insurance contract are tax-free except under contracts written on a per diem basis for proceeds that exceed a specified amount ($330 per day in 2015).

17. The typical eligibility rules (that is, full time, actively at work, and so on) apply to group long-term care products. At a minimum, coverage is available for an active employee and/or spouse. Many products also provide coverage to retirees and to other family

members, such as children, parents, parents-in-law, and possibly adult children. There is a maximum age for eligibility, but it is frequently as high as 85 and may be higher.

18. • Nursing home care encompasses skilled care, intermediate care, and custodial care in a licensed facility.

• Assisted-living care is provided in facilities that care for the frail elderly who are no longer able to care for themselves but do not need as high a level of care as a nursing home provides.

• Hospice care is devoted to easing the physical and psychological pain associated with death and does not attempt to cure medical conditions. In addition to providing services for the dying patient, a hospice may offer counseling to family members.

• Alzheimer's facilities are institutions that provide care for Alzheimer's disease and related forms of degenerative diseases and dementia. Where they are referred to separately in a policy, a policy refers to them separately but defines them as a facility that must meet the policy's definition of either a nursing home or an assisted-living facility.

• Home health care encompasses part-time skilled care, therapy, part-time services from home health aides, and help from homemakers. It may also include many other services such as the purchase or rental of needed medical equipment and emergency alert systems; modifications to the home; caregiver training; and prescription drugs and laboratory services.

• A respite caregiver is an alternate caregiver who provides long-term care services to relieve a primary caregiver from the physical and emotional stress of rendering care over a long period of time and/or to allow the primary caregiver to have some period of personal time.

• Adult day care is received at centers specifically designed for the elderly who live at home but whose spouses or families cannot be available during the day.

• Care coordination provides the services of a care coordinator who works with an insured, his or her family, and licensed health care practitioners. The coordinator assess a person's condition, evaluate care options, and develops an individualized plan of care that provides the most appropriate services.

• An alternative plan of care provides for types of care that might not be covered in the policy. For example, a policy covering nursing home care only might provide benefits for care in an assisted-living facility if these benefits are an appropriate and cost-effective alternative to care in a nursing home.

19. A facility-only policy provide benefits only if the insured in a nursing home or other institutional settings such as assisted-living facilities and hospices. In contrast, a home health care only policy is designed generally to provide benefits for care outside an institutional setting. As its name suggests, a comprehensive long-term care insurance policy, sometimes referred to as an integrated policy, combines benefits for facility care and home health care into a single contract.

20. • The majority of group policies pay benefits on a reimbursement basis. These contracts reimburse the insured for actual expenses up to the specified policy limit.

    • Some policies provide benefits on a per diem basis once the insured is actually receiving care. This means that a policy pays benefits regardless of the actual cost of care. In this case, a policy with a daily benefit of $200 will pay $200 even if actual long-term care charges for the day are only $150.

21. a. The obvious variation in waiting periods relates to relates to the number of days selected by an applicant from those offered by an insurer such as 20, 60, 100, or 180 days. Normally a single waiting period is satisfied by any combination of days during which the insured is in a long-term care facility or receiving home health care services.

    Significantly, there are several variations in the ways that home health care services can count toward the waiting period. Some policies count only those days when actual services are received for which charges are made and that will be covered after the waiting period is satisfied.

   b. Regarding types of variations found in long-term care insurance policies with respect to maximum duration of benefits:

    • Under one approach, the policy makes benefit payments for exactly the chosen benefit period. Thus, if the applicant selects a benefit period of 4 years and collects benefits for 4 years, the benefit payments cease.

    • A few policies use the concept of a shared benefit when a husband and wife have coverage under the same policy or with the same insurer. Under this concept, each spouse can access the other spouse's benefits.

22. The insured must meet one of two criteria for benefit eligibility. The first criterion is that the insured is expected to be unable, without substantial assistance from another person, to perform two of the six ADLs that are acceptable under HIPAA for a period of at least 90 days due to loss of functional capacity. The second criterion is that substantial supervision is required to protect the individual from threats to health and safety because of severe cognitive impairment.

23. These levels include guaranteed issue, modified guaranteed issue, simplified issue, and full underwriting as in the individual marketplace. From the standpoint of applicants, employees are often subject to less stringent underwriting than are their family members.

24. With a nonforfeiture benefit, the insured will receive some value for a policy if the policy lapses because a required premium is not paid in the future.

25. The insurer must provide the insured with a basis for continuation or conversion of coverage. Under a continuation of coverage, the insured retains coverage under the group contract but pays premiums directly to the insurer. Under a conversion of coverage, the insured is issued an individual policy that must be identical or equivalent to the group coverage.

26. a. Most comprehensive legal expense plans cover at least the following:

    - unlimited legal advice by telephone
    - document review and preparation
    - name changes
    - adoptions
    - purchase or sale of primary residences
    - eviction defense
    - civil actions
    - driver's license suspension
    - juvenile court proceedings
    - consumer protection
    - bankruptcy
    - IRS audits
    - debt collection
    - child custody and support
    - divorce, but possibly only for the covered employee and not dependents

    b. Common exclusions include the following:

    - business activities or transactions
    - preparation of tax returns
    - class-action suits

- actions involving the legal expense plan

- actions involving the employer

- actions involving the union that bargained for the coverage

- cases that have contingent fees

c. Many plans use a closed-panel approach, under which a panel of attorneys agrees to provide covered services at a predetermined fee or hourly rate for which they bill the plan. The plan member selects the attorney, and benefits are generally available at little or no additional cost.

    Other plans are open-panel in which a member can choose any licensed attorney; however, benefits are usually subject to scheduled dollar maximums.

    Still other plans are modified-panel plans, under which, a plan member may either choose a panel attorney as in a closed-panel plan or select his or her own attorney.

27. The cost of a legal expense plan is deductible for the employer. Employees, however, have taxable income to the extent of employer payments. If the employer prefunds the plan with an insurance contract or other arrangement, the employee has taxable income based on his or her share of the employer-paid premium and receives benefits tax free. If an employer self-funds a plan, the employee's taxable income is the value of the benefits the plan pays.

28. a. Most vacation plans are based on the employee's length of service, and the number of vacation days given to any particular employee normally increases over time. Some firms have different schedules for different classes of employees, with higher-paid employees tending to have more vacation time, particularly in the earlier years of service.

    b. One is the treatment of unused vacation days. Another issue is the question of when employees can take their vacations. In general, vacations may not be allowed during busy work times. Other issues that must be addressed are those of how unused vacation days are treated upon termination of employment if a state does not require payment for these days and whether sicknesses and holidays occurring during vacation periods are treated as vacation days.

29. Some companies adopt holiday plans that include a minimum number of scheduled holidays coupled with a specific number (often two or three) of floating holidays to be taken at an employee's option. Usually, there is no requirement that the days taken actually be holidays, so in effect they become additional vacation days in lieu of holidays.

30. The compensation employees receive during periods of vacation is treated the same as compensation for time worked and is taxed accordingly. Like vacation pay, holiday pay is taxed as regular income.

31. a. Laws sometimes require that employees get time off for reserve or National Guard duty, but there is no stipulation that pay continue during this period. However, many employers pay their employees the difference between their regular pay and any compensation received for reserve or National Guard duty of short duration.

    b. Most employers grant (and may be required to grant) time off for jury duty. Because employees are usually compensated for jury duty, some employers pay only the difference between this amount and an employee's regular pay.

    c. Employers often allow up to 5 days off with pay for the death of an immediate family member. At a minimum, this usually includes the death of a parent, child, spouse, or other relative residing in the household.

32. a. The legislation applies only to employers who have more than 50 employees within a 75-mile radius. To comply with the 50-employee requirement, an employer needs only to have that many employees during each workday of 20 or more calendar weeks during the current or preceding calendar year. Part-time employees and employees on unpaid leaves of absence are included in the calculation.

    b. With some exceptions, a worker must be allowed to take up to 12 weeks of unpaid leave in any 12-month period under the following circumstances:

        • because of the birth of the employee's child

        • because of the placement of a child in the employee's home for adoption or foster care

        • to care for the employee's child, spouse, or parent with a serious health condition

        • for the employee's own serious health condition that makes it impossible to work

        • because of a qualifying exigency arising if an employee's spouse, child, or parent is on (or has been called to) active duty in the armed forces in support of a contingency operation.

    c. An employer has no obligation to continue an employee's pay or most benefits except medical and dental benefits, and the employee is ineligible for unemployment compensation. The employee must continue to pay any required plan contributions and must be given a 30-day grace period for such payments.

33. a. The Internal Revenue Code provides favorable tax treatment to employees for the first $5,250 of annual education assistance received from their employers.

    b. Eligible benefits include tuition, fees, and books for courses, including graduate education. The costs of supplies and equipment are also included as long as they are not retained after completion of the course.

    c. In order for benefits to be tax free, the employer's plan cannot discriminate with respect to eligibility in favor of officers, shareholders, highly compensated employees, or their dependents. In addition, no more than 5 percent of the benefits may be paid to shareholders or owners (or their dependents) who are more-than-5-percent owners of the firm.

34. The employee must have moved because of a change in job location. In addition, the employee must satisfy both a distance test and a time test. The distance test requires that the employee's new workplace be at least 50 miles farther from the employee's old residence than the employee's old workplace (or old residence if the employee was previously unemployed). The time test requires that the employee work full time in the general location of the new residence for at least 39 weeks during the 12 months following the move.

35. a. This reimbursement is fully includible in Sam's income.

    b. The $4,500 for transportation of personal possessions and the $2,000 for travel and lodging expenses while moving are fully deductible by Sam in calculating his adjusted gross income. The other expenses are not deductible.

36. The cost of these services is not includible in an employee's gross income for tax purposes if:

    • The services cannot be provided on a basis that discriminates in favor of highly compensated employees.

    • The employer must not incur any significant additional cost or lost revenue in providing the services. For example, giving a standby ticket to an airline employee if there are unsold seats on a flight satisfies this requirement, but giving an airline ticket to an employee when potential paying customers are denied seats does not.

    • The services must be those that are provided in the employer's line of business in which the employee actually works. However, unrelated employers in the same line of business, such as airlines, may enter into reciprocal arrangements under which employees of any party to the arrangement may obtain services from the other parties.

37. a. Discounts on real estate cannot be given to employees on a tax-free basis.

    b. Discounts on merchandise can be given as long as they do not exceed the gross profit percentage of the price at which the merchandise is offered for sale to customers.

    c. Discounts on services, including insurance policies, can be received tax free as long as they do not exceed 20 percent of the normal selling price of the service to customers.

38. For a few employers, their child-care plan consists of maintaining on-site day-care centers. Some employers provide benefits by supporting a limited number of off-site child-care centers. Probably the most common approach is to provide reimbursements to employees who make their own arrangements for child care, either at child-care centers or in their own home or the home of a caregiver.

    Although an elder-care benefit may take a variety of forms, frequently it is much like the benefit provided under a child-care plan. Within limits, the employer may pay for costs associated with home care for elderly dependents or care at day-care facilities for the elderly.

39. a. Under the Internal Revenue Code, dependent care is a tax-free benefit to employees up to statutory limits as long as certain requirements are met. The amount of benefits that can be received tax free is limited to $5,000 for single persons and married persons who file jointly and to $2,500 for married persons who file separately.

    b. The plan must satisfy rules around eligibility, nondiscrimination, communications, and reporting.

        If the rules are not met, highly compensated employees are taxed on the amount of benefits received. However, the benefits for other employees still retain their tax-free status.

40. a. They include reasonable and necessary adoption fees, court costs, attorney's fees, travel expenses, and other expenses directly related to the legal adoption of an eligible child, defined as a child who is under age 18 or who is incapable of caring for himself or herself.

b.   For 2015, employer payments for qualified adoption expenses are excludible from an employee's gross income if an employer has an adoption-assistance program that satisfies IRS requirements.

41. a.   The costs of establishing and maintaining many of these programs are more than offset by the lower amounts paid for medical expense, disability, and death benefits. In addition, if long-term disabilities and premature deaths can be eliminated, the expenses associated with training new employees can be minimized. Many firms also feel these programs increase productivity by improving the employees' sense of well-being, their work attitudes, and their family relationships.

b.   In many instances, it is not possible to change an employee's lifestyle unless the lifestyle of his or her entire family also changes.

c.   Provisions of HIPAA affect wellness programs that provide rewards for adherence to health promotion and disease prevention programs. These rewards might be in the form of premium discounts or rebates, or modification of deductibles or copayments. Generally, HIPAA permits such rewards only if a wellness program meets certain specified requirements. These requirements limit the amount of an reward to no more than 20 percent of the cost of a participant's insurance coverage. Reward must also be available to all similarly situated individuals. The wellness program must be designed to promote good health or prevent disease as well as give eligible participants the opportunity to qualify for the reward at least once a year. The HIPAA regulations provide an exception to the requirements if a reward is based solely on an individual's participation in a wellness program.

d.   Employees have no taxable income as a result of participating in medical screening programs. The cost of providing lifestyle-management programs and other programs that promote general health, such as smoking cessation or weight control, are not considered medical expenses. Although the cost of providing these programs to employees is deductible by the employer, an employee incurs taxable income unless the purpose of the program is to alleviate a specific medical problem.

However, with some exceptions, premium discounts or rebates, or modification of deductibles and copayments are not taxable to employees. In addition, gifts of small value, such as a coffee mug, are tax free. Employees also incur no taxable income as a result of being provided with or using athletic facilities that are located on the employer's premises.

42. a.   These programs are designed to help employees with certain personal problems by providing:

- treatment for alcohol or drug abuse

- counseling for mental problems and stress

- counseling for family and marital problems

- financial, legal, and tax advice

- referrals for child care or elder care

- crisis intervention

b. Access to an employee-assistance program is through a counselor who may be a company employee, but most often an employer establishes the plan through a professional organization that specializes in such programs. Information provided to the counselor by the employee is kept confidential. Most plans have 24-hour counseling available, through either a telephone hot line or on-duty personnel. If the counselor cannot solve an employee's problem, it is the counselor's responsibility to make a preliminary determination about the type of professional help the employee should receive. In many cases, this treatment can be provided under existing medical expense or legal expense plans or through community agencies. The employer usually pays the costs of other types of treatment totally or in part.

c. As long as the treatment is for the purpose of alleviating medical conditions, including mental illness, an employee has no taxable income. If the treatment is for a nonmedical condition, the employee has taxable income as the result of employer payments.

43. a. A qualified transportation fringe includes the following:

- transportation in a commuter highway vehicle if such transportation is in connection with travel between the employee's residence and place of employment

- transit passes

- qualified parking

- qualified bicycle commuting reimbursement

b. For 2015, the value of a qualified transportation fringe is excludable from income up to the following amounts:

- $130 per month in the aggregate for any transit passes and transportation in a commuter highway vehicle

- $250 per month for qualified parking

- $20 per month for qualified bicycle commuting reimbursement. However, an employer cannot provide this benefit in any month that an employee receives reimbursement for any other type of qualified transportation fringe.

44. The most common method for valuing the car is for the employer to report an annual cost that is a percentage of the car's annual lease value.

   A second method is for the employer to annually report the entire lease value of the car as taxable income.

   A third alternative is to report a value that is based solely on the employee's use of the vehicle.

45. The subsidized value of meals served to employees is excluded from taxable income as long as the meals are (1) provided on the business premises and (2) furnished for the convenience of the employer.

Chapter 12

Employee Benefit Marketing, Plan Design, and Administration

Learning Objectives

An understanding of the material in this chapter should enable the student to

1. Identify the persons who make decisions regarding the purchase of group insurance, and explain how these persons tend to differ by the size of the group.

2. Identify the persons involved in the selling process of group insurance, and explain the role of each.

3. Describe the marketing process for group insurance, and explain how it differs by the size of the group insurance case.

4. Explain employee-benefit plan objectives and the methods to determine employee needs.

5. Analyze the high-level provisions contained in employee benefit plans for controlling costs.

6. Identify the objectives of an effective employee benefit communications program, and describe the methods by which it might be implemented.

7. Explain the reasons for outsourcing benefit administration, and describe the process by which it might be accomplished.

The marketing of employee benefits is a complex and specialized process that is subject to frequent changes because of the influences of employers, organized labor, and federal and state regulations. Many employers continually review benefit plans for ways to contain cost increases and to improve the services received from insurance companies or from other providers of benefits or services. Therefore, it is essential for agents, brokers, consultants, third-party administrators, and insurance companies to maintain a high level of technical competence and to provide continuous service.

PURCHASERS

The buyers of coverage for employees consist primarily of employers, trustees, and associations. Although it is difficult to precisely categorize the group benefit market by the size of groups, certain generalizations can be made.

Purchasers of group plan benefits include small employer groups, large employer groups, associations, and creditor-debtor groups.

Small employer groups account for over half of the number of groups, but they account for a small total premium volume for employee benefits. In some states, the small group market includes up to 50 employees. For other states, the small group definition of up to 100 employees established by the Affordable Care Act prevails. Decision makers in the small group market are the owners or chief executive officers of the organizations.

Groups of over 100 employees account for a smaller percentage of the total group benefit plans in existence, but they represent the bulk of the benefit dollars spent by employers. The larger the group, the more likely the group is to be self-funded. Decision makers in large groups may be persons in the benefits or human resources departments.

SELLERS

The sellers of employee benefit products and services consist primarily of insurance companies, HMOs, PPOs, third-party administrators, and the health insurance exchanges. Just as there are certain generalizations about who makes employee benefit decisions within an organization, there are generalizations about where employers purchase products and services. The breakdown by size is different.

Employers with fewer than 100 employees, or those considered to be a small group, often purchase coverage from insurance companies, HMOs, PPOs, and the health insurance exchanges. Benefit structures generally conform to the standardized bronze, silver, gold, and platinum plans approved for their states under the Affordable Care Act.

If an employer has more than 100 employees, or is considered to be a large group, coverage is purchased from insurance companies, HMOs, PPOs, or can be self-funded. The health insurance exchanges will be a viable option for coverage when implemented by the Affordable Care Act.

The following discussion looks at the functions and methods of compensation for each of the participants in the sales process for group benefits.

Agents

agent

An insurance company **agent** is a legal representative of the company and has certain powers to act on behalf of the insurer. Agents play a major role in marketing group insurance, particularly to groups that have fewer than 100 employees. Agents usually locate the prospective group insurance cases, but the extent of their further involvement in the sales process varies depending on the size of the group. For very small groups, the agent conducts virtually all sales activities. For larger groups, the agent is likely to call on the group representative of the insurance company for assistance in selling, installing, and servicing the case. To many agents, the selling of group insurance is not a specialty but is rather the selling of just another product in the portfolio of their insurance company.

standard (regular) commission schedule

level commission schedule

Insurance companies compensate agents in the form of commission payments. For most groups, two approaches are used. The larger the group, the more common it is for negotiation between the policyowner, the agent, and the insurance company to determine commissions. However, two basic types of commission schedules also frequently determine commissions. The **standard (or regular) commission schedule** has high first-year commission rates and lower rates in renewal years. The **level commission schedule** has the same commission rates for both the first year and any renewal years. These two schedules are typically designed so that over some period of time (often 10 years) the same overall commission is paid for a given amount of premium, regardless of which schedule is used. The following table shows an example of each type of schedule.

Table 12-1
Commission Schedules

Annual Premium		Standard Schedule		Level Schedule
		First Year	Renewal Years	
First	$ 1,000	20.0%	5.00%	6.50%
Next	4,000	20.0	3.00	4.70
"	5,000	15.0	1.50	2.85
"	10,000	12.5	1.50	2.60
"	10,000	10.0	1.50	2.35
"	20,000	5.0	1.50	1.85
"	200,000	2.5	1.00	1.15
"	250,000	1.0	0.50	0.55
"	2,000,000	0.5	0.25	0.25
Over	2,500,000	0.1	0.10	0.10

Note that these are sliding (or graded) scales based on additional increments of premium volume, not on the total premium volume.

Example

Using the regular scale previously shown, the first-year commission on a group case with an annual premium volume of $40,000 is calculated as follows:

$1,000	×	20.0%	=	$ 200
4,000	×	20.0	=	800
5,000	×	15.0	=	750
10,000	×	12.5	=	1,250
10,000	×	10.0	=	1,000
10,000	×	5.0	=	500
$40,000				$4,500 (or 11.25% of the total premium)

After the first year, insurers may subdivide the commissions under either of these schedules into selling commissions and service commissions, with the agent who sold the case receiving the latter only if he or she continues to service the case.

The standard schedule obviously produces a higher income for the agent in early years and generates a larger total income if the employer cancels or fails to renew the policy after a short period. However, the level schedule should be more beneficial if the agent expects substantial increases in premium volume in a case's renewal years. Insurance companies are concerned about using the standard commission schedule when there is a high probability that a group insurance case will either change insurers or lapse. The level schedule may also be mandatory for very large groups when competitive bidding requires that expenses be held to a minimum and be recoverable in the early years of a contract.

Brokers and Consultants

broker

consultant

The majority of large group insurance buyers retain a **broker** or employee benefit **consultant** to provide professional advice on group insurance matters and to aid them in dealing with insurance companies. Brokers and consultants are agents of the buyers and owe their allegiance to the buyers rather than to the insurance companies through which they place their clients' coverages. Traditionally, the major distinction between brokers and consultants was that brokers were compensated on a commission basis for the coverages they placed in behalf of clients, whereas consultants were compensated by fees charged to the clients. From a practical standpoint, the distinction between brokers and consultants has become blurred. The commission schedules insurance companies use for brokers and benefit consultants are usually the same as those used for agents. For large cases it is common for the commission to be a negotiated amount.

Over the last few years, many insurance companies have lowered the commission rates that they pay. As a result, brokers and consultants are more likely than in the past to do one or both of the following: charge fees for services that they previously performed at no additional cost or increase the fee levels they already charge for services.

Group Representatives

group representative

The **group representative** is an employee of the insurance company who specializes in the selling and servicing of his or her company's group insurance products. The group representative conducts sales activities through the agents, brokers, and consultants whom the group representative educates and motivates to place group insurance business with his or her company. In addition, the group representative aids the agents, brokers, or consultants in prospecting, securing necessary underwriting data, designing plans, and preparing and presenting group insurance proposals. After a plan is sold, the group representative is frequently involved in the enrolling of eligible employees, the administrative procedures of installing the case, and the providing of services necessary to keep the case in force. Group representatives almost always receive a salary, and most are eligible for bonuses based on performance.

Third-Party Administrators

third-party administrator (TPA)

A **third-party administrator** (frequently referred to as a **TPA**) is a person or organization that is hired to provide certain administrative services to group benefit plans. The functions of TPAs include receiving employee reports and contributions, keeping track of employee eligibility, preparing any reports required by state and federal laws, and handling complaints and grievances. In addition, the TPA is involved in certain aspects of the claims process. At a minimum, this probably involves the certification of eligibility and the processing of claim forms for submission to an insurance company, but it may also include paying claims from the trust's funds. Besides professional administrators, TPAs may be banks and insurance companies.

The increasing use of alternative funding methods, including total self-funding, has resulted in the need for employers to provide many of the services (such as claims handling) that are performed by an insurance company when traditional fully insured contracts are purchased. When employers have been unable to provide these services themselves in a cost-effective manner, they have often turned to TPAs. Over the last decade, the use of TPAs has increased dramatically, particularly for medical expense benefits.

Health Insurance Exchange Navigators

navigators

A navigator is a new role established by the Affordable Care Act. Navigators are employees of the health insurance exchanges who are licensed and trained to sell the products being offered through the health insurance exchanges by qualified health plans. Coverages offered include both group insurance plans and individual health insurance plans. The salaries and bonus arrangements for the navigators are paid by the health insurance exchanges. As employees of the exchanges, navigators may not be paid by both the health insurance exchange and the insurance carrier, HMO, PPO, or TPA.

MARKETING PROCESS

Although the main goal of employee benefit marketing is to "close the sale," the process involves two broad categories of activities: those that precede the sale and those that follow the sale. Presale activities include prospecting and the development and presentation of the group insurance proposal; postsale activities include the enrollment of employees and the actual installation, servicing, and renewal of the group insurance plan.

Prospecting

prospecting

Prospecting is the first step in the marketing process. It involves persuading the employer (or the employer's broker or consultant) to accept a group insurance proposal from the provider of benefits or services. Prospecting also involves convincing the employer to provide the information necessary for the preparation of the proposal.

The process of prospecting varies for different segments of the group insurance market. For very small groups sales, activities are conducted by agents who specialize in group insurance, but a large portion of the sales activities is conducted by agents, brokers, or consultants whose primary sales activities take place in the individual marketplace. It is also in the marketing to small groups that prospecting without known contacts (cold calling) is most likely to take place. Because of the modest premiums that these small groups generate, the agent, broker, or consultant usually carries out all of the sales activities (not just prospecting) with little direct involvement by representatives from the insurance company. Because of the limited and standardized products available for these small groups, training of agents, brokers, or consultants in this market is often oriented toward what products are available rather than toward group insurance planning in general.

As the size of groups increases, the chance of successful prospecting diminishes rapidly unless the agent, broker, or consultant (1) has a known contact who is a key person in an organization's decision-making process for group insurance matters and (2) has a more sophisticated understanding of group insurance. In these segments of the group insurance market, group representatives spend considerable time training agents, brokers, or consultants in the intricacies of group insurance and motivating them to develop prospects. For mid-sized groups, the agent, broker, or consultant may do the actual prospecting alone or with the group representative, or he or she may give qualified leads to the group representative who will perform this function.

For large groups, the situation is usually different because most large firms retain brokers or consultants to advise them on employee benefit programs and to aid them in the implementation of any decisions they make. Therefore, for this segment of the employee benefit market, prospecting is a two-part process. On one hand, there is intense competition among brokers and consultants to obtain the large firms as clients. On the other hand, clients are seldom successfully approached except through the broker or consultant. Therefore, prospecting includes the development of a close working relationship with the broker or consultant community.

Developing and Presenting the Proposal

proposal

In the broadest sense, the development of a **proposal** for a benefit plan involves designing the benefit plan, calculating the premium rate or rates, and putting the proposal in its final form for presentation. Managed care and the availability of varied types of medical expense plans make proposal development especially challenging. Prior to managed care, an insurance company proposal could concentrate on coverage, benefits, and premium with a focus on its reputation for stability and prompt payment of claims. With the advent of managed care, proposals for medical expense coverage needed to address questions on the delivery of care under the managed care plan. Thus, the adequacy of the provider network—including its size, scope of services, and access—became prominent issues. Quality—including the credentials of providers, the accreditation of the plan, and performance measures of the plan—also became selection criteria for employers and their employees.

It is at the proposal stage of the marketing process that insurers do the majority of the underwriting for a case that they ultimately write.

The premium rates presented in the group insurance proposal are based on the employee census that the employer provides prior to the development of the proposal, and thus they are usually only tentative rates, a fact that is clearly stated in the proposal. The final premium rates are usually determined at the time a group insurance plan is enrolled and are based on the census of employees covered under the plan at its inception and possibly on the health of the employees.

Although variations exist among insurance companies, most proposals contain at least the following information:

- a description of each coverage included in the plan
- a schedule of the tentative premium rates and the total premium for each coverage
- a description of the persons eligible for coverage under the plan
- any underwriting assumptions or conditions
- details for servicing the plan, such as the procedures and facilities for administering claims
- general information about the insurance company, including its size, financial strength, and products and services

For small groups, the preparation of a proposal is usually a relatively simple matter. Because little or no flexibility is available for the coverages offered, the plan design consists primarily of an agent, broker, or consultant describing the available options and determining the employer's preferences. Because the rate structure is fairly simplified, the agent, broker, or consultant also determines the tentative premium based on the census data provided by the employer. The proposal typically consists of (1) a standard brochure or packet of information that describes the benefits and (2) a brief premium-calculation presentation that contains a list of the covered employees and the tentative premium the employer must pay for the initial coverage period.

For large group insurance cases that are not controlled by brokers or consultants, the group representative plays a major role in the development of the proposal. The group representative must determine whether the employer is a serious prospect. In addition, the group representative must assess whether the employer is likely to meet the underwriting standards of the insurance company.

If the development of the proposal proceeds beyond the initial contact stage, the agent, broker, consultant, or group representative must (1) determine the employer's objectives, (2) aid the employer in designing the benefit plan for which the proposal will be made, and (3) obtain the information necessary to complete the development of the proposal. The rating and actual design of the proposal is normally conducted at the field office.

To complete the proposal, the insurance company obviously needs a description of the benefit plan desired and a census of employees (covered, not actively working, and on COBRA continuation) containing any information that affects underwriting or premium calculations. At a minimum, this information probably includes age and gender, but it may also include marital status, geographic location, income, and an indication of whether there are dependents. Most insurance companies commonly request the following information from the prospect or the prospect's agent, broker, or consultant:

- the reason for transferring (unless it is a new case)
- the nature of the employer's industry
- a history of changes in the number of employees over the least 2 or 3 years
- a statement indicating whether the plan is contributory and, if so, the amount of the employer's contribution
- the length of time with the current insurer
- premiums, rates, and claims experience with the current insurer for each line of coverage (usually for the previous 3 years)
- a statement indicating whether collective bargaining is involved
- copies of information about the current plan (such as benefit booklets or certificates of insurance)
- the most recent premium statement from the current insurer
- any renewal information from the current insurer for the past year or two
- any ongoing large claims

The bidding specifications are accompanied by a cover letter that invites the insurance company to bid and states the last date on which bids may be received or postmarked. This date is usually up to 90 days prior to the date coverage becomes effective. The specifications typically consist of a description of the plan desired, a census of employees, and any information the insurance company needs to properly underwrite and rate the case. Based on this data, the insurance company is asked to present a bid in the form of monthly and annual premiums for the coverage desired.

The insurance company is typically presented a rigid set of specifications on which it must bid. The following are only a few of the many questions that the specifications commonly contain:

- How are incurred claims defined?

- How is retention defined?

- How is the level of reserves determined?

- What is the interest rate credited to reserves?

- How are catastrophic losses handled in the experience-rating process?

- What charges are levied against the group's experience when coverage is converted?

- For what period of time are rates guaranteed?

- How much notice of rate changes is given at renewal?

- What is the procedure for handling claims?

- What services are provided in the area of cost containment?

- If you are selected to provide coverage, on what date will the master contract and certificates of insurance be delivered?

- Are there any additional costs for materials such as benefit booklets?

Challenges with Managed Care Plans

Managed care plans and employer sponsorship of plan options often make proposal development especially challenging.

Prior to managed care, an insurance company proposal could concentrate on coverage, benefits, and premium with a focus on its reputation for stability and prompt payment of claims. With the advent of managed care, proposals needed to address questions on the delivery of care under the managed care plan. Thus, the adequacy of the provider network, including its size, scope of services, and access became prominent issues. Quality, too, including the credentials of providers and the accreditation of the health plan overall by such organizations as NCQA, became paramount. All of these areas, along with performance measures, became plan selection criteria for employers and their employees.

Presenting the Proposal

The successful presentation of a proposal leads to a sale that closes when the employer submits a signed application and the first periodic premium. For small groups, the agent, broker, or consultant makes the presentation of the proposal directly to the employer. In general, there is little room for negotiations, and the employer either accepts or rejects the initial proposal. In some cases, however, the proposal may contain two or three choices in plan design.

For large groups when the employer is dealt with directly, the agent, broker, or consultant may present the proposal. However, because of the technical expertise necessary, the group representative is probably involved, and either presents the proposal or assists in its presentation. It is at this point that further negotiation on plan design and revision of the proposal are most likely to occur.

When a large broker or consultant puts a group insurance case out to bid, there is usually no direct contact between the insurance company and the employer in the initial stages of the presentation. Rather, the group representative usually makes the presentation to the broker or consultant, who then evaluates all such proposals and makes a recommendation to the employer. This consists of presenting an employer with two or three proposals that best meet the employer's objectives. The group representatives of the insurance companies involved are typically asked to meet with both the broker or consultant and the employer to further discuss the proposals. At this stage of the process, it is not unusual to give each company in contention a copy of the proposals that their competitors have submitted.

Enrollment

enrollment

The first step in the postsale activities of group marketing involves the **enrollment** of employees in the plan. If the plan is noncontributory, the employer must provide the insurance company with enrollment cards or a list of all employees to be covered and a certification that they have met all eligibility requirements, such as being actively at work or having satisfied a probationary period. If a plan is contributory, it must be properly marketed to the employees in order to encourage the maximum enrollment. Usually, the insurance company prepares the solicitation materials, such as letters or benefit booklets.

For small employers, these may be standardized materials. For large employers, they are custom designed. Although the actual solicitation always involves the employer in some capacity, it may consist only of the employer providing these materials to the employees. It is common for the employer to allow group meetings (during normal working hours) in which the agent, broker, consultant, or group representative can explain the plan to the employees and answer their questions.

The actual enrollment of employees consists of requesting the employees to complete enrollment forms supplied by the insurance company. These enrollment forms are usually brief, but they have more detail if the plan involves any individual underwriting of employees in addition to the usual group underwriting or if employees have a choice of alternative plans. It is common for the employer's supervisory personnel to carry out this activity.

Although proper marketing of a contributory plan to employees is crucial, a noncontributory plan must also be properly presented to employees if they are to fully understand and appreciate its provisions. In many cases, this means that the plan is presented to employees in virtually the same manner as if it were contributory.

Installation

When the enrollment procedure is completed, the insurance company calculates the final premium rates and prepares the master contract and any other administrative materials for the employer as well as the certificates of insurance for the employees. The agent, broker, or consultant usually delivers these materials to small employers. In larger cases, the group representative, accompanied by the agent, broker, or consultant, usually performs the task. The agent, broker, consultant, or group representative thoroughly reviews the plan at this point with the employer and explains its administrative aspects, such as premium billings, claims procedures, and the enrollment and termination of employees. The importance of this meeting with the employer should not be ignored because the future success of a group insurance case is often a function of how well these administrative procedures are explained and thus understood by the employer.

The prominence of managed care plans makes the prompt and accurate performance of these installation procedures even more important, especially for providers receiving capitation or incentive program payments per member. Premiums must also be collected promptly and accurately because such payments may have to be made in advance of the delivery of services to members. Network physicians unable to verify enrollment are unlikely to accept the plan's copayment amount from their patients, preferring instead to bill their usual charges for services.

Servicing the Case

The importance of properly servicing a group insurance case cannot be overlooked. Good service not only increases the employer's satisfaction, but it also minimizes the possibility that the employer will transfer the case to another insurance company at the time of renewal. In addition, it may also lead to other business for the insurance company or the agent, broker, or consultant when the employer adds a new coverage or renews an existing coverage.

The process of servicing a case begins at the initial sale and continues throughout its life. The agent, broker, or consultant—often with the assistance of the group representative—usually conducts the servicing. However, some insurance companies have trained personnel whose sole function is to service group insurance cases, which allows the group representative to devote more of his or her time to sales activities. Most requests for service relate to routine administrative matters that involve billing, claims, or enrollment procedures. As previously mentioned, proper installation minimizes these requests. To discover whether there is any difficulty with a group insurance case at its earliest stage, the group representative must develop a close working relationship with other functional departments of the insurance company. For example, correspondence between the employer and claims personnel may be the first indication of any potential dissatisfaction.

Even when no specific problems exist, the agent, broker, or consultant schedules periodic visits with the employer to discuss such items as the administration of the plan, claim trends, and new federal or state regulations that affect the plan. These visits may lead to suggestions that the employer make changes in the plan so that it better meets the employer's desires and needs.

GROUP BENEFIT PLAN DESIGN

If either a single type of group insurance plan or an overall employee benefit plan is to be properly designed and managed, many questions must be answered. There are six broad areas to address:

- What are the employer's objectives?
- What types of benefits should the plan provide?
- What provisions for controlling costs should the plan have?
- How should the plan be communicated to employees?
- To what extent should administrative functions be outsourced?

- How should the plan be funded?

EMPLOYER'S OBJECTIVES

No benefit plan is properly designed unless it meets the employer's objectives. Although these objectives may be unclear or nonexistent, particularly in small firms, most large corporations have (and all firms should have) specific written objectives. These objectives vary for each individual organization, depending on such factors as size, location, industry, the results of collective bargaining, and the employer's philosophy. Without such objectives, it is difficult for the agent, broker, benefit consultant, or third-party administrator to make recommendations or for the firm's in-house benefit staff (often part of the human resources department) to make decisions.

Types of Objectives

Objectives for benefit plans can be general and part of a firm's overall compensation objective (that is, cash and fringe benefits in the aggregate) in order to achieve a compensation package that is competitive within the firm's geographic area or industry. Such an "average" objective usually means that the firm wants both its wages and salaries and its fringe benefits to be similar to what the competition is offering its employees. Some firms have separate objectives for cash compensation and employee benefits.

A sample list of employer objectives for employee benefits plans include:

- to establish and maintain an employee benefit program that is based primarily on the employees' needs for leisure time and protection against the risks of old age, loss of health, and loss of life

- to establish and maintain an employee benefit program that complements the efforts of employees in their own behalf

- to evaluate the employee benefit plan annually for its effect on employee morale and productivity, giving consideration to turnover, unfilled positions, attendance, employee complaints, and employee opinions

- to compare the employee benefit plan annually with that of other leading companies in the same field and to maintain a benefit plan with an overall level of benefits (based on cost per employee) that falls within the second quintile of these companies

- to maintain a level of benefits for nonunion employees that represents the same level of expenditures per employee as for union employees

- to determine annually the cost of new, changed, and existing programs as a percentage of salaries and wages, and to maintain this percentage as much as possible
- to self-fund benefits to the extent that long-run cost savings can be expected for the firm and catastrophic losses can be avoided
- to coordinate all benefits with social insurance programs to which the company makes payments
- to maintain continual communications with all employees concerning benefit programs

Most lists of objectives establish guidelines—instead of specific performance goals—within which management must operate. The objectives also establish guidelines for the cost of providing benefits. Although the firm wants to have a better-than-average plan, it does not want to be a leader. There is a very specific statement about what the relationship between the cost of benefits for union and nonunion employees should be. However, there is no mention that the benefits for the two groups must also be identical. If the two groups have different needs, different types and levels of benefits may be desirable.

Three additional points about employer objectives should be made. First, as times change, benefit objectives may need revision. The rapidly rising cost of providing medical expense coverage has led many employers to focus more on objectives for slowing the increase in employer costs for benefits.

Second, the frequent lack of specific guidelines in benefit objectives gives the in-house benefit staff great creative latitude to come up with innovative solutions to benefit problems and to respond to the changing benefit environment. Such creativity can often lead to success and financial reward.

Third, a firm's primary objective may be to establish an overall employee benefit plan that channels as large a portion of the benefits as possible to the owner or owners. It is a reality that must be recognized, most commonly in small firms or in firms that have few owners. Large, publicly held corporations sometimes wish to provide better benefits for their executives than for other employees. However, employers are likely to provide these extra benefits under separate executive compensation plans, rather than under benefit plan that applies to all employees.

Who Should Receive Benefits?

As part of establishing its objectives, an employer must determine its responsibilities to various categories of persons who might be eligible for coverage under the firm's overall benefit program. The list is much longer than one might initially think. It includes

- active full-time employees and potentially their dependents
- retired employees and potentially their dependents
- part-time employees and potentially their dependents
- disabled employees and potentially their dependents
- survivors of deceased employees
- employees who have terminated employment and potentially their dependents
- employees who are temporarily separated from employment (for example, employees on family leave) and potentially their dependents

Obviously, employers give most benefits to employees and they give some benefits to their dependents, such as medical expense coverage. Whether other groups on the list receive any benefits depends on several factors. These include the attitude of the employer and the degree to which protection is available under other programs, such as Social Security. Federal and state laws also play a role. For example, employers must continue some benefits because of family leave legislation. In addition, employers must continue medical expense coverage in many cases because of COBRA.

TYPES OF BENEFITS A PLAN SHOULD PROVIDE

A major decision for any employer is what types and levels of benefits to include in an overall employee benefit plan. For those few firms that do not have an employee benefit program, this decision involves choosing which benefits to offer initially. However, in most cases, the decision is ongoing and involves either the offering of new or improved benefits or the redesigning of all or a major portion of the benefit plan. An objective of most employee benefit plans is to meet the "needs" of employees. If they vary for different groups of employees, should employers establish different benefits? Should the employer design a single plan in which employees can choose among alternative benefits?

Determining Needs

Traditional methods to determine employee needs include basing benefits on the following factors:

- the employer's perception of the employees' needs. Management's perception of employees' needs often differs from what the employees themselves feel they need.

- what competitors are doing. Employers may place the emphasis on having an employee benefit package that is virtually identical to that of the competition, even though the makeup of the workforce may be different and the employees may have different needs.

- collectively bargained benefits. Many employers pattern their benefit plans for salaried employees after their negotiated plans for union employees. Again, the needs of salaried employees may be substantially different and may call for a totally different plan.

- tax laws and regulations. Employers may design benefit plans to include those benefits that are best suited to the high tax brackets of top executives. The average employee who is in a modest tax bracket may actually have a preference for certain benefits even though they result in currently taxable income.

In the last few years, two trends have taken place. First, employers have increasingly taken a marketing-research approach to employee benefit planning. The employees' preferences for benefits are determined similarly to the way that consumers' demands for products are determined. For the most part, employers use this approach only for nonunion employees, because collective bargaining determines benefits for union employees. However, some employers and some unions use this procedure as a guide in their negotiations over benefits for union employees. Second, employers have increasingly turned to life-cycle and work/life approaches to benefit planning.

Use of Marketing Research

Employers can use a marketing-research approach to benefit planning for different purposes. Most often employers select it as a way to determine (1) how they should allocate funds to new types of benefits or (2) how they should use funds to improve current benefits. This can be for a one-time change in a firm's benefit plan or for changes that they implement over time.

Employers must use marketing-research techniques with caution. They can have a negative effect on employee morale unless the employer is committed to using the results of marketing research in benefit decision making.

Although employers can use a variety of marketing-research techniques in benefit planning, the techniques that they most commonly choose fall into three major categories: personal interviews, simplified questionnaires, and sophisticated research methods.

Personal Interviews. Personal interviews with employees are probably the most effective marketing-research technique for a small firm or for a benefit program that is limited to a small number of employees. On this scale, it is also usually the least expensive technique. An advantage of personal interviewing is that it can be used to collect the same type of information as do both simplified questionnaires and sophisticated research techniques. Because it is important in personal interviewing for the employees to feel they can speak candidly, it may be desirable to have the interviews conducted by someone outside the firm and to hold group interviews without the supervisor's presence.

Simplified Questionnaires. A simplified questionnaire often has two major parts: one determines benefit preferences; the other determines demographic data (such as age, gender, marital status, years of service, and salary range). The questionnaire is called "simplified" because employees are asked only to indicate and/or rank their preferences. It is important to use a clear, brief questionnaire that is not annoying to employees, so it is best that the questionnaire be initially given to a few employees in order to determine their reactions.

The questionnaire is essentially a structured one and is not open-ended. Employees must only rank their preferences, and they do not have the opportunity to state whether each benefit is important or whether it should be improved. They must also make their preferences known regarding possible trade-offs between benefits and pay. Even though the questionnaire is structured, employees still have the opportunity to make general comments. Any questionnaire should incorporate such a feature as a way of letting employees know that their opinions will be heard.

Sophisticated Research Methods. One difficulty with simplified questionnaires, and to some extent personal interviews, is that they fail to measure the intensity of employees' preferences. Consequently, some firms have used more sophisticated marketing-research techniques in an attempt to measure the degree of importance that employees place on various benefit alternatives. These more sophisticated research techniques are typically used only when the employer has formulated specific alternatives. Therefore, employers often use them as a follow-up to personal interviews and simplified questionnaires, and they frequently involve additional interviews and/or questionnaires.

Life-Cycle Approach to Benefit Planning

life-cycle approach

The design of employee benefit plans traditionally focused solely on providing active employees with protection against the financial consequences of illness, disability, retirement, and death. Over time, employers began to offer other types of benefits, but plan design tended to focus on the employee being part of a traditional family. Over the last two decades, the demographic makeup of the workforce has changed dramatically. As a result, many employers often take a **life-cycle approach** to benefit planning. Traditional benefits are still part of the core of most overall employee benefit plans. However, employers are increasingly designing benefit plans with the realization that benefit needs may differ for males and females, and may differ when employees are single, when they have and raise children, when they care for elderly parents, and when they retire. Different benefit needs also arise in today's society because of more family units containing children from prior marriages and more unmarried individuals (of either the same or opposite gender) living together.

Many of the benefits employees want at various stages in their lives are probably fairly obvious. However, many employers use questionnaires and personal interviews to determine these varying needs. Examples of benefit value to persons at different life-cycle stages are shown in the Table 12-2.

Work/Life Approach to Benefit Planning

work/life approach

Employers are increasingly taking a **work/life approach** to benefit planning. They have realized that employees are looking for employers who recognize that their employees have lives away from the workplace. Many of the benefits that appeal to this group of employees are those that have already been mentioned, such as flexible work schedules, child-care plans, elder-care benefits, family leave, and adoption assistance. All of these benefits have seen some growth in prevalence over the last two decades.

Table 12-2	
Sample Life-Cycle Benefits	
Life-Cycle Stage	**Desired Benefit**
Young, unmarried workers	Extra vacation
Newlyweds	Marriage leave
Employees in childbearing years	Prenatal courses
	Parental leave
	Adoption assistance
Workers during child-rearing years	Day-care centers
	Flexible work schedules
Employees dealing with divorce	Legal assistance
Workers in elder-care years	Long-term care insurance
	Support groups
Retirees	Medicare supplements
	Retiree job banks
	Preretirement counseling
Employees facing death	Grief counseling
	Funeral leave

PLAN PROVISIONS FOR CONTROLLING COSTS

Employers have always been concerned about the costs of providing employee benefits, which has led to plan provisions that transfer these costs to employees rather than
reducing the costs. These provisions include probationary periods, benefit limitations,
and contributory financing. Many recent attempts to control costs have been directed
primarily toward the rapidly increasing costs of medical care, and many of these provisions are designed to reduce administrative and claim costs without transferring them to
employees.

Probationary Periods

Probationary periods reduce costs to employers because any claims that employees incur
during this time must be borne by the employees themselves. In addition, probationary
periods reduce the adverse selection that would most likely exist without their use. Administrative costs are also minimized for employees who terminate employment shortly after
being hired. However, probationary periods do impose hardship on newer employees who
incur claims but find themselves without benefits. Primarily for competitive reasons in

attracting employees, the use and length of probationary periods, particularly in medical expense plans, have been decreasing except in high turnover situations.

Benefit Limitations

Benefit limitations in the form of deductibles, coinsurance, and exclusions for certain types of expenses are common in medical expense insurance. However, some of these techniques can also be used in other types of insurance, as in the following examples:

- the limiting of benefits to a maximum percentage of income in disability income plans. In addition to reducing the amount of the benefits paid by the employer, a maximum percentage also minimizes the possibility of feigned and unnecessarily prolonged disabilities.

- the setting of maximum benefits under dental plans for such expenses as orthodontics

Contributory Financing

Many benefit plans require that each employee pay a portion of the premium costs for his or her own coverage. This may lower the employer's costs and/or may enable the employer to use these saved dollars to provide additional or improved benefits. There are several arguments both for and against contributory financing.

When employers use contributory financing for benefits, employees are generally able to voluntarily elect or decline coverage. Adverse selection may be higher for contributory plans. Furthermore, having the option to decline coverage could mean that employees or their dependents will be without coverage should a loss occur. Finally, there tend to be greater administrative costs associated with a contributory plan than with a noncontributory plan.

Advocates of contributory plans feel that sharing in the cost increases the employees' awareness and appreciation of both the plan and the contribution the employer is making. Others counter this opinion with the argument that payroll deductions for benefits are a source of employee dissatisfaction because they may view the employer as "cheap" for not paying the entire cost of the plan.

BENEFIT PLAN COMMUNICATION

Traditionally, employers have placed a low priority on the communication of their benefit plans to employees. They have taken the attitude that employees appreciated any benefits given to them. The little information that was made available tended to be only the literature that the insurance companies providing the coverage had prepared.

Over the last few years, this situation has changed dramatically. Federal law requires employers to disclose a substantial amount of information to employees about their benefit plans. The Affordable Care Act requires more types of disclosures and communication to enrolled and prospective insureds.

Effective communication minimizes the dissatisfaction that arises from misunderstandings about the benefit program, and it may reduce turnover to the extent that employees realize the true value of their benefits. Employers have also learned that effective communication is necessary to obtain employee support if cost-containment efforts are to be successful.

Finally, benefit communication is increasingly important as employers give employees more choice with regard to their own benefits. This is occurring as more employees have alternative medical expense plans, cafeteria plans, and retirement plans that allow investment choices.

Most benefit consultants feel that an effective communication program should have four primary objectives:

- to create an awareness and appreciation of the way current benefits improve employees' financial security
- to provide a high level of understanding about available benefits
- to encourage the wise use of benefits
- to comply with legal requirements

Because many employees have coverage for dependents under their benefit plan, there is also an increasing awareness of the need to inform spouses of a firm's benefit programs. Therefore, spouses might be invited to benefit orientations.

Effective Communication

Good communication rarely just happens. It requires that the employer have objectives in a manner similar to that used for benefit plan design. Although any list of objectives is likely to include the clear and concise dissemination of information about current benefits, other objectives may change over time. For example, an employer may want to encourage employees to switch to a high deductible health plan.

Depending on the circumstances, communication may be ongoing or on a one-time basis. In either case, benefit consultants feel that it is important for employers to design communication materials so that employees are told that they and their needs are important to the firm, that the employer cares what employees think about benefits, and that the employer wants employees to understand their benefits. A successful long-run communication program also has a method for obtaining feedback so that the employer can determine the effectiveness of its communication. Steps can be taken to rectify inadequate information, and past experience can be of value in designing future communications.

Several factors can complicate the communication process. For example, an employer may have different benefit plans for different groups of employees and therefore may have to design alternative communication strategies. Although it may be possible to have the strategies be somewhat similar, the sophistication levels of the different employee groups may call for an entirely different approach. A similar problem may occur if an employer has multiple locations. In addition, employers must take the needs of employees who do not speak English into consideration. Finally, communication strategies may vary for new employees and existing employees.

Whatever form a communication plan may take, communication specialists recommend that several basic factors be present:

- The communication should be written in a style that is clear and understandable to the employees. Legalese and benefit jargon should be avoided.

- The communication should make it clear what a benefit means to an employee. For example, if an employer is trying to encourage enrollment in a managed care plan, the lack of any deductibles and minimal copayments should be emphasized.

- The communication should explain why changes are being made.

- The communication should make use of graphics and examples. Boring communication that lacks these features is less effective.

Methods of Communication

The communication of benefit plans to employees is a highly sophisticated task. No single method of communication is likely to accomplish all the desired objectives, so employers may use a combination of several methods. They can communicate benefit plans to employees in audiovisual presentations, in face-to-face meetings, through printed materials, and more recently with interactive communication through telephones and computers. Many employers hire communications experts who generally report to the person responsible for employee benefits. Other employers use the services of benefit-consulting firms, many of which have developed specialized units for advising their clients in this particular area.

Audiovisual Presentations

Audiovisual presentations are a very effective way to communicate benefit plans to new employees or to explain significant changes in existing benefit plans to current employees. It is much easier to require employees to view audiovisual presentations than to read printed materials. In addition, if properly done, audiovisual presentations can convey the employer's concern for the well-being of its employees, and they can explain proper benefit use more effectively than printed materials. Recently many employers view these presentations as a way of "advertising" their employee benefit plans. In fact, some employers have actually hired advertising firms to design not only their audiovisual programs but other aspects of their communication program as well.

Meetings with Employees

Face-to-face meetings with employees can also be an effective way to explain employee benefit plans and to answer employee questions. For small employers, this technique is generally used to present benefit plans to new employees or to explain the changes in existing plans. Large employers often combine meetings with audiovisual presentations. It is obvious that whoever conducts these meetings (be it the employer, agent, broker, consultant, or group representative) must be truly knowledgeable about the plan. In addition, it is just as important that he or she be able to effectively communicate this knowledge to employees.

The number of employees who attend a meeting may determine its effectiveness. A large meeting may be satisfactory if its purpose is primarily to present information. However, a series of small meetings may be more manageable and appropriate if the employer wants to solicit employee opinions or questions. These smaller-sized meetings can be in lieu of a large meeting or as follow-up meetings to a large group presentation. When employees must make decisions regarding their benefit plans, meetings with individual employees may also be necessary.

The success of face-to-face meetings may also depend to some degree on their time and location. To achieve maximum employee interest and attention, the facilities should be comfortable and not overcrowded. In addition, meetings should be held during normal working hours, not at the end of the working day, when many employees may be concerned about whether the meeting will end on time.

Printed Materials

benefit handbook

Virtually every employer provides employees with some printed materials about its employee benefit plans. Increasingly, this material is available online. At a minimum, this material consists of group insurance certificates and the information that is required under the disclosure provisions of ERISA. The next most commonly provided source of information is the **benefit handbook**. If there is a typical benefit handbook, it is best described as a reference book that summarizes the benefit plans that are available to all employees. In addition to describing group insurance benefits, it includes information about an organization's retirement plan, vacation policy, and possibly other benefits (such as educational assistance). The handbook describes each plan in terms of eligibility, benefits, and what employee contributions are required.

benefit statement

Because of the general nature of benefit handbooks, many employers also give each employee a personalized **benefit statement**, usually on an annual basis. Some employers feel that employees will better appreciate the value of their benefits if they are aware of the magnitude of the cost to the employer. The Table 12-3 is an example of one form that is used for reporting this information. However, the most common form of personalized benefit statement specifies the plans for which the employee is eligible and what benefits are available to that particular employee (or his or her family) under each of these plans. Table 12-4 shows a portion of a sample statement.

The Affordable Care Act requires the distribution of a standardized *four-page summary of benefits* to all plan participants and prospective enrollees. The Department of Health and Human Services manages the guidelines regarding the content of the document.

Vendors of employee benefit products and services may also make printed materials available for distribution to employees.

Table 12-3
Sample Current Benefit Statement

BENEFIT STATEMENT REVIEW FOR _____

Many of us forget that there is more to our paycheck than the amount we take home. The following are the "extras" that were provided in 20___ and their value as determined by the cost to your employer.

		Annual Value	Value per Hour
(1)	Social Security and Medicare (employer's contribution)	$_____	$ _____
(2)	Workers' Compensation Insurance Premium	$_____	$ _____
(3)	State Unemployment Insurance Premium	_____	_____
(4)	Paid Holidays	_____	_____
(5)	Vacation Days	_____	_____
(6)	Pension	_____	_____
(7)	Salary Continuation	_____	_____
(8)	Long-Term Disability Income Insurance	_____	_____
(9)	Life Insurance	_____	_____
(10)	Medical Expense Insurance (employer's contribution)	_____	_____
(11)	Others		
	_____	_____	_____
	_____	_____	_____

The $_____ value of those sometimes-forgotten benefits is equal to _____% of the $_____ you received as salary or wages in 20___. These benefits are provided to protect you and your family from certain financial risks and to help provide for your future retirement.

Interactive Voice-Response Systems

Employers are increasingly turning to newer technologies to communicate and manage benefit plans. One of these technologies is the telephone and the use of interactive voice-response systems. The system can allow employees, through a menu of options, to request general information and materials, such as enrollment forms. Carried even further, the system can enable employees to obtain specific information about their own benefits, such as the amount of life insurance they have or the balance in their 401(k) account. Of course, if personal information is available, employees need to have a personal identification number to access the information. At the most complex extreme, telephones can be used to allow employees to make benefit elections and changes—for example, to change investment options for a 401(k) plan or to change from one medical expense plan to another during open enrollment periods.

Table 12-4
Sample Current Benefit Statement

PERSONAL STATEMENT OF BENEFITS

This Personal Statement of Benefits lists the benefits that protect both you and your family now and provide security for your future. We know you will find this statement informative, and we hope it is useful in your personal planning.

Health Care Benefits

You have elected coverage for: ___ yourself ___ your family ___ You have not elected coverage

The highlights of your Comprehensive Medical Plan are summarized in the following table. See your employee handbook for further details.

In-Hospital Benefits	Out-of-Hospital Benefits	Special Benefits
$1,000 deductible per person each calendar year (3-deductible maximum per family)		100% of outpatient emergency treatment of accidental injury (no deductible)
100% of covered expenses, including maternity care, after the deductible is met	80% of first $3,000 of covered expenses, then 100% of remaining covered expenses; 50% of psychiatric treatment ($30-per-visit maximum benefit)	100% of diagnostic X-ray and laboratory tests (deductible applies)

Overall Plan Maximum: Unlimited

Disability Income Benefits

Salary Continuation Plan

- Your full salary continues for_____ weeks, then 3/4 of your salary continues for_____ weeks.

Long-Term Disability Income Plan

- If disabled over 26 weeks, you will receive_____ a month. This is 60 percent of your base pay and includes benefits under the corporation's plan and any Social Security benefits, other than family benefits, for which you are eligible.
- If you have eligible dependents, you can receive additional family benefits under Social Security of up to _____ a month.

If total long-term disability income from the above sources exceeds 80 percent of your base pay, disability benefits under the corporation's plan is reduced to bring the total to the 70 percent level.

There are both advantages and disadvantages to the use of telephone systems for benefit communication. Among the advantages are

- They can be designed to allow employee access on a 24-hour basis.

- They enable employees to get quick and accurate responses.

- They make it possible for employees to maintain a degree of anonymity without having to disclose information to in-house personnel.

- They allow human resources personnel to spend more time on issues other than routine phone inquiries.

However, there are also drawbacks and limitations, some of which can be overcome with proper planning and design:

- There is a lack of human interaction. This by itself will discourage some employees from using the telephone system if they can obtain the same information and perform the same transactions by calling someone personally. A well-designed system is simple to use and does not leave employees in an endless maze of pushing buttons. It also gives employees a method to speak to a real person when they feel it is necessary.

- Telephone systems can become increasingly expensive as they are expanded to allow employees a wider range of options. For some firms, the cost may outweigh the benefits.

- Because employees can make benefit changes and elections by merely pushing a button, they might make mistakes. Therefore, it is necessary for the telephone response system to confirm all transactions over the phone and allow employees to enter needed corrections. In addition, employers should send a written confirmation to employees, possibly requiring the return of a signed copy of the confirmation.

- Telephone systems are not conducive to inputting data, such as the name of a new dependent for purposes of obtaining medical expense coverage.

Computers

Although telephone systems can be used effectively for obtaining information and simple benefit plan enrollments, computers enable employers to use technology to a much greater extent.

The majority of computer benefits systems are intranet-based over a local area network of company computers. These have the advantage of speed and minimize security concerns. Firms can also use Internet-based systems over a public network secured by password access. A major advantage of the Internet is that employees can be allowed access from home or while they are traveling. In addition, the Internet is often better for providing employees with links to other useful Web sites because, for security reasons, a firm may not wish to have other links with its intranet site. Computerized benefit systems can be on either employees' personal computers at their workstations or computer terminals located at centralized stations. Employees may also be able to access these systems from their home computer or from other locations. By pressing the appropriate key, an employee can get a general description of the company's various plans. By inputting appropriate data (including an identification number), an employee may also be able to obtain information about his or her own particular situation. For example, an employee could determine a potential disability income or retirement benefit. An employee may also be able to obtain the answers to "what if" questions. For example, if I contribute $100 per month to a 401(k) plan that is expected to earn 5 percent annually, how much will I have at age 65? Or if I elect these options under a cafeteria plan, will any additional employer dollars remain for other benefits, or will I have to make an additional contribution through a payroll deduction?

Employers are increasingly using the computer to allow employees to make benefit selections. To have written verification, a form is either printed on the spot for an employee to sign and return or generated in the personnel office, reviewed, and sent to the employee for signing. Computers also facilitate data input, such as the name of a new beneficiary for life insurance coverage or the name of a new spouse for an employee's medical expense coverage. Computers can educate employees as well as provide benefit information. For example, employees can have access to information comparing the pros and cons of a managed care plan with those of a traditional indemnity plan. Employees also may have access to information to help them in their overall personal financial planning, often through links to other Internet sites.

Finally, employers are beginning to use computers to disseminate legally required information, such as summary plan descriptions.

BENEFIT OUTSOURCING

outsourcing

Historically, most organizations have fully administered their benefit programs with their own employees. However, it has not been unusual for an organization to turn to **outsourcing** whereby other parties perform some administrative functions. For example, third-party administrators may administer self-funded medical expense plans, and actuaries may perform some of the compliance functions for qualified retirement plans.

Recently, there has been a significant increase in the outsourcing of employee benefit administration, with estimates indicating that over half of all employers currently use outsourcing to some degree.

Reasons for Outsourcing Benefits

There are many reasons why an employer might decide to outsource benefit administration. The most common reason is that the organization lacks the technical and regulatory expertise to perform many of the necessary functions. For example, few employers have a staff with the expertise to perform actuarial calculations or utilization reviews. Closely correlated with this reason is the desire of firms to seek more value for the dollars spent on benefits. Although outsourcing costs money, it is often cheaper than performing the same functions in house. Some of this savings is because of the high cost of the hardware and software that the employer might need. An outside vendor can spread this cost over many customers.

Better service to employees is also an often-cited reason for outsourcing. Vendors frequently have toll-free numbers and a staff that specializes in specific benefit functions. Persons who answer telephones are typically trained to have the ability to handle 90 percent or more of the inquiries they receive. But more important, they have the ability to transfer the more complex calls to the appropriate person to handle the issue.

Outsourcing also buffers the employer from disgruntled employees. For example, if an employee is unhappy with disability, medical, or workers' compensation benefits, he or she may blame the outsourcing firm rather than the employer.

Another cited reason for outsourcing is so that the organization can focus its attention on the firm's core activities.

Functions Outsourced

Significant variations exist with respect to the benefit functions that are outsourced. Systems, staff, or both can be outsourced. *Systems outsourcing* refers to the use of an outsourcing organization's computer and other systems but retaining an in-house staff to perform administrative functions. *Staff outsourcing* refers to the outsourcing of people but the continued use of the organization's systems.

Outsourcing can also be classified as either partial or full. With *partial outsourcing,* an employer uses an outsourcing organization's personnel and/or staff for some benefit functions but continues other functions in house. The term *full outsourcing* refers to those situations where most benefit functions are outsourced. Even with full outsourcing, some functions, such as financial management of benefit plans and benefit plan design, remain the responsibility of senior personnel at the firm. Employees, however, typically deal with an outside firm by telephone, mail, or e-mail.

Most employers use partial outsourcing. Among the most common functions employers outsource are

- COBRA administration
- administration of medical and dental claims
- utilization review
- vision care programs
- government reporting
- record keeping and administration of defined-contribution retirement plans
- record keeping and administration of flexible spending accounts
- preretirement planning
- benefit communication

Vendors Used for Outsourcing

Employers may use several different vendors who specialize in a limited number of activities. In fact, some vendors may specialize in only one type of benefit, such as vision care.

The major providers of outsourcing services include benefit consulting firms, insurance companies, stock brokerage firms, mutual funds, and third-party administrators. Stock brokerage firms and mutual funds tend to be involved almost solely in functions relating to retirement plans. Although the other vendors often engage in a wide variety of activities, they may also specialize in a limited number of outsourcing services. For example, benefit consulting firms frequently focus their activities on regulatory compliance, eligibility determination, and enrollment.

The Decision to Outsource

The decision to outsource is not a simple task, and any such decision needs to incorporate sufficient lead time and preparation for the change. An organization must determine what functions it should outsource and what functions it can best perform in house. Consideration also needs to be given to the firm's personnel. Outsourcing often involves working with computers and other systems. It is important that people with expertise in these areas be involved. In addition, the help of the internal benefit staff is vital.

A formal outsourcing process begins with a request for proposal (RFP), in which vendors are asked to bid to provide services. The RFP should clearly spell out the goals of outsourcing and identify the major responsibilities of the potential parties to an outsourcing contract.

The outsourcing contract itself needs to clearly establish responsibilities of both the vendor and the employer, yet be flexible enough to address situations that may arise in the future. Proper planning must be done with respect to data to make sure the vendor does not destroy data important to the employer. It is also important for the employer to be able to retrieve data if the contract with the vendor terminates.

A good outsourcing contract contains performance guarantees. These guarantees may relate to such factors as timeliness, accuracy, productivity improvements, and employee complaints. Because the primary purpose of outsourcing is to save money in the long run, it is also very important to address vendor compensation. The contract should not be so open-ended that the vendor automatically passes on unforeseen costs to the employer. Even fixed-price contracts may prove to be expensive if a firm downsizes, but the vendor receives the same compensation for servicing a smaller number of employers.

Some other issues an employer must address include confidentiality and security of data, vendor responsibility for systems upgrades and employer responsibility to pay for them, insurance and/or bonding requirements, and procedures for resolving disputes among the parties.

CHAPTER REVIEW

Key Terms and Concepts

agent
standard (regular) commission
   schedule
level commission schedule
broker
consultant
group representative
third-party administrator (TPA)
navigator

prospecting
proposal
enrollment
life-cycle approach
work/life approach
benefit handbook
benefit statement
outsourcing

Review Questions

Review questions are based on the learning objectives in this chapter. For example, a [3] at the end of a questions means that the question is based on learning objective 3. If there are multiple objectives, they are all listed.

1. Identify the people within an organization who might make decisions regarding group insurance, and explain why these tend to be different people for different sizes of organizations. [1]

2. What types of companies sell employee benefit products? [1]

3. How do sales activities of agents differ for small groups as opposed to large groups? [2]

4. What types of commission schedules are used for employee benefit plans? [2]

5. What is the distinction between a broker and a consultant? [2]

6. What are the functions of a group representative? [2]

7. What services are provided by a third-party administrator? [2]

8. What is the role of the navigator in placing coverage for employee benefits? [2]

9. How does prospecting tend to vary for different-sized groups? [3]

10. What type of information do most group insurance proposals contain? [3]

11. How does the development of group insurance proposals vary for different-sized groups? [3]

12. What types of information does an insurer commonly request to complete a benefit proposal? [3]

13. What types of questions are commonly asked in the specifications when a group insurance case is put out for bid? [3]

14. How does managed care and the broad availability of medical expense plans make proposal development more challenging? [3]

15. How does the presentation of a group insurance proposal vary for different-sized groups? [3]

16. Describe the enrollment process for both contributory and noncontributory group insurance plans. [3]

17. Why doesn't the group insurance marketing process cease with the installation of a group insurance plan? [3]

18. Why is it important for an organization to have specific written objectives for its benefit plans? [4]

19. How may an organization's benefit objectives vary in both length and specific details? [4]

20. What are the various categories of persons to whom an employer might have responsibility for providing benefits? [4]

21. Describe the traditional approaches for determining the benefit needs of employees, and explain the drawbacks of each approach. [4]

22. What is the potential negative effect of using a marketing-research approach to determine the needs of employees? [4]

23. Regarding research interviews: [4]

    a. What are the advantages of using personal interviews to determine employee needs?

    b. Why should these interviews be conducted in the absence of an employee's supervisor?

24. What advantages does a structured questionnaire for determining employee needs have over an open-ended questionnaire? [4]

25. What is the purpose of life-cycle approach to benefit planning? [4]

26. What types of benefits might an employer provide under the work/life approach to benefit planning? [4]

27. Explain the ways in which each of the following provisions in group insurance plans may reduce costs to the employer: [5]

    a. probationary periods

    b. benefit limitations

28. What are the potential advantages of requiring employees to pay a portion of the premiums for their own coverage? [5]

29. What should be the objectives of an effective program for communicating benefit plans to employees? [6]

30. What factors should be present in communicating benefits? [6]

31. How can conducting meetings with employees be used to communicate benefits? [6]

32. Why might a personalized benefit statement be a more effective communication tool than a benefit handbook? [6]

33. Regarding the interactive voice-response systems: [6]

    a. How can interactive voice-response systems be used in benefit communication?

    b. What are their advantages and disadvantages?

34. What are the advantages of each of the following for benefit communications? [6]

    a. the intranet

    b. the Internet

35. What are some of the ways in which computers can be used to communicate employee benefit plans? [6]

36. Why might an employer decide to outsource benefit administration? [7]

37. Regarding outsourced functions: [7]

    a. What benefit administration functions are firms most likely to outsource?

    b. What types of vendors do they use?

Review Question Answers

1. In most cases, the person making group insurance decisions for groups up to 100 employees tends to be the organization's owner or chief executive officer.

    For groups of more than 100 employees, there may be one or more persons devoted full time to group insurance matters. These persons may be in a separate "insurance" or "benefit" department, or they may be part of a personnel, financial, or administrative department.

2. Sellers of employee benefit products consists primarily of insurance companies, HMOs, PPOs, third-party administrators, and the health insurance exchanges.

3. For all groups with less than 100 employees, agents usually locate the prospective group insurance cases, but the extent of their further involvement in the sales process varies depending on the size of the group. For very small groups, such as 25 or fewer employees, the agent also conducts virtually all sales activities. For larger groups up to 100 employees, the agent may call on the group representative of the insurance company for assistance in selling, installing, and servicing the case.

4. Commissions may be paid according to a standard commission schedule where the first year commission is higher with a lower commission payable for renewal years or according to a level commission level with the commissions for all years paid at the same percentage of premium.

5. Traditionally, the major distinction between brokers and consultants was that brokers were compensated on a commission basis for the coverages they placed in behalf of clients, whereas consultants were compensated by fees charged to the clients. From a practical standpoint, the distinction between brokers and consultants has become blurred and is now more semantic than real.

6. The group representative specializes in the selling and servicing of his or her company's group insurance products. The group representative's sales activities are conducted through the agents, brokers, and consultants whom the group representative educates and motivates to place group insurance business with his or her company. In addition, the group representative aids the agents, brokers, or consultants in prospecting, securing necessary underwriting data, designing plans, and preparing and presenting group insurance proposals. After a plan is sold, the group representative is frequently involved in the enrolling of eligible employees, the administrative procedures of installing the case, and the providing of services necessary to keep the case in force.

7. A third-party administrator provides administrative services to group benefit plans which can include receiving employee reports and contributions, tracking employee eligibility, preparing required reports, handling complaints and grievances, processing claims, and other functions.

8. Navigators are employed by the health insurance exchanges to sell the products being offered through the exchanges by qualified health plans. These products include both group insurance plans and individual health insurance plans.

9. Some of the sales activities for very small groups are conducted by agents who specialize in group insurance, but a large portion of the sales activities is conducted by agents, brokers, or consultants whose primary sales activities take place in the

individual marketplace. It is also in the marketing to small groups that prospecting without known contacts (cold calling) is most likely to take place.

For mid-sized groups, the agent, broker, or consultant may do the actual prospecting alone or with the group representative, or he or she may give qualified leads to the group representative who will perform this function.

For large groups, however, prospecting consists of group representatives who develop a close working relationship with the brokers or consultants to encourage the consideration of the group representatives' organization as a provider of group insurance or other employee benefit products or services.

10. Most proposals contain at least the following information:

   • a description of each coverage included in the plan

   • a schedule of the tentative premium rates and the total premium for each coverage

   • a description of the persons eligible for coverage under the plan

   • any underwriting assumptions or conditions

   • details for servicing the plan, such as the procedures and facilities for administering claims

   • general information about the insurance company, including its size, financial strength, and products and services

11. Because there is typically little or no flexibility in the design of plan options available to small groups, the preparation of proposals to such groups is usually a simple matter. As a result, the presentation of the small group proposals consists primarily of an agent, broker, or consultant describing the available options and determining the employer's preferences.

   For large group insurance cases that are not controlled by large brokers or consultants, the group representative plays a major role in the development of the proposal. In addition, the group representative assesses whether the employer is likely to meet the insurers underwriting standards prior to the proposal development.

12. Most insurance companies commonly request the following information from the prospect or the prospect's agent, broker, or consultant:

   • the reason for transferring (unless it is a new case)

   • the nature of the employer's industry

- a history of changes in the number of employees over the last 2 or 3 years
- a statement indicating whether the plan is contributory and, if so, the amount of the employer's contribution
- the length of time with the current insurer
- premiums, rates, and claims experience with the current insurer for each line of coverage (usually for the previous 3 years)
- a statement indicating whether collective bargaining is involved
- copies of information about the current plan (such as benefit booklets or certificates of insurance)
- the most recent premium statement from the current insurer
- any renewal information from the current insurer for the past year or two
- any ongoing large claims

13. A few of the many questions that the specifications commonly contain are:
    - How are incurred claims defined?
    - How is retention defined?
    - How is the level of reserves determined?
    - What is the interest rate credited to reserves?
    - How are catastrophic losses handled in the experience-rating process?
    - What charges are levied against the group's experience when coverage is converted?
    - For what period of time are rates guaranteed?
    - How much notice of rate changes is given at renewal?
    - What is the procedure for handling claims?
    - What services are provided in the area of cost containment?
    - If you are selected to provide coverage, on what date will the master contract and certificates of insurance be delivered?
    - Are there any additional costs for materials such as benefit booklets?

14. Managed care has made the adequacy of the provider network, including its availability of services, size, scope of services, and access a prominent issue. Quality, including the credentials of providers and the accreditation of the health plan through organizations such as NCQA, became paramount.

In addition, the broad availability of health plan options forces insurers to carefully evaluate the underwriting implications and loss potential of employee selection among the options offered.

15. For small groups, the agent, broker, or consultant makes the presentation of the proposal directly to the employer. In general, there is little room for negotiations, and the employer either accepts or rejects the initial proposal. In some cases, however, the proposal may contain two or three choices in plan design.

   For large groups because of the technical expertise necessary, the group representative is probably involved, and either presents the proposal or assists in its presentation. Further negotiation on plan design and revision of the proposal are most likely to occur at this point.

16. If the plan is noncontributory, the employer must provide the insurance company with enrollment cards or a list of all employees to be covered and a certification that they have met all eligibility requirements, such as being actively at work or having satisfied a probationary period.

   The enrollment of employees in contributory plans consists of requesting the employees to complete enrollment forms supplied by the insurance company. These enrollment forms are usually brief, but they are more detailed if the plan involves any individual underwriting of employees in addition to the usual group underwriting or if employees have a choice of alternative plans. Although the agent, broker, consultant, or group representative may conduct the actual enrollment, it is common for the employer's supervisory personnel to carry out this activity.

17. Marketing continues in the form of servicing a group insurance case. Good service not only increases the employer's satisfaction, but it also minimizes the possibility that the case will be transferred to another insurance company at the time of renewal. In addition, it may also lead to other business for the insurance company or the agent, broker, or consultant when the employer adds a new coverage or renews an existing coverage.

18. Without such objectives, it is difficult for the agent, broker, benefit consultant, or third-party administrator to make recommendations or for the firm's in-house benefit staff (often part of the human resources department) to make decisions.

19. Objectives for benefit plans can be general and part of a firm's overall compensation objective (that is, cash and fringe benefits), to achieve a compensation package that is competitive within the firm's geographic area or industry. However, this general

objective may make a distinction between cash compensation intended to be competitive and employee benefits intended to be better than average to attract new employees.

20. The categories include

- active full-time employees and potentially their dependents
- retired employees and potentially their dependents
- part-time employees and potentially their dependents
- disabled employees and potentially their dependents
- survivors of deceased employees
- employees who have terminated employment and potentially their dependents
- employees who are temporarily separated from employment (for example, employees on family leave) and potentially their dependents

21. The traditional approaches and their associated issues include the following:

- the employer's perception of the employees' needs. Management's perception of employees' needs often differs from what the employees themselves feel they need.
- what competitors are doing. The makeup of an employer's workforce may differ from competitors and the employees may have different needs.
- collectively bargained benefits. The needs of salaried employees may be substantially different and may call for a totally different plan.
- tax laws and regulations. The average employee who is in a modest tax bracket may actually have a preference for certain benefits even though they result in currently taxable income.

22. Marketing-research techniques can have a negative effect on employee morale unless the employer is committed to using the results of marketing research in benefit decision making.

23. a. An advantage of personal interviewing is that it can be used to collect the same type of information as do both simplified questionnaires and sophisticated research techniques.

    b. Because it is important in personal interviewing for the employees to feel they can speak candidly, it may be desirable to have the interviews conducted by someone outside the firm and to hold group interviews without the supervisor's presence.

24. In a structured questionnaire, employees are requested only to rank their preferences, and they are not given the opportunity to state whether each benefit is important or whether it should be improved. They are also required to make their preferences known regarding possible trade-offs between benefits and pay.

25. Employers are increasingly designing benefit plans with the realization that the demographic makeup of the workforce has changed dramatically. Benefit needs may differ for males and females, and may differ when employees are single, when they have and raise children, when they care for elderly parents, and when they retire. Different benefit needs also arise in today's society because of more family units containing children from prior marriages and more unmarried individuals living together.

26. Some of the benefits that might be provided are flexible work schedules, child-care plans, elder-care benefits, family leave, and adoption assistance.

    Employers are also increasingly making on-site personal services available. Some of the more common services are ATMs and other banking activities, access to postal services, travel agencies, and dry cleaning pickup.

27. a. Any claims that employees incur during this time must be borne by the employees themselves. In addition, probationary periods reduce the adverse selection that would most likely exist without their use. Administrative costs are also minimized for employees who terminate employment shortly after being hired.

    b. Benefit limitations may reduce costs to the employer as follows:

    - Limiting benefits to a maximum percentage of income in disability income plans, for example, reduces the amount of the benefits paid by the employer. A maximum percentage also minimizes the possibility of feigned and unnecessarily prolonged disabilities.

    - Setting maximum benefits under dental plans for such expenses as orthodontics limits costs

28. - Contributory financing lowers the employer's costs and/or may enable the employer to use these saved dollars to provide additional or improved benefits.

    - Sharing in the cost increases the employees' awareness and appreciation of both the plan and the contribution the employer is making.

29. - to create an awareness and appreciation of the way current benefits improve employees' financial security

    - to provide a high level of understanding about available benefits

- to encourage the wise use of benefits
- to comply with legal requirements

30. • The communication should be written in a style that is clear and understandable to the employees.

   • The communication should make it clear what a benefit means to an employee.

   • The communication should explain why changes are being made.

   • The communication should make use of graphics and examples.

31. Face-to-face meetings with employees can be an effective way to explain employee benefit plans and to answer employee questions, and can be held periodically to re-explain benefits, to answer employee questions, or to listen to employee concerns and suggestions. When employees must make decisions regarding their benefit plans, meetings with individual employees may also be necessary.

   Employers should regard these meetings as a way to communicate their concern about the security of their employees and the benefits with which they are provided.

32. Employees are more likely to better appreciate the value of their benefits if they are aware of the magnitude of the cost to the employer as presented in a personalized benefit statement. It also gives the employee a full description of what benefits are available to the particular employee and his/her dependents.

33. a. A basic system can give information to all employees about such matters as times for employee meetings, enrollment deadlines, and plan changes. A more sophisticated system allows employees, through a menu of options, to request general information and materials, such as enrollment forms. Today's fully developed systems enable employees to obtain specific information about their own benefits and can be used to allow employees to make benefit elections and changes.

   b. The advantages are:

   • They can be designed to allow employee access on a 24-hour basis.

   • They enable employees to get quick and accurate responses.

   • They make it possible for employees to maintain a degree of anonymity without having to disclose information to in-house personnel.

   • They allow human resources personnel to spend more time on issues other than routine phone inquiries.

   There are also disadvantages:

- There is a lack of human interaction.

- Telephone systems can become increasingly expensive as they are expanded to allow employees a wider range of options.

- Because employees can make benefit changes and elections by merely pushing a button, they might make mistakes.

- Telephone systems are not conducive to inputting data, such as the name of a new dependent for purposes of obtaining medical expense coverage.

34. a. The intranet, which uses a local area network of company computers, has the advantage of speed and minimizes security concerns.

b. Employees are allowed access from home or while they are traveling. In addition, the Internet enables employees to link with other useful Web sites because, for security reasons, a firm may not wish to have other links with its intranet site.

35. • Employees can get a general and specific information on an employer's various plans, including benefit information.

- Employees may also be able to obtain information relevant to his or her own particular situation.

- Employees can make benefit selections.

- Employees can input information, such as the name of a new beneficiary for life insurance coverage or the name of a new spouse being added for medical expense coverage.

- Employees can also be given information to help them in their overall personal financial planning.

- Employers are beginning to use computers to disseminate legally required information, such as summary plan descriptions.

36. • An employer may lack the technical and regulatory expertise to perform many of the necessary functions.

- Outsourcing is often cheaper than performing the same functions in house.

- Employees may receive better service as vendors frequently have 800 numbers and a staff that specializes in specific benefit functions.

- Outsourcing buffers the employer from disgruntled employees.

- An employer can focus its attention on the firm's core activities.

- An employer may decrease the size of the staff that administers its benefits or at least have the staff remain stable or grow more slowly even as benefit administration is becoming increasingly complex.

37. a. Among the most common functions employers outsource are

   - COBRA administration

   - administration of medical and dental claims

   - utilization review

   - vision care programs

   - government reporting

   - record keeping and administration of defined-contribution retirement plans

   - record keeping and administration of flexible spending accounts

   - preretirement planning

   - benefit communication

   b. The major providers of outsourcing services include benefit consulting firms, insurance companies, stock brokerage firms, mutual funds, and third-party administrators.

Chapter 13

Alternative Funding Methods

Learning Objectives

An understanding of the material in this chapter should enable the student to

1. **Explain the reasons why employers may use alternative funding methods.**

2. **Describe the characteristics and appropriateness of funding methods that modify traditional group insurance arrangements.**

3. **Describe the characteristics and appropriateness of self-funding methods.**

In recent years, employers have increasingly considered—and often adopted—benefit funding methods that are alternatives to the traditional fully insured group insurance contract. Under the traditional group insurance contract, the employer pays premiums in advance to the insurance company, which then has the financial responsibility both for paying claims (if and when they occur) and for assuming the administrative expenses associated with the contract. In addition, the insurance company bears the risk that claims will be larger than anticipated.

REASONS FOR ALTERNATIVE FUNDING

The increasing interest in alternatives to the traditional fully insured group arrangement has focused on two factors: cost savings and improved cash flow. To a large extent, this interest has grown in response to the rising cost of medical care that has resulted in an increase in the cost of providing medical expense benefits. Even though employers most commonly use alternative funding methods for providing medical expense benefits, many of the methods described here are also appropriate for other types of benefits.

Cost Savings

Savings result to the extent that either claims or the insurance company's retention can be reduced. Retention—the portion of the insurance company's premium over and above the incurred claims and dividends—includes such items as commissions, premium taxes, risk charges, and profit. Traditionally, alternative funding methods have not focused on reducing claims because the same benefits are normally provided (and therefore the same claims are paid) regardless of which funding method is used. However, this focus has changed as federal and state laws and regulations increasingly mandate the types and levels of benefits that must be contained in medical expense contracts. To the extent that these laws and regulations apply only to benefits that are included in insurance contracts, employers can avoid providing these mandated benefits by using alternative funding methods that do not involve insurance contracts. Some federal mandates apply to benefit plans, not just insurance contracts, and employers cannot avoid them by self-funding.

Modifications of fully insured contracts are usually designed either to lower or eliminate premium taxes or to reduce the insurance company's risk and consequently the risk charge. Alternative funding methods that involve a degree of self-funding also may be designed to reduce other aspects of retention and to reduce claims by excluding mandated benefits.

Improved Cash Flow

Under a standard fully insured contract, an employer generally is able to improve cash flow because the insurer collects premiums before the funds are actually needed to pay claims. Alternative funding arrangements that are intended to improve cash flow either postpone the payment of premiums to the insurance company or keep the funds that would otherwise be held in reserves in the employer's hands until the insurance company needs them. Such an arrangement is particularly advantageous to the employer when the employer can invest these funds at a rate of return.

METHODS OF ALTERNATIVE FUNDING

Under totally self-funded plans, the employer is responsible for paying claims, administering the plan, and bearing the risk that actual claims will exceed those expected. However, very few employee benefit plans that use alternative methods of funding have actually turned to total self-funding. Rather, the methods used typically fall somewhere between the two extremes.

The methods of alternative funding fall into two general categories: those that primarily modify traditional fully insured group insurance contracts and those that have some self-funding (either partial or total). The first category includes

- premium-delay arrangements
- reserve-reduction arrangements
- minimum-premium plans
- cost-plus arrangements
- retrospective-rating arrangements

These alternative funding methods are modifications of traditional fully insured plans because the insurance company has the ultimate responsibility for paying all benefits promised under the contract. Although practices differ among insurance companies, generally a group insurance plan must generate between $150,000 and $250,000 in claims or have a minimum number of covered persons, such as 50 or 100, before these funding methods are available to the employer.

The second category of alternative funding methods includes

- total self-funding from current revenue and self-administration
- self-funding with stop-loss coverage and/or administrative-services-only arrangements
- funding through a 501(c)(9) trust

Premium-Delay Arrangements

premium-delay arrangement

A **premium-delay arrangement** allows the employer to defer payment of monthly premiums for some time beyond the usual 30-day grace period. In fact, this arrangement lengthens the grace period, most commonly by 60 or 90 days. The practical effect of a premium-delay arrangement is that it enables the employer to have continuous use of the portion of the annual premium that is approximately equal to the claim reserve. For example, a 90-day premium delay allows the employer to use 3 months (or 25 percent) of the annual premium for other purposes. This amount roughly corresponds to what is usually in the claim reserve for medical expense coverage. Generally, the larger this reserve is on a percentage basis, the longer the employer can delay the premium payment. Because the insurance company still has a statutory obligation to maintain the claim reserve, it must use other assets besides the employer's premiums for this purpose. In most cases, these assets come from the insurance company's surplus.

A premium-delay arrangement has a financial advantage to the extent that an employer can earn a higher return by investing the delayed premiums than by accruing interest on the claim reserve.

On termination of an insurance contract with a premium-delay arrangement, the employer is responsible for paying any deferred premiums. However, the insurance company is legally responsible for paying all claims incurred prior to termination, even if the employer fails to pay the deferred premiums. Consequently, most insurance companies are concerned about the employer's financial position and credit rating. For many insurance companies, the final decision of whether to enter into a premium-delay arrangement, or any other alternative funding arrangement that leaves funds in the hands of the employer, is made by the insurer's financial experts after a thorough analysis of the employer. In some cases, this may mean that the insurance company will require the employer to submit a letter of credit or some other form of security.

Reserve-Reduction Arrangements

reserve-reduction arrangement

A **reserve-reduction arrangement** is similar to a premium-delay arrangement. Under the usual reserve-reduction arrangement, the employer is allowed (at any given time) to retain an amount of the annual premium that is equal to the claim reserve. Generally, an insurer allows such an arrangement only after the contract's first year, when it can more accurately estimate the pattern of claims and the appropriate amount of the reserve. In succeeding years, if the contract is renewed, the amount the insurer retains is adjusted according to changes in the size of the reserve. As with a premium-delay arrangement, the employer must pay the monies it retains to the insurance company on termination of the contract. Again, the advantage of this approach lies in the employer's ability to earn more on these funds than it would earn under the traditional insurance arrangement.

Minimum-Premium Plans

minimum-premium plan

A **minimum-premium plan** is designed primarily to reduce state premium taxes. However, many minimum-premium plans also improve the employer's cash flow.

Under the typical minimum-premium plan, the employer assumes the financial responsibility for paying claims up to a specified level, usually from 80 to 95 percent of estimated claims (with 90 percent most common). The specified level may be determined on either a monthly or an annual basis. The funds necessary to pay these claims are deposited into a bank account that belongs to the employer. However, the actual payment of claims is made from this account by the insurance company, which acts as an agent of the employer. When claims exceed the specified level, the insurance company pays the balance from own funds. No premium tax is levied by the states on the amounts the employer deposits into such an account, as it would have been if these deposits had been paid directly to the insurance company. In effect, for premium-tax purposes, the insurance company is considered to be only the administrator of these funds and not a provider of insurance. Minimum-premium plans are used to insure disability income and medical expense benefits.

Under a minimum-premium plan, the employer pays a substantially reduced premium, subject to premium taxation, to the insurance company for administering the entire plan and for bearing the cost of claims above the specified level. Because such a plan may be slightly more burdensome for an insurance company to administer than would a traditional group arrangement, the retention charge may also be slightly higher. Under a minimum-premium arrangement, the insurance company is ultimately responsible for seeing that all claims are paid, and it must maintain the same reserves that would have been required if the plan had been funded under a traditional group insurance arrangement. Consequently, the premium includes a charge for the establishment of these reserves, unless the employer also negotiates some type of reserve-reduction arrangement.

Cost-Plus Arrangements

cost-plus arrangement

A **cost-plus arrangement** (often referred to by other names, such as flexible funding) may be used to fund other types of employee benefits, but large employers generally use this to provide life insurance benefits. Under such an arrangement, the employer's monthly premium is based on the claims paid by the insurance company during the preceding month, plus a specified retention charge that is uniform throughout the policy period. To the extent that an employer's loss experience is less than that assumed in a traditional premium arrangement, the employer's cash flow is improved. However, an employer with worse-than-expected experience, either during the early part of the policy period or during the entire policy period, could also have a more unfavorable cash flow than if a traditional insurance arrangement were used. To prevent this from occurring, many insurance companies place a maximum limit on the employer's monthly premium. The effect of this limit is that the aggregate monthly premiums paid at any time during the policy period do not exceed the aggregate monthly premiums that would have been paid if the cost-plus arrangement had not been used.

Retrospective-Rating Arrangements

retrospective-rating arrangement

Under a **retrospective-rating arrangement**, the insurance company charges the employer an initial premium that is less than what would be justified by the expected claims for the year. In general, this reduction is between 5 and 10 percent of the premium for a traditional group insurance arrangement. However, if claims plus the insurance company's retention exceed the initial premium, the employer must pay an additional amount at the end of the policy year. Because an employer will usually have to pay this additional premium, one advantage of a retrospective-rating arrangement is the employer's ability to use these funds during the year.

This potential additional premium is subject to a maximum amount based on some percentage of expected claims. For example, assume that a retrospective-rating arrangement bases the initial premium on the fact that claims will be 93 percent of those actually expected for the year. If claims in fact are below this level, the employer receives an experience refund. If they exceed 93 percent, the retrospective-rating arrangement is "triggered," and the employer has to reimburse the insurance company for any additional claims paid, up to some percentage of those expected, such as 112 percent.

The insurance company bears claims in excess of 112 percent, so some of the risk associated with claims fluctuations is passed on to the employer. This reduces both the insurance company's risk charge and any reserve for claims fluctuations. The amount of these reductions depends on the actual percentage specified in the contract, above which the insurance company is responsible for claims. This percentage and the one that triggers the retrospective-rating arrangement are subject to negotiations between the insurance company and the employer. In general, the lower the percentage that triggers the retrospective arrangement, the higher the percentage above which the insurance company is fully responsible for claims. In addition, the better the cash-flow advantage of the employer, the greater the risk of claims fluctuations.

In all other respects, a retrospective-rating arrangement is identical to the traditional group insurance contract.

Total Self-Funding and Self-Administration

The purest form of a self-funded benefit plan is one in which the employer pays benefits from current revenue (rather than from a trust), administers all aspects of the plan, and bears the risk that benefit payments will exceed those expected. In addition to eliminating state premium taxes, avoiding state-mandated benefits, and improving cash flow, the employer has the potential to reduce its operating expenses to the extent that the plan can be administered at a lower cost than the insurance company's retention (other than premium taxes). A decision to use this kind of self-funding plan is generally considered most desirable when all of the following conditions are present:

- predictable claims. Budgeting is an integral part of the operation of any organization, and it is necessary to budget for benefit payments that will need to be paid in the future. This can best be done when a specific type of benefit plan has a claim pattern that is either stable or shows a steady trend. Such a pattern is most likely to occur in those types of benefit plans that have a relatively high frequency of low-severity claims. Although a self-funded plan may still be appropriate when the level of future benefit payments is difficult to predict, the plan will generally be designed to include stop-loss coverage (discussed later in this chapter).

- a noncontributory plan. Several difficulties arise if a self-funded benefit plan is contributory. Some employees may resent paying "their" money to the employer for benefits that are contingent on the firm's future financial ability to pay claims. If claims are denied, employees under a contributory plan are more likely to be bitter toward the employer than they would be if the benefit plan were noncontributory. Finally, ERISA requires that a trust must be established to hold employee contributions until the plan uses the funds. Both the establishment and maintenance of the trust result in increased administrative costs to the employer.

- a nonunion situation. Self-funding of benefits for union employees may not be feasible if a firm is subject to collective bargaining. Self-funding (at least by the employer) may be used if benefits are provided through a negotiated trusteeship. Even when collective bargaining results in benefits being provided through an individual employer plan, unions often insist that benefits be insured in order to guarantee that union members actually receive them. An employer's decision about whether to use self-funding is most likely motivated by the potential to save money. When unions approve of self-funding, they also frequently insist that some of these savings be passed on to union members through additional or increased benefits.

- the ability to effectively and efficiently handle claims. One reason that many employers do not use totally self-funded and self-administered benefit plans is the difficulty in handling claims as efficiently and effectively as an insurance company or other benefit-plan administrator would handle them. Unless an employer is extremely large, only one person or a few persons are needed to handle claims. Who in the organization can properly train and supervise these people? Can they be replaced if they should leave? Will anyone have the expertise to properly handle the unusual or complex claims that might occur? Many employers want some insulation from their employees in the handling of claims. If employees are unhappy with claim payments under a self-administered plan, dissatisfaction (and possibly legal actions) is directed toward the employer rather than toward the insurance company. The employer's inability to handle claims, or its lack of interest in wanting to handle them, does not completely rule out the use of self-funding. As discussed later, employers can have claims handled by another party through an administrative-services-only contract.

- the ability to provide other administrative services. In addition to claims, the employer must determine whether the other administrative services normally included in an insured arrangement can be provided in a cost-effective manner. These services are associated with plan design, actuarial calculations, statistical reports, communication with employees, compliance with government regulations, and the preparation of government reports. As with claims administration, an employer can purchase needed services from other sources.

- the ability to obtain discounts from medical care providers if medical expense benefits are self-funded. In order to obtain much of the cost savings associated with managed care plans, the employer must be able to secure discounts from the providers of medical care. Large employers whose employees live in a relatively concentrated geographic region may be able to enter into contracts with local providers. Other employers often use the services of third-party administrators who have either entered into contracts with managed care plans to use their networks or possibly established their own networks.

The extent of total self-funding and self-administration differs significantly among the different types of group benefit plans. Plans that provide life insurance or accidental death and dismemberment benefits do not usually lend themselves to self-funding because of infrequent and large claims that are difficult to predict. Only very large employers can expect stable and predictable claims on an annual basis. In addition, federal income tax laws impede the use of self-funding for death benefits because any payments to beneficiaries are taxable income to the beneficiaries. Such a limitation does not exist if the plan is insured.

The most widespread use of self-funding and self-administration occurs in short-term disability income plans, particularly those that limit the maximum duration of benefits to 6 months or less. For employers of almost any size, the number and average length of short-term absences from work are relatively predictable. In addition, the payment of claims is fairly simple because benefits can be (and usually are) made through the employer's usual payroll system as a salary continuation plan.

Large employers occasionally fund long-term disability income benefits. Like death claims, long-term disability income claims are difficult to predict for small employers because of their infrequent occurrence and potentially large size. In addition, because small employers receive only a few claims of this type, they become economically unjustifiable to self-administer.

Statistics indicate that 63 percent of all covered workers receive medical expense benefits form plans that are partially or totally self-funded. For employers with fewer than 200 employees, the percentage is only about 17 percent, but this increases to almost 94 percent for employers with 5,000 or more employees.[1] All types of medical expense plans are self-funded, but the most prevalent use of this technique occurs with PPO plans.[2]

Type of Plan	Percent of Employees Covered By Self-Funding
PPOs	70%
HDHPs	68%
HMOs	38%
POSs	36%

The major problem with a self-funded medical expense plan is not the prediction of claims frequency but rather the prediction of the average severity of claims. Although infrequent, claims of $500,000, $1,000,000, or more do occasionally occur. Most small- and medium-sized employers are unwilling to assume the risk that they might have to pay such a large claim. Only employers with several thousand employees are large enough to anticipate that such claims will regularly occur and to have the resources necessary to pay any unexpectedly large claims. This does not mean that smaller employers cannot self-fund medical benefits. To avoid the uncertainty of catastrophic claims, these employers often self-fund basic medical expense benefits and insure major medical expense benefits or self-fund their entire coverage but purchase stop-loss protection. Many employers that self-fund, regardless of size, also purchase at least some administrative services.

It is not unusual to use self-funding and self-administration in other types of benefit plans, such as those providing coverage for dental care, vision care, prescription drugs, or legal expenses. Initially, it may be difficult to predict the extent to which these plans will be utilized. However, once the plans have "matured," the level of claims tends to be fairly stable. Furthermore, these plans are commonly subject to maximums so that the employer has little or no risk of catastrophic claims. Although larger employers may be able to economically administer the plans themselves, smaller employers commonly purchase administrative services.

1.   The Henry J. Kaiser Foundation and Health Research & Educational Trust, Employer Health Benefits Survey, 2015, 09-22-15, page 8.
2.   Ibid: Section Ten; Plan Funding.

Self-Funding with Stop-Loss Coverage and/or ASO Arrangements

Two of the problems associated with self-funding and self-administration are the risk of catastrophic claims and the employer's inability to provide administrative services in a cost-effective manner. For each of these problems, however, solutions have evolved—namely stop-loss coverage and administrative-services-only (ASO) contracts—that still allow an employer to use elements of self-funding. Although an ASO contract and stop-loss coverage can be provided separately, they are commonly written together. In fact, most insurance companies require an employer with stop-loss coverage to have a self-funded plan administered under an ASO arrangement, either by the insurance company or by a third-party administrator.

Until recently, stop-loss coverage and ASO contracts were generally provided by insurance companies and were available only to employers with at least several hundred employees. However, these arrangements are increasingly becoming available to smaller employers, and in many cases the administrative services are purchased from third-party administrators who operate independently from insurance companies.

Stop-Loss Coverage

aggregate stop-loss coverage

Aggregate stop-loss coverage is one form of protection for employers against an unexpectedly high level of claims. If total claims exceed a specified dollar limit, the insurance company assumes the financial responsibility for those claims that are over the limit, subject to the maximum reimbursement specified in the contract. The limit is usually applied on an annual basis and is expressed as some percentage of expected claims (typically between 115 percent and 135 percent). The employer is responsible for the paying of all claims to employees, including any payments that it receives from the insurance company under the stop-loss coverage. In fact, because the insurance company has no responsibility to the employees, no reserve for claims must be established.

Aggregate stop-loss coverage results in (1) an improved cash flow for the employer and (2) a minimization of premium taxes because they must be paid only on the stop-loss coverage. However, these advantages are partially (and perhaps totally) offset by the cost of the coverage. In addition, many insurance companies insist that the employer purchase other insurance coverages or administrative services to obtain aggregate stop-loss coverage.

specific stop-loss coverage

Stop-loss plans may also be written on a "specific" basis, similar to the way an insured plan with a deductible is written. In fact, this **specific stop-loss coverage** is usually applied on an annual basis and pertains to each person insured under the contract.

The deductible specified in the stop-loss coverage is the amount the employer must assume before the stop-loss carrier is responsible for claims and is different from the deductible that an employee must satisfy under the medical expense plan. For example, employees may have a medical expense plan with a $1,000 annual deductible and an 80 percent coinsurance provision. If the employer purchases stop-loss coverage with a $5,000 stop-loss limit, an employee assumes the first $1,000 in annual medical expenses, and the plan will then pay 80 percent of any additional expenses until it has paid a total of $5,000. At that time, the stop-loss carrier reimburses the plan for any additional amounts that the plan must pay to the employee. The stop-loss carrier has no responsibility to pay the employer's share of claims under any circumstances, and most insurance companies require that employees be made aware of this fact.

Misunderstandings often arise over two variations in specific stop-loss contracts. Most contracts settle claims on a paid basis, which means that only those claims paid during the stop-loss period under a benefit plan are taken into consideration in determining the liability of the stop-loss carrier. Some stop-loss contracts, however, settle claims on an incurred basis. In these cases, the stop-loss carrier's liability is determined on the basis of the date a loss took place rather than when the benefit plan actually made payment. For example, assume an employee was hospitalized last December, but the claim was not paid until this year. This is an incurred claim for last year but a paid claim for this year.

A second variation affects an employer's cash flow. Assume an employer has a medical expense plan with a $20,000 stop-loss limit and that an employee has a claim of $38,000. If the stop-loss contract is written on a reimbursement basis, the employer's plan must pay the $38,000 claim before the plan's administrator can submit an $18,000 claim to the stop-loss carrier. If the stop-loss contract is written on an advance-funding basis, the employer's plan does not actually have to pay the employee before seeking reimbursement.

ASO Contracts

ASO contract

Under an **ASO contract**, the employer purchases specific administrative services from an insurance company or from an independent third-party administrator. These services usually include the administration of claims, but they may also include a broad array of other services, such as COBRA administration, prescription drug cards, employee communications, and government reporting. In effect, the employer has the option to purchase services for those administrative functions that can be handled more cost effectively by another party. Note that an employer might purchase different administrative services from more than one source. In addition, third-party administrators often subcontract some of the services they provide employers to other administrators that provide specialized services, such as case management and hospital audits.

Under ASO contracts, the administration of claims is performed in much the same way as it is under a minimum-premium plan; that is, the administrator has the authority to pay claims from a bank account that belongs to the employer or from segregated funds in the administrator's hands. However, the administrator is not responsible for paying claims from its own assets if the employer's account is insufficient.

In addition to listing the services that are provided, an ASO contract also stipulates the administrator's authority and responsibility, the length of the contract, the provisions for terminating and amending the contract, and the manner in which disputes between the employer and the administrator are settled. The charges for the services provided under the contract may be stated in one or some combination of the following ways:

- a percentage of the amount of claims paid
- a flat amount per processed claim
- a flat charge per employee
- a flat charge for the employer

Payments for ASO contracts are regarded as fees for services performed, and they are therefore not subject to state premium taxes. However, one similarity to a traditional insurance arrangement may be present: The administrator may agree to continue paying any unsettled claims after the contract's termination but only with funds provided by the employer.

Funding through a 501(c)(9) Trust

501(c)(9) trust

Sec. 501(c)(9) of the Internal Revenue Code provides for the establishment of *voluntary employees' beneficiary associations* (commonly called **501(c)(9) trusts** or *VEBAs*), which are funding vehicles for the employee benefits that are offered to members. The trusts have been allowed for many years, but until the passage of the 1969 Tax Reform Act, they were primarily used by negotiated trusteeships and association groups. The liberalized tax treat-ment of the funds accumulated by these trusts resulted in their increased use by employers as a method of self-funding employee benefit plans. However, the Tax Reform Act of 1984 imposed more restrictive provisions on 501(c)(9) trusts, and their use has diminished somewhat, particularly by smaller employers who previously had overfunded their trusts primarily as a method to shelter income from taxation.

Advantages

The use of a 501(c)(9) trust offers the employer some advantages over a benefit plan that it self-funds from current revenue. Contributions can be made to the trust and can be deducted for federal income tax purposes at that time, just as if the trust were an insurance company. Appreciation in the value of the trust assets or investment income earned on the trust assets is also free of taxation. The trust is best suited for an employer who wishes to establish either a fund for claims that have been incurred but not paid or a fund for possible claims fluctuations. Unless the employer uses a 501(c)(9) trust to establish these funds, the employer cannot deduct contributions for federal income tax purposes until the fund pays benefits to employees. In addition, fund earnings are subject to taxation.

The Internal Revenue Code requires that certain fiduciary standards be maintained regarding the investment of the trust assets. The employer, however, does have some latitude and does have the potential for earning a return on the trust assets that is higher than what is earned on the reserves held by insurance companies. A 501(c)(9) trust also lends itself to use by a contributory self-funded plan because ERISA requires that, under a self-funded benefit plan, a trust must be established to hold employees' contributions until they are used to pay benefits.

There is also flexibility regarding contributions to the trust. Although the Internal Revenue Service does not permit a tax deduction for "overfunding" a trust, there is no requirement that the trust must maintain enough assets to pay claims that have been incurred but not yet paid. Consequently, an employer can "underfund" the trust in bad times and make up for this underfunding in good times with larger-than-normal contributions. However, any underfunding must be shown as a contingent liability on the employer's balance sheet.

Disadvantages

A 501(c)(9) also has its drawbacks. The cost of establishing and maintaining the trust may be prohibitive, especially for small employers. In addition, the employer must be con-cerned about the administrative aspects of the plan and the fact that claims might deplete the trust's assets. However, as long as the trust is properly funded, the employer can purchase ASO contracts and stop-loss coverage.

Requirements for Establishment

To qualify under Sec. 501(c)(9), a trust must meet certain requirements— some of which may hinder its establishment—including the following:

- Membership in the trust must be objectively restricted to those persons who share a common employment-related bond. Internal Revenue Service regulations interpret this broadly to include active employees and their dependents, surviving dependents, and employees who are retired, laid off, or disabled. Except for plans maintained pursuant to collective-bargaining agreements, benefits must be provided under a classification of employees that the IRS does not find to be discriminatory in favor of highly compensated individuals.

- With two exceptions, membership in the trust must be voluntary on the part of employees. Members can be required to participate (1) as a result of collective bargaining or (2) when participation is not detrimental to them. In general, participation is not regarded as detrimental if the employee is not required to make any contributions.

- The trust must provide only eligible benefits. The list of eligible coverages is broad enough that a trust can provide benefits because of death, medical expenses, disability, and unemployment. Retirement benefits, deferred compensation, and group property and liability insurance cannot be provided.

- The sole purpose of the trust must be to provide benefits to its members or their beneficiaries. Trust assets can be used to pay the administrative expenses of the trust, but they cannot revert to the employer. If the trust is terminated, any assets that remain after all existing liabilities have been satisfied must either be used to provide other benefits or be distributed to members of the trust.

- The trust must be controlled by (1) its membership, (2) independent trustees (such as a bank), or (3) trustees or other fiduciaries, at least some of whom are designated by or on behalf of the members. Independent trustees selected by the employer control most 501(c)(9) trusts.

CHAPTER REVIEW

Key Terms and Concepts

premium-delay arrangement	aggregate stop-loss coverage
reserve-reduction arrangement	specific stop-loss coverage
minimum-premium plan	ASO contract
cost-plus arrangement	501(c)(9) trust
retrospective-rating arrangement	

Review Questions

Review questions are based on the learning objectives in this chapter. For example, a [3] at the end of a questions means that the question is based on learning objective 3. If there are multiple objectives, they are all listed.

1. Regarding alternative funding methods: [1]

   a. What are the two major objectives in using alternative funding methods?

   b. Briefly explain how alternative funding methods meet these objectives.

2. Under what circumstances does an employer have a financial advantage by using a premium-delay arrangement? [1]

3. Why is an insurance company concerned with the financial position and credit rating of an employer to whom it issues a group insurance contract that contains a premium-delay arrangement? [2]

4. With respect to reserve-reduction arrangements, answer the following: [2]

   a. Why are they usually not used during the first year of a group insurance contract?

   b. What is the responsibility of the employer upon termination of the contract?

5. How do minimum-premium plans reduce the cost of providing group benefits? [2]

6. Why are minimum-premium plans used to insure disability income and medical expense benefits rather than life insurance benefits? [2]

7. With respect to minimum-premium plans, answer the following: [2]

   a. How do they minimize premium taxes?

   b. What is the responsibility of the insurance company for paying claims and maintaining reserves?

8. Explain the mechanics of a retrospective-rating arrangement. [2]

9. What conditions are generally desirable before an employer should use total self-funding? [3]

10. Why are employers more likely to self fund short-term disability income plans than long-term disability income plans? [3]

11. What is the difference between aggregate stop-loss coverage and specific stop-loss coverage? [3]

12. How are claims administered under an ASO contract? [3]

13. What are the advantages and disadvantages of using a 501(c)(9) trust to fund an employee benefit plan? [3]

14. What conditions must a 501(c)(9) trust satisfy in order to meet Internal Revenue Service requirements? [3]

Review Question Answers

1. a. The increasing interest in alternatives to the traditional fully insured group arrangement has focused on two factors: cost savings and improved cash flow.

   b. State laws and regulations increasingly mandate the types and levels of benefits that must be contained in medical expense contracts. To the extent that these laws and regulations apply only to benefits that are included in insurance contracts, employers can avoid providing these mandated benefits and therefore achieve cost savings by using alternative funding methods that do not involve insurance contracts.

   Alternative funding arrangements also improve cash flow by postponing the payment of premiums to the insurance company or keeping the funds that would otherwise be held in reserves in the employer's hands until the insurance company needs them. The employer can invest these funds at a rate of return that is higher than the interest rate credited by the insurance company to reserves.

2. A premium-delay arrangement has a financial advantage to the extent that an employer can earn a higher return by investing the delayed premiums than by accruing interest on the claim reserve.

3. On termination of an insurance contract with a premium-delay arrangement, the employer is responsible for paying any deferred premiums. However, the insurance

company is legally responsible for paying all claims incurred prior to termination, even if the employer fails to pay the deferred premiums. Consequently, most insurance companies are concerned about the employer's financial position and credit rating.

4. a. Generally, such an arrangement is allowed only after the contract's first year, when the pattern of claims and the appropriate amount of the reserve can be more accurately estimated.

    b. As with a premium-delay arrangement, the employer must pay the monies it retains to the insurance company on termination of the contract. Again, the advantage of this approach lies in the employer's ability to earn more on these funds than it would earn under the traditional insurance arrangement.

5. A minimum-premium plan is designed primarily to reduce state premium taxes. However, many minimum-premium plans also improve the employer's cash flow.

6. The IRS considers these funds to belong to the employer, and death benefits represent taxable income to beneficiaries. Consequently, minimum-premium plans are used to insure disability income and medical expense benefits rather than life insurance benefits.

7. a. The employer's substantially reduced premium also reduces the amount subject to premium taxation.

    b. The insurance company is ultimately responsible for seeing that all claims are paid, and it must maintain the same reserves that would have been required if the plan had been funded under a traditional group insurance arrangement.

8. Under a retrospective-rating arrangement, the employer pays an initial premium that is generally between 5 and 10 percent less than what would be justified by the expected claims for the year. If claims in fact are below this level, the employer receives an experience refund. If they exceed the initial premium, the retrospective-rating arrangement is "triggered," and the employer has to reimburse the insurance company for additional claims paid. In the meantime, the employer has the advantage of using of these funds during the year. However, the potential additional premium is subject to a maximum amount based on some percentage of expected claims, such as 112 percent. The insurance company would bear the risk for claims in excess of that percentage.

9. Desirable conditions for employer use of total self-funding generally include the following:

    •   predictable claims

- a noncontributory plan

- a nonunion situation

- the ability to effectively and efficiently handle claims

- the ability to provide other administrative services

- the ability to obtain discounts from medical care providers if medical expense benefits are self-funded

10. For employers of almost any size, the number and average length of short-term absences from work are relatively predictable. In addition, the payment of claims is fairly simple because benefits can be (and usually are) made through the employer's usual payroll system.

11. Under Aggregate stop-loss coverage, if total claims exceed a specified dollar limit, the insurance company assumes the financial responsibility for those claims that are over the limit, subject to the maximum reimbursement specified in the contract. The limit is usually applied on an annual basis and is expressed as some percentage of expected claims (typically between 115 percent and 135 percent). The employer is responsible for the payment of all claims to employees under the limit.

    Specific stop-loss coverage applies to the annual claims incurred by each person insured under the contract subject to a deductible that is most commonly in the range of $10,000 to $20,000. The stop-loss carrier reimburses the plan for any additional amounts that the plan must pay to the employee above the stated deductible.

12. Under ASO contracts, the administrator has the authority to pay claims from a bank account that belongs to the employer or from segregated funds in the administrator's hands. However, the administrator is not responsible for paying claims from its own assets if the employer's account is insufficient.

13. The advantages are:

    - Contributions can be made to the trust and deducted for federal income tax purposes at that time, just as if the trust were an insurance company.

    - Appreciation in the value of the trust assets or investment income earned on the trust assets is also free of taxation.

    - An employer has the flexibility to "underfund" the trust in bad times and make up for this underfunding in good times with larger-than-normal contributions.

    There are also disadvantages:

- The cost of establishing and maintaining the trust may be prohibitive, especially for small employers.

- The employer must be concerned about the administrative aspects of the plan and the fact that claims might deplete the trust's assets.

14. • Membership in the trust must be objectively restricted to those persons who share a common employment-related bond.

- With two exceptions, membership in the trust must be voluntary on the part of employees. Members can be required to participate (1) as a result of collective bargaining or (2) when participation is not detrimental to them.

- The trust must provide only eligible benefits. Retirement benefits, deferred compensation, and group property and liability insurance cannot be provided.

- The trust must be controlled by (1) its membership, (2) independent trustees (such as a bank), or (3) trustees or other fiduciaries, at least some of whom are designated by or on behalf of the members.

Chapter 14

Underwriting and Group Insurance Pricing

Learning Objectives

An understanding of the material in this chapter should enable the student to

1. **Understand the process of underwriting and its importance to group insurance rates.**

2. **Describe the purpose of rate making.**

3. **Explain the process by which manual premium rates are calculated and used to determine group insurance premiums.**

4. **Explain the rationale for experience rating and describe the process of using experience rating to calculate premiums.**

5. **Describe a medical loss ratio and how it is applied by the Affordable Care Act.**

GROUP UNDERWRITING

underwriting

evidence of insurability

Underwriting is the process of evaluating an insurance applicant, making decisions about the applicant's acceptability for insurance coverage, and determining the appropriate basis on which to determine the price for the coverage. The applicant for individual insurance must generally provide **evidence of insurability**. This means that the applicant must meet the standards that the insurance company has determined are necessary before it will issue a policy. For group insurance, on the other hand, individual members of the group are usually not required to show any evidence of insurability when initially eligible for coverage. This is not to say that there is no underwriting, but rather that underwriting focuses on the characteristics of the group instead of on the insurability of individual members of the group.

adverse selection

The purpose of group insurance underwriting is twofold: (1) to minimize the problem of **adverse selection** (meaning that those who are likely to have claims are also those who are most likely to seek insurance) and (2) to minimize the administrative costs associated with group insurance. Because of group underwriting, insurers can provide coverage through group insurance arrangements at a lower cost than through individual insurance.

Underwriting considerations unique to specific types of group insurance are discussed throughout the book where appropriate. However, there are certain general underwriting considerations applicable to all or most types of group insurance that affect the contractual provisions in group insurance contracts as well as insurance company practices pertaining to group insurance. These general underwriting considerations include

- the reason for the group's existence
- the stability of the group
- the persistency of the group
- the method of determining benefits
- the provisions for determining eligibility
- the source and method of premium payments
- the administrative aspects of the group insurance plan
- the prior experience of the plan
- the size of the group
- the composition of the group
- the industry represented by the group
- the geographic location of the group

Reason for Existence

Probably the most fundamental group underwriting principle is that a group must have been formed for some purpose other than to obtain insurance for its members. Such a rule protects the group insurance company against the adverse selection that would likely exist if poor risks were to form a group just to obtain insurance. Groups based on an employer-employee relationship present little difficulty with respect to this rule.

Stability

probationary period

Ideally, an underwriter would like to see a reasonable but steady flow of persons through a group. A higher-than-average turnover rate among employees results in increased administrative costs for the insurance company as well as for the employer. If high turnover exists among recently hired employees, the resulting costs can be minimized by requiring employees to wait a certain period before becoming eligible for coverage. However, such a **probationary period** leaves newly hired employees without protection if their previous group insurance coverage has terminated.

mortality

morbidity

A lower-than-average turnover rate often results in an increasing average age for the members of a group. To the extent that a plan's premium is a function of the **mortality** (death rates) and the **morbidity** (sickness and disability rates) of the group, such an increase in average age results in an increasing premium rate for that group insurance plan. This high rate may cause the better risks to drop out of a plan, if they are required to contribute to its cost, and may ultimately force the employer to terminate the plan because of its increasing cost.

Persistency

persistency

An underwriter is concerned with **persistency**, which is the length of time a group insurance contract will remain on the insurance company's books. Initial acquisition expenses of an insurer frequently cause an insurance company to lose money during the first year the group insurance contract is in force. These acquisition expenses include costs associated with marketing and the enrollment of members in a group insurance plan. Only through the renewal of the contract for a period of time, often 3 or 4 years, can insurers recover these acquisition expenses. For this reason, insurers often avoid firms with a history of frequently changing insurance carriers or those with financial difficulty.

Determination of Benefits

In most types of group insurance, the underwriter requires that benefit levels for individual members of the group be determined in a manner that precludes individual selection by either the employees or the employer. If employees choose their own benefit levels, there would be a tendency for the poorer risks to select greater amounts of coverage than the better risks would select. Adverse selection could also exist if the employer was able to choose a separate benefit level for each individual member of the group. As a result, this underwriting rule has led to benefit levels that are either identical for all employees or determined by a benefit formula that bases benefit levels on some specific criterion, such as salary or position which may still have rules for determining the maximum benefit that may be provided for any individual employee without evidence of insurability. Additional amounts of coverage either are not provided or are subject to individual evidence of insurability.

The general level of benefits for all employees is also of interest to the underwriter. For example, benefit levels that are too high may encourage overutilization and malingering, and benefit levels that are unusually low may lead to low participation if a plan is voluntary or requires a partial contribution.

Determination of Eligibility

eligibility provision

The underwriter is also concerned with the **eligibility provision** in a group insurance plan. This provision determines who will be eligible for coverage under the plan and when coverage will begin. As previously mentioned, many group insurance plans contain probationary periods that must be satisfied before an employee is eligible for coverage. In addition to minimizing administrative costs, a probationary period also discourages persons with known medical conditions from seeking employment primarily because of a firm's group insurance benefits. This latter problem can also be addressed in other ways—for example, by including a requirement that an employee be actively at work before coverage commences or by limiting coverage for preexisting conditions to the extent allowed by federal and state laws.

Most group insurance plans limit eligibility to regular full-time employees because the coverage of part-time, seasonal, and temporary employees may not be desirable from an underwriting standpoint. In addition to having a high turnover rate, these employees are more likely to seek employment primarily to obtain group insurance benefits.

Premium Payments

contributory plan

noncontributory plan

Group insurance plans may be contributory or noncontributory. Members of a **contributory plan** pay a portion, or possibly all, of the cost of their own coverage. When employees pay the entire portion, these plans are often referred to as fully contributory, employee-pay-all, or voluntary plans. Under a **noncontributory plan**, the policyowner pays the entire cost, and all eligible employees are usually covered. This type of plan is desirable from an underwriting standpoint because it minimizes adverse selection. In fact, most insurance companies and the laws of many states require 100 percent participation of eligible employees under noncontributory plans.

Most state laws prohibit an employer from requiring an employee to participate in a contributory plan. The insurance company is therefore faced with the possibility of adverse selection because those who elect coverage tend to be the poorer risks. From a practical standpoint, 100 percent participation in a contributory plan is unrealistic because for many reasons some employees neither desire nor need the coverage provided under the plan. However, insurance companies require that a minimum percentage of the eligible members of a group elect to participate before the contract is issued. A common requirement is 75 percent, although a lower percentage is often acceptable for large groups and a higher percentage may be required for small groups.

Administration

To minimize the expenses associated with group insurance, the underwriter often requires that the employer carry out certain administrative functions, either with its own employees or through outsourcing. These commonly include communicating the plan to employees, handling enrollment procedures, collecting employee contributions on a payroll-deduction basis, and keeping certain types of records. In addition, employers are often involved in the claims process. Underwriters are concerned not only with the employer's ability to carry out these functions but also with the employer's willingness to cooperate with the insurance company.

Size

The size of a group is a significant factor in the underwriting process. With large groups, historically there is prior group insurance experience insurers can use as a factor in determining the premium, and considerable flexibility also exists with respect to both rating and plan design.

For small groups, coverage is sometimes being written for the first time. Administrative expenses tend to be high in relation to the premium. There is also an increased possibility that the owner or major stockholder might be interested in coverage primarily because he or she or a family member has a medical problem that will result in large immediate claims. As a result, contractual provisions and the benefits available are quite standardized in order to control administrative costs. Furthermore, because past experience for small groups is not necessarily a realistic indicator of future experience, most insurance companies use pooled rates under which they apply a uniform rate to all groups that have a specific coverage.

The Affordable Care Act definition of "small group" as a group up to 100 employees has been repealed by President Obama. The individual states will determine the maximum size of a small group independently.

RATE MAKING

One of the least understood aspects of group insurance is the underwriting and pricing process. In the simplest sense, group insurance pricing is no different from pricing in other industries. The insurance company must generate enough revenue to cover its costs (claims and expenses) and to contribute to the net worth of the company. However, this similarity is often overlooked because of the unique terminology that is associated with insurance pricing and because the price of a group insurance product is initially determined on the basis of expected, but uncertain, future events rather than on current tangible cost estimates. In addition, a group insurance plan may be subject to experience rating so that the final price to the consumer can be determined only after the coverage period has ended.

rate making

 Rate making consists of two distinct steps:

rate

premium

- the determination of a unit price, referred to as a **rate** or *premium rate*, for each unit of benefit (such as each $1,000 of life insurance)
- the determination of the total price, or **premium**, that the policyowner will pay for the entire amount of coverage purchased

manual rating

experience rating

 The mechanics of rate making differ, depending on whether a particular group is subject to manual rating or experience rating. When **manual rating** is used, the premium rate is determined independently of a particular group's claims; when **experience rating** is used, the past claims experience of a group is considered in determining future premiums for the group and/or in adjusting past premiums after a policy period has ended.

adequate rates

The major objective of rate making for all types of group insurance is to develop premium rates that are both adequate and equitable. **Adequate rates** must be sufficient enough to cover both incurred claims and expenses and to generate the desired profit or contribution to the insurance company's surplus. Obviously, the success and solvency of any group insurance operation is contingent on the long-term adequacy of premium rates. Several states, concerned about the solvency of insurance companies, have laws and regulations regarding the adequacy of rates.

equitable rates

Equitable rates require that each group pay a premium that reflects the expected cost of providing coverage to that group. Again, practical considerations and state regulations act to encourage equity. Overpricing group coverage for some segments of the market results in lost business; underpricing for other segments attracts unprofitable business. Most states also have laws and regulations that try to encourage equity by prohibiting unfair discrimination in insurance rates. The objective of equity has resulted in group insurance rates that differ because of such factors as the age, gender, and income distribution of a group's members as well as the size of a group, its geographic location, its occupational hazards, and its claims experience. As discussed later, the factors that are considered vary with the type of group insurance coverage.

The role of competition in the rate making process should not be overlooked. If there is little or no competition, an insurer may develop rates to generate a higher-than-usual profit. In a very competitive market, rates may need to be lower than justified to obtain and retain business.

MANUAL RATING

In the manual-rating process, insurance companies establish premium rates only for broad classes of group insurance business, and they do not consider the past claims experience of a particular group when determining that group's rates. However, claims experience is not entirely ignored, because insurers use the aggregate claims experience for a class of business to determine the premium rates for that class.

Insurers use manual rating with small groups for which no credible individual loss experience is available. This lack of credibility exists because the group's size makes it impossible to determine whether other-than-average loss experience is due to random chance or is truly reflective of the group. Manual rating is also frequently used to determine the initial premiums for groups that are subject to experience rating, particularly when a group's past experience is unobtainable or when a group is being written for the first time. In addition, experience rating typically uses a weighting of manual rates and the actual experience of a group to determine the premium. (Rates for very large groups may be based solely on a group's own experience.)

Rating Basis

rating basis

Prior to the actual calculation of manual premium rates, insurers develop a basis on which the rates are determined. This **rating basis** involves a decision regarding (1) what benefit unit to use, (2) the extent to which rates are refined by factors affecting claims, and (3) the frequency with which premiums are paid.

Benefit Unit

Subject to certain adjustments, insurers calculate the premium for a group by multiplying the premium rate by the number of benefit units provided. Although variations do occasionally exist, the benefit units predominantly used for the most common types of group insurance are shown in the following table.

Table 14-1 Benefit Units	
Type of Group Insurance	**Benefit Unit**
Term life (including accidental death and dismemberment)	Each $1,000 of death benefit
Short-term disability income	Each $10 of weekly income
Long-term disability income	Each $100 of monthly income
Medical expense (including dental)	Each employee and each category of dependents

Factors Affecting Pricing

Rates reflect those factors that result in different claims experience for different groups. Although there are variations among insurance companies, the following discussion indicates the factors used by most insurance companies to determine rates for most types of group insurance plans. Medical expense factors will be discussed in more detail in a later section.

Gender. Gender of insured persons is taken into account for determining rates for all the types of insurance mentioned in the previous paragraph.

Age. Age is also used as a rating factor for group coverage although dental insurance rates usually do not take age into consideration.

Geographic Location. At one time, geographic location was a rating factor for medical expense insurance and dental insurance only. However, an increasing number of insurance companies use geographic variations for determining life insurance and disability income insurance rates. For these latter types of insurance, rates may not be determined separately for a wide variety of locations. Instead, the insurance company may have only two or three rate schedules, with each schedule applying to several different geographic locations on the basis of past experience.

Occupation. Occupation is virtually always reflected in life insurance rates, accidental death and dismemberment, and disability income insurance rates. It may also be reflected in dental insurance rates. Some companies ignore it as a rating factor but may not write coverage when certain occupations are involved.

Income. At one time, the income level of group members was commonly used as a factor in establishing disability income, medical expense, and dental insurance rates. Currently, income level is still a factor in determining dental insurance premiums, but it is more likely to be an underwriting consideration only in disability income and medical expense insurance.

Size. The size of a group also affects rates because the proportion of the premium needed for expenses decreases as the size of a group increases. All manual premium rates are based on an assumption that the size of a group falls within a certain range. If the size of a group varies from this range, insurers make an appropriate rate adjustment to reflect this differential. In addition, many insurers reserve the right to rerate a group during the period of the contract or cancel the contract at renewal if the group changes in size by a certain percentage. This is particularly important in an era of downsizing and mergers.

The small group definition of medical expense groups up to 100 employees established by the Affordable Care Act was repealed at the federal level in October of 2015. The states now have independent authority to define a small medical expense group as a group with up to 50 employees or up to 100 employees.

Time. A final factor considered in the calculation of rates is the length of time for which the rates will be in effect. This is a concern primarily for coverages that involve medical and dental claims, which over time are expected to increase in severity because of inflation. In inflationary times, monthly rates that are guaranteed for three months can be lower than those guaranteed for one year.

Frequency of Premium Payment Period

Because employers usually pay group insurance premiums monthly, insurers generally determine rates for this period. When premiums can be paid less frequently (such as annually), they are usually slightly lower than the sum of the monthly premiums for the same period of coverage. This results from the extra investment earnings the insurer can get by collecting premiums earlier. In addition, the annual expense of processing premiums is lower if employers pay them less frequently.

Calculation of Manual Premium Rates

manual premium rate

final premium rate

Manual rating involves the calculation of the **manual premium rate** (also called *tabular rate*), which is quoted in an insurance company's rate book. The manual rate is applied to a specific group insurance case in order to determine a **final premium rate** (sometimes called an *average premium rate*) that is then multiplied by the number of benefit units to obtain a premium for the group.

There are three manual-rating methods. However, if identical assumptions are used, each method should result in approximately the same premium for any given group. The first method determines separate manual rates for groups with certain characteristics that an insurance company feels affect claims experience. A second approach establishes a single "standard manual rate" that is adjusted in the premium-calculation process to compensate for any characteristics that deviate from those of the standard group. A third method merely combines the first two approaches and considers some factors in determining the manual rate and other factors in determining the final premium rate.

net premium rate

The first step in the calculation of manual premium rates is the determination of the **net premium rate**, which is the amount necessary to support the cost of expected claims. For any given classification, the net premium rate is generally calculated by multiplying the probability (frequency) of a claim occurring by the expected amount (severity) of the claim. For example, if the probability that an employee aged 50 will die in the next month is .0005, then the net monthly premium for each $1,000 of coverage is .0005 × $1,000, or $.50. Because insurers collect premiums before claims are paid, they adjust this figure downward for anticipated interest earnings on these funds.

In general, insurance companies that write a large volume of any given type of group insurance rely on their own experience in determining the frequency and severity of future claims. Insurance companies that do not have enough past data for reliable future projections can turn to many sources for useful statistics. Probably the major source is the Society of Actuaries, which regularly collects and publishes aggregate data on the group insurance business that is written by a number of large group insurance companies. Other sources of information are industry trade organizations and various agencies of the federal government.

risk charge

The second step in the calculation of manual premium rates is the adjustment of the net premium rates for expenses, a risk charge, and a contribution to surplus. Expenses include commissions, premium taxes, claims settlement costs, and other costs associated with the acquisition and servicing of group insurance business. The **risk charge** represents a contribution to the insurance company's contingency reserve as a cushion against unanticipated and catastrophic amounts of claims. The contribution to surplus or net worth represents the profit margin of the insurance company. Although mutual companies are legally non-profit, they, like stock insurance companies, require a contribution to net worth that is a source of financing for future growth.

From the standpoint of equity, the adjustment of the net premium rate is complex. Some factors, such as premium taxes and commissions, vary with the premium charge. However, the size of a group does not affect the premium tax rate, whereas the commission rate generally decreases as the size of a group increases. To a large degree, the expenses of settling claims vary with the number, and not the size, of claims. It costs just as much administratively to pay a $10,000 claim under a group life insurance plan as it does to pay a $100,000 claim. Certain other costs also tend to be fixed regardless of the size of a group. For simplicity, some insurance companies adjust or load their net premium rates by a constant percentage. However, other insurance companies consider the different patterns of expenses by using a percentage plus a constant charge. For example, if the net premium rate is $.60, this might be increased by 20 percent plus $.10 to arrive at a manual premium rate of $.82 (that is, $.60 × 1.2 + $.10). Because neither approach adequately accounts for the difference in expenses as a result of a group's size, another adjustment based on the size of the group is made in the calculation of the final premium rate.

Calculation of Premiums

Probably the best way to explain the actual calculation of group insurance premiums is through examples. The following analysis begins with group term life insurance, then discusses how the structure of manual premium rates and the premium calculation process differ for certain other types of group insurance.

Group Term Life Insurance

The mechanics of calculating a final premium rate and the premium for a particular group vary among insurance companies because of the differences in methods of preparing manual premium rates and the process by which insurers make adjustments to these rates.

The following example begins with the table below, which is an abbreviated version of a set of rates on a monthly basis per $1,000 of coverage at selected ages.

Table 14-2 Term Insurance Rates		
Age at Nearest Birthday	**Male Rate**	**Female Rate**
20	$0.16	$0.10
25	0.18	0.11
30	0.21	0.12
35	0.24	0.15
40	0.37	0.21
45	0.48	0.30
50	0.81	0.48
55	1.24	0.75
60	1.87	1.12
65	2.83	1.70
70	4.35	2.52

These rates are loaded for expenses, and they assume that the coverage contains a waiver-of-premium provision on disabled lives, accidental death and dismemberment coverage, and a conversion privilege so the sample rates are higher than if none of these additional benefits were included. When an employee converts coverage to an individual policy, a charge is assessed against the group insurance business of an insurance company to reflect the increased death claims that result from adverse selection on conversions. The amount of this assessment (commonly $50 to $75 per $1,000 of converted insurance) is transferred to the individual insurance department of the company to compensate it for having to write the converted business at too low a rate.

The premium-calculation process starts with the determination of an "unadjusted cost," based on a census of the covered employees and the manual rates.

The unadjusted cost is calculated as the total of the

> # of employees in each age bracket
>
> x the amount of coverage in $1,000s
>
> x the applicable male or female rate

The next step is to reduce the sum of the total unadjusted cost by a percentage based on the volume of a group insurance plan as determined by its monthly premium. This reduction results from the fact that the expenses associated with a group insurance plan decrease on a percentage basis as the size (premium volume) of the plan increases.

An example of the initial monthly premium for a group of 230 employees with $25,000 of life insurance each could be calculated as follows:

Unadjusted cost	$1,725.00
Minus expense reduction (7 percent)	−120.75
Adjusted monthly premium	$1,604.25

The initial monthly premium is also used to calculate the final monthly premium rate per $1,000 of protection for the group:

$$\frac{\text{Monthly premium}}{\text{rate per thousand}} = \frac{\text{Adjusted monthly premium}}{\text{Total volume (in thousands)*}}$$

$$= \frac{\$1,604.25}{(230** \times \$25,000***)/\$1,000}$$

$$= \frac{\$1,604.25}{5750}$$

$$= \$0.28$$

> *(# of employees x face amount) / $1,000
> ** number of employees
> *** amount of life insurance each employee has

This final monthly premium rate (usually rounded to either the nearest cent or one-tenth of a cent) is used throughout the first policy year and is multiplied each month by the amount of insurance in force to calculate the monthly premium due. Insurance companies may charge adjusted higher rates for employers in industries that they considered hazardous. Adjustments to the final monthly premium rate because of changes in the makeup of employees by age or gender are not made until the beginning of the next policy year as part of the renewal process. Insurance companies generally guarantee the initial rate for at least one year, assuming that there is no change in the benefit structure of the plan. However, 2- and 3-year rate guarantees are not unusual.

Variations for Large Groups. Some insurance companies do not incorporate a charge for a waiver of premium or accidental death and dismemberment coverage into their manual rates. Rather, an extra charge, which usually differs by industry, is added for this coverage. Also, some companies use (and are required to use in a few states) manual rates that vary by age but not gender. These unisex rate tables are based on assumptions about the ratio of males to females in the group. However, insurers usually make an adjustment the premium-calculation process if the actual group ratio differs from this assumption.

Variations for Small Groups. The manual-rating process for small groups differs from that of large groups in several ways. In general, insurers band the manual rates by age, typically in 5-year intervals. The following table is an example of one such monthly rate table for each $1,000 of coverage.

Table 14-3 Banded Rates		
Age at Nearest Birthday	Male Rate	Female Rate
Under 30	$0.24	$0.10
30–34	0.24	0.13
35–39	0.25	0.15
40–44	0.36	0.20
45–49	0.58	0.36
50–54	0.91	0.54
55–59	1.55	0.79
60–64	1.93	1.02
65–69	3.30	1.81
70 and over	6.80	3.23

An unadjusted cost is developed based on a census of the employees by age and by gender unless unisex rates are used. Because the manual rates are loaded for most expenses, and because the groups written tend to be reasonably close in size, typically no adjustment for size is made. However, to compensate for the expenses of periodic billings, most insurance companies apply a flat fee to all groups, commonly between $10 and $20 per billing. Some companies do not levy this charge if the premium is paid annually. To reflect the administrative costs associated with record keeping, some insurance companies also levy a modest one-time expense charge when a plan adds coverage for a new employee.

Accidental Death and Dismemberment Insurance

Accidental death and dismemberment insurance is usually not written as a separate coverage unless coverage is voluntary. Rather, it is added by an endorsement to a group term insurance contract. A single manual rate typically applies to all employees regardless of age or gender, but it varies depending on whether coverage is written (1) for nonoccupational accidents only or (2) on a 24-hour basis for both nonoccupational and occupational accidents. The rate for nonoccupational coverage generally does not vary by industry and ranges from $.02 to $.05 per $1,000 of principal sum per month. However, the rate for coverage on a 24-hour basis does vary by industry, and although it falls within this same range for low-risk industries, it may be several times higher for hazardous ones. Some companies calculate a separate cost for the accidental death and dismemberment coverage and add it to the charge for the group term life insurance. However, most employers purchase accidental death and dismemberment coverage. As a result, other insurance companies incorporate the cost into the manual rates for group term life insurance, making the principal sum equal to the amount of life insurance protection purchased, and an additional charge is levied only if the employer desires a higher level of accidental death and dismemberment coverage.

Dependent Life Insurance

Dependent life insurance may be added as additional coverage to a group life insurance contract that provides protection for employees. Because dependent life insurance coverage is usually a modest fixed amount (such as $2,000 on the spouse and $1,000 on each child) that generates a relatively small additional premium, insurers tend to use a very simplified rate structure. However, several variations do exist. Some insurance companies have a single flat rate, independent of the type or number of dependents, for each employee who has dependent coverage. Other companies have two separate flat rates: one for the spouse's coverage and the other for children's coverage. The rate for the children's coverage is a family rate regardless of the number of children, and it is based upon an average-sized family.

Flat rates are based on the assumption that the group has an average age mix of employees. If the group of employees is older than average, the flat rate for dependent coverage may be adjusted (particularly when it applies to spouses) to reflect the likelihood that the dependents are also above average in age when compared to the dependents of most other groups. A flat rate is commonly used when employees pay the entire cost of dependent coverage. The uniform charge is easy to communicate to employees, and it simplifies the payroll-deduction process for the employer.

Some insurance companies also use a rate for dependent coverage that varies with the employee's age, thereby assuming that older employees have older dependents. Basing the rate on the employee's age may seem illogical, but it is administratively simpler and less expensive than having to determine the ages of dependents. A single variable rate may apply to the total family coverage for the spouse and all children, or it may apply only to the spouse. In this latter case, a flat rate is generally used if coverage for children is also provided.

It is becoming less common to see dependent life insurance added to the basic group life coverage for an employee. Instead, this coverage is more frequently being written as an employee-pay-all voluntary benefit, with higher amounts of coverage available.

Short-Term Disability Income Insurance

In addition to varying by age, by gender, and possibly by geographic location, manual rates for short-term disability income insurance also differ according to (1) the maximum benefit period, (2) the length of the waiting period, and (3) the writing of coverage either on a 24-hour basis or only for nonoccupational disabilities.

Some insurance companies (particularly those for small groups) have only a single standard short-term disability income plan that they sell, and therefore they only need a single manual rate table. On the other hand, some companies allow the employer to exercise a degree of flexibility in designing the plan. Rather than make adjustments to a single rate table, these companies usually have several rate tables. These tables vary by such factors as maximum benefit period (such as 13 or 26 weeks) and waiting period (such as 7 days for all disabilities or 7 days for illnesses and no waiting period for injuries). If they allow any other variations, they make appropriate rate adjustments.

Insurers adjust for the nature of the industry the group represents. Ignoring the occupational injuries and diseases that are covered under workers' compensation, a few occupations are still characterized by higher-than-average disability income claims. As an alternative to a rate adjustment, some insurance companies have underwriting standards that prohibit the writing of coverage for these groups.

In contrast to group life insurance rates, which are lower for females than for males, disability income rates are higher for females. Ignoring pregnancy-related disabilities, the claims of females at younger ages still somewhat exceed those of males. However, because male and female claims are comparable at older ages, the rates for later years seldom vary. The following table, which illustrates one insurance company's monthly manual rates per $10 of weekly benefit for 26 weeks following a 7-day waiting period, shows how this rate differential is even more pronounced at younger ages if maternity coverage is included.

Table 14-4
Disability Income Rates

Age	Male	Female
Under 30	$0.48	$1.25
30–34	0.52	1.25
35–39	0.56	1.25
40–44	0.72	1.21
45–49	0.81	1.21
50–54	1.01	1.31
55–59	1.21	1.53
60–64	1.61	1.61
65–69	2.01	2.01
70 and over	2.16	2.16

In the past, it was common for short-term disability income rates to be expressed on the basis of each $10 of weekly benefit. This is probably still the norm, but some insurance companies are now expressing their rates in terms of a higher weekly benefit, such as $50 or $100.

Long-Term Disability Income Insurance

Like short-term disability income rates, the manual rates for long-term coverage vary by age, gender, the length of the benefit period, the length of the waiting period, and possibly geographic location. In addition, the manual rates reflect the fact that benefits are coordinated with Social Security and certain other disability income benefits for which an employee might be eligible. To the extent that insurers allow variations in the coordination provision that was assumed in developing the manual rates, they adjust the premium-calculation process. As is also the case with short-term rates, insurers might adjust for certain occupations.

Unlike short-term disability income rates, which are commonly expressed on the basis of a weekly benefit, long-term rates are typically expressed on the basis of a monthly benefit, usually per $100. Unlike the coverages previously discussed, long-term disability claims fluctuate with general economic conditions. Consequently, insurance companies review and possibly revise their manual rates (and/or their underwriting standards) as economic conditions change.

The period for which insurers guarantee rates may vary from one to 3 years, depending on the industry in which the employees work.

Medical Expense Insurance

The Affordable Care Act changed the underwriting and rating practices for medical expense coverage in the United States. Medical expense plans are guaranteed issue with no pre-existing condition exclusions. In general, the only factors which may be considered for rating purposes are age, geographic location, tobacco use, and family size. The rating for medical expense plans is also now based on community rates.

community rating

With **community rating** each plan uses the same rate structure for all members, regardless of their past or potential loss experience and regardless of whether the plan writes coverage on an individual or a group basis. Usually, the only variations in the rate structure result from variations in coverage, whether it is for an individual, a couple without children, or a family. The philosophy behind the community-rating approach is that coverage should be available to the widest range of persons possible at an affordable cost. Charging lower premium rates to segments of the community with better-than-average loss experience is thought to result in higher and possibly unaffordable premium rates for other segments of the community.

Geographic location is a variable in rates because of the significant differences in medical costs across the country. Each county (or other geographic subdivision) where coverage is written is assigned a factor that is based on the cost of health care in that location compared with the "average" cost that is assumed in the manual rates. For example, if

Seattle were 20 percent higher than average, it would have a factor of 1.2. If all of a firm's employees are there, the manual rates for that group is multiplied by a location factor of 1.2 in the process of determining the group's premium. If employees are in several locations, a composite factor is calculated.

Dental Insurance

The rating of dental insurance has its own unique rating criteria. Most insurance companies do not vary their manual rates by the ages of group members. Instead, an adjustment is often made for the income levels of employees, because higher-paid persons are much more likely to obtain dental care. This adjustment is usually in the form of a percentage based on the extent to which the portion of employees with incomes higher than some figure (such as $30,000) exceeds the proportion of such employees that is assumed in the manual rates. There is also an adjustment for certain occupations (such as salespeople or teachers) that use dental services more frequently than average. Finally, insurers usually increase the manual rates when a plan is new (or expands benefits) if the employees have been informed of the change beforehand. Under these circumstances, there is a tendency to postpone needed dental care until the new plan is in effect increasing the adverse selection potential.

EXPERIENCE RATING

With experience rating, an insurance company considers a group's claims experience, either at the issue date or at the end of a policy period, when determining the premium rate for that group. When applied prospectively (that is, to future periods), experience rating is used to determine (1) adjustments in renewal premiums (either upward or downward) for those groups whose claims experience has deviated from what was expected and (2) initial premiums for large groups that change insurance carriers.

dividend

retrospective rate credit

In addition to determining the premium rate for the next policy period (usually 12 months), experience rating is also used to compute the refund payable to the policyowner (usually the employer) for those groups that had better claims experience than anticipated. Mutual insurance companies refer to this refund as a **dividend**, and stock insurance companies call it a **retrospective rate credit** or *premium refund*. Under some experience-rating arrangements, the premium at the end of a policy period may also be retroactively adjusted upward if a group's claims experience has been worse than anticipated, and an additional premium is charged. These arrangements are not very common.

Rationale for Experience Rating

One argument in favor of experience rating is that it achieves the ultimate degree of premium equity among policyowners. Even though manual rating also results in equity because it considers the obvious factors that affect claims, it is impossible to measure and make adjustments in the manual rates for such factors as lifestyle, working conditions, and morale, all of which contribute to the level of claims experience. Experience rating is also the most cost-effective way to reflect the general health of a group in the premium that is charged.

Probably the major reason for using experience rating is the competition that exists in the group insurance marketplace. If an insurance company were to use identical rates for all groups regardless of their experience, the employers with good experience would soon seek out insurance companies that offered lower rates, or they would turn to self-funding as a way to reduce costs. The insurance company that did not consider claims experience would therefore be left with only the poor risks. Experience rating allows an insurance company to acquire and retain the better cases (from a claims-experience standpoint) and to determine an appropriate premium for the groups that have worse-than-average claims experience.

Stop-Loss Limit

stop-loss limit

The **stop-loss limit**—the maximum amount of any claim that is charged to the group in the experience-rating calculation. Its purpose is to minimize the effect of any chance fluctuations that might occur from year to year because of catastrophic losses within the group. These chance fluctuations tend to become relatively smaller as the size of a group increases, and insurers may not use a stop-loss limit for very large groups.

The stop-loss limit in medical expense insurance is usually expressed as a dollar amount per claim, and the actual figure is subject to negotiation between the policyowner and the insurance company. In this illustration, $250,000 is used. Therefore, if a claim of $400,000 is incurred because of a premature birth, only the first $250,000 of the claim will be used in the experience-rating calculation.

Obviously, a charge must be made somewhere for incorporating a stop-loss provision into an experience-rating contract, because the insurance company is obligated to pay any excess amount over the stop-loss limit. In effect, this charge for stop-loss coverage can be viewed as a manual-rate charge for losses in excess of some limit, with only those losses below the limit subject to experience rating.

Incurred Claims

experience period

incurred claims

The concept of incurred claims, which are those claims attributable to the recently ended period of coverage that was subject to experience rating (that is, the **experience period**) is another factor in experience rating. The incurred claims are those claims that were paid during the experience period. Unfortunately, it is not that simple. Some of the claims that were paid during the experience period may actually be attributable to previous periods and must be subtracted from the incurred claims. In addition, other claims that are attributable to the experience period may not have been reported or may be in the course of settlement. However, insurance companies need to estimate their value. Therefore, an appropriate determination of **incurred claims** is as follows:

$$
\begin{aligned}
\text{incurred claims} \quad = \quad & \text{claims paid during the experience period} \\
- \quad & \text{claims paid during the experience period but incurred} \\
& \text{during previous periods} \\
+ \quad & \text{estimate of claims incurred during the experience period} \\
& \text{but to be paid in future periods}
\end{aligned}
$$

or

$$
\begin{aligned}
\text{incurred claims} \quad = \quad & \text{paid claims} \\
+ \quad & \text{change in claim reserve}
\end{aligned}
$$

claim reserve

This **claim reserve**, which is often referred to as the *open-and-unreported claim reserve,* represents an estimate by the insurance company for (1) claims that have been approved but not yet paid, (2) claims that are in the course of settlement, and (3) claims that have been incurred but not yet reported (often referred to as *IBNR*). In addition, when coverage is experience rated, an additional amount is added to this estimate for any claims that have been incurred, reported, and approved but are not yet payable. Essentially, these claims can arise from claims that will continue beyond the experience period.

In general, the claim reserve is based either on a percentage of the annual premium (before experience rating) or on a percentage of claims paid. The first approach is most common for small groups, and the latter approach tends to be used for large groups.

Expected Claims

expected claims

The amount of **expected claims** represents the portion of the premiums paid that the insurance company has anticipated would be necessary to pay claims during the experience period. This amount may have been derived either from average experience as in manual rating or from the past experience of the particular group.

Credibility

credibility

The **credibility** factor, which can vary from zero to one, is a statistical measure of the reliability of the group's past experience. In other words, it is a measure of the probability that the group's actual experience is a true reflection of the group and is not the result of chance occurrences. In general, the larger the group is, the greater the reliability of estimates is (because of the law of large numbers).

Insurers may adjust these factors to reflect any characteristics of either the group or the insurance contract that deviate from the norm. For example, an older group of employees might be assigned a higher credibility factor than a younger group whose claims are more likely to be due to random fluctuations. In addition, the level of any stop-loss limit may have an effect. As the stop-loss charge is increased (meaning the stop-loss limit is lowered), the credibility that can be assigned to the remaining claims below the stop-loss limit also increases.

Retention

retention

The **retention** in a group insurance contract is usually defined as the excess of premiums paid over claims payments and dividends. It consists of charges for (1) the stop-loss coverage, (2) expenses (commissions, premium taxes, and administrative expenses), (3) a risk charge, and (4) a contribution to the insurance company's surplus. For large groups, insurers calculate each item in the retention separately, based on the group's actual experience. For small groups, the insurance company usually applies a formula based on insurance company averages. This formula varies according to the size of a group and the type of coverage involved; most often it is either a percentage of the claims charge or a flat charge plus a percentage of the claims charge.

Renewal Rating

Insurers often use experience rating to develop future premiums for group insurance cases based on the past experience of the group. In most cases, the experience-rating period is 3 to 5 years so cumulative premiums and charges for this period are used. A conservative (that is, lower) credibility factor is normally applied. Because a premium is being developed for the future, it is also necessary to adjust past claims and the retention, not only to reflect current cost levels but also to include expected trends for the next year. Adjustments must also be made to account for any changes in the coverage.

MEDICAL LOSS RATIO REQUIREMENTS

medical loss ratio (MLR)

The term **medical loss ratio (MLR)** refers to the percentage of premium dollars that an insurance company spends on providing health care and improving the quality of care versus how much is spent on administrative and overhead costs. The Affordable Care Act requires insurance companies and health plans to spend at least 85 percent of premium on medical care services for large groups and at least 80 percent of premium on medical care services for small groups and individual coverage. Medicare has a medical loss ratio for its Medicare Advantage plans of 85 percent. If the medical loss ratio level is not met, the insurer will have to rebate the difference to the purchaser. The medical loss ratio requires medical expense premiums to be set at a higher accuracy level.

CHAPTER REVIEW

Key Terms and Concepts

underwriting	mortality
evidence of insurability	morbidity
adverse selection	persistency
probationary period	eligibility provisions
community rating	contributory plans

noncontributory plans
rate making
rate premium
manual rating
experience rating
adequate rates
equitable rates
rating basis
manual premium rate
final premium rate
net premium rate
risk charge

dividend
retrospective rate credit
stop-loss limit
experience period
incurred claims
claim reserve
expected claims
credibility
claims charge
retention
medical loss ratio (MLR)

Review Questions

Review questions are based on the learning objectives in this chapter. For example, a [3] at the end of a questions means that the question is based on learning objective 3. If there are multiple objectives, they are all listed.

1. Why are group insurance underwriters concerned about the purpose for which a group was formed? [1]

2. What is adverse selection? [1]

3. What is the underwriting rationale for not allowing each member of a group to elect his or her own level of benefits? [1]

4. Explain why eligibility requirements for coverage are of concern to the group insurance underwriter. [1]

5. Define the following: [1]

    a. underwriting

    b. mortality

    c. morbidity

    d. probationary period

    e. persistency

6. From an underwriting standpoint, why is it desirable for a group insurance plan to be noncontributory? [1]

7. The major objective of rate making is to develop rates that are adequate and equitable. What is meant by adequate and equitable? [2]

8. One decision that an insurer must make in determining manual rates is to select the benefit unit to use. How do insurers usually measure the benefit unit for each of the following types of group insurance? [3]

    a. term life

    b. short-term disability income

    c. long-term disability income

9. In addition to determining the benefit unit, what decisions must an insurer make in developing a basis on which it will establish manual premium rates? [3]

10. Describe the steps in the calculation of manual premium rates. [2]

11. Explain how the manual-rating process for group term life insurance may vary for [2]

    a. large groups

    b. small groups

12. How do insurers express rates for dependent life insurance coverage? [3]

13. What group characteristics do insurers usually consider to determine disability income rates versus group term life insurance rates [3]?

14. What is community rating? [3]

15. What are the factors that insurers usually consider in determining dental insurance rates for a group? [3]

16. What are the situations in which an insurer may use experience rating? [4]

17. What is the rationale for the use of experience rating? [4]

18. What is the purpose of a stop-loss limit? [4]

19. Why do paid claims differ from incurred claims? [4]

20. How does the credibility factor for a group vary by the size of the group and the characteristics of the insurance coverage? [4]

21. How do insurers usually calculate the retention charge for a large group? For a small group? [4]

22. What is a medical loss ratio and how does the Affordable Care Act apply it? [5]

Review Question Answers

1. Probably the most fundamental group underwriting principle is that a group must have been formed for some purpose other than to obtain insurance for its members. Such a rule protects the group insurance company against the adverse selection that would likely exist if poor risks were to form a group just to obtain insurance.

2. Adverse selection is the concept that those who are likely to have claims are also those who are most likely to seek insurance.

3. If employees could choose their own benefit levels, there would be a tendency for the poorer risks to select greater amounts of coverage than the better risks would select. Adverse selection could also exist if the employer could choose a separate benefit level for each individual member of the group. As a result, benefit levels are either identical for all employees or determined by a benefit formula that bases benefit levels on some specific criterion, such as salary or position.

4. An eligibility provision determines who will be eligible for coverage under the plan and when coverage will begin. Many group insurance plans contain probationary period that must be satisfied before an employee is eligible for coverage. Such a period discourages persons with known medical conditions from seeking employment primarily because of a firm's group insurance benefits.

5. a. Underwriting is the process of evaluating an insurance applicant, making decisions about the applicant's acceptability and determining the appropriate price for the coverage.

   b. Mortality is the measure of human death rates.

   c. Morbidity is the measure of sickness and disability rates.

   d. The probationary period is the waiting period for employees before becoming eligible for coverage.

   e. Persistency is the length of time a group insurance contract remains on the insurance company's books.

6. Under a noncontributory plan, the policyowner pays the entire cost. Because all eligible employees are usually covered, this type of plan is desirable from an underwriting standpoint because it minimizes adverse selection.

7. Adequate rates must be sufficient to cover both incurred claims and expenses and to generate the desired profit or contribution to the insurance company's surplus.

    Equitable rates require that each group pay a premium that reflects the expected cost of providing coverage to that group.

8. a. For term life insurance, including accidental death and dismemberment, the usual benefit unit is each $1,000 of death benefit.

    b. For short-term disability income insurance, the usual benefit unit is each $10 of weekly income.

    c. For long-term disability income insurance, the usual benefit is each $100 of monthly income.

9. Decisions must also be made about the factors affecting claims which result in different claims experience for different groups and the frequency of the premium payment period that affect investment earnings and processing expenses. The factors affecting claims include the gender, age, income, and occupation of the insureds as well as the geographic location, and size of the insured group. The length of time for which the rates are to be applicable also affects claims.

10. The first step in the calculation of manual premium rates is the determination of the net premium rate, which is the amount necessary to support the cost of expected claims. The net premium rate is calculated by multiplying the probability (frequency) of a claim occurring by the expected amount (severity) of the claim. Because premiums are collected before claims are paid, the insurance company adjusts this figure downward for anticipated interest earnings on these funds.

    The second and final step in the calculation of manual premium rates is the adjustment of the net premium rates for expenses, a risk charge, and a contribution to surplus. Expenses include commissions, premium taxes, claims settlement costs, and other costs associated with the acquisition and servicing of group insurance business. The risk charge represents a contribution to the insurance company's contingency reserve as a cushion against unanticipated and catastrophic amounts of claims. The contribution to surplus or net worth represents the profit margin of the insurance company.

11. a. For groups over a certain size, that may be considered large groups, some insurance companies do not incorporate a charge for a waiver of premium or accidental death and dismemberment coverage into their manual rates. Rather, an extra charge, which usually differs by industry, is added for this coverage. Also,

some companies use (and are required to use in a few states) manual rates that vary by age but not gender. However, an adjustment is usually made in the premium-calculation process if the actual group ratio differs from an assumed male to female ratio.

In the final premium-calculation process, an adjustment for expenses is made; larger groups receive an expense reduction and smaller groups receive an expense surcharge.

b. In general, for small groups, the manual rates are banded by age, typically in 5-year intervals.

To compensate for the expenses of periodic billings, most insurance companies apply a flat fee to all groups, commonly between $10 and $20 per billing. This fee may be waived if the group pays its premium annually. Some insurance companies also levy a modest one-time administrative expense charge when coverage is added for a new employee.

Although most insurance companies guarantee that the manual rates used when the group was initially written (and any future manual rates applicable to the group) remain applicable for some period of time, such as 12 months, small groups are more likely to have shorter premium guarantee periods. For these groups, the monthly premium rate for small groups may be recalculated each month based not only on the volume of insurance but also on changes in the makeup of employees by age and gender (unless unisex rates are used).

12. Some insurance companies have a single flat rate, independent of the type or number of dependents, for each employee who has dependent coverage. Other companies have two separate flat rates: one for the spouse's coverage and the other for children's coverage. The rate for the children's coverage is a family rate regardless of the number of children, and it is based upon an average-sized family.

Some insurance companies also use a rate for dependent coverage that varies with the employee's age, thereby assuming that older employees have older dependents.

13. In contrast to life insurance rates, manual rates for short-term disability income insurance also consider (1) the maximum benefit period, (2) the length of the waiting period, and (3) the writing of coverage either on a 24-hour basis or only for nonoccupational disabilities. An adjustment also may be made for the nature of the industry the group represents. Disability income rates are higher for females compared to males rather than lower as they are for life insurance. However, because male and female claims are comparable at older ages, the rates for later years seldom vary.

In addition, the manual rates for long-term disability coverage reflect the fact that benefits are coordinated with Social Security and certain other disability income benefits for which an employee might be eligible. To the extent that variations are allowed in the coordination provision that was assumed in developing the manual rates, an adjustment is made in the premium-calculation process. As is also the case with short-term rates, an adjustment might be made for certain occupations.

14. With community rating, each plan uses the same rate structure for all members, regardless of past or potential claims and whether the plan is for an individual or group coverage.

15. An adjustment is often made for the income levels of employees, because higher-paid persons are much more likely to obtain dental care. An adjustment is also made for certain occupations (such as salespeople or teachers) that use dental services more frequently than average. Finally, the manual rates are usually increased when a plan is new (or expands benefits) if the employees have been informed beforehand. Under these circumstances, there is a tendency to postpone needed dental care until the plan is installed.

16. An insurance company considers a group's dental claims experience, either at the issue date or at the end of a policy period, when determining the premium rate for that group. When applied prospectively (that is, to future periods), experience rating is used to determine (1) adjustments in renewal premiums for those groups whose claims experience has deviated from what was expected and (2) initial premiums for large groups that change insurance carriers.

    In addition to determining the premium rate for the next policy period (usually 12 months), experience rating is also used to compute the refund payable to the policy-owner (usually the employer) for those groups that had better claims experience than anticipated.

17. The major reason for using experience rating is the competition that exists in the group insurance marketplace. If an insurance company were to use identical rates for all groups regardless of their experience, the employers with good experience would soon seek out insurance companies that offered lower rates, or they would turn to self-funding as a way to reduce costs. Experience rating is also the most cost-effective way to reflect the general health of a group in the premium that is charged.

18. The purpose of a stop-loss limit is to minimize the effect of any chance fluctuations that might occur from year to year because of catastrophic losses within the group.

19. Some of the claims that were paid during the experience period may actually be attributable to previous periods and must be subtracted from the incurred claims. In addition, other claims that are attributable to the experience period may not have been reported or may be in the course of settlement.

20. In general, the larger the group is, the greater the reliability of estimates is (because of the law of large numbers). In addition, actual experience tends to deviate less from the estimates of expected claims (on a relative basis) as the frequency of claims rises.

21. Retention in group insurance consists of charges for (1) the stop-loss coverage, (2) expenses (commissions, premium taxes, and administrative expenses), (3) a risk charge, and (4) a contribution to the insurance company's surplus. For large groups, each item in the retention is calculated separately, based on the group's actual experience. For small groups, a formula based on insurance company averages is usually applied. This formula varies according to the size of a group and the type of coverage involved; most often it is either a percentage of the claims charge or a flat charge plus a percentage of the claims charge.

22. The medical loss ratio is the percentage of premium dollars an insurance company spends on providing health care and improving the quality of care versus how much is spent on administrative and overhead costs. The Affordable Care Act requires at least 85 percent of the premium for large groups and at least 80 percent of the premium for small groups and individual coverage to be spent on medical care services. For Medicare Advantage plans, the medical loss ratio is 85 percent. If the required medical loss ratio is not met, the insurer will have to rebate the difference to the purchaser.

Index